ANOTHER VIEW: TO BE BLACK IN AMERICA

ANOTHER VIEW:

Edited by Gerald Messner

Cañada College

To Be Black in America

HARCOURT, BRACE & WORLD, INC.

New York Chicago San Francisco Atlanta

FOR BOB AND MARY HOOVER

ANOTHER VIEW: TO BE BLACK IN AMERICA, *edited by Gerald Messner*

ISBN: 0-15-502810-3

Library of Congress Catalog Card Number: 72-111322

Printed in the United States of America

COVER: *The Wall of Respect,* Chicago; photographed by Michael Mauney/Black Star

PREFACE

Another View: To Be Black in America is a collection of twenty-eight readings that describe the present condition of the black man in this country. Most of the selections are in essay form; in addition, parts of two novels and one poem are included. The selections take the reader inside the black community to hear the voices of black leaders confronting the major issues involved in being black in America today. The book also includes several "overview" studies, such as E. Franklin Frazier's *Behind the Masks* and Stanley Elkins' *Slavery and Personality*, by writers whose ideas have played a significant part in characterizing the black experience. The attitude of the white man toward blacks is explored in several essays by both black and white writers. Finally, two important historical documents—the Supreme Court's *Brown v. Board of Education* decision and the Kerner Commission Report—are included.

Although the emphasis of the book is contemporary, several nineteenth- and early twentieth-century writers have been represented to enable the student to see the development of ideas in black thought. The selections are arranged chronologically for historical continuity, but the book need not be read in a linear fashion. Nearly every writer in the anthology recapitulates the important themes of blackness. Changes in emphasis are frequent, however; and to deal with a subject at once gigantic and subtle, blocks of at least five or six readings should be undertaken.

Each selection is introduced by a brief headnote identifying the author and is followed by discussion questions designed to elicit careful reading and interpretation from the student. The questions also ask the reader to compare the ideas and opinions of several writers.

I would like to thank several people for their help in putting together *Another View*. Many suggestions came from former students in the College of San Mateo's College Readiness Program—most especially, from Ludia Washington. Bob Hoover, whom I worked with in the program, taught me what it meant to believe in the young and to fight for them. David Arovola of the Speech Department of San Jose State College helped editorially in preparing the manuscript. The greatest assistance came from my wife, Nancy, who gave unsparingly of her time, energies, and emotions in order that *Another View* might come about.

Gerald Messner

CONTENTS

ANOTHER VIEW: TO BE BLACK IN AMERICA

RAFFLE

Mr. Joseph Jennings respectfully informs his friends and the public that, at the request of many acquaintances, he has been induced to purchase from Mr. Osborne, of Missouri, the celebrated

DARK BAY HORSE, "STAR,"

Aged five years, square trotter and warranted sound; with a new light Trotting Buggy and Harness; also, the dark, stout

MULATTO GIRL, "SARAH,"

Aged about twenty years, general house servant, valued at *nine hundred dollars*, and guaranteed, and

Will be Raffled for

At 4 o'clock P. M., February first, at the selection hotel of the subscribers. The above is as represented, and those persons who may wish to engage in the usual practice of raffling, will, I assure them, be perfectly satisfied with their destiny in this affair.

The whole is valued at its just worth, fifteen hundred dollars; fifteen hundred

CHANCES AT ONE DOLLAR EACH.

The Raffle will be conducted by gentlemen selected by the interested subscribers present. Five nights will be allowed to complete the Raffle. BOTH OF THE ABOVE DESCRIBED CAN BE SEEN AT MY STORE, No. 78 Common St., second door from Camp, at from 9 o'clock A. M. to 2 P. M.

Highest throw to take the first choice; the lowest throw the remaining prize, and the fortunate winners will pay twenty dollars each for the refreshments furnished on the occasion.

N. B. No chances recognized unless paid for previous to the commencement.

JOSEPH JENNINGS.

Raffle poster (about 1830).
New-York Historical Society

World War I veteran returns.
United Press International

Black nationalist bookstore in Harlem.
United Press International

THE HOUSE OF COMMON SENSE
OME OF PROPER PROPAGANDA.
WORLD HISTORY
BOOK OUTLET ON
JOMO KENYATTA
Hon. MARCUS GARVEY
2,000,000,000
(TWO BILLION)
AFRICANS AND NON-WHITE PEOPLES
AFRICAN CHIEFS OF STATES
ETHIOPIA
LIBERIA
EGYPT
SUDAN
GHANA
GUINEA
CAMEROON
TOGOLAND
CONGO
SOMALIA
NIGERIA
EAST NIGERIA
BLACK MAN'S GOD
REPATRIATION HEADQUARTERS
BACK TO AFRICA MOVEMENT
RECRUITING
REGISTER HERE!
HARLEM
SQUARE
WHITE MAN'S GOD
A HISTORY OF NEGRO PEOPLE IN AMERICA
Get Away JORDAN
LET GODS CHULLUN BY
WE MUST PASS OVER TO THE PROMISE LAND OR DIE
DIANA SANDS

"Separate but equal" facilities in a Southern town.
Eliot Erwitt, Magnum

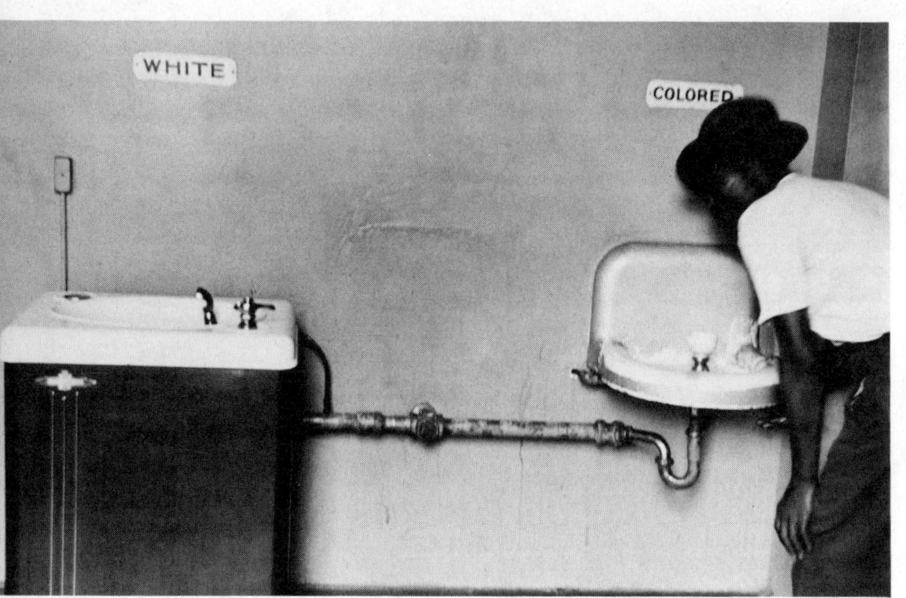

Marcher at rally following the death of Martin Luther King, Jr.
Reginald McGhee

March on Jackson, Mississippi (1966). *From left:* Dr. Martin Luther King, James Meredith, Stokely Carmichael, Floyd McKissick.
United Press International

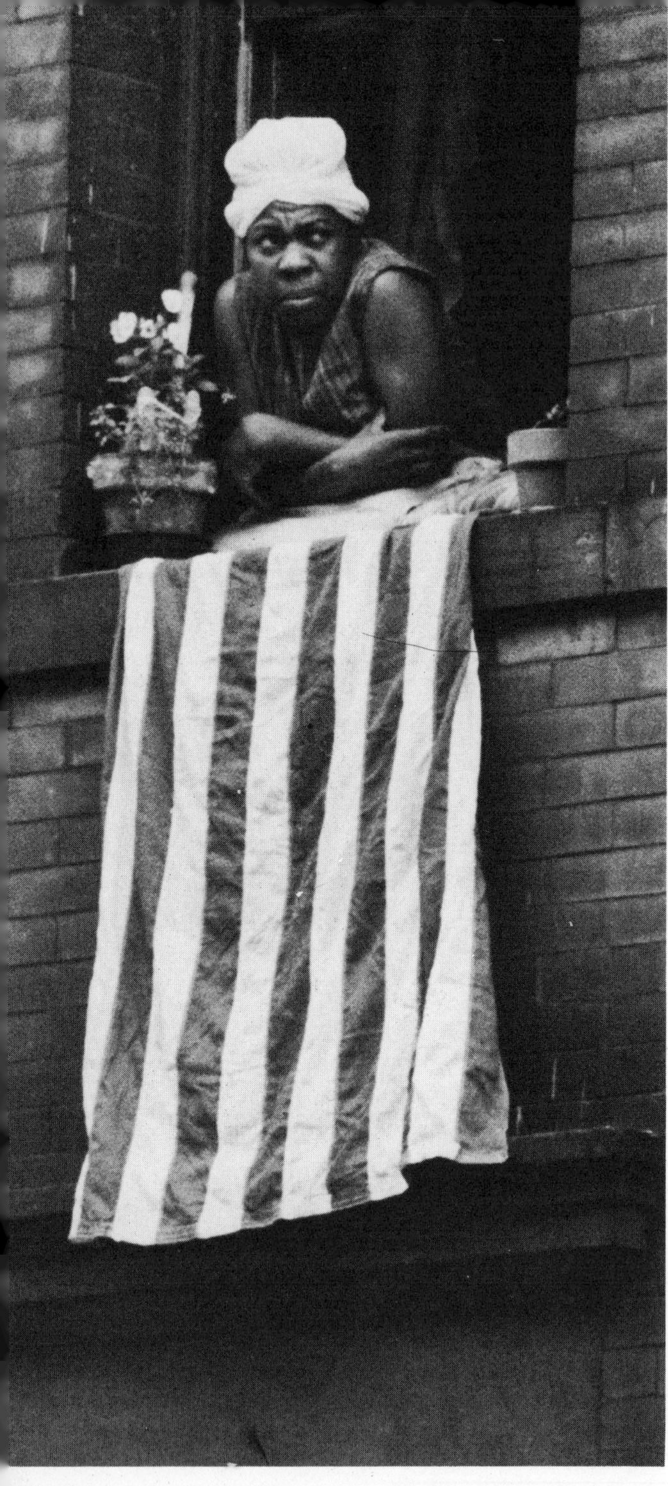

Harlem tenement.
Bruce Davidson,
Magnum

ON JULY 29, 1967, PRESIDENT LYNDON JOHNSON APPOINTED A SPECIAL INVESTIGATING COMMITTEE TO DETERMINE THE CAUSES OF RACIAL STRIFE AND DISORDER AND TO SUGGEST SOLUTIONS TO THE PROBLEM. THE COMMITTEE WAS HEADED BY GOVERNOR OTTO KERNER OF ILLINOIS AND WAS CALLED THE NATIONAL ADVISORY COMMISSION ON CIVIL DISORDERS, OR KERNER COMMISSION. ITS REPORT WAS PUBLISHED IN MARCH 1968.

KERNER COMMISSION

REJECTION AND PROTEST: AN HISTORICAL SKETCH

Introduction

The events of the summer of 1967 are in large part the culmination of 300 years of racial prejudice. Most Americans know little of the origins of the racial schism separating our white and Negro citizens. Few appreciate how central the problem of the Negro has been to our social policy. Fewer still understand that today's problems can be solved only if white Americans comprehend the rigid social, economic, and educational barriers that have prevented Negroes from participating in the mainstream of American life. Only a handful realize that Negro accommodation to the patterns of prejudice in American culture has been but one side of the coin—for as slaves and as free men,

REJECTION AND PROTEST: AN HISTORICAL SKETCH From *The Report of the National Advisory Commission on Civil Disorders* (1968), Chapter 5.

Negroes have protested against oppression and have persistently sought equality in American society.

What follows is neither a history of the Negro in the United States nor a full account of Negro protest movements. Rather, it is a brief narrative of a few historical events that illustrate the facts of rejection and the forms of protest.

We call on history not to justify, but to help explain, for black and white Americans, a state of mind.

The Colonial Period

Twenty years after Columbus reached the New World, African Negroes, transported by Spanish, Dutch, and Portuguese traders, were arriving in the Caribbean Islands. Almost all came as slaves. By 1600, there were more than half a million slaves in the Western Hemisphere.

In Colonial America the first Negroes landed at Jamestown in August 1619. Within 40 years Negroes had become a group apart, separated from the rest of the population by custom and law. Treated as servants for life, forbidden to intermarry with whites, deprived of their African traditions, and dispersed among Southern plantations, American Negroes lost tribal, regional, and family ties.

Through massive importation, their numbers increased rapidly. By 1776, some 500,000 Negroes were held in slavery and indentured servitude in the United States. Nearly one of every six persons in the country was a slave.

Americans disapproved a preliminary draft of the Declaration of Independence that indicted the King of England for waging "cruel war against human nature itself, violating its most sacred rights of life and liberty in the persons of a distant people who never offended him, captivating and carrying them into slavery in another hemisphere, or to incur miserable death in their transportation thither." Instead, they approved a document that proclaimed "all men are created equal."

The statement was an ideal, a promise. But it excluded the Negroes who were held in bondage, as well as the few who were free men.

The conditions in which Negroes lived had already led to protest. Throughout the 18th century, the danger of Negro revolts obsessed many white Americans. Slave plots of considerable scope were uncovered in New York in 1712 and 1741, and they resulted in bloodshed—whites and Negroes were slain.

Racial violence was present almost from the beginning of the American experience.

The Revolution

Negroes were at first barred from serving in the Revolutionary Army, recruiting officers having been ordered in July 1775 to enlist no "stroller, Negro, or vagabond." Yet Negroes were already actively involved in the struggle for independence. Crispus Attucks, a Boston Negro, was perhaps the first American to die for freedom, and Negroes had already fought in the battles at Lexington and Concord. They were among the soldiers at Bunker Hill.

Fearing that Negroes would enlist in the British Army, which welcomed them, and facing a manpower shortage, the Continental Army accepted free Negroes. Slaves joined the British, and according to an estimate by Thomas Jefferson, more than 30,000 Virginia slaves ran away in 1778 alone, presumably to enlist. The states were enrolling both free and slave Negroes, and finally Congress authorized military service for slaves, who were to be emancipated in return for their service. By the end of the war, about 5,000 Negroes had been in the ranks of the Continental Army. Those who had been slaves became free.

But the liberty and equality implicit in American independence had meaning rather than application to them.

The Constitution and the Laws

Massachusetts abolished slavery in 1783, and Connecticut, Rhode Island, New Jersey, Pennsylvania, and New York soon provided for gradual liberation. But relatively few Negroes lived in these states. The bulk of the Negro population was in the South, where white Americans had fortunes invested in slaves. Although the Congress banned slavery in the Northwest Territory, delegates at the Constitutional Convention compromised with the institution—a slave counted as three-fifths of a person for determining the number of representatives from a state to Congress; Congress was prohibited from restricting the slave trade until after 1808, and the free states were required to return fugitive slaves to their Southern owners.

Growing numbers of slaves in the South became permanently fastened in bondage, and slavery spread into the new Southern regions. When more slaves were needed for the cotton and sugar plantations in the Southwest, they were ordered from the "Negro-raising" states of the Old South or, despite Congressional prohibition of the slave trade, imported from Africa.

The laws of bondage became even more institutionalized. Masters retained absolute authority over their Negroes, who were unable to leave their masters' properties without written permission. Any white person, even those who owned no slaves—and they outnumbered slaveholders six to one—could challenge a truant slave and turn him over to a public official. Slaves could own no property, could enter into no contract, not even a contract of marriage, and had no right to assemble in public unless a white person was present. They had no standing in the courts. Without legal means of defense, slaves were susceptible to the premise that any white person could threaten their lives or take them with impunity.

Discrimination as Doctrine

The situation was hardly better for free Negroes. A few achieved material success, several owned slaves themselves, but the vast majority knew only poverty and suffered the indignity of rejection by white society. Forbidden to settle in some areas, segregated in others, they were targets of prejudice and discrimination. In the South, they were denied freedom of movement, severely restricted in their choice of occupation, and forbidden to associate with whites or with slaves. They lived in constant danger of being enslaved—whites could challenge their freedom and an infraction of the law could put them into bondage. In both North and South, they were regularly victims of mobs. In 1829, for example, white residents invaded Cincinnati's "Little Africa," killed Negroes, burned their property, and ultimately drove half the colored population from the city.

Some Americans, Washington and Jefferson among them, advocated the gradual emancipation of slaves, and in the 19th century, a movement to abolish slavery grew in importance and strength. A few white abolitionist leaders wanted full equality for Negroes, but others sought only to eliminate the institution itself. And some anti-slavery societies, fearing that Negro members would unnecessarily offend those who were unsympathetic with abolitionist principles, denied entrance to Negro abolitionists.

Most Americans were, in fact, against abolishing slavery. They refused to rent their halls for anti-slavery meetings. They harassed abolitionist leaders who sought to educate white and Negro children together. They attacked those involved in the movement. Mobs sometimes killed abolitionists and destroyed their property.

A large body of literature came into existence to prove that the Negro was imperfectly developed in mind and body, that he belonged to a lower order of man, that slavery was right on ethnic, economic, and social grounds—and quoted the Scriptures in support.

Spreading rapidly during the first part of the 19th century, the institution enslaved less than one million Negroes in 1800, but almost four million in 1860. Although some few white Americans had freed their slaves, most increased their holdings, for the invention of the cotton gin had made the cotton industry profitable. In mid-century, slavery in the South was a systematic and aggressive way of treating a whole race of people.

The despair of Negroes was evident. Malingering and sabotage tormented every slaveholder. The problem of runaway slaves was endemic. Some slaves—Gabriel Prosser in 1800, Denmark Vesey in 1822, Nat Turner in 1831, and others—turned to violence, and the sporadic uprisings that flared demonstrated a deep protest against a demeaning way of life.

Negroes who had material resources expressed their distress in other ways. Paul Cuffee, Negro philanthropist and owner of a fleet of ships, transported in 1816 a group of Negroes to a new home in Sierra Leone. Forty years later Martin R. Delany, Negro editor and physician, urged Negroes to settle elsewhere. When Frederick Douglass, the distinguished Negro abolitionist, addressed the citizens of Rochester on Independence Day, 1852, he told them:

> The Fourth of July is *yours*, not mine. *You* may rejoice, *I* must mourn. To drag a man into the grand illuminated temple of liberty, and call upon him to join you in joyous anthems, were inhuman mockery and sacrilegious irony. . . . Fellow citizens, above your national tumultuous joy, I hear the mournful wail of millions, whose chains, heavy and grievous yesterday, are today rendered more intolerable by the jubilant shouts that reach them. . . .

The Path Toward Civil War

The 1850's brought Negroes increasing despair, as the problem of slavery was debated by the nation's leaders. The Compromise of 1850 and the Kansas-Nebraska Act of 1854 settled no basic issues. And the *Dred Scott* case in 1857 confirmed Negroes in their understanding that they were not "citizens" and thus not entitled to the constitutional safeguards enjoyed by other Americans.

But the abolitionist movement was growing. *Uncle Tom's Cabin* appeared in 1852 and sold more than 300,000 copies that year. Soon presented on the stage throughout the North, it dramatized the cruelty of slave masters and overseers and condemned a culture based on human degradation and exploitation. John Brown's raids, then the election of Abraham Lincoln to the Presidency on an anti-slavery platform gave hope that the end of slavery was near.

But by the time Lincoln took office, seven Southern states had seceded from the Union, and four more soon joined them.

Even the abolitionist movement had disappointed perceptive Negroes who saw that white leaders were less than altogether sincere. A few were genuinely interested in the Negro, but most were paternalistic and prejudiced. Whites were motivated at best by pity, at worst by economic self-interest.

Equality of treatment and acceptance by the society at large were myths, and Negro protest during the first half of the 19th century took the form of rhetoric, spoken and written, which combined denunciation of undemocratic oppression together with pleas to the conscience of white Americans for the redress of grievances and the recognition of their constitutional rights.

A few Negroes joined white Americans who believed that only Negro emigration to Africa would solve racial problems. But most Negroes equated that program with banishment and felt themselves "entitled to participate in the blessings" of America. The National Negro Convention Movement, formed in 1830, held conferences to publicize on a national scale the evils of slavery and the indignities heaped on free Negroes.

The American Moral Reform Society, founded by Negroes in 1834, rejected racial separatism and advocated uplifting "the whole human race, without distinction as to . . . complexion." Other Negro reformers pressed for stronger racial consciousness and solidarity as the means to overcome racial barriers. Many took direct action to help slaves escape through the Underground Railroad. A few resisted discrimination by political action, even though most Negroes were barred from voting. Some few called for, but made no effort to organize, slave rebellions and mass violence.

Frustration, disillusionment, anger, and fantasy marked the Negro protest against the place in American society assigned to them. "I was free," Harriet Tubman said, "but there was no one to welcome me in the land of freedom. I was a stranger in a strange land."

The Civil War and Emancipation renewed Negro faith in the vision of a racially egalitarian and integrated American society. But Americans, after having been roused by wartime crisis, would again fail to destroy what abolitionists had described as the "sins of caste."

Civil War and "Emancipation"

Negroes volunteered for military service during the Civil War, the struggle, as they saw it, between the slave states and the free states. They were rejected.

Not until a shortage of troops plagued the Union Army late in 1862, were segregated units of "United States Colored Troops" formed. Not until 1864 did these men receive the same pay as white soldiers. A total of 186,000 Negroes served.

The Emancipation Proclamation of 1863 freed few slaves at first, but had immediate significance as a symbol. Negroes could hope again for equality.

But there were, at the same time, bitter signs of racial unrest. Violent rioting occurred in Cincinnati in 1862, when Negro and Irish hands competed for work on the riverboats. Lesser riots took place in Newark, New Jersey, and in Buffalo and Troy, New York, the result of combined hostility to the war and fear that Negroes would take white jobs.

The most violent of the troubles took place in New York City Draft Riots in July 1863, when white workers, mainly Irish-born, embarked on a three-day rampage.

> Desperately poor and lacking real roots in the community, they had the most to lose from the draft. Further, they were bitterly afraid that even cheaper Negro labor would flood the North if slavery ceased to exist.

> All the frustrations and prejudices the Irish had suffered were brought to a boiling point. . . . At pitiful wages, they had slaved on the railroads and canals, had been herded into the most menial jobs as carters and stevedores. . . . Their crumbling frame tenements . . . were the worst slums in the city.

Their first target was the office of the provost-marshal in charge of conscription, and 700 people quickly ransacked the building and set it on fire. The crowd refused to permit firemen into the area, and the whole block was gutted. Then the mob spilled into the Negro area, where many were slain and thousands forced to flee town. The police were helpless until federal troops arrived on the third day and restored control.

Union victory in the Civil War promised the Negroes freedom but hardly equality or immunity from white aggression. Scarcely was the war ended when racial violence erupted in New Orleans. Negroes proceeding to an assembly hall to discuss the franchise were charged by police and special troops, who routed the Negroes with guns, bricks, and stones, killed some at once, pursued and killed others who were trying to escape.

Federal troops restored order. But 34 Negroes and four whites were reported dead and over 200 people were injured. General Sheridan later said:

> At least nine-tenths of the casualties were perpetrated by the police and citizens by stabbing and smashing in the heads of many who had already been wounded or killed by policemen. . . . It was not just a riot but "an absolute massacre by the police . . . ," a murder which the mayor and police . . . perpetrated without the shadow of necessity.

Reconstruction

Reconstruction was a time of hope, the period when the 13th, 14th, and 15th Amendments were adopted, giving Negroes the vote and the promise of equality.

But campaigns of violence and intimidation accompanied these optimistic expressions of a new age, as the Ku Klux Klan and other secret organizations sought to suppress the emergence into society of the new Negro citizens. Major riots occurred in Memphis, Tennessee, where 46 Negroes were reported killed and 75 wounded, and in the

Louisiana centers of Colfax and Coushatta, where more than 100 Negro and white Republicans were massacred.

Nevertheless, Reconstruction reached a legislative climax in 1875 with passage of the first civil rights law. Negroes now had the right to equal accommodations, facilities, and advantages of public transportation, inns, theaters, and places of public amusement, but the law had no effective enforcement provisions and was, in fact, poorly enforced. Although bills to provide federal aid to education for Negroes were prepared, none passed, and educational opportunities remained meager.

But Negroes were elected to every Southern legislature, 20 served in the U.S. House of Representatives, two represented Mississippi in the U.S. Senate, and a prominent Negro politician was Governor of Louisiana for 40 days.

Opposition to Negroes in state and local government was always open and bitter. In the press and on the platform they were described as ignorant and depraved. Critics made no distinction between Negroes who had graduated from Dartmouth and those who had graduated from the cotton fields. Every available means was employed to drive Negroes from public life. Negroes who voted or held office were refused jobs or punished by the Ku Klux Klan. One group in Mississippi boasted of having killed 116 Negroes and of having thrown their bodies into the Tallahatchie River. In a single South Carolina county, six men were murdered and more than 300 whipped during the first six months of 1870.

The federal government seemed helpless. Having withdrawn the occupation troops as soon as the Southern states organized governments, the President was reluctant to send them back. In 1870 and 1871, after the 15th Amendment was ratified, Congress enacted several laws to protect the right of citizens to vote. They were seldom enforced, and the Supreme Court struck down most of the important provisions in 1875 and 1876.

The End of Reconstruction

As Southern white governments returned to power, beginning with Virginia in 1869 and ending with Louisiana in 1877, the program of relegating the Negro to a subordinate place in American life was accelerated. Disfranchisement was the first step. Negroes who defied the Klan and tried to vote faced an array of deceptions and obstacles—

polling places were changed at the last minute without notice to Negroes, severe time limitations were imposed on marking complicated ballots, votes cast incorrectly in a maze of ballot boxes were nullified. The suffrage provisions of state constitutions were rewritten to disenfranchise Negroes who could not read, understand, or interpret the Constitution. Some state constitutions permitted those who failed the tests to vote if their ancestors had been eligible to vote on January 1, 1860, when no Negro could vote anywhere in the South.

In 1896, Negroes registered in Louisiana totalled 130,344. In 1900, after the state rewrote the suffrage provisions of its constitution, Negroes on the registration books numbered only 5,320. Essentially the same thing happened in the other states of the former Confederacy.

Segregation by Law

When the Supreme Court, in 1883, declared the Civil Rights Act of 1875 unconstitutional, Southern states began to enact laws to segregate the races. In 1896, the Supreme Court in *Plessy* v. *Ferguson* approved "separate but equal" facilities; it was then that segregation became an established fact, by law and by custom. Negroes and whites were separated on public carriers and in all places of public accommodation, including hospitals and churches. In courthouses, whites and Negroes took oaths on separate Bibles. In most communities, whites were separated from Negroes in cemeteries.

Segregation invariably meant discrimination. On trains all Negroes, including those holding first-class tickets, were allotted a few seats in the baggage car. Negroes in public buildings had to use freight elevators and toilet facilities reserved for janitors. Schools for Negro children were at best a weak imitation of those for whites, as states spent 10 times more to educate white youngsters than Negroes. Discrimination in wages became the rule, whether between Negro and white teachers of similar training and experience or between common laborers on the same job.

Some Northern states enacted civil rights laws in the 1880's, but Negroes in fact were treated little differently in the North than in the South. As Negroes moved north in substantial numbers toward the end of the century, they discovered that equality of treatment was only a dream in Massachusetts, New York, or Illinois. They were crowded by local ordinances into one section of the city where housing and public services were generally sub-standard. Overt discrimination in employment was a general practice. Employment opportunities apart from menial tasks were few. Most labor unions excluded Negroes from membership—or granted membership in separate and powerless Jim Crow locals. Yet when Negroes secured employment during strikes, labor leaders castigated them for not understanding the principles of trade unionism. And when Negroes sought to move into the mainstream of community life by seeking membership in the organizations around them—educational, cultural, and religious—they were invariably rebuffed.

That Northern whites would resort to violence was made clear in anti-Negro riots in New York, 1900; Springfield, Ohio, 1904; Greensburg, Indiana, 1906; Springfield, Illinois, 1908.

The latter was a three-day riot, initiated by a white woman's claim of violation by a Negro, inflamed by newspapers, intensified by crowds of whites gathered around the jail demanding that the Negro, arrested and imprisoned, be lynched. When the sheriff transferred the accused and another Negro to a jail in a nearby town, rioters headed for the Negro section and attacked homes and businesses owned by or catering to Negroes. White owners who showed handkerchiefs in their windows averted harm to their stores. One Negro was summarily lynched, others were dragged from houses and streetcars and beaten. By the time National Guardsmen could reach the scene, six persons were dead—four whites and two Negroes; property damage was extensive. Many Negroes left Springfield, hoping to find better conditions elsewhere, especially in Chicago.

By the 20th century, the Negro was at the bottom of American society. Disfranchised, Negroes throughout the country were excluded by employers and labor unions from white collar jobs and skilled trades. Jim Crow laws and farm tenancy characterized Negro existence in the South. About 100 lynchings occurred every year in the 1880's and 1890's; there were 161 lynchings in 1892. As increasing numbers of Negroes migrated to Northern cities, race riots became commonplace. Northern whites, even many former abolitionists, began to accept the white South's views on race relations.

Booker T. Washington

Between his famous Atlanta Exposition Address in 1895 and his death in 1915, Booker T. Washington, principal of the Tuskegee

Normal and Industrial Institute in Alabama and the most prominent Negro in America, secretly spent thousands of dollars fighting disfranchisement and segregation laws; publicly he advocated a policy of accommodation, conciliation, and gradualism. Largely blaming Negroes themselves for their condition, Washington believed that by helping themselves, by creating and supporting their own businesses, by proving their usefulness to society through the acquisition of education, wealth, and morality, Negroes would earn the respect of the white man and thus eventually gain their constitutional rights.

Self-help and self-respect appeared a practical and sure, if gradual, way of ultimately achieving racial equality. Washington's doctrines also gained support because they appealed to race pride—if Negroes believed in themselves, stood together, and supported each other, they would be able to shape their destinies.

The Niagara Movement

In the early years of the century, a small group of Negroes, led by W. E. B. DuBois, formed the Niagara Movement to oppose Washington's program, which they claimed had failed. Washington had put economic progress before politics, had accepted the separate-but-equal theory, and opposed agitation and protest. DuBois and his followers stressed political activity as the basis of the Negro's future, insisted on the inequity of Jim Crow laws, and advocated agitation and protest.

In sharp language, the Niagara group placed responsibility for the race problem squarely on the whites. The aims of the movement were voting rights and "the abolition of all caste distinctions based simply on race and color."

Although Booker T. Washington tried to crush his critics, DuBois and the Negro "radicals," as they were called, enlisted the support of a small group of influential white liberals and socialists. Together, in 1909–1910, they formed the National Association for the Advancement of Colored People.

The NAACP

The NAACP hammered at the walls of prejudice by organizing Negroes and well-disposed whites, by aiming propaganda at the whole nation, by taking legal action in courts and legislatures. Almost at the outset of its career, the NAACP prevailed upon the Supreme Court to declare unconstitutional two discriminatory statutes. In 1915, the Court overruled the Oklahoma "grandfather clause," a provision in several Southern state constitutions that excluded from the vote those whose ancestors were ineligible to vote in 1860. Two years later, the Supreme Court outlawed municipal residential segregation ordinances. These NAACP victories were the first legal steps in a long fight against disfranchisement and segregation.

The Federal Government

During the first quarter of the 20th century, the federal government enacted no new legislation to ensure equal rights or opportunities for Negroes and made little attempt to enforce existing laws despite flagrant violations of Negro civil rights.

In 1913, members of Congress from the South introduced bills to federalize the Southern segregation policy. They wished to ban interracial marriages in the District of Columbia, segregate white and Negro federal employees, and introduce Jim Crow laws in the public carriers of the District. The bills did not pass, but segregation practices were extended in federal offices, shops, restrooms, and lunchrooms. The nation's capital became as segregated as any in the former Confederate states.

East St. Louis, 1917

Elsewhere there was violence. In East St. Louis, Illinois, a riot in July 1917 claimed the lives of 39 Negroes and nine whites, as a result of fear by white working men that Negro advances in economic, political and social status were threatening their own security and status.

When the labor force of an aluminum plant went on strike, the company hired Negro workers. A labor union delegation called on the mayor and asked that further migration of Negroes to East St. Louis be stopped. As the men were leaving City Hall, they heard that a Negro had accidentally shot a white man during a holdup. In a few minutes rumor had replaced fact: the shooting was intentional—a white woman had been insulted—two white girls were shot. By this time 3,000 people had congregated and were crying for vengeance.

Mobs roamed the streets, beating Negroes. Policemen did little more than take the injured to hospitals and disarm Negroes.

The National Guard restored order. When the governor withdrew the troops, tensions were still high, and scattered episodes broke the peace. The press continued to emphasize the incidence of Negro crimes, white pickets and Negro workers at the aluminum company skirmished and, on July 1, some whites drove through the main Negro neighborhood firing into homes. Negro residents armed themselves. When a police car drove down the street Negroes riddled it with gunshot.

The next day a Negro was shot on the main street and a new riot was under way. The authority on the event records that the area became a "bloody half mile" for three or four hours; streetcars were stopped, and Negroes, without regard to age or sex, were pulled off and stoned, clubbed and kicked, and mob leaders calmly shot and killed Negroes who were lying in blood in the street. As the victims were placed in an ambulance, the crowds cheered and applauded.

Other rioters set fire to Negro homes, and by midnight the Negro section was in flames and Negroes were fleeing the city. There were 48 dead, hundreds injured, and more than 300 buildings destroyed.

World War I

When the United States entered World War I in 1917, the country again faced the question whether American citizens should have the right to serve, on an equal basis, in defense of their country. More than two million Negroes registered under the Selective Service Act, and some 360,000 were called into service.

The Navy rejected Negroes except as menials. The Marine Corps rejected them altogether. The Army formed them into separate units commanded, for the most part, by white officers. Only after enormous pressure did the Army permit Negro candidates to train as officers in a segregated camp. Mistreated at home and overseas, Negro combat units performed exceptionally well under French commanders, who refused to heed American warnings that Negroes were inferior people.

Mobbed for attempting to use facilities open to white soldiers, Negro soldiers returning home suffered indignities. Of the 70 Negroes lynched during the first year after the war, a substantial number were soldiers. Some were lynched in uniform.

Postwar Violence

Reorganized in 1915, the Ku Klux Klan was flourishing again by 1919. Its program "for uniting native-born white Christians for concerted action in the preservation of American institutions and the supremacy of the white race," was implemented by flogging, branding with acid, tarring and feathering, hanging and burning. It destroyed the elemental rights of many Negroes, and of some whites.

Violence took the form of lynchings and riots, and major riots by whites against Negroes took place in 1917 in Chester, Pennsylvania, and Philadelphia; in 1919 in Washington, D.C., Omaha, Charleston, Longview, Texas, Chicago, and Knoxville; in 1921 in Tulsa.

The Chicago riot of 1919 flared from the increase in Negro population, which had more than doubled in 10 years. Jobs were plentiful, but housing was not. Black neighborhoods expanded into white sections of the city, and trouble developed. Between July 1917 and March 1921, 58 Negro houses were bombed, and recreational areas were sites of racial conflict.

The riot itself started on Sunday, July 27, with stone throwing and sporadic fighting at adjoining white and Negro beaches. A Negro boy swimming off the Negro beach drifted into water reserved for whites and drowned. Young Negroes claimed he had been struck by stones and demanded the arrest of a white man. Instead, police arrested a Negro. When Negroes attacked policemen, a riot was in the making. News spread to the city, white and Negro groups clashed in the streets, two persons died, and 50 were wounded. On Monday, Negroes coming home from work were attacked; later, when whites drove cars through Negro neighborhoods and fired weapons, Negroes retaliated. Twenty more were killed and hundreds wounded. On Tuesday, a handful more were dead, 129 injured. On Wednesday, losses in life and property declined further. Rain began to fall; the mayor finally called in the state militia. After nearly a week of violence, the city quieted down.

The 1920's and the New Militancy

In the period between the two World Wars, the NAACP dominated the strategy of racial advancement. The NAACP drew its strength from large numbers of Southern Negroes who had migrated to Northern cities; from a small but growing Negro group of professionals and businessmen who served them; from an upsurge of confidence among the "New Negro," race-proud and self-reliant, believing in racial cooperation and self-help and determined to fight for his constitutional rights; from writers and artists known as the "Harlem Renaissance" who used their own cultural tradition and experience as materials for their works. W. E. B. DuBois, editor of the *Crisis*, the NAACP publication, symbolized the new mood and exerted great influence.

The NAACP did extraordinary service, giving legal defense to victims of race riots and unjust judicial proceedings. It obtained the release of the soldiers who had received life sentences on charges of rioting against intolerable conditions at Houston in 1917. It successfully defended Negro sharecroppers in Elaine, Arkansas, who in 1919 had banded together to gain fairer treatment, who had become the objects of a massive armed hunt by whites to put them "in their place," and who were charged with insurrection when they resisted. It secured the acquittal, with the help of Clarence Darrow, of Dr. Ossian Sweet and his family who had moved into a white neighborhood in Detroit, shot at a mob attacking their home, killed a man, and were eventually judged to have committed the act in self-defense.

The NAACP tried vainly to promote passage of an anti-lynching bill, but its most important activity was its campaign to secure enforcement of the 14th and 15th Amendments. It conducted sustained litigation against disfranchisement and segregation, and embarked upon a long fight against the white primaries in the Southern states. The NAACP attacked one aspect of discrimination at a time, hacking away at the structure of discrimination. Local branches in Northern and border cities won a number of important victories, but full recognition of the Negroes' constitutional rights was still a future prospect.

Less successful were attempts to prevent school segregation in Northern cities, which followed the migration of large numbers of rural black folk from the South. Gerrymandering of school boundaries and other devices by boards of education were fought with written petitions, verbal protests to school officials, legal suits and, in several cities, school boycotts. All proved of no avail.

The thrust of the NAACP was primarily political and legal, but the National Urban League, founded in 1911 by philanthropists and social workers, sought an economic solution to the Negroes' problems.

Sympathetic with Booker T. Washington's point of view, believing in conciliation, gradualism, and moral suasion, the Urban League searched out industrial opportunities for Negro migrants to the cities, using arguments that appealed to the white businessman's sense of economic self-interest and also to his conscience.

Also espousing an economic program to ameliorate the Negroes' condition was A. Philip Randolph, an editor of the *Messenger*. He regarded the NAACP as a middle-class organization unconcerned about pressing economic problems. Taking a Marxist position on the causes of prejudice and discrimination, Randolph called for a new and radical Negro unafraid to demand his rights as a member of the working class. He advocated physical resistance to white mobs, but he believed that only united action of black and white workers against capitalists would achieve social justice.

Although Randolph addressed himself to the urban working masses, few of them ever read the *Messenger*. The one man who reached the masses of frustrated and disillusioned migrants in the Northern ghettos was Marcus Garvey.

Separatism

Garvey, founder in 1914 of the Universal Negro Improvement Association (UNIA), aimed to liberate both Africans and American Negroes from their oppressors. His utopian method was the wholesale migration of American Negroes to Africa. Contending that whites would always be racist, he stressed racial pride and history, denounced integration, and insisted that the black man develop "a distinct racial type of civilization of his own and . . . work out his salvation in his motherland." On a more practical level he urged support of Negro businesses, and through the UNIA organized a chain of groceries, restaurants, laundries, a hotel, printing plant, and steamship line. When several prominent Negroes called the attention of the United States Government to irregularities in the management of the steamship line, Garvey was jailed, then deported for having used the mails to defraud.

But Garvey dramatized, as no one before, the bitterness and alienation of the Negro slum dwellers who, having come North with great expectations, found only overcrowded and deteriorated housing, mass unemployment, and race riots.

The Depression

Negro labor, relatively unorganized and the target of discrimination and hostility, was hardly prepared for the depression of the 1930's. To a disproportionate extent, Negroes lost their jobs in cities and worked for starvation wages in rural areas. Although organizations like the National Urban League tried to improve employment opportunities, 65 percent of Negro employables were in need of public assistance by 1935.

Public assistance was given on a discriminatory basis, especially in the South. For a time Dallas and Houston gave no relief at all to Negro families. In general, Negroes had more difficulty than whites in obtaining assistance, and the relief benefits were smaller. Some religious and charitable organizations excluded Negroes from their soup kitchens.

The New Deal

The New Deal marked a turning point in American race relations. Negroes found much in the New Deal to complain about: discrimination existed in many agencies; federal housing programs expanded urban ghettos; money from the Agricultural Adjustment Administration went in the South chiefly to white landowners, while crop restrictions forced many Negro sharecroppers off the land. Nevertheless, Negroes shared in relief, jobs, and public housing, and Negro leaders, who felt the open sympathy of many highly placed New Dealers, held more prominent political positions than at any time since President Taft's administration. The creation of the Congress of Industrial Organizations (CIO), with its avowed philosophy of non-discrimination, made the notion of an alliance of black and white workers something more than a visionary's dream.

The depression, the New Deal, and the CIO reoriented Negro protest to concern with economic problems. Negroes conducted "Don't Buy Where You Can't Work" campaigns in a number of cities, boycotted and picketed commercial establishments owned by whites, and sought equality in American society through an alliance with white labor.

The NAACP came under attack from Negroes. DuBois resigned as editor of the *Crisis* in 1934 because, believing in the value of collective racial economic endeavor, he saw little point in protesting disfranchisement and segregation without pursuing economic goals. Younger critics also disagreed with [the] NAACP's gradualism on economic issues.

Undeterred, the NAACP broadened the scope of its legal work, fought a vigorous though unsuccessful campaign to abolish the poll tax, and finally won its attack on the white primaries in 1944 through the Supreme Court. But the heart of its litigation was a long-range campaign against segregation and the most obvious inequities in the Southern school systems: the lack of professional and graduate schools and the low salaries received by Negro teachers. Not until about 1950 would the NAACP make a direct assault against school segregation on the legal ground that separate facilities were inherently unequal.

World War II

During World War II, Negroes learned again that fighting for their country brought them no nearer to full citizenship. Rejected when they tried to enlist, they were accepted into the Army according to the proportion of the Negro population to that of the country as a whole—but only in separate units—and those mostly noncombat. The United States thus fought racism in Europe with a segregated fighting force. In some instances at home, Negro soldiers were unable to secure food, even though German prisoners of war were being served. The Red Cross, with the government's approval, separated Negro and white blood in banks established for wounded servicemen—even though the blood banks were largely the work of a Negro physician, Charles Drew.

Not until 1949 would the Armed Forces begin to adopt a firm policy against segregation.

Negroes seeking employment in defense industries were embittered by policies like that of a West Coast aviation factory which declared openly that "the Negro will be considered only as janitors and in other similar capacities. . . . Regardless of their training as aircraft workers, we will not employ them."

Two new movements marked Negro protest: the March on

Washington, and the Congress of Racial Equality (CORE). In 1941, consciously drawing on the power of the Negro vote and concerned with the economic problems of the urban slum dweller, A. Philip Randolph threatened a mass Negro convergence on Washington unless President Roosevelt secured employment for Negroes in the defense industries. The President's Executive Order 8802 establishing a federal Fair Employment Practices Commission forestalled the demonstration. Even without enforcement powers, the FEPC set a precedent for treating fair employment practice as a civil right.

CORE, founded in 1942–43, grew out of the Fellowship Reconciliation, a pacifist organization, when certain leaders became interested in the use of nonviolent direct action to fight racial discrimination. CORE combined Gandhi's techniques with the sit-in, derived from the sit-down strikes of the 1930's. Until about 1959, CORE's main activity was attacking discrimination in places of public accommodation in the cities of the Northern and border states, and as late as 1961, two-thirds of its membership and most of its national officers were white.

Meanwhile, racial disorders had broken out sporadically—in Mobile, Los Angeles, Beaumont, Texas, and elsewhere. The riot in Detroit in 1943 was the most destructive. The Negro population in the city had risen sharply and more than 50,000 recent arrivals put immense pressures on the housing market. Neighborhood turnover at the edge of the ghetto bred bitterness and sometimes violence, and recreational areas became centers of racial abrasion. The federal regulations requiring employment standards in defense industries also angered whites, and several unauthorized walk-outs had occurred in automobile plants after Negro workers were upgraded. Activities in the city of several leading spokesmen for white supremacy—Gerald L. K. Smith, Frank J. Norris, and Father Charles Coughlin—inflamed many white southerners who migrated to Detroit during the war.

On Sunday, June 20, rioting broke out on Belle Isle, a recreational spot used by both races, but predominantly by Negroes. Fist fights escalated into a major conflict. The first wave of looting and bloodshed began in the Negro ghetto "Paradise Valley" and later spread to other sections of the city. Whites began attacking Negroes as they emerged from the city's all-night movie theaters in the downtown area. White forays into Negro residential areas by car were met by sniping. By the time federal troops arrived to halt the racial conflict, 25 Negroes and nine whites were dead, property damage exceeded $2 million, and a legacy of fear and hate became part of the city.

In Harlem, New York, a riot erupted also in 1943, following the attempt of a white policeman to arrest a Negro woman defended by a Negro soldier. Negro rioters assaulted white passersby, overturned parked automobiles, tossed bricks and bottles at policemen, but the major emphasis was on destroying property, looting and burning stores. Six persons died, over 500 were injured, more than 100 were jailed.

The Postwar Period

White opinion in some quarters of America had begun to shift to a more sympathetic regard for Negroes during the New Deal, and the war had accelerated that movement. Thoughtful whites had been painfully aware of the contradiction in opposing Nazi racial philosophy with racially segregated military units. In the postwar years, American racial attitudes became more liberal as new nonwhite nations emerged in Asia and Africa and took increasing responsibilities in international councils.

Against this background, the growing size of the Northern Negro vote made civil rights a major issue in national elections and, ultimately, in 1957, led to the federal Civil Rights Commission, which had the power to investigate discriminatory conditions throughout the country and to recommend corrective measures to the President. Northern and Western states outlawed discrimination in employment, housing, and public accommodations, while the NAACP, in successive court victories, ended racially restrictive covenants in housing, segregation in interstate transportation, and discrimination in publicly-owned recreational facilities. The NAACP helped register voters, and in 1954, *Brown* v. *Board of Education* became the triumphant climax to the NAACP's campaign against educational segregation in the public schools of the South.

CORE, demonstrating in the Border states, its major focus on public accommodations, began experimenting with direct-action techniques to open employment opportunities. In 1947, in conjunction with the Fellowship of Reconciliation, CORE conducted a "Journey of Reconciliation"—what would later be called a "Freedom Ride"—in the states of the Upper South to test compliance with the Supreme

Court decision outlawing segregation on interstate buses. The resistance met by riders in some areas, the sentencing of two to 30 days on a North Carolina road gang, dramatized the gap between American democratic theory and practice.

But what captured the imagination of the nation and of the Negro community in particular, and what was chiefly responsible for the growing use of direct-action techniques, was the Montgomery, Alabama, bus boycott of 1955–1956, which catapulted into national prominence the Reverend Martin Luther King, Jr. Like the founders of CORE, King held to a Gandhian belief in the principles of pacifism.

Even before a court decision obtained by NAACP attorneys in November 1956 desegregated the Montgomery buses, a similar movement had started in Tallahassee, Florida. Afterward another one developed in Birmingham, Alabama. In 1957, the Tuskegee Negroes undertook a three-year boycott of local merchants after the state legislature gerrymandered nearly all of the Negro voters outside of the town's boundaries. In response to a lawsuit filed by the NAACP, the Supreme Court ruled the Tuskegee gerrymander illegal.

These events were widely heralded. A "new negro" had emerged in the South—militant, no longer fearful of white hoodlums or mobs, and ready to use his collective weight to achieve his ends. In this mood, King established the Southern Christian Leadership Conference in 1957 to coordinate direct-action activities in Southern cities.

Negro protest had now moved in a vigorous fashion into the South, and like similar activities in the North, it was concentrated in the urban ghettos.

The Persistence of Discrimination

Nonviolent direct action attained popularity not only because of the effectiveness of King's leadership but because the older techniques of legal and legislative action had had limited success. Impressive as the advances in the 15 years after World War II were, in spite of state laws and Supreme Court decisions, something was still clearly wrong. Negroes were disfranchised in most of the South, though in the 12 years following the outlawing of the white primary in 1944, the number of Negroes registered in Southern states had risen from about 250,000 to nearly a million and a quarter. Supreme Court decisions desegregating transportation facilities were still being largely ignored in the South. Discrimination in employment and housing continued, not only in the South but also in Northern states with model civil rights laws. The Negro unemployment rate steadily moved upward after 1954. The South reacted to the Supreme Court's decision on school desegregation by outlawing the NAACP, intimidating civil rights leaders, bringing "massive resistance" to the Court's decision, curtailing Negro voter registration, and forming White Citizens' Councils.

Revolution of Rising Expectations

At the same time, Negro attitudes were changing. Negroes were gaining a new sense of self-respect and a new self-image as a result of the civil rights movement and their own advancement. King and others were demonstrating that nonviolent direct action could succeed in the South. New laws and court decisions and increasing support of white public opinion gave American Negroes a new confidence in the future. There occurred what has been described as a "revolution in expectations."

Negroes no longer felt that they had to accept the humiliations of second-class citizenship, which consequently appeared more intolerable than ever. Ironically, it was the very successes in the legislatures and the courts that, more perhaps than any other single factor, led to intensified Negro expectations and resulting dissatisfaction with the limitations of legal and legislative programs. Increasing Negro impatience accounted for the rising tempo of nonviolent direct action in the late 1950's, culminating in the student sit-ins of 1960 and the inauguration of what is popularly known as the "Civil Rights Revolution" or the "Negro Revolt."

Many believe that the Montgomery boycott ushered in this Negro Revolt, and its importance, by projecting the image of King and his techniques, is great. But the decisive break with traditional techniques came with the college student sit-ins that swept the South in the winter and spring of 1960. In dozens of communities in the Upper South, the Atlantic coastal states, and Texas, student demonstrations secured the desegregation of lunch counters in drug and variety stores. Arrests were numbered in the thousands, and brutality was evident in scores of communities. In the Deep South the campaign ended in failure, even in instances where hundreds had been arrested, as in Montgomery; Orangeburg, South Carolina; and Baton Rouge. But the youth had captured the imagination of the Negro community and to a remarkable extent of the whole nation.

Student Involvement

The Negro protest movement would never be the same again. The Southern college students shook the power structure of the Negro community, made direct action temporarily pre-eminent as a civil rights tactic, speeded up the process of social change in race relations, and ultimately turned the Negro protest organizations toward a deep concern with the economic and social problems of the masses.

Involved in this was a gradual shift in both tactics and goals: from legal to direct action, from middle and upper class to mass action, from attempts to guarantee the Negro's constitutional rights to efforts to secure economic policies giving him equality of opportunity in a changing society, from appeals to the sense of fair play of white Americans to demands based upon power in the black ghetto.

The successes of the student movement threatened existing Negro leadership and precipitated a spirited rivalry among civil rights organizations. The NAACP and SCLC associated themselves with the student movement. The organizing meeting of the Student Nonviolent Coordinating Committee (SNCC)[1] at Raleigh, North Carolina, in April 1960 was called by Martin Luther King, but within a year the youth considered King too cautious and broke with him.

The NAACP now decided to make direct action a major part of its strategy and organized and reactivated college and youth chapters in the Southern and Border states.

CORE, still unknown to the general public, installed James Farmer as national director in January 1961, and that spring joined the front rank of civil rights organizations with the famous Freedom Ride to Alabama and Mississippi that dramatized the persistence of segregated public transportation. A bus-burning resulted in Alabama, and hundreds of demonstrators spent a month or more in Mississippi

[1] [SNCC now stands for Student National Coordinating Committee—G. M.]

prisons. Finally, a new order from the Interstate Commerce Commission desegregating all interstate transportation facilities received partial compliance.

Organizational Rivalries

Disagreement over strategy and tactics inevitably became intertwined with personal and organizational rivalries. Each civil rights group felt the need for proper credit in order to obtain the prestige and financial contributions necessary to maintain and expand its own programs. The local and national, individual and organizational clashes only stimulated competition and activity that further accelerated the pace of social change.

Yet there were differences in style. CORE was the most interracial. SCLC appeared to be the most deliberate. SNCC staff workers lived on subsistence allowances and seemed to regard going to jail as a way of life. The NAACP continued the most varied programs, retaining a strong emphasis on court litigation, maintaining a high effective lobby at the national capital, and engaging in direct-action campaigns. The National Urban League, under the leadership of Whitney M. Young, Jr., appointed executive director in 1961, became more outspoken and talked more firmly to businessmen who had previously been treated with utmost tact and caution.

The Role of Whites

The role of whites in the protest movement gradually changed. Instead of occupying positions of leadership, they found themselves relegated to the role of followers. Whites were likely to be suspect in the activist organizations. Negroes had come to feel less dependent on whites, more confident of their own power, and they demanded that their leaders be black. The NAACP had long since acquired Negro leadership but continued to welcome white liberal support. SCLC and SNCC were from the start Negro-led and Negro-dominated. CORE became predominantly Negro as it expanded in 1962 and 1963; today all executives are Negro, and a constitutional amendment adopted in 1965 officially limited white leadership in the chapters.

The Black Muslims

A major factor intensifying the civil rights movement was widespread Negro unemployment and poverty; an important force in awakening Negro protest was the meteoric rise to national prominence of the Black Muslims, established around 1930. The organization reached the peak of its influence when more progress toward equal rights was being made than ever before in American history while at the same time economic opportunity for the poorest groups in the urban ghettos was stagnating.

Increasing unemployment among Negroes, combined with the revolution in expectations, created a climate in which the Black Muslims thrived. They preached a vision of the doom of the white "devils" and the coming dominance of the black man, promised a utopian paradise of a separate territory within the United States for a Negro state, and offered a practical program of building Negro business through hard work, thrift, and racial unity. To those willing to submit to the rigid discipline of the movement, the Black Muslims organization gave a sense of purpose and dignity.

"Freedom Now!"

As the direct-action tactics took more dramatic form, as the civil rights groups began to articulate the needs of the masses and draw some of them to their demonstrations, the protest movement in 1963 assumed a new note of urgency, a demand for complete "Freedom Now!" Direct action returned to the Northern cities, taking the form of massive protests against economic, housing and educational inequities, and a fresh wave of demonstrations swept the South from Cambridge, Maryland, to Birmingham, Alabama. Northern Negroes launched street demonstrations against discrimination in the building trade unions and, the following winter, school boycotts against de facto segregation.

In the North, 1963 and 1964 brought the beginning of the waves of civil disorders in Northern urban centers. In the South, incidents occurred of brutal white resistance to the civil rights movement, beginning with the murder of Mississippi Negro leader Medgar Evers and four Negro schoolgirls in a church in Birmingham. . . .

The March on Washington

The massive anti-Negro actions in Birmingham and numerous other Southern cities during the spring of 1963 compelled the nation to face the problem of race prejudice in the South. President Kennedy affirmed that racial discrimination was a moral issue and asked Congress for a major civil rights bill. But a major impetus for what was to be the Civil Rights Act of 1964 was the March on Washington in August 1963.

Early in the year, A. Philip Randolph issued a call for a March on Washington to dramatize the need for jobs and to press for a federal commitment to job action. At about the same time, Protestant, Jewish, and Catholic churches sought and obtained representation on the March committee. Although the AFL-CIO national council refused to endorse the March, a number of labor leaders and international unions participated.

Reversing an earlier stand, President Kennedy approved the March. A quarter of a million people, about 20 percent of them white, participated. It was more than a summation of the past years of struggle and aspiration. It symbolized certain new directions: a deeper concern for the economic problems of the masses; more involvement of white moderates; and new demands from the most militant, who implied that only a revolutionary change in American institutions would permit Negroes to achieve the dignity of citizens.

President Kennedy had set the stage for the Civil Rights Act of 1964. After his death President Johnson took forceful and effective action to secure its enactment. The law settled the public accommodations issue in the South's major cities. Its voting section, however, promised more than it could accomplish. Martin Luther King and SCLC dramatized the issue locally with demonstrations at Selma, Alabama, in the spring of 1965. Again the national government was forced to intervene, and a new and more effective voting law was passed.

Failures of Direct Action

Birmingham had made direct action respectable, but Selma, which drew thousands of white moderates from the North, made direct action fashionable. Yet as early as 1964, it was becoming evident that, like legal action, direct action was an instrument of limited usefulness. This was the result of two converging developments.

In Deep South states like Mississippi and Alabama, direct action had failed to desegregate public accommodations in the sit-ins of 1960–1961. A major reason was that Negroes lacked the leverage of the vote. The demonstrations of the early 1960's had been successful principally in places like Atlanta, Nashville, Durham, Winston-Salem, Louisville, Savannah, New Orleans, Charleston, and Dallas—where Negroes voted and could swing elections. Beginning in 1961 Robert Moses of SNCC, with the cooperation of CORE and NAACP, established voter registration projects in the cities and county seats of Mississippi. He succeeded in registering only a handful of Negroes, but by 1964, he had generated enough support throughout the country to enable the Mississippi Freedom Democratic Party, which he had created, to challenge dramatically the seating of the official white delegates from the state at the Democratic National Convention.

In the black ghettos of the North direct action also largely failed. Street demonstrations did compel employers, from supermarkets to banks, to add many Negroes to their work force in Northern and Western cities, in some Southern cities, and even in some Southern towns where the Negroes had considerable buying power. However, separate and inferior schools, slum housing, and police hostility proved invulnerable to direct attack.

New Directions

But while Negroes were being hired in increasing numbers, mass unemployment and underemployment remained. As economist Vivian Henderson pointed out in his testimony before the Commission:

> No one can deny that all Negroes have benefited from civil rights laws and desegregation in public life in one way or another.

> The fact is, however, that the masses of Negroes have not experienced tangible benefits in a significant way. This is so in education and housing. It is critically so in the area of jobs and economic security. Expectations of Negro masses for equal job opportunity programs have fallen far short of fulfillment.
>
> Negroes have made gains. . . . There have been important gains. But . . . the masses of Negroes have been virtually untouched by those gains.

Faced with the intransigence of the deep South and the inadequacy of direct action to solve the problems of the slum dwellers, Negro protest organizations began to diverge. The momentum toward unity, apparent in 1963, was lost. At the very time that white support for the protest movement was rising markedly, militant Negroes felt increasingly isolated from the American scene. On two things, however, all segments of the protest movement agreed: (1) future civil rights activity would have to focus on the economic and social discrimination in the urban ghettos and (2) while demonstrations would still have a place, the major weapon would have to be the political potential of the black masses.

By the middle of the decade, many militant Negro members of SNCC and CORE began to turn away from American society and the "middle-class way of life." Cynical about the liberals and the leaders of organized labor, they regarded compromise, even as a temporary tactical device, as anathema. They talked more of "revolutionary" changes in the social structure, of retaliatory violence, and increasingly rejected white assistance. They insisted that Negro power alone could compel the white "ruling class" to make concessions. Yet they also spoke of an alliance of Negroes and unorganized lower-class whites to overthrow the "power structure" of capitalists, politicians and bureaucratic labor leaders who exploited the poor of both races by dividing them through an appeal to race prejudice.

At the same time that their activities declined, other issues, particularly Vietnam, diverted the attention of the country, including some Negro leaders, from the issue of equality. Reduced financing made it increasingly difficult to support staff personnel, even on a subsistence basis. Most important was the increasing frustration of expectations that affected the direct-action advocates of the early 1960's—the sense of futility growing out of the feeling that progress had turned out to be "tokenism," that the compromises of the white community were sedatives rather than solutions and that the current methods of Negro protest were doing little for the masses of the race.

As frustration grew, the ideology and rhetoric of a number of civil rights activists became angrier. One man more than any other—a black man who grew up believing whites had murdered his father—became the spokesman for this anger: Malcolm X, who perhaps best embodied the belief that racism was so deeply ingrained in white America that appeals to conscience would bring no fundamental change.

"Black Power"

In this setting the rhetoric of "Black Power" developed. The precipitating occasion was the Meredith March from Memphis to Jackson in June 1966, but the slogan expressed tendencies that had been present for a long time and had been gaining strength in the Negro community.

Black Power first articulated a mood rather than a program—disillusionment and alienation from white America and independence, race pride, and self-respect, or "black consciousness." Having become a household phrase, the term generated intense discussion of its real meaning, and a broad spectrum of ideologies and programmatic proposals emerged.

In politics, Black Power meant independent action—Negro control of the political power of the black ghettos and its conscious use to better slum dwellers' conditions. It could take the form of organizing a black political party or controlling the political machinery within the ghetto without the guidance or support of white politicians. Where predominantly Negro areas lacked Negroes in elective office, whether in the rural Black Belt of the South or in the urban centers, Black Power advocates sought the election of Negroes by voter registration campaigns, by getting out the vote, and by working for redrawing electoral districts. The basic belief was that only a well-organized and cohesive bloc of Negro voters could provide for the needs of the black masses. Even some Negro politicians allied to the major political parties adopted the term "Black Power" to describe their interest in the Negro vote.

In economic terms, Black Power meant creating independent, self-sufficient Negro business enterprise, not only by encouraging

Negro entrepreneurs but also by forming Negro cooperatives in the ghettos and in the predominantly black rural counties of the South. In the area of education, Black Power called for local community control of the public schools in the black ghettos.

Throughout, the emphasis was on self-help, racial unity, and, among the most militant, retaliatory violence, the latter ranging from the legal right of self-defense to attempts to justify looting and arson in ghetto riots, guerrilla warfare and armed rebellion.

Phrases like "Black Power," "Black Consciousness," and "Black is Beautiful," enjoyed an extensive currency in the Negro community, even within the NAACP and among relatively conservative politicians, but particularly among young intellectuals and Afro-American student groups on predominantly white college campuses. Expressed in its most extreme form by small, often local, fringe groups, the Black Power ideology became associated with SNCC and CORE.

Generally regarded as the most militant among the important Negro protest organizations, they have different interpretations of the Black Power doctrine. SNCC calls for totally independent political action outside the established political parties, as with the Black Panther Party in Lowndes County, Alabama; questions the value of political alliances with other groups until Negroes have themselves built a substantial base of independent political power; applauds the idea of guerrilla warfare; and regards riots as rebellions.

CORE has been more flexible. Approving the SNCC strategy, it also advocates working within the Democratic Party, forming alliances with other groups and, while seeking to justify riots as the natural explosion of an oppressed people against intolerable conditions, advocates violence only in self-defense. Both groups favor cooperatives, but CORE has seemed more inclined toward job-training programs and developing a Negro entrepreneurial class, based upon the market within the black ghettos.

Old Wine in New Bottles

What is new about "Black Power" is phraseology rather than substance. Black consciousness has roots in the organization of Negro churches and mutual benefit societies in the early days of the republic, the antebellum Negro convention movement, the Negro colonization schemes of the 19th century, DuBois' concept of Pan-Africanism,

Booker T. Washington's advocacy of race pride, self-help, and racial solidarity, the Harlem Renaissance, and the Garvey movement. The decade after World War I—which saw the militant, race-proud "new negro," the relatively widespread theory of retaliatory violence, and the high tide of the Negro-support-of-Negro-business ideology—exhibits striking parallels with the 1960's.

Similarly, there are striking parallels between both of these periods and the late 1840's and 1850's when ideologies of self-help, racial solidarity, separatism and nationalism, and the advocacy of organized rebellion were widespread.

The theme of retaliatory violence is hardly new for American Negroes. Most racial disorders in American history until recent years were characterized by white attacks on Negroes. But Negroes retaliated violently during Reconstruction, just after World War I, and in the last four years.

Black Power rhetoric and ideology actually express a lack of power. The slogan emerged when the Negro protest movement was slowing down, when it was finding increasing resistance to its changing goals, when it discovered that nonviolent direct action was no more a panacea than legal action, when CORE and SNCC were declining in terms of activity, membership, and financial support. This combination of circumstances provoked anger deepened by impotence. Powerless to make any fundamental changes in the life of the masses—powerless, that is, to compel white America to make those changes—many advocates of Black Power have retreated into an unreal world, where they see an outnumbered and poverty-stricken minority organizing itself independently of whites and creating sufficient power to force white America to grant its demands. To date, the evidence suggests that the situation is much like that of the 1840's, when a small group of intellectuals advocated slave insurrections, but stopped short of organizing them.

The Black Power advocates of today consciously feel that they are the most militant group in the Negro protest movement. Yet they have retreated from a direct confrontation with American society on the issue of integration and, by preaching separatism, unconsciously function as an accommodation to white racism. Much of their economic program, as well as their interest in Negro history, self-help, racial solidarity and separation, is reminiscent of Booker T. Washington. The rhetoric is different, but the programs are remarkably similar.

The Meaning

By 1967, whites could point to the demise of slavery, the decline of illiteracy among Negroes, the legal protection provided by the constitutional amendments and civil rights legislation, and the growing size of the Negro middle class. Whites would call it Negro progress from slavery to freedom toward equality.

Negroes could point to the doctrine of white supremacy, its widespread acceptance, its persistence after emancipation, and its influence on the definition of the place of Negroes in American life. They could point to their long fight for full citizenship, when they had active opposition from most of the white population and little or no support from the government. They could see progress toward equality accompanied by bitter resistance. Perhaps most of all, they could feel the persistent, pervasive racism that kept them in inferior segregated schools, restricted them to ghettos, barred them from fair employment, provided double standards in courts of justice, inflicted bodily harm on their children, and blighted their lives with a sense of hopelessness and despair.

In all of this and in the context of professed ideals, Negroes would find more retrogression than progress, more rejection than acceptance.

Until the middle of the 20th century, the course of Negro protest movements in the United States except for slave revolts, was based in the cities of the North, where Negroes enjoyed sufficient freedom to mount a sustained protest. It was in the cities, North and South, that Negroes had their greatest independence and mobility. It was natural, therefore, for black protest movements to be urban-based—and, until the last dozen years or so, limited to the North. As Negroes migrated from the South, the mounting strength of their votes in Northern cities became a vital element in drawing the federal government into the defense of the civil rights of Southern Negroes. While rural Negroes today face great racial problems, the major unsolved questions that touch the core of Negro life stem from discrimination embedded in urban housing, employment, and education.

Over the years the character of Negro protest has changed. Originally it was a white liberal and Negro upper-class movement aimed at securing the constitutional rights of Negroes through propaganda, lawsuits, and legislation. In recent years the emphasis in tactics shifted first to direct action and then—among the most militant—to the rhetoric of "Black Power." The role of white liberals declined as Negroes came to direct the struggle. At the same time the Negro protest movement became more of a mass movement, with increasing participation from the working classes. As these changes were occurring, and while substantial progress was being made to secure constitutional rights for the Negroes, the goals of the movement were broadened. Protest groups now demand special efforts to overcome the Negro's poverty and cultural deprivation—conditions that cannot be erased simply by ensuring constitutional rights.

The central thrust of Negro protest in the current period has aimed at the inclusion of Negroes in American society on a basis of full equality rather than at a fundamental transformation of American institutions. There have been elements calling for a revolutionary overthrow of the American social system or for a complete withdrawal of Negroes from American society. But these solutions have had little popular support. Negro protest, for the most part, has been firmly rooted in the basic values of American society, seeking not their destruction but their fulfillment.

QUESTIONS FOR DISCUSSION AND WRITING

1. The Kerner report calls upon history "not to justify, but to help explain, for black and white Americans, a state of mind." How can a "state of mind" be related to the history of black people in America? Whose "state of mind" is more relevant to an understanding of that history? Why?
2. According to the report, what motives are most characteristic of white segregationists? Of black separatists? Have these motives changed to any great extent in the past two hundred years? How?
3. What is the pattern of "civil disorders" (riots) involving racial confrontation in the United States? How can their causes be best accounted for?
4. The Commission states that "a revolution in expectations" has created a drastic change in black hopes and demands. How has the

shift manifested itself within the "movement"? Has a similar revolution taken place in other contemporary protests? How?

5. The report suggests, in general terms, the parallels between the ideologies of previous times of black protest and those of the present. Compare and contrast the specific views of the following men regarding the cause of the Negro's plight, segregation, poverty, proper tactics, and the American economy: Douglass (p. 45) and King (p. 341), Garvey (p. 103) and Malcolm X (p. 317), Carmichael (p. 329) and DuBois (p. 91).

HARRIET BEECHER STOWE PUBLISHED *Uncle Tom's Cabin, or Life Among the Lowly* IN 1852, WHEN SHE WAS FORTY-ONE. MRS. STOWE LIVED FOR NEARLY TWENTY YEARS IN CINCINNATI, OHIO, THEN A CENTER FOR THE "UNDERGROUND RAILWAY." THE NOVEL BECAME A WORLDWIDE BEST SELLER, COMBINING MRS. STOWE'S OWN RELIGIOUS FERVOR WITH THE SUBJECT OF SLAVERY, AN ISSUE NOT MUCH WRITTEN ABOUT IN NOVEL FORM PRIOR TO THAT TIME.

HARRIET BEECHER STOWE

THE MARTYR

"Deem not the just by Heaven forgot!
  Though life its common gifts deny,—
Though, with a crushed and bleeding heart,
  And spurned of man, he goes to die!
For God hath marked each sorrowing day,
  And numbered every bitter tear;
And heaven's long years of bliss shall pay
  For all his children suffer here."

Bryant

The longest way must have its close,—the gloomiest night will wear on to a morning. An eternal, inexorable lapse of moments is ever hurrying the day of the evil to an eternal night, and the night of the

THE MARTYR From *Uncle Tom's Cabin, or Life Among the Lowly* (1852) by Harriet Beecher Stowe, Chapter 40.

just to an eternal day. We have walked with our humble friend thus far in the valley of slavery; first through flowery fields of ease and indulgence, then through heart-breaking separations from all that man holds dear. Again, we have waited with him in a sunny island, where generous hands concealed his chains with flowers; and, lastly, we have followed him where the last ray of earthly hope went out in night, and seen how, in the blackness of earthly darkness, the firmament of the unseen has blazed with stars of new and significant lustre.

The morning star now stands over the tops of the mountains, and gales and breezes, not of earth, show that the gates of day are unclosing.

The escape of Cassy and Emmeline irritated the before surly temper of Legree to the last degree; and his fury, as was to be expected, fell upon the defenceless head of Tom. When he hurriedly announced the tidings among his hands, there was a sudden light in Tom's eye, a sudden upraising of his hands, that did not escape him. He saw that he did not join the muster of the pursuers. He thought of forcing him to do it; but, having had, of old, experience of his inflexibility when commanded to take part in any deed of inhumanity, he would not, in his hurry, stop to enter into any conflict with him.

Tom, therefore, remained behind, with a few who had learned of him to pray, and offered up prayers for the escape of the fugitives.

When Legree returned, baffled and disappointed, all the long-working hatred of his soul towards his slave began to gather in a deadly and desperate form. Had not this man braved him,—steadily, powerfully, resistlessly,—ever since he bought him? Was there not a spirit in him which, silent as it was, burned on him like the fires of perdition?

"I *hate* him!" said Legree, that night, as he sat up in his bed; "I *hate* him! And isn't he MINE? Can't I do what I like with him? Who's to hinder, I wonder?" And Legree clenched his fist, and shook it, as if he had something in his hands that he could rend in pieces.

But, then, Tom was a faithful, valuable servant; and, although Legree hated him the more for that, yet the consideration was still somewhat of a restraint to him.

The next morning, he determined to say nothing, as yet; to assemble a party, from some neighboring plantations, with dogs and guns; to surround the swamp, and go about the hunt systematically. If it succeeded, well and good; if not, he would summon Tom before him, and—his teeth clenched and his blood boiled—*then* he would break that fellow down, or——there was a dire inward whisper, to which his soul assented.

Ye say that the *interest* of the master is a sufficient safeguard for the slave. In the fury of man's mad will, he will wittingly, and with open eye, sell his own soul to the devil to gain his ends; and will he be more careful of his neighbor's body?

"Well," said Cassy, the next day, from the garret, as she reconnoitred through the knot-hole, "the hunt's going to begin again, to-day!"

Three or four mounted horsemen were curvetting about, on the space front of the house; and one or two leashes of strange dogs were struggling with the Negroes who held them, baying and barking at each other.

The men were, two of them, overseers of plantations in the vicinity; and others were some of Legree's associates at the tavern-bar of a neighboring city, who had come for the interest of the sport. A more hard-favored set, perhaps, could not be imagined. Legree was serving brandy, profusely, round among them, as also among the Negroes, who had been detailed from the various plantations for this service; for it was an object to make every service of this kind, among the Negroes, as much of a holiday as possible.

Cassy placed her ear at the knot-hole; and, as the morning air blew directly towards the house, she could overhear a good deal of the conversation. A grave sneer overcast the dark, severe gravity of her face, as she listened, and heard them divide out the ground, discuss the rival merits of the dogs, give orders about firing, and the treatment of each, in case of capture.

Cassy drew back; and, clasping her hands, looked upward, and said, "O, great Almighty God! we are *all* sinners; but what have *we* done, more than all the rest of the world, that we should be treated so?"

There was a terrible earnestness in her face and voice, as she spoke.

"If it wasn't for *you,* child," she said, looking at Emmeline, "I'd *go* out to them; and I'd thank any one of them that *would* shoot me down; for what use will freedom be to me? Can it give me back my children, or make me what I used to be?"

Emmeline, in her child-like simplicity, was half afraid of the dark moods of Cassy. She looked perplexed, but made no answer. She only took her hand, with a gentle, caressing movement.

"Don't!" said Cassy, trying to draw it away; "you'll get me to loving you; and I never mean to love anything, again!"

"Poor Cassy!" said Emmeline, "don't feel so! If the Lord gives us liberty, perhaps he'll give you back your daughter; at any rate, I'll be like a daughter to you. I know I'll never see my poor old mother again! I shall love you, Cassy, whether you love me or not!"

The gentle, child-like spirit conquered, Cassy sat down by her, put her arm round her neck, stroked her soft brown hair; and Emmeline then wondered at the beauty of her magnificent eyes, now soft with tears.

"O, Em!" said Cassy, "I've hungered for my children, and thirsted for them, and my eyes fail with longing for them! Here! here!" she said, striking her breast, "it's all desolate, all empty! If God would give me back my children, then I could pray."

"You must trust him, Cassy," said Emmeline; "he is our Father!"

"His wrath is upon us," said Cassy; "he has turned away in anger."

"No, Cassy! He will be good to us! Let us hope in Him," said Emmeline,—"I always have had hope."

. . .

The hunt was long, animated, and thorough, but unsuccessful; and, with grave, ironic exultation, Cassy looked down on Legree, as, weary and dispirited, he alighted from his horse.

"Now, Quimbo," said Legree, as he stretched himself down in the sitting-room, "you jest go and walk that Tom up here, right away! The old cuss is at the bottom of this yer whole matter; and I'll have it out of his old black hide, or I'll know the reason why!"

Sambo and Quimbo, both, though hating each other, were joined in one mind by a no less cordial hatred of Tom. Legree had told them, at first, that he had bought him for a general overseer, in his absence; and this had begun an ill will, on their part, which had increased, in their debased and servile natures, as they saw him becoming obnoxious to their master's displeasure. Quimbo, therefore, departed, with a will, to execute his orders.

Tom heard the message with a forewarning heart; for he knew all the plan of the fugitives' escape, and the place of their present concealment;—he knew the deadly character of the man he had to deal with, and his despotic power. But he felt strong in God to meet death, rather than betray the helpless.

He sat his basket down by the row, and, looking up, said, "Into thy hands I commend my spirit! Thou hast redeemed me, oh Lord God of truth!" and then quietly yielded himself to the rough, brutal grasp with which Quimbo seized him.

"Ay, ay!" said the giant, as he dragged him along; "ye'll cotch it, now! I'll boun' Mas'r's back's up *high!* No sneaking out, now! Tell ye, ye'll get it, and no mistake! See how ye'll look, now, helpin' Mas'r's niggers to run away! See what ye'll get!"

The savage words none of them reached that ear!—a higher voice there was saying, "Fear not them that kill the body, and, after that, have no more that they can do." Nerve and bone of that poor man's body vibrated to those words, as if touched by the finger of God; and he felt the strength of a thousand souls in one. As he passed along, the trees and bushes, the huts of his servitude, the whole scene of his degradation, seemed to whirl by him as the landscape by the rushing car. His soul throbbed,—his home was in sight,—and the hour of release seemed at hand.

"Well, Tom!" said Legree, walking up, and seizing him grimly by the collar of his coat, and speaking through his teeth, in a paroxysm of determined rage, "do you know I've made up my mind to KILL you?"

"It's very likely, Mas'r," said Tom, calmly.

"I *have*," said Legree, with grim, terrible calmness, "*done—just—that—thing*, Tom, unless you'll tell me what you know about these yer gals!"

Tom stood silent.

"D'ye hear!" said Legree, stamping, with a roar like that of an incensed lion. "Speak!"

"I han't got nothing to tell, Mas'r," said Tom, with a slow, firm, deliberate utterance.

"Do you dare to tell me, ye old black Christian, ye don't *know*?" said Legree.

Tom was silent.

"Speak!" thundered Legree, striking him furiously. "Do you know anything?"

"I know, Mas'r; but I can't tell anything. *I can die!*"

Legree drew in a long breath; and, suppressing his rage, took Tom by the arm, and, approaching his face almost to his, said, in a terrible voice, "Hark 'e, Tom!—ye think, 'cause I've let you off before, I don't mean what I say; but, this time, I've *made up my mind,* and counted the cost. You've always stood it out agin' me: now, I'll *conquer ye, or kill ye!*—one or t'other. I'll count every drop of blood there is in you, and take 'em, one by one, till ye give up!"

Tom looked up to his master, and answered, "Mas'r, if you was sick, or in trouble, or dying, and I could save ye, I'd *give* ye my heart's blood; and if taking every drop of blood in this poor old body would save your precious soul, I'd give 'em freely, as the Lord gave his for me. O, Mas'r! don't bring this great sin on your soul! It will hurt you more than 'twill me! Do the worst you can, my troubles'll be over soon; but if you don't repent, yours won't *never* end!"

Like a strange snatch of heavenly music, heard in the lull of a tempest, this burst of feeling made a moment's blank pause. Legree stood aghast, and looked at Tom; and there was such a silence, that the tick of the old clock could be heard, measuring, with silent touch, the last moments of mercy and probation to that hardened heart.

It was but a moment. There was one hesitating pause,—one irresolute, relenting thrill,—and the spirit of evil came back, with seven-fold vehemence; and Legree, foaming with rage, smote his victim to the ground.

. . .

Scenes of blood and cruelty are shocking to our ear and heart. What man has nerve to do, man has not nerve to hear. What brother-man and brother-Christian must suffer, cannot be told us, even in our secret chamber, it so harrows up the soul! And yet, oh my country; these things are done under the shadow of thy laws! O, Christ! thy church sees them, almost in silence!

But, of old, there was One whose suffering changed an instrument of torture, degradation and shame, into a symbol of glory, honor, and immortal life; and, where His spirit is, neither degrading stripes, nor blood, nor insults, can make the Christian's last struggle less than glorious.

Was he alone, that long night, whose brave, loving spirit was bearing up, in that old shed, against buffeting and brutal stripes?

Nay! There stood by him One,—seen by him alone,—"like unto the Son of God."

The tempter stood by him, too,—blinded by furious, despotic will,—every moment pressing him to shun that agony by the betrayal of the innocent. But the brave, true heart was firm on the Eternal Rock. Like his Master, he knew that, if he saved others, himself he could not save; nor could utmost extremity wring from him words, save of prayer and holy trust.

"He's most gone, Mas'r," said Sambo, touched, in spite of himself, by the patience of his victim.

"Pay away, till he give up! Give it to him!—give it to him!" shouted Legree. "I'll take every drop of blood he has, unless he confesses!"

Tom opened his eyes, and looked upon his master. "Ye poor miserable crittur!" he said, "there an't no more ye can do! I forgive ye, with all my soul!" and he fainted entirely away.

"I b'lieve, my soul, he's done for, finally," said Legree, stepping forward, to look at him. "Yes, he is! Well, his mouth's shut up, at last, —that's one comfort!"

Yes, Legree; but who shall shut up that voice in thy soul? that soul, past repentance, past prayer, past hope, in whom the fire that never shall be quenched is already burning!

Yet Tom was not quite gone. His wondrous words and pious prayers had struck upon the hearts of the imbruted blacks, who had been the instruments of cruelty upon him; and, the instant Legree withdrew, they took him down, and, in their ignorance, sought to call him back to life,—as if *that* were any favor to him.

"Sartin, we's been doin' a drefful wicked thing!" said Sambo; "hopes Mas'r'll have to 'count for it, and not we."

They washed his wounds,—they provided a rude bed, of some refuse cotton, for him to lie down on; and one of them, stealing up to the house, begged a drink of brandy of Legree, pretending that he was tired, and wanted it for himself. He brought it back, and poured it down Tom's throat.

"O, Tom!" said Quimbo, "we's been awful wicked to ye!"

"I forgive ye, with all my heart!" said Tom, faintly.

"O, Tom! do tell us who is *Jesus,* anyhow?" said Sambo;—"Jesus, that's been a standin' by you so, all this night!—Who is he?"

The word roused the failing, fainting spirit. He poured forth a few energetic sentences of that wondrous One,—his life, his death, his everlasting presence, and power to save.

They wept,—both the two savage men.

"Why didn't I never hear this before?" said Sambo; "but I do believe!—I can't help it! Lord Jesus, have mercy on us!"

"Poor critturs!" said Tom, "I'd be willing to b'ar all I have, if it'll only bring ye to Christ! O, Lord! give me these two more souls, I pray!"

That prayer was answered!

QUESTIONS FOR DISCUSSION AND WRITING

1. Mrs. Stowe's characterization of Uncle Tom provided the white world with a long-lasting stereotype of the American Negro. What aspects of this stereotype are still *effectively* present in white thinking? In black thinking?
2. *Uncle Tom's Cabin* offers the reader an assortment of white stereotypes in addition to the black ones. Simon Legree is meant to represent an extreme—a thoroughly cruel, thoroughly evil man; yet even Legree is affected by his persecution of Tom. Is Legree's viewpoint representative of current white thinking in America? Does Legree perceive Tom as a human being or as a curse? Why?
3. Evaluate Mrs. Stowe's attitudes toward black Christianity. Does her antislavery plea seem to be based on a recognition of the evils of slavery or on a religious point of view? What *is* her apparent religious view?
4. In *The Sentimental Novel in America* Herbert Brown points out that *Uncle Tom's Cabin* is a profound document of religious-emotional attitudes. The novel provided great impetus to the anti-slavery campaign, which culminated in the Civil War. What kind of sentiment is aroused by the section of the novel presented in the text? What is the reader asked to accept as the "good" and the "bad" in this melodramatic situation?
5. Contrast Mrs. Stowe's characterization of Negroes with that presented in Helper's essay (p. 59) and in Governor Barnett's speech (p. 217). What similarity in attitudes becomes clear? Is that attitude echoed in Ellison (p. 113) and Washington (p. 65)?

FREDERICK DOUGLASS, BORN INTO SLAVERY IN 1817, BECAME A CENTRAL FIGURE IN THE ABOLITIONIST MOVEMENT THROUGH HIS WRITINGS AND HIS SPEECHES. BILLED ON THE LECTURE CIRCUIT AS "AN ESCAPED SLAVE," DOUGLASS SPOKE WITH AUTHORITY ON THE SUBJECT OF SLAVERY. HIS WRITINGS WERE PUBLISHED BOTH IN PERIODICALS AND IN HIS OWN NEWSPAPER, *North Star*. HIS INFLUENCE WAS LATER ACKNOWLEDGED BY HIS APPOINTMENT AS AMBASSADOR TO HAITI.

FREDERICK DOUGLASS

ON FREEDOM AND PREJUDICE

Give Us the Freedom Intended for Us

We are often cautioned against demanding too much for the colored people of this country. This cautioning is invariably accompanied with a full narration of what has already been done for our people, and we are further exhorted to remember that within the past decade we were slaves without any rights entitled to respect, and that in this short space of time we have been freed and transformed into American citizens, with the right to exercise the elective franchise extended to us by amendment to the National Constitution. Having been the recipients of these very valuable gifts, it is asserted by some who have taken an active part in the giving, that we should be satisfied at least

ON FREEDOM AND PREJUDICE "Give Us the Freedom Intended for Us" is reprinted from *The New National Era* (December 5, 1872). "The Color Line" is reprinted from *The North American Review*, Vol. 132 (June 1881).

long enough to allow the nation to take breath after its strenuous exertions in the accomplishment of the results so beneficial to us. To such persons the fact that we have been oppressed, outraged, and wronged for more than two centuries seems to be no argument why the nation should hasten to undo the wrong it has sanctioned against us, now that it fully admits the evil perpetrated upon us.

The elective franchise without protection in its exercise amounts to almost nothing in the hands of a minority with a vast majority determined that no exercise of it shall be made by the minority. Freedom from the auction block and from legal claim as property is of no benefit to the colored man without the means of protecting his rights. The black man is not a free American citizen in the sense that a white man is a free American citizen; he cannot protect himself against encroachments upon the rights and privileges already allowed him in a court of justice without an impartial jury. If accused of crime, he is tried by men who have a bias against him by reason of his race, color, or previous condition of servitude. If he attempts to send his children to the nearest public school where a free white American citizen, who pays no more taxes, can have the privilege without question, he is driven away and has no redress at law. If, after purchasing tickets for a ride in a first-class railway carriage, a colored person is hustled out into a smoking car, he or she has no redress at law because a custom prevails which allows injustice in this respect to colored persons.

We claim that the thirteenth, fourteenth, and fifteenth amendments to the Constitution of the United States were intended to give full freedom to every person without regard to race or color in the United States; and, in order that this intention should be carried out and acted upon, power for that purpose was given by conferring upon Congress the right to enforce the amendments by appropriate legislation. It cannot be denied that the violent interference with the black man to prevent him from exercising the elective franchise in accordance with his own views is an abridgement of his freedom as is also the refusal of a trial by a jury of his peers; nor can it be denied that the forcing of colored men to pay for what they do not get by railroad corporations or the refusal to allow the same accommodation to them as to other citizens of the United States, is an invidious discrimination amounting to an abridgement of citizenship rights.

We cannot be asking too much when we ask this Congress to carry out the intention of this Nation as expressed in the thirteenth, fourteenth and fifteenth amendments. We are not free. We cannot be free without the appropriate legislation provided for in the above amendments. We say to those who think we are demanding too much that it is idle to point us to the amendments and ask us to be satisfied with them and wait until the nation is educated up to giving us something more. The amendments are excellent but they need to be enforced. The result intended to be reached by the nation has not been reached. Congress has neglected to do its full duty. The people one month ago reiterated in thunder tones their demand "that complete liberty and *exact equality* in the enjoyment of all civil, political, and public rights should be established and effectually maintained throughout the Union by efficient and appropriate State and Federal legislation." We join in this demand those who think we are asking too much to the contrary notwithstanding.

The people on the 5th of November last ratified the following: "The recent amendments to the national Constitution should be cordially sustained because they are right, not merely tolerated because they are law, and should be carried out *according to their spirit* by appropriate legislation." The Liberal Democratic platform took similar ground as follows, and all the voters in the country voted for similar principles: "We recognize the equality of all men before the law and hold that it is the duty of Government in its dealings with the people to mete out equal and exact justice to all of whatever nativity, race, color or persuasion religious or political. We pledge ourselves to maintain the Union of these States, emancipation and enfranchisement and to oppose any reopening of the questions settled by the thirteenth, fourteenth, and fifteenth amendments to the Constitution." In view of this can a Republican Congress longer refuse to enact into law such a bill as Senator Sumner brought forward in the last session of Congress and which is by far the best measure yet proposed for establishing "complete liberty and exact equality in the enjoyment of all civil, political, and public rights."

December 5, 1872

The Color Line

Few evils are less accessible to the force of reason, or more tenacious of life and power, than a long-standing prejudice. It is a moral disorder, which creates the conditions necessary to its own existence, and fortifies itself by refusing all contradiction. It paints a hateful picture according to its own diseased imagination, and distorts the features of the fancied original to suit the portrait. As those who believe in the visibility of ghosts can easily see them, so it is always easy to see repulsive qualities in those we despise and hate.

Prejudice of race has at some time in their history afflicted all nations. "I am more holy than thou" is the boast of races, as well as that of the Pharisee. Long after the Norman invasion and the decline of Norman power, long after the sturdy Saxon had shaken off the dust of his humiliation and was grandly asserting his great qualities in all directions, the descendants of the invaders continued to regard their Saxon brothers as made of coarser clay than themselves, and were not well pleased when one of the former subject race came between the sun and their nobility. Having seen the Saxon a menial, a hostler, and a common drudge, oppressed and dejected for centuries, it was easy to invest him with all sorts of odious peculiarities, and to deny him all manly predicates. Though eight hundred years have passed away since Norman power entered England, and the Saxon has for centuries been giving his learning, his literature, his language, and his laws to the world more successfully than any other people on the globe, men in that country still boast their Norman origin and Norman perfections. This superstition of former greatness serves to fill out the shriveled sides of a meaningless race-pride which holds over after its power has vanished. With a very different lesson from the one this paper is designed to impress, the great Daniel Webster once told the people of Massachusetts (whose prejudices in the particular instance referred to were right) that they "had conquered the sea, and had conquered the land," but that "it remained for them to conquer their prejudices." At one time we are told that the people in some of the towns of Yorkshire cherished a prejudice so strong and violent against strangers and foreigners that one who ventured to pass through their streets would be pelted with stones.

Of all the races and varieties of men which have suffered from this feeling, the colored people of this country have endured most. They can resort to no disguises which will enable them to escape its deadly aim. They carry in front the evidence which marks them for persecution. They stand at the extreme point of difference from the Caucasian race, and their African origin can be instantly recognized, though they may be several removes from the typical African race.

They may remonstrate like Shylock—"Hath not a Jew eyes? Hath not a Jew hands, organs, dimensions, senses, affections, passions; fed with the same food, hurt with the same weapons, subject to the same diseases, healed by the same means, warmed and cooled by the same summer and winter, as a Christian is?"—but such eloquence is unavailing. They are Negroes—and that is enough, in the eye of this unreasoning prejudice, to justify indignity and violence. In nearly every department of American life they are confronted by this insidious influence. It fills the air. It meets them at the workshop and factory, when they apply for work. It meets them at the church, at the hotel, at the ballot-box, and worst of all, it meets them in the jury-box. Without crime or offense against law or gospel, the colored man is the Jean Valjean of American society. He has escaped from the galleys, and hence all presumptions are against him. The workshop denies him work, and the inn denies him shelter, the ballot-box a fair vote, and the jury-box a fair trial. He has ceased to be the slave of an individual, but has in some sense become the slave of society. He may not now be bought and sold like a beast in the market, but he is the trammeled victim of a prejudice, well calculated to repress his manly ambition, paralyze his energies, and make him a dejected and spiritless man, if not a sullen enemy to society, fit to prey upon life and property and to make trouble generally.

When this evil spirit is judge, jury, and prosecutor, nothing less than overwhelming evidence is sufficient to overcome the force of unfavorable presumptions.

Everything against the person with the hated color is promptly taken for granted; while everything in his favor is received with suspicion and doubt.

A boy of this color is found in his bed tied, mutilated, and bleeding, when forthwith all ordinary experience is set aside, and he is presumed to have been guilty of the outrage upon himself; weeks and months he is kept on trial for the offense, and every effort is made to entangle the poor fellow in the confused meshes of expert testimony (the least trustworthy of all evidence). This same spirit, which promptly assumes everything against us, just as readily denies or explains away everything in our favor. We are not, as a race, even permitted to appropriate the virtues and achievements of our individual representatives. Manliness, capacity, learning, laudable ambition, heroic service, by any of our number, are easily placed to the credit of the superior race. One drop of Teutonic blood is enough to account for all good and great qualities occasionally coupled with a colored skin; and on the other hand, one drop of Negro blood, though in the veins of a man of Teutonic whiteness, is enough on which to predicate all offensive and ignoble qualities. In presence of this spirit, if a crime is committed, and the criminal is not positively known, a suspicious-looking colored man is sure to have been seen in the neighborhood. If an unarmed colored man is shot down and dies in his tracks, a jury, under the influence of this spirit, does not hesitate to find the murdered man the real criminal, and the murderer innocent.

Now let us examine this subject a little more closely. It is claimed that this wonder-working prejudice—this moral magic that can change virtue into vice, and innocence to crime; which makes the dead man the murderer, and holds the living homicide harmless—is a natural, instinctive, and invincible attribute of the white race, and one that cannot be eradicated; that even evolution itself cannot carry us beyond or above it. Alas for this poor suffering world (for four-fifths of mankind are colored), if this claim be true! In that case men are forever doomed to injustice, oppression, hate, and strife; and the religious sentiment of the world, with its grand idea of human brotherhood, its "peace on earth and good-will to men," and its golden rule, must be voted a dream, a delusion, and a snare.

But is this color prejudice the natural and inevitable thing it claims to be? If it is so, then it is utterly idle to write against it, preach, pray, or legislate against it, or pass constitutional amendments against it. Nature will have her course, and one might as well preach and pray to a horse against running, to a fish against swimming, or to a bird against flying. Fortunately, however, there is good ground for calling in question this high pretension of a vulgar and wicked prepossession.

If I could talk with all my white fellow-countrymen on this subject, I would say to them, in the language of Scripture: "Come and let us reason together." Now, without being too elementary and formal, it may be stated here that there are at least seven points which candid men will be likely to admit, but which, if admitted, will prove fatal to the popular thought and practice of the times.

First. If what we call prejudice against color be natural, *i.e.*, a part of human nature itself, it follows that it must be co-extensive with human nature, and will and must manifest itself whenever and wherever the two races are brought into contact. It would not vary with either latitude, longitude, or altitude; but like fire and gunpowder, whenever brought together, there would be an explosion of contempt, aversion, and hatred.

Second. If it can be shown that there is anywhere on the globe any considerable country where the contact of the African and the Caucasian is not distinguished by this explosion of race-wrath, there is reason to doubt that the prejudice is an ineradicable part of human nature.

Thirdly. If this so-called natural, instinctive prejudice can be satisfactorily accounted for by facts and considerations wholly apart from the color features of the respective races, thus placing it among the things subject to human volition and control, we may venture to deny the claim set up for it in the name of human nature.

Fourthly. If any considerable number of white people have overcome this prejudice in themselves, have cast it out as an unworthy sentiment, and have survived the operation, the fact shows that this prejudice is not at any rate a vital part of human nature, and may be eliminated from the race without harm.

Fifthly. If this prejudice shall, after all, prove to be, in its essence and in its natural manifestation, simply a prejudice against condition, and not against race or color, and that it disappears when this or that condition is absent, then the argument drawn from the nature of the Caucasian race falls to the ground.

Sixthly. If prejudice of race and color is only natural in the sense that ignorance, superstition, bigotry, and vice are natural, then it has no better defense than they, and should be despised and put away from human relations as an enemy to the peace, good order, and happiness of human society.

Seventhly. If, still further, this aversion to the Negro arises out of the fact that he is as we see him, poor, spiritless, ignorant, and degraded, then whatever is humane, noble, and superior, in the mind of the superior and more fortunate race, will desire that all arbitrary barriers against his manhood, intelligence, and elevation shall be removed, and a fair chance in the race of life be given him.

The first of these propositions does not require discussion. It commends itself to the understanding at once. Natural qualities are common and universal, and do not change essentially on the mountain or in the valley. I come therefore to the second point—the existence of countries where this malignant prejudice, as we know it in America, does not prevail; where character, not color, is the passport to consideration; where the right of the black man to be a man, and a man among men, is not questioned; where he may, without offense, even presume to be a gentleman. That there are such countries in the world there is ample evidence. Intelligent and observing travelers, having no theory to support, men whose testimony would be received without question in respect of any other matter, and should not be questioned in this, tell us that they find no color prejudice in Europe, except among Americans who reside there. In England and on the Continent, the colored man is no more an object of hate than any other person. He mingles with the multitude unquestioned, without offense given or received. During the two years which the writer spent abroad, though he was much in society, and was sometimes in the company of lords and ladies, he does not remember one word, look, or gesture that indicated the slightest aversion to him on account of color. His experience was not in this respect exceptional or singular. Messrs. Remond, Ward, Garnet, Brown, Pennington, Crummell, and Bruce,[1] all of them colored, and some of them black, bear the same testimony. If what these gentlemen say (and it can be corroborated by a thousand witnesses) is true there is no prejudice against color in England, save as it is carried there by Americans—carried there as a moral disease from an infected country. It is American, not European; local, not general; limited, not universal, and must be ascribed to artificial conditions, and not to any fixed and universal law of nature.

The third point is: Can this prejudice against color, as it is called, be accounted for by circumstances outside and independent of race or color? If it can be thus explained, an incubus may be removed from the breasts of both the white and the black people of this country, as well as from that large intermediate population which has sprung up between these alleged irreconcilable extremes. It will help us to see that it is not necessary that the Ethiopian shall change his skin, nor needful that the white man shall change the essential elements of his nature, in order that mutual respect and consideration may exist between the two races.

Now it is easy to explain the conditions outside of race or color from which may spring feelings akin to those which we call prejudice. A man without the ability or the disposition to pay a just debt does not feel at ease in the presence of his creditor. He does not want to meet him on the street, or in the market-place. Such meeting

[1] [Acquaintances of Douglass' who wrote testimonials about social conditions in England—G. M.]

makes him uncomfortable. He would rather find fault with the bill than pay the debt, and the creditor himself will soon develop in the eyes of the debtor qualities not altogether to his taste.

Someone has well said, we may easily forgive those who injure us, but it is hard to forgive those whom we injure. The greatest injury this side of death, which one human being can inflict on another, is to enslave him, to blot out his personality, degrade his manhood, and sink him to the condition of a beast of burden; and just this has been done here during more than two centuries. No other people under heaven, of whatever type or endowments, could have been so enslaved without falling into contempt and scorn on the part of those enslaving them. Their slavery would itself stamp them with odious features, and give their oppressors arguments in favor of oppression. Besides the long years of wrong and injury inflicted upon the colored race in this country, and the effect of these wrongs upon that race, morally, intellectually, and physically, corrupting their morals, darkening their minds, and twisting their bodies and limbs out of all approach to symmetry, there has been a mountain of gold—uncounted millions of dollars—resting upon them with crushing weight. During all the years of their bondage, the slave master had a direct interest in discrediting the personality of those he held as property. Every man who had a thousand dollars so invested had a thousand reasons for painting the black man as fit only for slavery. Having made him the companion of horses and mules, he naturally sought to justify himself by assuming that the Negro was not much better than a mule. The holders of twenty hundred million dollars' worth of property in human chattels procured the means of influencing press, pulpit, and politician, and through these instrumentalities they belittled our virtues and magnified our vices, and have made us odious in the eyes of the world. Slavery had the power at one time to make and unmake Presidents, to construe the law, dictate the policy, set the fashion in national manners and customs, interpret the Bible, and control the church; and, naturally enough, the old masters set themselves up as much too high as they set the manhood of the Negro too low. Out of the depths of slavery has come this prejudice and this color line. It is broad enough and black enough to explain all the malign influences which assail the newly emancipated millions to-day. In reply to this argument it will perhaps be said that the Negro has no slavery now to contend with, and that having been free during the last sixteen years, he ought by this time to have contradicted the degrading qualities which slavery formerly ascribed to him. All very true as to the letter, but utterly false as to the spirit. Slavery is indeed gone, but its shadow still lingers over the country and poisons more or less the moral atmosphere of all sections of the republic. The money motive for assailing the Negro which slavery represented is indeed absent, but love of power and dominion, strengthened by two centuries of irresponsible power, still remains.

Having now shown how slavery created and sustained this prejudice against race and color, and the powerful motive for its creation, the other four points made against it need not be discussed in detail and at length, but may only be referred to in a general way.

If what is called the instinctive aversion of the white race for the colored, when analyzed, is seen to be the same as that which men feel or have felt toward other objects wholly apart from color; if it should be the same as that sometimes exhibited by the haughty and rich to the humble and poor, the same as the Brahmin feels toward the lower caste, the same as the Norman felt toward the Saxon, the same as that cherished by the Turk against Christians, the same as Christians have felt toward the Jews, the same as that which murders a Christian in Wallachia, calls him a "dog" in Constantinople, oppresses and persecutes a Jew in Berlin, hunts down a socialist in St. Petersburg, drives a Hebrew from an hotel at Saratoga, that scorns the Irishman in London, the same as Catholics once felt for Protestants, the same as that which insults, abuses, and kills the Chinaman on the Pacific slope—then may we well enough affirm that this prejudice really has nothing whatever to do with race or color, and that it has its motive and mainspring in some other source with which the mere facts of color and race have nothing to do.

After all, some very well informed and very well meaning people will read what I have now said, and what seems to me so just and reasonable, and will still insist that the color of the Negro has something to do with the feeling entertained toward him; that the white man naturally shudders at the thought of contact with one who is black—that the impulse is one which he can neither resist nor control. Let us see if this conclusion is a sound one. An argument is unsound when it proves too little or too much, or when it proves nothing. If color is an offense, it is so, entirely apart from the manhood it envelops. There must be something in color of itself to kindle rage and inflame hate, and render the white man generally uncomfortable. If the white man were really so constituted that color were, in itself, a torment to him, this grand old earth of ours would be no place for him. Colored objects confront him here at every point of the compass. If he should shrink and shudder every time he sees anything dark, he would have little time for anything else. He would require a colorless world to live in—a world where flowers, fields, and floods should all be of snowy whiteness; where rivers, lakes, and oceans should all be white; where islands, capes, and continents should all be white; where all the men, and women, and children should be white; where all the fish of the sea, all the birds of the air, all the "cattle upon a thousand hills," should be white; where the heavens above and the earth beneath should be white, and where day and night should not be divided by light and darkness, but the world should be one eternal scene of light. In such a white world, the entrance of a black man would be hailed with joy by the inhabitants. Anybody or anything would be welcome that would break the oppressive and tormenting monotony of the all-prevailing white.

In the abstract, there is no prejudice against color. No man shrinks from another because he is clothed in a suit of black, nor offended with his boots because they are black. We are told by those who have resided there that a white man in Africa comes to think that ebony is about the proper color for man. Good old Thomas Whitson—a noble old Quaker—a man of rather odd appearance—used to say that even he would be handsome if he could change public opinion.

Aside from the curious contrast to himself, the white child feels nothing on the first sight of a colored man. Curiosity is the only feeling. The office of color in the color line is a very plain and subordinate one. It simply advertises the objects of oppression, insult, and persecution. It is not the maddening liquor, but the black letters on the sign telling the world where it may be had. It is not the hated Quaker, but the broad brim and the plain coat. It is not the hateful Cain, but the mark by which he is known. The color is innocent enough, but things with which it is coupled make it hated. Slavery, ignorance, stupidity, servility, poverty, dependence, are undesirable conditions. When these shall cease to be coupled with color, there will be no color line drawn. It may help in this direction to observe a few of the inconsistencies of the color-line feeling, for it is neither uniform in its operations nor consistent in its principles. Its contradictions in the latter respect would be amusing if the feeling itself were not so deserving of unqualified abhorrence. Our Californian brothers, of Hibernian descent, hate the Chinaman, and kill him, and when asked why they do so, their answer is that a Chinaman is so industrious he will do all the work, and can live by wages upon which other people would starve. When the same people and others are asked why they hate the colored people, the answer is that they are indolent and wasteful, and cannot take care of themselves. Statesmen of the South will tell you that the Negro is too ignorant and stupid properly to exercise the elective franchise, and yet his greatest offense is that he acts with the only party intelligent enough in the eyes of the nation to legislate for the country. In one breath they tell us that the Negro is so weak in intellect, and so destitute of manhood, that he is but the echo of designing white men, and yet in another they will virtually tell you that the Negro is so clear in his moral perceptions, so firm in purpose, so steadfast in his convictions, that he cannot be persuaded by arguments or intimidated by threats, and that nothing but the shot-gun can restrain him from voting for the men and measures he approves. They shrink back in horror from contact with the Negro as a man and a gentleman, but like him very well as a barber, waiter, coachman, or cook. As a slave, he could ride anywhere, side by side with his white master, but as a freeman, he must be thrust into the smoking-car. As a slave, he could go into the first cabin; as a freeman, he was not allowed abaft the wheel. Formerly it was said he was incapable of learning, and at the same time it was a crime against the State for any man to teach him to read. To-day he is said to be originally and permanently inferior to the white race, and yet wild apprehensions are expressed lest six millions of this inferior race will somehow or other manage to rule over thirty-five millions of the superior race. If inconsistency can prove the hollowness of anything, certainly the emptiness of this pretense that color has any terrors is easily shown. The trouble is that most men, and especially mean men, want to have something under them. The rich man would have the poor man, the white would have the black, the Irish would have the Negro, and the Negro must have a dog, if he can get nothing higher in the scale of intelligence to dominate. This feeling is one of the vanities which enlightenment will dispel. A good but simple-minded Abolitionist said to me that he was not ashamed to walk with me down Broadway arm-in-arm, in open daylight, and evidently thought he was saying something that must be very pleasing to my self-importance, but it occurred to me, at the moment, this man does not dream of any reason why I might be ashamed to walk arm-in-arm with him through Broadway in open daylight. Riding in a stage-coach from Concord, New Hampshire, to Vergennes, Vermont, many years ago, I found myself on very pleasant terms with all the passengers through the night, but the morning light came to me as it comes to the stars; I was as Dr. Beecher says he was at the first fire he witnessed, when a bucket of cold water was poured down his back—"the fire was not put out, but he was." The fact is, the higher the colored man rises in the scale of society, the less prejudice does he meet.

The writer has met and mingled freely with the leading great men of his time,—at home and abroad, in public halls and private houses, on the platform and at the fireside,—and can remember no instance when among such men has he been made to feel himself an object of aversion. Men who are really great are too great to be small. This was gloriously true of the late Abraham Lincoln, William H. Seward, Salmon P. Chase, Henry Wilson, John P. Hale, Lewis Tappan, Edmund Quincy, Joshua R. Giddings, Gerrit Smith, and Charles Sumner, and many others among the dead. Good taste will not permit me now to speak of the living, except to say that the number of those who rise superior to prejudice is great and increasing. Let those who wish to see what is to be the future of America, as relates to races and race relations, attend, as I have attended, during the administration of President Hayes, the grand diplomatic reception at the executive mansion, and see there, as I have seen, in its splendid east room the wealth, culture, refinement, and beauty of the nation assembled, and with it the eminent representatives of other nations,—the swarthy Turk with his "fez," the Englishman shining with gold, the German, the Frenchman, the Spaniard, the Japanese, the Chinaman, the Caucasian, the Mongolian, the Sandwich Islander and the Negro,—all moving about freely, each respecting the rights and dignity of the other, and neither receiving nor giving offense.

"Then let us pray that come it may,
As come it will for a' that,
That sense and worth, o'er a' the earth,
May bear the gree, and a' that;

"That man to man, the world o'er,
Shall brothers be, for a' that."

June, 1881

QUESTIONS FOR DISCUSSION AND WRITING

1. Frederick Douglass asserts that in point of fact freedom did not exist for the black man after his emancipation. What factors operating to prevent freedom in 1872 are still present today? Are they equally important in today's definition of freedom?
2. Does Douglass provide an argument for people today who claim that blacks want too much too fast? Analyze the effectiveness of his argument in present-day circumstances.
3. Is the concept of "color line" as forceful a comment on contemporary life as it was in 1881? What aspects of current racial prejudice are connected with the present-day black stereotype? Is the 1881 stereotype similar? How?
4. "To-day he is said to be originally and permanently inferior to the white race, and yet wild apprehensions are expressed lest six millions of this inferior race will somehow or other manage to rule over thirty-five millions of the superior race." To what extent is Douglass' statement, despite its quaint population statistics, valid today? How?
5. Is "the problem of identity" a problem of the majority race as well as of the minority race(s)? Compare Douglass' statements (pp. 48, 49, 51, 56) with Grier and Cobbs' (p. 300).

HINTON ROWAN HELPER (1829–1909) SERVED AS CONSUL IN RIO DE JANEIRO BY APPOINTMENT OF PRESIDENT ABRAHAM LINCOLN. *The Negroes in Negroland,* PUBLISHED IN 1868, DIFFERS EMPHATICALLY FROM HELPER'S EARLIER WORK *The Impending Crisis* (1859), WHICH INSISTED THAT SLAVERY AS AN INSTITUTION WAS EVIL. IN *The Negroes in Negroland* HELPER ASSERTS THAT BLACKS ARE "NATURALLY INFERIOR."

HINTON ROWAN HELPER

THE NEGROES IN NEGROLAND

There are now in the United States of America thirty millions of white people, who are (or ought to be) bound together by the ties of a kindred origin, by the affinities of a sameness of noble purpose, by the links of a common nationality, and by the cords of an inseparable destiny. We have here also, unfortunately for us all, four millions of black people, whose ancestors, like themselves, were never known (except in very rare instances, which form the exceptions to a general rule) to aspire to any other condition than that of base and beastlike slavery. These black people are, by nature, of an exceedingly low and groveling disposition. They have no trait of character that is lovely or admirable. They are not high-minded, enterprising,

THE NEGROES IN NEGROLAND From *The Negroes in Negroland, the Negro in America, and Negroes Generally* (1868), by Hinton Rowan Helper, pp. viii–x and xii–xiv.

nor prudent. In no age, in no part of the world, have they, of themselves, ever projected or advanced any public or private interest, nor given expression to any thought or sentiment that could worthily elicit the praise, or even the favorable mention, of the better portion of mankind. Seeing, then, that the negro does, indeed, belong to a lower and inferior order of beings, why, in the name of Heaven, why should we forever degrade and disgrace both ourselves and our posterity by entering, of our own volition, into more intimate relations with him? May God, in his restraining mercy, forbid that we should ever do this most foul and wicked thing!

Acting under the influence of that vile spirit of deception and chicanery which is always familiar with every false pretence, the members of a Radical Congress, the editors of a venal press, and other peddlers of perverted knowledge, are now loudly proclaiming that nowhere in our country, henceforth, must there be any distinction, any discrimination, on account of color; thereby covertly inculcating the gross error of inferring or supposing that color is the only difference—and that a very trivial difference—between the whites and the blacks! Now, once and for all, in conscientious deference to truth, let it be distinctly made known and acknowledged, that, in addition to the black and baneful color of the negro, there are numerous other defects, physical, mental, and moral, which clearly mark him, when compared with the white man, as a very different and inferior creature. While, therefore, with an involuntary repugnance which we cannot control, and with a wholesome antipathy which it would be both unnatural and unavailing in us to attempt to destroy, we behold the crime-stained blackness of the negro, let us, also, at the same time, take cognizance of

His low and compressed Forehead;
His hard, thick Skull;
His small, backward-thrown Brain;
His short, crisp Hair;
His flat Nose;
His thick Lips;
His projecting, snout-like mouth;
His strange, Eunuch-toned Voice;
The scantiness of Beard on his Face;
The Toughness and Unsensitiveness of his Skin;
The Thinness and Shrunkenness of his Thighs;

His curved Knees;
His calfless Legs;
His low, short Ankles;
His long, flat Heels;
His glut-shaped Feet;
The general Angularity and Oddity of his Frame;
The Malodorous Exhalations from his Person;
His Puerility of Mind;
His Inertia and Sleepy-headedness;
His proverbial Dishonesty;
His predisposition to fabricate Falsehoods; and
His Apathetic Indifference to all Propositions and Enterprises of Solid Merit.

Many other differences might be mentioned; but the score and more of obvious and undeniable ones here enumerated ought to suffice for the utter confusion and shame of all those disingenuous politicians and others, who, knowing better, and who are thus guilty of the crime of defeating the legitimate ends of their own knowledge, would, for mere selfish and partisan purposes, convey the delusive impression that there is no other difference than that of color.

. . .

There are many points of general dissatisfaction and dispute, which should not, on any account, be overlooked in the discussion of the subjects here presented. One of these is, that white people, whose reason and honor have not been vitiated, object to close relationship with negroes, not wishing to live with them in the same house; not wishing to fellowship with them in the same society, assembly, or congregation; not wishing to ride with them in the same omnibus, car, or carriage; and not wishing to mess with them at the same table, whether at a hotel, in a restaurant, on a steamer, or elsewhere. Now, any and every white person who does not think and act in strict accordance with the just and pure promptings here indicated, is, in reality, a most unworthy and despicable representative of his race. Even the lower animals, the creatures of mere instinct—the beasts, the birds, and the fishes—many distinct species of which are apparently quite similar, set us daily and hourly examples of the eminent propriety of each kind forming and maintaining separate communities of their own; and so we always find them—in herds, in flocks, and in shoals. How can the negro be a fit person to occupy, in any capacity, our houses or our hotels, our theatres or our churches, our schools or our colleges, our steamers or our vehicles, or any other place or places of uncommon comfort and convenience, which owe their creation, their proper uses, and their perpetuity, to the whites alone—places and improvements about which the negro, of himself, is, and always has been, absolutely ignorant and indifferent? Neither in his own country nor elsewhere has the negro ever built a house or a theatre; he has never erected a church nor a college; he has never constructed a steamer nor a railroad, nor a railroad-car—nor, except when under the special direction and control of superior intelligence, has he ever invented or manufactured even the minutest appendage of any one of the distinctive elements or realities of human progress. Yet, let this not, by any means, be understood as an argument, nor even as a hint, in behalf of slavery. It is to the great and lasting honor of the Republic that slavery in the United States is abolished forever. In losing her slaves, the South lost nothing that was worth the keeping. Had slavery only been abolished by law many years ago, our whole country would be infinitely better off to-day.

Never will it be possible for the compiler to erase from his memory the feelings of weighty sadness and disgust which overcame him, a few months since, when, while sojourning in the city of Washington, he walked, one day, into the Capitol, and, leisurely passing into the galleries of the two houses of Congress, beheld there, uncouthly lounging and dozing upon the seats, a horde of vile, ignorant, and foul-scented negroes. He was perplexed, shocked, humiliated, and indignant—and could not sit down. With merited emotions of bitterness and contempt for those narrow-minded white men, through whose detestable folly and selfishness so great an outrage against public propriety and decency had been perpetrated, he turned away—indeed, it was not in his power to contemplate with calmness that motley and monstrous manifestation of national incongruity, ugliness, and disgrace. Then it was that, for the first time in his life, he wished himself a Hercules, in order that he might be able to clean, thoroughly and at once, those Augean stables of the black ordure and Radical filth which, therein and elsewhere, had already accumulated to an almost insufferable excess. It was the powerful and long-lingering momentum of the impressions received on that occasion, more than any other circumstance, that gave definite form and resolution to the purpose (although the idea had been previously entertained) of preparing this compilation. The object of the compiler will have been well attained if the work aids materially in more fully convincing his countrymen, North, South, East and West, that negro equality, negro supremacy, and negro domination, as now tyrannically enforced at the point of the bayonet, are cruel and atrocious innovations, which ought to be speedily terminated.

QUESTIONS FOR DISCUSSION AND WRITING

1. What manner of support does Helper use for his argument?
2. What type of solution does Helper offer for the "Negroes in Negroland"?
3. What aspects of the characterization presented by Helper are found in the present-day Negro stereotype?
4. Does Helper seem to have much knowledge of black African culture and civilization? Would he be likely to give it much value? Why?
5. Compare and contrast Helper's view with that of Douglass (p. 47) and Washington (p. 75). What assumptions do the three writers share? Whose viewpoint is most persistently reflected in American thought? Why?

BOOKER T. WASHINGTON, WELL KNOWN AS A SPEAKER AND WRITER, WAS THE ORGANIZER AND PRINCIPAL OF THE TUSKEGEE INSTITUTE, A NEGRO TRADE SCHOOL IN TUSKEGEE, ALABAMA. WASHINGTON WAS THE FIRST BLACK MAN TO BE ACCORDED A POSITION OF SOCIAL PROMINENCE IN THE UNITED STATES. HE DELIVERED HIS *Atlanta Exposition Address* ON THE OPENING DAY OF THE COTTON STATES AND INTERNATIONAL EXPOSITION IN SEPTEMBER 1895. THE SPEECH WAS WIDELY PRAISED, AND IT EARNED WASHINGTON ACCLAIM AS A NEGRO SPOKESMAN.

BOOKER T. WASHINGTON

THE ATLANTA EXPOSITION ADDRESS

The Atlanta Exposition, at which I had been asked to make an address as a representative of the Negro race, . . . was opened with a short address from Governor Bullock. After other interesting exercises, including an invocation from Bishop Nelson, of Georgia, a dedicatory ode by Albert Howell, Jr., and addresses by the President of the Exposition and Mrs. Joseph Thompson, the President of the Woman's Board, Governor Bullock introduced me with the words, "We have with us to-day a representative of Negro enterprise and Negro civilization."

When I arose to speak, there was considerable cheering, especially from the coloured people. As I remember it now, the thing that was uppermost in my mind was the desire to say something that

THE ATLANTA EXPOSITION ADDRESS From *Up from Slavery* (1901) by Booker T. Washington, Chapter 14.

would cement the friendship of the races and bring about hearty coöperation between them. So far as my outward surroundings were concerned, the only thing that I recall distinctly now is that when I got up, I saw thousands of eyes looking intently into my face. The following is the address which I delivered:—

Mr. President and Gentlemen
of the Board of Directors and Citizens

One-third of the population of the South is of the Negro race. No enterprise seeking the material, civil, or moral welfare of this section can disregard this element of our population and reach the highest success. I but convey to you, Mr. President and Directors, the sentiment of the masses of my race when I say that in no way have the value and manhood of the American Negro been more fittingly and generously recognized than by the managers of this magnificent Exposition at every stage of its progress. It is a recognition that will do more to cement the friendship of the two races than any occurrence since the dawn of our freedom.

Not only this, but the opportunity here afforded will awaken among us a new era of industrial progress. Ignorant and inexperienced, it is not strange that in the first years of our new life we began at the top instead of at the bottom; that a seat in Congress or the state legislature was more sought than real estate or industrial skill; that the political convention of stump speaking had more attractions than starting a dairy farm or truck garden.

A ship lost at sea for many days suddenly sighted a friendly vessel. From the mast of the unfortunate vessel was seen a signal, "Water, water; we die of thirst!" The answer from the friendly vessel at once came back, "Cast down your bucket where you are." A second time the signal, "Water, water; send us water!" ran up from the distressed vessel, and was answered, "Cast down your bucket where you are." And a third and fourth signal for water was answered, "Cast down your bucket where you are." The captain of the distressed vessel, at last heeding the injunction, cast down his bucket, and it came up full of fresh, sparkling water from the mouth of the Amazon River. To those of my race who depend on bettering their condition in a foreign land or who underestimate the importance of cultivating friendly relations with the Southern white man, who is their next-door neighbour, I would say: "Cast down your bucket where you are"—cast it down in making friends in every manly way of the people of all races by whom we are surrounded.

Cast it down in agriculture, mechanics, in commerce, in domestic service, and in the professions. And in this connection it is well to bear in mind that whatever other sins the South may be called to bear, when it comes to business, pure and simple, it is in the South that the Negro is given a man's chance in the commercial world, and in nothing is this Exposition more eloquent than in emphasizing this chance. Our greatest danger is that in the great leap from slavery to freedom we may overlook the fact that the masses of us are to live by the productions of our hands, and fail to keep in mind that we shall prosper in proportion as we learn to dignify and glorify common labor and put brains and skill into the common occupations of life; shall prosper in proportion as we learn to draw the line between the superficial and the substantial, the ornamental gewgaws of life and the useful. No race can prosper till it learns that there is as much dignity in tilling a field as in writing a poem. It is at the bottom of life we must begin, and not at the top. Nor should we permit our grievances to overshadow our opportunities.

To those of the white race who look to the incoming of those of foreign birth and strange tongue and habits for the prosperity of the South, were I permitted I would repeat what I say to my own race, "Cast down your bucket where you are." Cast it down among the eight millions of Negroes whose habits you know, whose fidelity and love you have tested in days when to have proved treacherous meant the ruin of your firesides. Cast down your bucket among these people who have, without strikes and labour wars, tilled your fields, cleared your forests, builded your railroads and cities, and brought forth treasures from the bowels of the earth, and helped make possible this magnificent representation of the progress of the South. Casting down your bucket among my people, helping and encouraging them as you are doing on these grounds, and to education of head, hand, and heart, you will find that they will buy your surplus land, make blossom the waste places in your fields, and run your factories. While doing this, you can be sure in the future, as in the past, that you and your families will be surrounded by the most patient, faithful, law-abiding, and unresentful people that the world has seen. As we have proved our loyalty to you in the past, in nursing your children, watching by the sick-bed of your mothers and fathers, and often following them with tear-dimmed eyes to their graves, so in the future, in our humble way, we shall stand by you with a devotion that no foreigner can approach, ready to lay down our lives, if need be, in defence of yours, interlacing our industrial, commercial, civil, and religious life with yours in a way that shall make the interests of both races one. In all things that are purely social we can be as separate as the fingers, yet one as the hand in all things essential to mutual progress.

There is no defence or security for any of us except in the highest intelligence and development of all. If anywhere there are efforts tending to curtail the fullest growth of the Negro, let these efforts be turned into stimulating, encouraging, and making him the most useful and intelligent citizen. Effort or means so invested will pay a thousand per cent interest. These efforts will be twiced blessed—"blessing him that gives and him that takes."

There is no escape through law of man or God from the inevitable:—

> The laws of changeless justice bind
>   Oppressor with oppressed;
> And close as sin and suffering joined
>   We march to fate abreast.

Nearly sixteen millions of hands will aid you in pulling the load upward, or they will pull against you the load downward. We shall constitute one-third and more of the ignorance and crime of the South, or one-third its intelligence and progress; we shall contribute one-third to the business and industrial prosperity of the South, or we shall prove a veritable body of death, stagnating, depressing, retarding every effort to advance the body politic.

Gentlemen of the Exposition, as we present to you our humble effort at an exhibition of our progress, you must not expect overmuch. Starting thirty years ago with ownership here and there in a few quilts and pumpkins and chickens (gathered from miscellaneous sources), remember the path that has led from these to the inventions and production of agricultural implements, buggies, steam-engines, newspapers, books, statuary, carving, paintings, the management of drug-stores and banks, has not been trodden without contact with thorns and thistles. While we take pride in what we exhibit as a result of our independent efforts, we do not for a moment forget that our part in this exhibition would fall far short of your expectations but for the constant help that has come to our educational life, not only from the Southern states, but especially from Northern philanthropists, who have made their gifts a constant stream of blessing and encouragement.

The wisest among my race understand that the agitation of questions of social equality is the extremest folly, and that progress in the enjoyment of all the privileges that will come to us must be the result of severe and constant struggle rather than of artificial forcing. No race that has anything to contribute to the markets of the world is long in any degree ostracized. It is important and right that all privileges of the law be ours, but it is vastly more important that we be prepared for the exercises of these privileges. The opportunity to earn a dollar in a factory just now is worth infinitely more than the opportunity to spend a dollar in an opera-house.

In conclusion, may I repeat that nothing in thirty years has given us more hope and encouragement, and drawn us so near to you of the white race, as this opportunity offered by the Exposition; and here bending, as it were, over the altar that represents the results of the struggles of your race and mine, both starting practically empty-handed three decades ago, I pledge that in your effort to work out the great and intricate problem which God has laid at the doors of the South, you shall have at all times the patient, sympathetic help of my race; only let this be constantly in mind, that, while from representations in these buildings of the product of field, of forest, of mine, of factory, letters, and art, much good will come, yet far above and beyond material benefits will be that higher good, that, let us pray God, will come, in a blotting out of sectional differences and racial animosities and suspicions, in a determination to administer absolute justice, in a willing obedience among all classes to the mandates of law. Thus, this, coupled with our material prosperity, will bring into our beloved South a new heaven and a new earth.

The first thing that I remember, after I had finished speaking, was that Governor Bullock rushed across the platform and took me by the hand, and that others did the same. I received so many and such hearty congratulations that I found it difficult to get out of the building. I did not appreciate to any degree, however, the impression which my address seemed to have made, until the next morning, when I went into the business part of the city. As soon as I was recognized, I was surprised to find myself pointed out and surrounded by a crowd of men who wished to shake hands with me. This was kept up on every street on to which I went, to an extent which embarrassed me so much that I went back to my boarding-place. The next morning I returned to Tuskegee. At the station in Atlanta, and at almost all of the stations at which the train stopped between that city and Tuskegee, I found a crowd of people anxious to shake hands with me.

The papers in all parts of the United States published the address in full, and for months afterward there were complimentary editorial references to it. Mr. Clark Howell, the editor of the Atlanta *Constitution*, telegraphed to a New York paper, among other words, the following, "I do not exaggerate when I say that Professor Booker T. Washington's address yesterday was one of the most notable speeches, both as to character and as to the warmth of its reception, ever delivered to a Southern audience. The address was a revelation. The whole speech is a platform upon which blacks and whites can stand with full justice to each other."

The Boston *Transcript* said editorially: "The speech of Booker T. Washington at the Atlanta Exposition, this week, seems to have dwarfed all the other proceedings and the Exposition itself. The sensation that it has caused in the press has never been equalled."

I very soon began receiving all kinds of propositions from lecture bureaus, and editors of magazines and papers, to take the lecture platform, and to write articles. One lecture bureau offered me fifty thousand dollars, or two hundred dollars a night and expenses, if I would place my services at its disposal for a given period. To all these communications I replied that my life-work was at Tuskegee; and that whenever I spoke it must be in the interests of the Tuskegee school and my race, and that I would enter into no arrangements that seemed to place a mere commercial value upon my services.

Some days after its delivery I sent a copy of my address to the President of the United States, the Hon. Grover Cleveland. I received from him the following autograph[ed] reply:—

GRAY GABLES, BUZZARD'S BAY, MASS.
October 6, 1895

BOOKER T. WASHINGTON, ESQ.

MY DEAR SIR: I thank you for sending me a copy of your address delivered at the Atlanta Exposition.

I thank you with much enthusiasm for making the address. I have read it with intense interest, and I think the Exposition would be fully justified if it did not do more than furnish the opportunity for its delivery. Your words cannot fail to delight and encourage all who wish well for your race; and if our coloured fellow-citizens do not from your utterances gather new hope and form new determinations to gain every valuable advantage offered them by their citizenship, it will be strange indeed.

Yours very truly,
GROVER CLEVELAND

Later I met Mr. Cleveland, for the first time, when, as President, he visited the Atlanta Exposition. At the request of myself and others he consented to spend an hour in the Negro Building, for the purpose of inspecting the Negro exhibit and of giving the coloured people in attendance an opportunity to shake hands with him. As soon as I met Mr. Cleveland I became impressed with his simplicity, greatness, and rugged honesty. I have met him many times since then, both at public functions and at his private residence in Princeton, and the more I see of him the more I admire him. When he visited the Negro Building in Atlanta he seemed to give himself up wholly, for that hour, to the coloured people. He seemed to be as careful to shake hands with some old coloured "auntie" clad partially in rags, and to take as much pleasure in doing so, as if he were greeting some millionaire. Many of the coloured people took advantage of the occasion to get him to write his name in a book or on a slip of paper. He was as careful and patient in doing this as if he were putting his signature to some great state document.

Mr. Cleveland has not only shown his friendship for me in many personal ways, but has always consented to do anything I have asked of him for our school. This he has done, whether it was to make a personal donation or to use his influence in securing the donations of others. Judging from my personal acquaintance with Mr. Cleveland, I do not believe that he is conscious of possessing any colour prejudice. He is too great for that. In my contact with people I find that, as a rule, it is only the little, narrow people who live for themselves, who never read good books, who do not travel, who never open up their souls in a way to permit them to come into contact with other souls—with the great outside world. No man whose vision is bounded by colour can come into contact with what is highest and best in the world. In meeting men, in many places, I have found that the happiest people are those who do the most for others; the most miserable are those who do the least. I have also found that few things, if any, are capable of making one so blind and narrow as race prejudice. I often say to our students, in the course of my talks to them on Sunday evenings in the chapel, that the longer I live and the more experience I have of the world, the more I am convinced that, after all, the one thing that is most worth living for—and dying for, if need be—is the opportunity of making some one else more happy and more useful.

The coloured people and the coloured newspapers at first seemed to be greatly pleased with the character of my Atlanta address, as well as with its reception. But after the first burst of enthusiasm began to die away, and the coloured people began reading the speech in cold type, some of them seemed to feel that they had been hypnotized. They seemed to feel that I had been too liberal in my remarks toward the Southern whites, and that I had not spoken out strongly enough for what they termed the "rights" of the race. For a while there was a reaction, so far as a certain element of my own race was concerned, but later these reactionary ones seemed to have been won over to my way of believing and acting.

While speaking of changes in public sentiment, I recall that about ten years after the school at Tuskegee was established, I had an experience that I shall never forget. Dr. Lyman Abbott, then the pastor of Plymouth Church, and also editor of the *Outlook* (then the *Christian Union*), asked me to write a letter for his paper giving my opinion of the exact condition, mental and moral, of the coloured ministers in the South, as based upon my observations. I wrote the letter, giving the exact facts as I conceived them to be. The picture painted was a rather black one—or, since I am black, shall I say "white"? It could not be otherwise with a race but a few years out of slavery, a race which had not had time or opportunity to produce a competent ministry.

What I said soon reached every Negro minister in the country, I think, and the letters of condemnation which I received from them were not few. I think that for a year after the publication of this article every association and every conference or religious body of any kind, of my race, that met, did not fail before adjourning to pass a resolution condemning me, or calling upon me to retract or modify what I had said. Many of these organizations went so far in their resolutions as to advise parents to cease sending their children to Tuskegee. One association even appointed a "missionary" whose duty it was to warn the people against sending their children to Tuskegee. This missionary had a son in the school, and I noticed that, whatever the "missionary" might have said or done with regard to others, he was careful not to take his son away from the institution. Many of the coloured papers, especially those that were the organs of religious bodies, joined in the general chorus of condemnation or demands for retraction.

During the whole time of the excitement, and through all the criticism, I did not utter a word of explanation or retraction. I knew that I was right, and that time and the sober second thought of the people would vindicate me. It was not long before the bishops and other church leaders began to make a careful investigation of the conditions of the ministry, and they found out that I was right. In fact, the oldest and most influential bishop in one branch of the Methodist Church said that my words were far too mild. Very soon public sentiment began making itself felt, in demanding a purifying of the ministry. While this is not yet complete by any means, I think I may say, without egotism, and I have been told by many of our most influential ministers, that my words had much to do with starting a demand for the placing of a higher type of men in the pulpit. I have had the satisfaction of having many who once condemned me thank me heartily for my frank words.

The change of the attitude of the Negro ministry, so far as regards myself, is so complete that at the present time I have no warmer friends among any class than I have among the clergymen. The improvement in the character and life of the Negro ministers is one of the most gratifying evidences of the progress of the race. My experience with them, as well as other events in my life, convince me that the thing to do, when one feels sure that he has said or done the right thing, and is condemned, is to stand still and keep quiet. If he is right, time will show it.

In the midst of the discussion which was going on concerning my Atlanta speech, I received the letter which I give below, from Dr. Gilman, the President of Johns Hopkins University, who had been made chairman of the judges of award in connection with the Atlanta Exposition:—

JOHNS HOPKINS UNIVERSITY, BALTIMORE
President's Office, September 30, 1895

DEAR MR. WASHINGTON: Would it be agreeable to you to be one of the Judges of Award in the Department of Education at Atlanta?

If so, I shall be glad to place your name upon the list. A line by telegraph will be welcomed.

Yours very truly,

D. C. GILMAN

I think I was even more surprised to receive this invitation than I had been to receive the invitation to speak at the opening of the Exposition. It was to be a part of my duty, as one of the jurors, to pass not only upon the exhibits of the coloured schools, but also upon those of the white schools. I accepted the position, and spent a month in Atlanta in performance of the duties which it entailed. The board of jurors was a large one, consisting in all of sixty members. It was about equally divided between Southern white people and Northern white people. Among them were college presidents, leading scientists and men of letters, and specialists in many subjects. When the group of jurors to which I was assigned met for organization, Mr. Thomas Nelson Page, who was one of the number, moved that I be made secretary of that division, and the motion was unanimously adopted. Nearly half of our division were Southern people. In performing my duties in the inspection of the exhibits of white schools I was in every case treated with respect, and at the close of our labours I parted from my associates with regret.

I am often asked to express myself more freely than I do upon the political condition and the political future of my race. These recollections of my experience in Atlanta give me the opportunity to do so briefly. My own belief is, although I have never before said so in so many words, that the time will come when the Negro in the South will be accorded all the political rights which his ability, character, and material possessions entitle him to. I think, though, that the opportunity to freely exercise such political rights will not come in any large degree through outside or artificial forcing, but will be accorded to the Negro by the Southern white people themselves, and that they will protect him in the exercise of those rights. Just as soon as the South gets over the old feeling that it is being forced by "foreigners," or "aliens," to do something which it does not want to do, I believe that the change in the direction that I have indicated is going to begin. In fact, there are indications that it is already beginning in a slight degree.

Let me illustrate my meaning. Suppose that some months before the opening of the Atlanta Exposition there had been a general demand from the press and public platform outside the South that a Negro be given a place on the opening programme, and that a Negro be placed upon the board of jurors of award. Would any such recognition of the race have taken place? I do not think so. The Atlanta officials went as far as they did because they felt it to be a pleasure, as well as a duty, to reward what they considered merit in the Negro race. Say what we will, there is something in human nature which we cannot blot out, which makes one man, in the end, recognize and reward merit in another, regardless of colour or race.

I believe it is the duty of the Negro—as the greater part of the race is already doing—to deport himself modestly in regard to political claims, depending upon the slow but sure influences that proceed from the possession of property, intelligence, and high character for the full recognition of his political rights. I think that the according of the full exercise of political rights is going to be a matter of natural, slow growth, not an over-night, gourd-vine affair. I do not believe that the Negro should cease voting, for a man cannot learn the exercise of self-government by ceasing to vote any more than a boy can learn to swim by keeping out of the water, but I do believe that in his voting he should more and more be influenced by those of intelligence and character who are his next-door neighbours.

I know coloured men who, through the encouragement, help, and advice of Southern white people, have accumulated thousands of dollars' worth of property, but who, at the same time, would never think of going to those same persons for advice concerning the casting of their ballots. This, it seems to me, is unwise and unreasonable, and should cease. In saying this I do not mean that the Negro should truckle, or not vote from principle, for the instant he ceases to vote from principle he loses the confidence and respect of the Southern white man even.

I do not believe that any state should make a law that permits an ignorant and poverty-stricken white man to vote, and prevents a black man in the same condition from voting. Such a law is not only unjust, but it will react, as all unjust laws do, in time; for the effect of such a law is to encourage the Negro to secure education and property, and at the same time it encourages the white man to remain in ignorance and poverty. I believe that in time, through the operation of intelligence and friendly race relations, all cheating at the ballot box in the South will cease. It will become apparent that the white man who begins by cheating a Negro out of his ballot soon learns to cheat a white man out of his, and that the man who does this ends his career of dishonesty by the theft of property or by some equally serious crime. In my opinion, the time will come when the South will encourage all of its citizens to vote. It will see that it pays better, from every standpoint, to have healthy, vigorous life than to have that political stagnation which always results when one-half of the population has no share and no interest in the Government.

As a rule, I believe in universal, free suffrage, but I believe that in the South we are confronted with peculiar conditions that justify the protection of the ballot in many of the states, for a while at least, either by an educational test, a property test, or by both combined; but whatever tests are required, they should be made to apply with equal and exact justice to both races.

QUESTIONS FOR DISCUSSION AND WRITING

1. Washington's speech sets out a line of argument for the value of blacks to the South. How does he feel blacks can be valuable to that portion of the country?
2. Why do many blacks disagree with Washington's opinions about black economic progress and political freedom?
3. Generally, the most effective speeches are those given by speakers who have the ability to analyze their audiences. An individual speaker can give a successful speech by telling his audience what it wants to hear. The success of Washington's address indicates that he followed this prime rule for effective speech. What, then, does the *Atlanta Exposition Address* reveal about its audience?
4. Washington states that "the wisest among my race understand that the agitation of questions of social equality is the extremest folly, and that progress in the enjoyment of all the privileges that will come to us must be the result of severe and constant struggle rather than artificial forcing." Compare this point of view with that expressed by Douglass (p. 45). How do their opinions differ?
5. Compare and contrast Washington's view of "self-reliance" with that of Carmichael (p. 329) and of Browne (p. 385).

W. E. B. DUBOIS FOUNDED THE NATIONAL ASSOCIATION FOR THE ADVANCEMENT OF COLORED PEOPLE (NAACP) IN 1909. DUBOIS WAS A HIGHLY PERSUASIVE WRITER AND A DEVOTED EDUCATOR. IN 1961, AT THE AGE OF NINETY-THREE, HE EMIGRATED TO GHANA, WHERE HE DIED TWO YEARS LATER. HIS WORKS INCLUDE *The Philadelphia Negro* AND *The Souls of Black Folk,* FROM WHICH THE FOLLOWING SELECTION IS TAKEN.

W. E. B. DUBOIS

OF MR. BOOKER T. WASHINGTON AND OTHERS

From birth till death enslaved; in word, in deed, unmanned!

. . .

Hereditary bondsmen! Know ye not
Who would be free themselves must strike the blow?

Byron

OF MR. BOOKER T. WASHINGTON AND OTHERS From *The Souls of Black Folk* (1903) by W. E. B. DuBois, Chapter 3.

Easily the most striking thing in the history of the American Negro since 1876 is the ascendancy of Mr. Booker T. Washington. It began at the time when war memories and ideals were rapidly passing; a day of astonishing commercial development was dawning; a sense of doubt and hesitation overtook the freedmen's sons,—then it was that his leading began. Mr. Washington came, with a single definite programme, at the psychological moment when the nation was a little ashamed of having bestowed so much sentiment on Negroes, and was concentrating its energies on Dollars. His programme of industrial education, conciliation of the South, and submission and silence as to civil and political rights, was not wholly original; the Free Negroes from 1830 up to war-time had striven to build industrial schools, and the American Missionary Association had from the first taught various trades; and Price and others had sought a way of honorable alliance with the best of the Southerners. But Mr. Washington first indissolubly linked these things; he put enthusiasm, unlimited energy, and perfect faith into this programme, and changed it from a by-path into a veritable Way of Life. And the tale of the methods by which he did this is a fascinating study of human life.

It startled the nation to hear a Negro advocating such a programme after many decades of bitter complaint; it startled and won the applause of the South, it interested and won the admiration of the North; and after a confused murmur of protest, it silenced if it did not convert the Negroes themselves.

To gain the sympathy and coöperation of the various elements comprising the white South was Mr. Washington's first task; and this, at the time Tuskegee was founded, seemed, for a black man, well-nigh impossible. And yet ten years later it was done in the words spoken at Atlanta: "In all things that are purely social we can be as separate as five fingers, yet one as the hand in all things essential to mutual progress." This "Atlanta Compromise" is by all odds the most notable thing in Mr. Washington's career. The South interpreted it in different ways: the radicals received it as a complete surrender of the demand for civil and political equality; the conservatives, as a generously conceived working basis for mutual understanding. So both approved it, and to-day its author is certainly the most distinguished Southerner since Jefferson Davis, and the one with the largest personal following.

Next to this achievement comes Mr. Washington's work in gaining place and consideration in the North. Others less shrewd and tactful had formerly essayed to sit on these two stools and had fallen between them; but as Mr. Washington knew the heart of the South from birth and training, so by singular insight he intuitively grasped the spirit of the age which was dominating the North. And so thoroughly did he learn the speech and thought of triumphant commercialism, and the ideals of material prosperity, that the picture of a lone black boy poring over a French grammar amid the weeds and dirt of a neglected home soon seemed to him the acme of absurdities. One wonders what Socrates and St. Francis of Assisi would say to this.

And yet this very singleness of vision and thorough oneness with his age is a mark of the successful man. It is as though Nature must needs make men narrow in order to give them force. So Mr. Washington's cult has gained unquestioning followers, his work has wonderfully prospered, his friends are legion, and his enemies are confounded. To-day he stands as the one recognized spokesman of his ten million fellows, and one of the most notable figures in a nation of seventy millions. One hesitates, therefore, to criticise a life which, beginning with so little, has done so much. And yet the time is come when one may speak in all sincerity and utter courtesy of the mistakes and shortcomings of Mr. Washington's career, as well as of his triumphs, without being thought captious or envious, and without forgetting that it is easier to do ill than well in the world.

The criticism that has hitherto met Mr. Washington has not always been of this broad character. In the South especially has he had to walk warily to avoid the harshest judgments,—and naturally so, for he is dealing with the one subject of deepest sensitiveness to that section. Twice—once when at the Chicago celebration of the Spanish-American War he alluded to the color-prejudice that is "eating away the vitals of the South," and once when he dined with President Roosevelt—has the resulting Southern criticism been violent enough to threaten seriously his popularity. In the North the feeling has several times forced itself into words, that Mr. Washington's counsels of submission overlooked certain elements of true manhood, and that his educational programme was unnecessarily narrow. Usually, however, such criticism has not found open expression, although, too, the spiritual sons of the Abolitionists have not been prepared to acknowledge that the schools founded before Tuskegee, by men of broad ideals and self-sacrificing spirit, were wholly failures or worthy of ridicule. While, then, criticism has not failed to follow Mr. Washington, yet the prevailing public opinion of the land has been but too willing to deliver the solution of a wearisome problem into his hands, and say, "If that is all you and your race ask, take it."

Among his own people, however, Mr. Washington has encountered the strongest and most lasting opposition, amounting at times to bitterness, and even to-day continuing strong and insistent even though largely silenced in outward expression by the public opinion of the nation. Some of this opposition is, of course, mere envy; the disappointment of displaced demagogues and the spite of narrow minds. But aside from this, there is among educated and thoughtful colored men in all parts of the land a feeling of deep regret, sorrow, and apprehension at the wide currency and ascendancy which some of Mr. Washington's theories have gained. These same men admire his sincerity of purpose, and are willing to forgive much to honest endeavor which is doing something worth the doing. They coöperate with Mr. Washington as far as they conscientiously can; and, indeed, it is no ordinary tribute to this man's tact and power that, steering as he must between so many diverse interests and opinions, he so largely retains the respect of all.

But the hushing of the criticism of honest opponents is a dangerous thing. It leads some of the best of the critics to unfortunate silence and paralysis of effort, and others to burst into speech so passionately and intemperately as to lose listeners. Honest and earnest criticism from those whose interests are most nearly touched,—criticism of writers by readers, of government by those governed, of leaders by those led,—this is the soul of democracy and the safeguard of modern society. If the best of the American Negroes receive by outer pressure a leader whom they had not recognized before, manifestly there is here a certain palpable gain. Yet there is also irreparable loss,—a loss of that peculiarly valuable education which a group receives when by search and criticism it finds and commissions its own leaders. The way in which this is done is at once the most elementary and the nicest problem of social growth. History is but the record of such group-leadership; and yet how infinitely changeful is its type and character! And of all types and kinds, what can be more instructive than the leadership of a group within a group?—that curious double movement where real progress may be negative and actual advance be relative retrogression. All this is the social student's inspiration and despair.

Now in the past the American Negro has had instructive experience in the choosing of group leaders, founding thus a peculiar dynasty which in the light of present conditions is worth while studying. When sticks and stones and beasts form the sole environment of a people, their attitude is largely one of determined opposition to and conquest of natural forces. But when to earth and brute force is added an environment of men and ideas, then the attitude of the imprisoned group may take three main forms,—a feeling of revolt and revenge; an attempt to adjust all thought and action to the will of the greater group; or, finally, a determined effort at self-realization and self-development despite environing opinion. The influence of all of these attitudes at various times can be traced in the history of the American Negro, and in the evolution of his successive leaders.

Before 1750, while the fire of African freedom still burned in the veins of the slaves, there was in all leadership or attempted leadership but the one motive of revolt and revenge,—typified in the terrible Maroons, the Danish blacks, and Cato of Stono, and veiling all the Americas in fear of insurrection. The liberalizing tendencies of the latter half of the eighteenth century brought, along with kindlier relations between black and white, thoughts of ultimate adjustment and assimilation. Such aspiration was especially voiced in the earnest songs of Phyllis, in the martyrdom of Attucks, the fighting of Salem and Poor, the intellectual accomplishments of Banneker and Derham, and the political demands of the Cuffes.

Stern financial and social stress after the war cooled much of the previous humanitarian ardor. The disappointment and impatience of the Negroes at the persistence of slavery and serfdom voiced itself in two movements. The slaves in the South, aroused undoubtedly by vague rumors of the Haytian revolt, made three fierce attempts at insurrection,—in 1800 under Gabriel in Virginia, in 1822 under Vesey in Carolina, and in 1831 again in Virginia under the terrible Nat Turner. In the Free States, on the other hand, a new and curious attempt at self-development was made. In Philadelphia and New York color-prescription led to a withdrawal of Negro communicants from white churches and the formation of a peculiar socio-religious institution among the Negroes known as the African Church,—an organization still living and controlling in its various branches over a million of men.

Walker's wild appeal against the trend of the times showed how the world was changing after the coming of the cotton-gin. By 1830 slavery seemed hopelessly fastened on the South, and the slaves thoroughly cowed into submission. The free Negroes of the North, inspired by the mulatto immigrants from the West Indies, began to change the basis of their demands; they recognized the slavery of slaves, but insisted that they themselves were freemen, and sought assimilation and amalgamation with the nation on the same terms with other men. Thus, Forten and Purvis of Philadelphia, Shad of Wilmington, DuBois of New Haven, Barbadoes of Boston, and others, strove singly and together as men, they said, not as slaves; as "people of color," not as "Negroes." The trend of the times, however, refused them recognition save in individual and exceptional cases, considered them as one with all the despised blacks, and they soon found themselves striving to keep even the rights they formerly had of voting and working and moving as freemen. Schemes of migration and colonization arose among them; but these they refused to entertain, and they eventually turned to the Abolition movement as a final refuge.

Here, led by Remond, Nell, Wells-Brown, and Douglass, a new period of self-assertion and self-development dawned. To be sure, ultimate freedom and assimilation was the ideal before the leaders, but the assertion of the manhood rights of the Negro by himself was the main reliance, and John Brown's raid was the extreme of its logic. After the war and emancipation, the great form of Frederick Douglass, the greatest of American Negro leaders, still led the host. Self-assertion, especially in political lines, was the main programme, and behind Douglass came Elliot, Bruce, and Langston, and the Reconstruction politicians, and, less conspicuous but of greater social significance, Alexander Crummell and Bishop Daniel Payne.

Then came the Revolution of 1876, the suppression of the Negro votes, the changing and shifting of ideals, and the seeking of new lights in the great night. Douglass, in his old age, still bravely stood for the ideals of his early manhood,—ultimate assimilation *through* self-assertion, and on no other terms. For a time Price arose as a new leader, destined, it seemed, not to give up, but to re-state the old ideals in a form less repugnant to the white South. But he passed away in his prime. Then came the new leader. Nearly all the former ones had become leaders by the silent suffrage of their fellows, had sought to lead their own people alone, and were usually, save Douglass, little known outside their race. But Booker T. Washington arose as essentially the leader not of one race but of two,—a compromiser between the South, the North, and the Negro. Naturally the Negroes resented, at first bitterly, signs of compromise which surrendered their civil and political rights, even though this was to be exchanged for larger chances of economic development. The rich and dominating North, however, was not only weary of the race problem, but was investing largely in Southern enterprises, and welcomed any method of peaceful coöperation. Thus, by national opinion, the Negroes began to recognize Mr. Washington's leadership; and the voice of criticism was hushed.

Mr. Washington represents in Negro thought the old attitude of adjustment and submission; but adjustment at such a peculiar time as to make his programme unique. This is an age of unusual economic development, and Mr. Washington's programme naturally takes an economic cast, becoming a gospel of Work and Money to such an extent as apparently almost completely to overshadow the higher aims of life. Moreover, this is an age when the more advanced races are coming in closer contact with the less developed races, and the race-feeling is therefore intensified; and Mr. Washington's programme practically accepts the alleged inferiority of the Negro races. Again, in our own land, the reaction from the sentiment of war time has given impetus to race-prejudice against Negroes, and Mr. Washington withdraws many of the high demands of Negroes as men and American citizens. In other periods of intensified prejudice all the Negro's tendency to self-assertion has been called forth; at this period a policy of submission is advocated. In the history of nearly all other races and peoples the doctrine preached at such crises has been that manly self-respect is worth more than lands and houses, and that a people who voluntarily surrender such respect, or cease striving for it, are not worth civilizing.

In answer to this, it has been claimed that the Negro can survive only through submission. Mr. Washington distinctly asks that black people give up, at least for the present, three things,—

First, political power,

Second, insistence on civil rights,

Third, higher education of Negro youth,—

and concentrate all their energies on industrial education, the accumulation of wealth, and the conciliation of the South. This policy has been courageously and insistently advocated for over fifteen years, and has been triumphant for perhaps ten years. As a result of this tender of the palm-branch, what has been the return? In these years there have occurred:

1. The disfranchisement of the Negro.

2. The legal creation of a distinct status of civil inferiority for the Negro.

3. The steady withdrawal of aid from institutions for the higher training of the Negro.

These movements are not, to be sure, direct results of Mr. Washington's teachings; but his propaganda has, without a shadow of doubt, helped their speedier accomplishment. The question then comes: Is it possible, and probable, that nine millions of men can make effective progress in economic lines if they are deprived of political rights, made a servile caste, and allowed only the most meagre chance for developing their exceptional men? If history and reason give any distinct answer to these questions, it is an emphatic *No*. And Mr. Washington thus faces the triple paradox of his career:

1. He is striving nobly to make Negro artisans business men and property-owners; but it is utterly impossible, under modern competitive methods, for workingmen and property-owners to defend their rights and exist without the right of suffrage.

2. He insists on thrift and self-respect, but at the same time counsels a silent submission to civic inferiority such as is bound to sap the manhood of any race in the long run.

3. He advocates common-school and industrial training, and depreciates institutions of higher learning; but neither the Negro common schools, nor Tuskegee itself, could remain open a day were it not for teachers trained in Negro colleges, or trained by their graduates.

This triple paradox in Mr. Washington's position is the object of criticism by two classes of colored Americans. One class is spiritually descended from Toussaint the Savior, through Gabriel, Vesey, and Turner, and they represent the attitude of revolt and revenge; they hate the white South blindly and distrust the white race generally, and so far as they agree on definite action, think that the Negro's only hope lies in emigration beyond the borders of the United States. And yet, by the irony of fate, nothing has more effectually made this programme seem hopeless than the recent course of the United States toward weaker and darker peoples in the West Indies, Hawaii, and the Philippines,—for where in the world may we go and be safe from lying and brute force?

The other class of Negroes who cannot agree with Mr. Washington has hitherto said little aloud. They deprecate the sight of scattered counsels, of internal disagreement; and especially they dislike making their just criticism of a useful and earnest man an excuse for a general discharge of venom from small-minded opponents. Nevertheless, the questions involved are so fundamental and serious that it is difficult to see how men like the Grimkes, Kelly Miller, J. W. E. Bowen, and other representatives of this group, can much longer be silent. Such men feel in conscience bound to ask of this nation three things:

1. The right to vote.
2. Civic equality.
3. The education of youth according to ability.

They acknowledge Mr. Washington's invaluable service in counselling patience and courtesy in such demands; they do not ask that ignorant black men vote when ignorant whites are debarred, or that any reasonable restrictions in the suffrage should not be applied; they know that the low social level of the mass of the race is responsible for much discrimination against it, but they also know, and the nation knows, that relentless color-prejudice is more often a cause than a result of the Negro's degradation; they seek the abatement of this relic of barbarism, and not its systematic encouragement and pampering by all agencies of social power from the Associated Press to the Church of Christ. They advocate, with Mr. Washington, a broad system of Negro common schools supplemented by thorough industrial training; but they are surprised that a man of Mr. Washington's insight cannot see that no such educational system ever has rested or can rest on any other basis than that of the well-equipped college and university, and they insist that there is a demand for a few such institutions throughout the South to train the best of the Negro youth as teachers, professional men, and leaders.

This group of men honor Mr. Washington for his attitude of conciliation toward the white South; they accept the "Atlanta Compromise" in its broadest interpretation; they recognize, with him, many signs of promise, many men of high purpose and fair judgment, in this section; they know that no easy task has been laid upon a region already tottering under heavy burdens. But, nevertheless, they insist that the way to truth and right lies in straightforward honesty, not in indiscriminate flattery; in praising those of the South who do well and criticising uncompromisingly those who do ill; in taking advantage of the opportunities at hand and urging their fellows to do the same, but at the same time in remembering that only a firm adherence to their higher ideals and aspirations will ever keep those ideals within the realm of possibility. They do not expect that the free right to vote, to enjoy civic rights, and to be educated, will come in a moment; they do not expect to see the bias and prejudices of years disappear at the blast of a trumpet; but they are absolutely certain that the way for a people to gain their reasonable rights is not by voluntarily throwing them away and insisting that they do not want them; that the way for a people to gain respect is not by continually belittling and ridiculing themselves; that, on the contrary, Negroes must insist continually, in season and out of season, that voting is necessary to modern manhood, that color discrimination is barbarism, and that black boys need education as well as white boys.

In failing thus to state plainly and unequivocally the legitimate demands of their people, even at the cost of opposing an honored leader, the thinking classes of American Negroes would shirk a heavy responsibility,—a responsibility to themselves, a responsibility to the struggling masses, a responsibility to the darker races of men whose future depends so largely on this American experiment, but especially a responsibility to this nation,—this common Fatherland. It is wrong to encourage a man or a people in evil-doing; it is wrong to aid and abet a national crime simply because it is unpopular not to do so. The growing spirit of kindliness and reconciliation between the North and South after the frightful difference of a generation ago ought to be a source of deep congratulation to all, and especially to those whose mistreatment caused the war; but if that reconciliation is to be marked by the industrial slavery and civic death of those same black men, with permanent legislation into a position of inferiority, then those black men, if they are really men, are called upon by every consideration of patriotism and loyalty to oppose such a course by all civilized methods, even though such opposition involves disagreement with Mr. Booker T. Washington. We have no right to sit silently by while the inevitable seeds are sown for a harvest of disaster to our children, black and white.

First, it is the duty of black men to judge the South discriminatingly. The present generation of Southerners are not responsible for the past, and they should not be blindly hated or blamed for it. Furthermore, to no class is the indiscriminate endorsement of the recent course of the South toward Negroes more nauseating than to the best thought of the South. The South is not "solid"; it is a land in the ferment of social change, wherein forces of all kinds are fighting for supremacy; and to praise the ill the South is to-day perpetrating is just as wrong as to condemn the good. Discriminating and broad-minded criticism is what the South needs,—needs it for the sake of her own white sons and daughters, and for the insurance of robust, healthy mental and moral development.

To-day even the attitude of the Southern whites toward the blacks is not, as so many assume, in all cases the same; the ignorant Southerner hates the Negro, the workingmen fear his competition, the money-makers wish to use him as a laborer, some of the educated see a menace in his upward development, while others—usually the sons of the masters—wish to help him to rise. National opinion has enabled this last class to maintain the Negro common schools, and to protect the Negro partially in property, life, and limb. Through the pressure of the money-makers, the Negro is in danger of being reduced to semi-slavery, especially in the country districts; the workingmen, and those of the educated who fear the Negro, have united to disfranchise him, and some have urged his deportation; while the passions of the ignorant are easily aroused to lynch and abuse any black man. To praise this intricate whirl of thought and prejudice is nonsense; to inveigh indiscriminately against "the South" is unjust; but to use the same breath in praising Governor Aycock, exposing Senator Morgan, arguing with Mr. Thomas Nelson Page, and denouncing Senator Ben Tillman, is not only sane, but the imperative duty of thinking black men.

It would be unjust to Mr. Washington not to acknowledge that in several instances he has opposed movements in the South which were unjust to the Negro; he sent memorials to the Louisiana and Alabama constitutional conventions, he has spoken against lynching, and in other ways has openly or silently set his influence against sinister schemes and unfortunate happenings. Notwithstanding this, it is equally true to assert that on the whole the distinct impression left by Mr. Washington's propaganda is, first, that the South is justified in its present attitude toward the Negro because of the Negro's degradation; secondly, that the prime cause of the Negro's failure to rise more quickly is his wrong education in the past; and, thirdly, that his future rise depends primarily on his own efforts. Each of these propositions is a dangerous half-truth. The supplementary truths must never be lost sight of: first, slavery and race-prejudice are potent if not sufficient causes of the Negro's position; second, industrial and common-school training were necessarily slow in planting because they had to await the black teachers trained by higher institutions,—it being extremely doubtful if any essentially different development was possible, and certainly a Tuskegee was unthinkable before 1880; and, third, while it is a great truth to say that the Negro must strive and strive mightily to help himself, it is equally true that unless his striving be not simply seconded, but rather aroused and encouraged, by the initiative of the richer and wiser environing group, he cannot hope for great success.

In his failure to realize and impress this last point, Mr. Washington is especially to be criticized. His doctrine has tended to make the whites, North and South, shift the burden of the Negro problem to the Negro's shoulders and stand aside as critical and rather pessimistic spectators; when in fact the burden belongs to the nation, and the hands of none of us are clean if we bend not our energies to righting these great wrongs.

The South ought to be led, by candid and honest criticism, to assert her better self and do her full duty to the race she has cruelly wronged and is still wronging. The North—her co-partner in guilt—cannot salve her conscience by plastering it with gold. We cannot settle this problem by diplomacy and suaveness, by "policy" alone. If worse come to worst, can the moral fibre of this country survive the slow throttling and murder of nine millions of men?

The black men of America have a duty to perform, a duty stern and delicate,—a forward movement to oppose a part of the work of their greatest leader. So far as Mr. Washington preaches Thrift, Patience, and Industrial Training for the masses, we must hold up his hands and strive with him, rejoicing in his honors and glorying in the strength of this Joshua called of God and of man to lead the headless host. But so far as Mr. Washington apologizes for injustice, North or South, does not rightly value the privilege and duty of voting, belittles the emasculating effects of caste distinctions, and opposes the higher training and ambition of our brighter minds,—so far as he, the South, or the Nation, does this,—we must unceasingly and firmly oppose them. By every civilized and peaceful method we must strive for the rights which the world accords to men, clinging unwaveringly to those great words which the sons of the Fathers would fain forget: "We hold these truths to be self-evident: that all men are created equal;

that they are endowed by their Creator with certain unalienable rights; that among these are life, liberty, and the pursuit of happiness."

QUESTIONS FOR DISCUSSION AND WRITING

1. What specific complaints does DuBois make about Washington's point of view? Why does he consider that point of view to be dangerous for the future of black people?
2. According to DuBois, what does Washington's leadership symbolize?
3. DuBois' essay, written in the early twentieth century, asserts that emigration cannot be a major hope for the black man. What evidence does he cite to support this point of view? What assumptions does he make about American foreign policy?
4. DuBois introduces the terms "guilt" and "sentiment" into his discussion of racial relationships. To what extent have these psychological factors determined the direction of white attitudes?
5. The theme of "manly self-respect" runs throughout DuBois' essay. What conditions are necessary for this self-respect? Compare DuBois' definition of self-respect with that presented by Grier and Cobbs (p. 307).

BETWEEN 1896 AND 1898 W. E. B. DUBOIS (SEE P. 77) INVESTIGATED ONE OF THE FIRST BLACK URBAN GHETTOS, PHILADELPHIA'S SEVENTH WARD. HIS BOOK *The Philadelphia Negro* DOCUMENTS THIS STUDY AND IS A LANDMARK IN SOCIOLOGY.

W. E. B. DUBOIS

A FINAL WORD

The Meaning of All This

Two sorts of answers are usually returned to the bewildered American who asks seriously: What is the Negro problem? The one is straightforward and clear: it is simply this, or simply that, and one simple remedy long enough applied will in time cause it to disappear. The other answer is apt to be hopelessly involved and complex—to indicate no simple panacea, and to end in a somewhat hopeless—There it is; what can we do? Both of these sorts of answers have something of truth in them: the Negro problem looked at in one way is but the old world questions of ignorance, poverty, crime, and the dislike of the stranger. On the other hand it is a mistake to think that

A FINAL WORD From *The Philadelphia Negro* (1899) by W. E. B. DuBois, Chapter 18.

attacking each of these questions single-handed without reference to the others will settle the matter: a combination of social problems is far more than a matter of mere addition,—the combination itself is a problem. Nevertheless the Negro problems are not more hopelessly complex than many others have been. Their elements despite their bewildering complication can be kept clearly in view: they are after all the same difficulties over which the world has grown gray: the question as to how far human intelligence can be trusted and trained; as to whether we must always have the poor with us; as to whether it is possible for the mass of men to attain righteousness on earth; and then to this is added that question of questions: after all who are Men? Is every featherless biped to be counted a man and brother? Are all races and types to be joint heirs of the new earth that men have striven to raise in thirty centuries and more? Shall we not swamp civilization in barbarism and drown genius in indulgence if we seek a mythical Humanity which shall shadow all men? The answer of the early centuries to this puzzle was clear: those of any nation who can be called Men and endowed with rights are few: they are the privileged classes—the well-born and the accidents of low-birth called up by the King. The rest, the mass of the nation, the *pöbel*, the mob, are fit to follow, to obey, to dig and delve, but not to think or rule or play the gentleman. We who were born to another philosophy hardly realize how deep-seated and plausible this view of human capabilities and powers once was; how utterly incomprehensible this republic would have been to Charlemagne or Charles V or Charles I. We rather hasten to forget that once the courtiers of English kings looked upon the ancestors of most Americans with far greater contempt than these Americans look upon Negroes—and perhaps, indeed, had more cause. We forget that once French peasants were the "Niggers" of France, and that German princelings once discussed with doubt the brains and humanity of the *bauer*.

Much of this—or at least some of it—has passed and the world has glided by blood and iron into a wider humanity, a wider respect for simple manhood unadorned by ancestors or privilege. Not that we have discovered, as some hoped and some feared, that all men were created free and equal, but rather that the differences in men are not so vast as we had assumed. We still yield the well-born the advantages of birth, we still see that each nation has its dangerous flock of fools and rascals; but we also find most men have brains to be cultivated and souls to be saved.

And still this widening of the idea of common Humanity is of slow growth and to-day but dimly realized. We grant full citizenship in the World-Commonwealth to the "Anglo-Saxon" (whatever that may mean), the Teuton and the Latin; then with just a shade of reluctance we extend it to the Celt and Slav. We half deny it to the yellow races of Asia, admit the brown Indians to an ante-room only on the strength of an undeniable past; but with the Negroes of Africa we come to a full stop, and in its heart the civilized world with one accord denies that these come within the pale of nineteenth century Humanity. This feeling, widespread and deep-seated, is, in America, the vastest of the Negro problems; we have, to be sure, a threatening problem of ignorance but the ancestors of most Americans were far more ignorant than the freedmen's sons; these ex-slaves are poor but not as poor as the Irish peasants used to be; crime is rampant but not more so, if as much, as in Italy; but the difference is that the ancestors of the English and the Irish and the Italians were felt to be worth educating, helping and guiding because they were men and brothers, while in America a census which gives a slight indication of the utter disappearance of the American Negro from the earth is greeted with ill-concealed delight.

Other centuries looking back upon the culture of the nineteenth would have a right to suppose that if, in a land of freemen, eight millions of human beings were found to be dying of disease, the nation would cry with one voice, "Heal them!" If they were staggering on in ignorance, it would cry, "Train them!" If they were harming themselves and others by crime, it would cry, "Guide them!" And such cries are heard and have been heard in the land; but it was not one voice and its volume has been ever broken by counter-cries and echoes, "Let them die!" "Train them like slaves!" "Let them stagger downward!"

This is the spirit that enters in and complicates all Negro social problems and this is a problem which only civilization and humanity can successfully solve. Meantime we have the other problems before us—we have the problems arising from the uniting of so many social questions about one centre. In such a situation we need only to avoid underestimating the difficulties on the one hand and overestimating them on the other. The problems are difficult, extremely difficult, but they are such as the world has conquered before and can conquer again. Moreover the battle involves more than a mere altruistic interest in an alien people. It is a battle for humanity and human culture. If in the hey-day of the greatest of the world's civilizations, it is possible for one people ruthlessly to steal another, drag them helpless across the water, enslave them, debauch them, and then slowly murder them by economic and social exclusion until they disappear from the face of the earth—if the consummation of such a crime be possible in the twentieth century, then our civilization is vain and the republic is a mockery and a farce.

But this will not be; first, even with the terribly adverse circumstances under which Negroes live, there is not the slightest likelihood of their dying out; a nation that has endured the slave-trade, slavery, reconstruction, and present prejudice three hundred years, and under it increased in numbers and efficiency, is not in any immediate danger of extinction. Nor is the thought of voluntary or involuntary emigration more than a dream of men who forget that there are half as many Negroes in the United States as Spaniards in Spain. If this be so then a few plain propositions may be laid down as axiomatic:

1. The Negro is here to stay.
2. It is to the advantage of all, both black and white, that every Negro should make the best of himself.
3. It is the duty of the Negro to raise himself by every effort to the standards of modern civilization and not to lower those standards in any degree.
4. It is the duty of the white people to guard their civilization against debauchment by themselves or others; but in order to do this is not necessary to hinder and retard the efforts of an earnest people to rise, simply because they lack faith in the ability of that people.
5. With these duties in mind and with a spirit of self-help, mutual aid and co-operation, the two races should strive side by side to realize the ideals of the republic and make this truly a land of equal opportunity for all men.

The Duty of the Negroes

That the Negro race has an appalling work of social reform before it need hardly be said. Simply because the ancestors of the present white inhabitants of America went out of their way barbarously to mistreat and enslave the ancestors of the present black inhabitants, gives those blacks no right to ask that the civilization and morality of the land be seriously menaced for their benefit. Men have a right to demand that the members of a civilized community be civilized; that the fabric of human culture, so laboriously woven, be not wantonly or ignorantly destroyed. Consequently a nation may rightly demand, even of a people it has consciously and intentionally wronged, not indeed complete civilization in thirty or one hundred years, but at least every effort and sacrifice possible on their part toward making themselves fit members of the community within a reasonable length of time; that thus they may early become a source of strength and help instead of a national burden. Modern society has too many problems of its own, too much proper anxiety as to its own ability to survive under its present organization, for it lightly to shoulder all the burdens of a less advanced people, and it can rightly demand that as far as possible and as rapidly as possible the Negro bend his energy to the solving of his own social problems—contributing to his poor, paying his share of the taxes and supporting the schools and public administration. For the accomplishment of this the Negro has a right to demand freedom for self-development, and no more aid from without than is really helpful for furthering that development. Such aid must of necessity be considerable: it must furnish schools and reformatories, and relief and preventive agencies; but the bulk of the work of raising the Negro must be done by the Negro himself, and the greatest help for him will be not to hinder and curtail and discourage his efforts. Against prejudice, injustice and wrong the Negro ought to protest energetically and continuously, but he must never forget that he protests because those things hinder his own efforts, and that those efforts are the key to his future.

And those efforts must be mighty and comprehensive, persistent, well-aimed and tireless; satisfied with no partial success, lulled to sleep by no colorless victories; and, above all, guided by no low selfish ideals; at the same time they must be tempered by common sense and rational expectation. In Philadelphia those efforts should first be directed toward a lessening of Negro crime; no doubt the amount of crime imputed to the race is exaggerated, no doubt features of the Negro's environment over which he has no control excuse much that is committed; but beyond all this the amount of crime that can without doubt rightly be laid at the door of the Philadelphia Negro is large and is a menace to a civilized people. Efforts to stop this crime must commence in the Negro homes; they must cease to be, as they often are, breeders of idleness and extravagance and complaint. Work, continuous and intensive; work, although it be menial and poorly rewarded; work, though done in travail of soul and sweat of brow, must be so impressed upon Negro children as the road to salvation, that a child would feel it a greater disgrace to be idle than to do the humblest labor. The homely virtues of honesty, truth and chastity must be instilled in the cradle, and although it is hard to teach self-respect to a people whose million fellow-citizens half-despise them, yet it must be taught as the surest road to gain the respect of others.

It is right and proper that Negro boys and girls should desire to rise as high in the world as their ability and just desert entitle them. They should be ever encouraged and urged to do so, although they should be taught also that idleness and crime are beneath and not above the lowest work. It should be the continual object of Negroes to open up better industrial chances for their sons and daughters. Their success here must of course rest largely with the white people, but not entirely. Proper co-operation among forty or fifty thousand colored people ought to open many chances of employment for their sons and daughters in trades, stores and shops, associations and industrial enterprises.

Further, some rational means of amusement should be furnished young folks. Prayer meetings and church socials have their place, but they cannot compete in attractiveness with the dance halls and gambling dens of the city. There is a legitimate demand for amusement on the part of the young which may be made a means of education, improvement and recreation. A harmless and beautiful amusement like dancing might with proper effort be rescued from its low and unhealthful associations and made a means of health and recreation. The billiard table is no more wedded to the saloon than to the church if good people did not drive it there. If the Negro homes and churches cannot amuse their young people, and if no other efforts are made to satisfy this want, then we cannot complain if the saloons and clubs and bawdy-houses send these children to crime, disease and death.

There is a vast amount of preventive and rescue work which the Negroes themselves might do: keeping little girls off the street at night, stopping [to do] the escorting of unchaperoned young ladies to church and elsewhere, showing the dangers of the lodging system, urging the buying of homes and removal from crowded and tainted neighborhoods, giving lectures and tracts on health and habits, exposing the dangers of gambling and policy-playing, and inculcating respect for women. Day-nurseries and sewing-schools, mothers' meetings, the parks and airing places, all these things are little known or appreciated among the masses of Negroes, and their attention should be directed to them.

The spending of money is a matter to which Negroes need to give especial attention. Money is wasted to-day in dress, furniture, elaborate entertainments, costly church edifices, and "insurance" schemes, which ought to go toward buying homes, educating children, giving simple healthful amusement to the young, and accumulating something in the savings bank against a "rainy day." A crusade for the savings bank as against the "insurance" society ought to be started in the Seventh Ward without delay.

Although directly after the war there was great and remarkable enthusiasm for education, there is no doubt but that this enthusiasm has fallen off, and there is to-day much neglect of children among the Negroes, and failure to send them regularly to school. This should be looked into by the Negroes themselves and every effort made to induce full regular attendance.

Above all, the better classes of the Negroes should recognize their duty toward the masses. They should not forget that the spirit of the twentieth century is to be the turning of the high toward the lowly, the bending of Humanity to all that is human; the recognition that in the slums of modern society lie the answers to most of our puzzling problems of organization and life, and that only as we solve those problems is our culture assured and our progress certain. This the Negro is far from recognizing for himself; his social evolution in cities like Philadelphia is approaching a mediaeval stage when the centrifugal forces of repulsion between social classes are becoming more powerful than those of attraction. So hard has been the rise of the better class of Negroes that they fear to fall if now they stoop to lend a hand to their fellows. This feeling is intensified by the blindness of those outsiders who persist even now in confounding the good and bad, the risen and fallen in one mass. Nevertheless the Negro must learn the lesson that other nations learned so laboriously and imperfectly, that his better classes have their chief excuse for being in the work they may do toward lifting the rabble. This is especially true in a city like Philadelphia which has so distinct and creditable a Negro aristocracy; that they do something already to grapple with these social problems of their race is true, but they do not yet do nearly as much as they must, nor do they clearly recognize their responsibility.

Finally, the Negroes must cultivate a spirit of calm, patient persistence in their attitude toward their fellow citizens rather than of loud and intemperate complaint. A man may be wrong, and know he is wrong, and yet some finesse must be used in telling him of it. The white people of Philadelphia are perfectly conscious that their Negro citizens are not treated fairly in all respects, but it will not improve matters to call names or impute unworthy motives to all men. Social reforms move slowly and yet when Right is reinforced by calm but persistent Progress we somehow all feel that in the end it must triumph.

The Duty of the Whites

There is a tendency on the part of many white people to approach the Negro question from the side which just now is of least pressing importance, namely, that of the social intermingling of races. The old query: Would you want your sister to marry a Nigger? still stands as a grim sentinel to stop much rational discussion. And yet few white women have been pained by the addresses of black suitors, and those who have, easily got rid of them. The whole discussion is little less than foolish; perhaps a century from to-day we may find ourselves seriously discussing such questions of social policy, but it is certain that just as long as one group deems it a serious *mésalliance* to marry with another just so long few marriages will take place, and it will need neither law nor argument to guide human choice in such a matter. Certainly the masses of whites would hardly acknowledge that an active propaganda of repression was necessary to ward off intermarriage. Natural pride of race, strong on one side and growing on the other, may be trusted to ward off such mingling as might in this stage of development prove disastrous to both races. All this therefore is a question of the far-off future.

To-day, however, we must face the fact that a natural repugnance to close intermingling with unfortunate ex-slaves has descended to a discrimination that very seriously hinders them from being anything better. It is right and proper to object to ignorance and consequently to ignorant men; but if by our actions we have been responsible for their ignorance and are still actively engaged in keeping them ignorant, the argument loses its moral force. So with the Negroes: men have a right to object to a race so poor and ignorant and inefficient as the mass of the Negroes; but if their policy in the past is parent of much of this condition, and if to-day by shutting black boys and girls out of most avenues of decent employment they are increasing pauperism and vice, then they must hold themselves largely responsible for the deplorable results.

There is no doubt that in Philadelphia the centre and kernel of the Negro problem so far as the white people are concerned is the narrow opportunities afforded Negroes for earning a decent living. Such discrimination is morally wrong, politically dangerous, industrially wasteful, and socially silly. It is the duty of the whites to stop it, and to do so primarily for their own sakes. Industrial freedom of opportunity has by long experience been proven to be generally best for all. Moreover the cost of crime and pauperism, the growth of slums, and the pernicious influences of idleness and lewdness, cost the public far more than would the hurt to the feelings of a carpenter to work beside a black man, or a shop-girl to stand beside a darker mate. This does not contemplate the wholesale replacing of white workmen for Negroes out of sympathy or philanthropy; it does mean that talent should be rewarded, and aptness used in commerce and industry whether its owner be black or white; that the same incentive to good, honest, effective work be placed before a black office boy as before a white one—before a black porter as before a white one; and that unless this is done the city has no right to complain that black boys lose interest in work and drift into idleness and crime. Probably a change in public opinion on this point to-morrow would not make very much difference in the positions occupied by Negroes in the city: some few would be promoted, some few would get new places—the mass would remain as they are; but it would make one vast difference: it would inspire the young to try harder, it would stimulate the idle and discouraged and it would take away from this race the omnipresent excuse for failure: prejudice. Such a moral change would work a revolution in the criminal rate during the next ten years. Even a Negro bootblack could black boots better if he knew he was a menial not because he was a Negro but because he was best fitted for that work.

We need then a radical change in public opinion on this point; it will not and ought not to come suddenly, but instead of thoughtless acquiescence in the continual and steadily encroaching exclusion of Negroes from work in the city, the leaders of industry and opinion ought to be trying here and there to open up new opportunities and give new chances to bright colored boys. The policy of the city to-day simply drives out the best class of young people whom its schools have educated and social opportunities trained, and fills their places with idle and vicious immigrants. It is a paradox of the times that young men and women from some of the best Negro families of the city—families born and reared here and schooled in the best traditions of this municipality have actually had to go to the South to get work, if they wished to be aught but chambermaids and bootblacks. Not that such work may not be honorable and useful, but that it is as wrong to make scullions of engineers as it is to make engineers of scullions. Such a situation is a disgrace to the city—a disgrace to its Christianity, to its spirit of justice, to its common sense; what can be the end of such a policy but increased crime and increased excuse for crime? Increased poverty and more reason to be poor? Increased political serfdom of the mass of black voters to the bosses and rascals who divide the spoils? Surely here lies the first duty of a civilized city.

Secondly, in their efforts for the uplifting of the Negro the people of Philadelphia must recognize the existence of the better class of Negroes and must gain their active aid and co-operation by generous and polite conduct. Social sympathy must exist between what is best in both races and there must no longer be the feeling that the Negro who makes the best of himself is of least account to the city of Philadelphia, while the vagabond is to be helped and pitied. This better class of Negro does not want help or pity, but it does want a generous recognition of its difficulties, and a broad sympathy with the problem of life as it presents itself to them. It is composed of men and women educated and in many cases cultured; with proper co-operation they could be a vast power in the city, and the only power that could successfully cope with many phases of the Negro problems. But their active aid cannot be gained for purely selfish motives, or kept by churlish and ungentle manners; and above all they object to being patronized.

Again, the white people of the city must remember that much of the sorrow and bitterness that surrounds the life of the American Negro comes from the unconscious prejudice and half-conscious actions of men and women who do not intend to wound or annoy.

One is not compelled to discuss the Negro question with every Negro one meets or to tell him of a father who was connected with the Underground Railroad; one is not compelled to stare at the solitary black face in the audience as though it were not human; it is not necessary to sneer, or be unkind or boorish, if the Negroes in the room or on the street are not all the best behaved or have not the most elegant manners; it is hardly necessary to strike from the dwindling list of one's boyhood and girlhood acquaintances or school-day friends all those who happen to have Negro blood, simply because one has not the courage now to greet them on the street. The little decencies of daily intercourse can go on, the courtesies of life be exchanged even across the color line without any danger to the supremacy of the Anglo-Saxon or the social ambition of the Negro. Without doubt social differences are facts not fancies and cannot lightly be swept aside; but they hardly need to be looked upon as excuses for downright meanness and incivility.

A polite and sympathetic attitude toward these striving thousands; a delicate avoidance of that which wounds and embitters them; a generous granting of opportunity to them; a seconding of their efforts, and a desire to reward honest success—all this, added to proper striving on their part, will go far even in our day toward making all men, white and black, realize what the great founder of the city meant, when he named it the City of Brotherly Love.

QUESTIONS FOR DISCUSSION AND WRITING

1. DuBois suggests that "denial of Humanity" is the greatest Negro problem. What solutions does he suggest for this problem?
2. In what sense is the recognition of and solution to the Negro problem a "battle for Humanity and human culture"?
3. What must Negroes do in order to help themselves?
4. According to DuBois, how can recognition of the Negro's problems and work toward their solutions be helpful to whites?
5. What is DuBois' attitude toward the future of the black man in America? How does he indicate his point of view? Compare this viewpoint with that of Carmichael (p. 329).

MARCUS GARVEY ORGANIZED THE UNIVERSAL NEGRO IMPROVEMENT ASSOCIATION IN 1914 IN HIS NATIVE JAMAICA, BUT THE ORGANIZATION DID NOT GAIN LARGE MEMBERSHIP IN THE UNITED STATES UNTIL AFTER WORLD WAR I. THE UNIA WAS THE FIRST "BACK TO AFRICA" MOVEMENT TO RECEIVE WIDE SUPPORT WITHIN THE BLACK COMMUNITY AND ONE OF THE FIRST BLACK ORGANIZATIONS TO EXCLUDE WHITES. THE FOLLOWING SELECTION IS A SPEECH DELIVERED BY GARVEY AT LIBERTY HALL, NEW YORK CITY, ON NOVEMBER 25, 1922. GARVEY DIED IN 1940, AT THE AGE OF FIFTY-THREE.

MARCUS GARVEY

THE PRINCIPLES OF THE UNIVERSAL NEGRO IMPROVEMENT ASSOCIATION

Over five years ago, the Universal Negro Improvement Association placed itself before the world as the movement through which the new and rising Negro would give expression of his feelings. This Association adopts an attitude not of hostility to other races and peoples of the world, but an attitude of self-respect, of manhood rights on behalf of 400,000,000 Negroes of the world.

We represent peace, harmony, love, human sympathy, human rights and human justice, and that is why we fight so much. Wheresoever human rights are denied to any group, wheresoever justice is denied to any group, there the U.N.I.A. finds a cause. And at this time among all the peoples of the world, the group that suffers most from injustice, the group that is denied most of those rights that be-

THE PRINCIPLES OF THE UNIVERSAL NEGRO IMPROVEMENT ASSOCIATION From *The Philosophy and Opinions of Marcus Garvey* (1925), Vol. 2.

long to all humanity, is the black group of 400,000,000. Because of that injustice, because of that denial of our rights, we go forth under the leadership of the One who is always on the side of right to fight the common cause of humanity; to fight as we fought in the Revolutionary War, as we fought in the Civil War, as we fought in the Spanish-American War, and as we fought in the war between 1914–18 on the battle plains of France and of Flanders. As we fought on the heights of Mesopotamia, even so under the leadership of the U.N.I.A., we are marshaling the 400,000,000 Negroes of the world to fight for the emancipation of the race and of the redemption of the country of our fathers.

We represent a new line of thought among Negroes. Whether you call it advanced thought or reactionary thought, I do not care. If it is reactionary for people to seek independence in government, then we are reactionary. If it is advanced thought for people to seek liberty and freedom, then we represent the advanced school of thought among the Negroes of this country. We of the U.N.I.A. believe that what is good for the other folks is good for us. If government is something that is worth while; if government is something that is appreciable and helpful and protective to others, then we also want to experiment in government. We do not mean a government that will make us citizens without rights or subjects without consideration. We mean a kind of government that will place our race in control, even as other races are in control of their own governments.

That does not suggest anything that is unreasonable. It was not unreasonable for George Washington, the great hero and father of the country, to have fought for the freedom of America, giving to us this great republic and this great democracy; it was not unreasonable for the Liberals of France to have fought against the Monarchy to give to the world French Democracy and French Republicanism; it was no unrighteous cause that led Tolstoi to sound the call of liberty in Russia, which has ended in giving to the world the social democracy of Russia, an experiment that will probably prove to be a boon and a blessing to mankind. If it was not an unrighteous cause that led Washington to fight for the independence of this country, and led the Liberals of France to establish the Republic, it is therefore not an unrighteous cause for the U.N.I.A. to lead 400,000,000 Negroes all over the world to fight for the liberation of our country.

Therefore the U.N.I.A. is not advocating the cause of church building, because we have a sufficiently large number of churches among us to minister to the spiritual needs of the people, and we are not going to compete with those who are engaged in so splendid a work; we are not engaged in building any new social institutions, any Y.M.C.A. or Y.W.C.A., because there are enough social workers engaged in those praise-worthy efforts. We are not engaged in politics because we have enough local politicians, Democrats, Socialists, Soviets, etc., and the political situation is well taken care of. We are not engaged in domestic politics, in church building or in social uplift work, but we are engaged in nation building.

In advocating the principles of this Association we find we have been very much misunderstood and very much misrepresented by men from within our own race, as well as others from without. Any reform movement that seeks to bring about changes for the benefit of humanity is bound to be misrepresented by those who have always taken it upon themselves to administer to, and lead the unfortunate, and to direct those who may be placed under temporary disadvantages. It has been so in all other movements whether social or political; hence those of us in the Universal Negro Improvement Association who lead, do not feel in any way embarrassed about this misrepresentation, about this misunderstanding as far as the Aims and Objects of the Universal Negro Improvement Association go. But those who probably would have taken kindly notice of this great movement, have been led to believe that this movement seeks, not to develop the good within the race, but to give expression to that which is most destructive and most harmful to society and to government.

I desire to remove the misunderstanding that has been created in the minds of millions of peoples throughout the world in their relationship to the organization. The Universal Negro Improvement Association stands for the Bigger Brotherhood; the Universal Negro Improvement Association stands for human rights, not only for Negroes, but for all races. The Universal Negro Improvement Association believes in the rights of not only the black race, but the white race, the yellow race and the brown race. The Universal Negro Improvement Association believes that the white man has as much right to be considered, the yellow man has as much right to be considered, the brown man has as much right to be considered as well as the black man of Africa. In view of the fact that the black man of Africa has contributed as much to the world as the white man of Europe, and the brown man and yellow man of Asia, we of the Universal Negro Improvement Association demand that the white, yellow and brown races give to the black man his place in the civilization of the world. We ask for nothing more than the rights of 400,000,000 Negroes. We are not seeking, as I said before, to destroy or disrupt the society or the government of other races, but we are determined that 400,-000,000 of us shall unite ourselves to free our motherland from the grasp of the invader. We of the Universal Negro Improvement Association are determined to unite 400,000,000 Negroes for their own industrial, political, social and religious emancipation.

We of the Universal Negro Improvement Association are determined to unite the 400,000,000 Negroes of the world to give expression to their own feeling; we are determined to unite the 400,000,000 Negroes of the world for the purpose of building a civilization of their own. And in that effort we desire to bring together the 15,000,-000 of the United States, the 180,000,000 in Asia, the West Indies and Central and South America, and the 200,000,000 in Africa. We are looking toward political freedom on the continent of Africa, the land of our fathers.

The Universal Negro Improvement Association is not seeking to build up another government within the bounds or borders of the United States of America. The Universal Negro Improvement Association is not seeking to disrupt any organized system of government, but the Association is determined to bring Negroes together for the building up of a nation of their own. And why? Because we have been forced to it. We have been forced to it throughout the world; not only in America, not only in Europe, not only in the British Empire, but wheresoever the black man happens to find himself, he has been forced to do for himself.

To talk about Government is a little more than some of our people can appreciate just at this time. The average man does not think that way, just because he finds himself a citizen or a subject of some country. He seems to say, "Why should there be need for any other government?" We are French, English or American. But we of the U.N.I.A. have studied seriously this question of nationality among Negroes—this American nationality, this British nationality, this French, Italian or Spanish nationality, and have discovered that it counts for nought when that nationality comes in conflict with the racial idealism of the group that rules. When our interests clash with those of the ruling faction, then we find that we have absolutely no rights. In times of peace, when everything is all right, Negroes have a hard time, wherever we go, wheresoever we find ourselves, getting those rights that belong to us, in common with others whom we claim as fellow citizens; getting that consideration that should be ours by right of the constitution, by right of the law; but in the time of trouble they make us all partners in the cause, as happened in the last war, when we were partners, whether British, French or American Negroes. And we were told that we must forget everything in an effort to save the nation.

We have saved many nations in this manner, and we have lost our lives doing that before. Hundreds of thousands—nay, millions of black men, lie buried under the ground due to that old-time camouflage of saving the nation. We saved the British Empire; we saved the French empire; we saved this glorious country more than once; and all that we have received for our sacrifices, all that we have received for what we have done, even in giving up our lives, is just what you are receiving now, just what I am receiving now.

You and I fare no better in America, in the British Empire, or in any other part of the white world; we fare no better than any black man wheresoever he shows his head. And why? Because we have been satisfied to allow ourselves to be led, educated, to be directed by the other fellow, who has always sought to lead in the world in that direction that would satisfy him and strengthen his position. We have allowed ourselves for the last 500 years to be a race of followers, following every race that has led in the direction that would make them more secure.

The U.N.I.A. is reversing the old-time order of things. We refuse to be followers any more. We are leading ourselves. That means, if any saving is to be done, later on, whether it is saving this one nation or that one government, we are going to seek a method of saving Africa first. Why? And why Africa? Because Africa has become the grand prize of the nations. Africa has become the big game of the nation hunters. To-day Africa looms as the greatest commercial, industrial and political prize in the world.

The difference between the Universal Negro Improvement Association and the other movements of this country, and probably the world, is that the Universal Negro Improvement Association seeks independence of government, while the other organizations seek to make the Negro a secondary part of existing governments. We differ from the organizations in America because they seek to subordinate the Negro as a secondary consideration in a great civilization, knowing that in America the Negro will never reach his highest ambition, knowing that the Negro in America will never get his constitutional rights. All those organizations which are fostering the improvement of Negroes in the British Empire know that the Negro in the British Empire will never reach the height of his constitutional rights. What do I mean by constitutional rights in America? If the black man is to reach the height of his ambition in this country—if the black man is to get all of his constitutional rights in America—then the black man should have the same chance in the nation as any other man to become president of the nation, or a street cleaner in New York. If the black man in the British Empire is to have all his constitutional rights it means that the Negro in the British Empire should have at least the same right to become premier of Great Britain as he has to become street cleaner in the city of London. Are they prepared to give us such political equality? You and I can live in the United States of America for 100 more years, and our generations may live for 200 years or for 5000 more years, and so long as there is a black and white population, when the majority is on the side of the white race, you and I will never get political justice or get political equality in this country. Then why should a black man with rising ambition, after preparing himself in every possible way to give expression to that highest ambition, allow himself to be kept down by racial prejudice within a country? If I am as educated as the next man, if I am as prepared as the next man, if I have passed through the best schools and colleges and universities as the other fellow, why should I not have a fair chance to compete with the other fellow for the biggest position in the nation? I have feelings, I have blood, I have senses like the other fellow; I have ambition, I have hope. Why should he, because of some racial prejudice, keep me down and why should I concede to him the right to rise above me, and to establish himself as my permanent master? That is where the U.N.I.A. differs from other organizations. I refuse to stultify my ambition, and every true Negro refuses to stultify his ambition to suit any one, and therefore the U.N.I.A. decides if America is not big enough for two presidents, if England is not big enough for two kings, then we are not going to quarrel over the matter; we will leave one president in America, we will leave one king in England, we will leave one president in France and we will have one president in Africa. Hence, the Universal Negro Improvement Association does not seek to interfere with the social and political systems of France, but by the arrangement of things today the U.N.I.A. refuses to recognize any political or social system in Africa except that which we are about to establish for ourselves.

We are not preaching a propaganda of hate against anybody. We love the white man; we love all humanity, because we feel that we cannot live without the other. The white man is as necessary to the existence of the Negro as the Negro is necessary to his existence. There is a common relationship that we cannot escape. Africa has certain things that Europe wants, and Europe has certain things that Africa wants, and if a fair and square deal must bring white and black with each other, it is impossible for us to escape it. Africa has oil, diamonds, copper, gold and rubber and all the minerals that Europe wants, and there must be some kind of relationship between Africa and Europe for a fair exchange, so we cannot afford to hate anybody.

The question often asked is what does it require to redeem a race and free a country? If it takes man power, if it takes scientific intelligence, if it takes education of any kind, or if it takes blood, then the 400,000,000 Negroes of the world have it.

It took the combined man power of the Allies to put down the mad determination of the Kaiser to impose German will upon the world and upon humanity. Among those who suppressed his mad ambition were two million Negroes who have not yet forgotten how to drive men across the firing line. Surely those of us who faced German shot and shell at the Marne, at Verdun, have not forgotten the order of our Commander-in-Chief. The cry that caused us to leave America in such mad haste, when white fellow citizens of America refused to fight and said, "We do not believe in war and therefore, even though we are American citizens, and even though the nation is in danger, we will not go to war." When many of them cried out and said, "We are German-Americans and we can not fight," when so many white men refused to answer to the call and dodged behind all kinds of excuses, 400,000 black men were ready without a question. It was because we were told it was a war of democracy; it was a war for the liberation of the weaker peoples of the world. We heard the cry of Woodrow Wilson, not because we liked him so, but because the things he said were of such a nature that they appealed to us as men. Wheresoever the cause of humanity stands in need of assistance, there you will find the Negro ever ready to serve.

He has done it from the time of Christ up to now. When the whole world turned its back upon the Christ, the man who was said to be the Son of God, when the world cried out "Crucify Him," when the world spurned Him and spat upon Him, it was a black man, Simon, the Cyrenian, who took up the cross. Why? Because the cause of humanity appealed to him. When the black man saw the suffering Jew, struggling under the heavy cross, he was willing to go to His assistance, and he bore that cross up to the heights of Calvary. In the spirit of Simon, the Cyrenian, 1900 years ago we answered the call of Woodrow Wilson, the call of a larger humanity, and it was for that that we willingly rushed into the war from America, from the West Indies, over 100,000; it was for that that we rushed into the war from Africa, 2,000,000 of us. We met in France, Flanders and in Mesopotamia. We fought unfalteringly. When the white men faltered and fell back on their battle lines, at the Marne and at Verdun, when they ran away from the charge of the German hordes, the black hell fighters stood before the cannonade, stood before the charge, and again they shouted, "There will be a hot time in the old town tonight."

We made it so hot a few months after our appearance in France and on the various battle fronts, we succeeded in driving the German hordes across the Rhine, and driving the Kaiser out of Germany, and out of Potsdam into Holland. We have not forgotten the prowess of war. If we have been liberal minded enough to give our life's blood in France, in Mesopotamia and elsewhere, fighting for the white man, whom we have always assisted, surely we have not forgotten to fight for ourselves, and when the time comes that the world will again give Africa an opportunity for freedom, surely 400,000,000 black men will march out on the battle plains of Africa, under the colors of the red, the black and the green.

We shall march out, yes, as black American citizens, as black British subjects, as black French citizens, as black Italians or as black Spaniards, but we shall march out with a greater loyalty, the loyalty of race. We shall march out in answer to the cry of our fathers, who cry out to us for the redemption of our own country, our motherland, Africa.

We shall march out, not forgetting the blessings of America. We shall march out, not forgetting the blessings of civilization. We shall march out with a history of peace before and behind us, and surely that history shall be our breastplate, for how can man fight better than knowing that the cause for which he fights is righteous? How can man fight more gloriously than by knowing that behind him is a history of slavery, a history of bloody carnage and massacre inflicted upon a race because of its inability to protect itself and fight? Shall we not fight for the glorious opportunity of protecting and forever more establishing ourselves as a mighty race and nation, never more to be disrespected by men. Glorious shall be the battle when the time comes to fight for our people and our race.

We should say to the millions who are in Africa to hold the fort, for we are coming 400,000,000 strong.

QUESTIONS FOR DISCUSSION AND WRITING

1. What reasons does Garvey give for the formation and policy of the UNIA?
2. Why does Garvey feel that emigration is imperative?
3. Why is race a principal factor in political control?
4. According to Garvey, what is self-respect? How does his definition differ from DuBois' (p. 85)?
5. In what ways are the viewpoints of Garvey and Malcolm X (p. 317) similar? How do their solutions to the black man's problems differ? Why?

RALPH ELLISON IS ONE OF AMERICA'S BEST-KNOWN BLACK NOVELISTS. THE FOLLOWING SELECTION IS TAKEN FROM HIS AWARD-WINNING NOVEL *Invisible Man,* WHICH WAS PUBLISHED IN 1953, WHEN ELLISON WAS THIRTY-NINE.

RALPH ELLISON

Prologue to INVISIBLE MAN

I am an invisible man. No, I am not a spook like those who haunted Edgar Allan Poe; nor am I one of your Hollywood-movie ectoplasms. I am a man of substance, of flesh and bone, fiber and liquids—and I might even be said to possess a mind. I am invisible, understand, simply because people refuse to see me. Like the bodiless heads you see sometimes in circus sideshows, it is as though I have been surrounded by mirrors of hard, distorting glass. When they approach me they see only my surroundings, themselves, or figments of their imagination—indeed, everything and anything except me.

Nor is my invisibility exactly a matter of a bio-chemical accident to my epidermis. That invisibility to which I refer occurs because of a peculiar disposition of the eyes of those with whom I come in contact.

A matter of the construction of their *inner* eyes, those eyes with which they look through their physical eyes upon reality. I am not complaining, nor am I protesting either. It is sometimes advantageous to be unseen, although it is most often rather wearing on the nerves. Then too, you're constantly being bumped against by those of poor vision. Or again, you often doubt if you really exist. You wonder whether you aren't simply a phantom in other people's minds. Say, a figure in a nightmare which the sleeper tries with all his strength to destroy. It's when you feel like this that, out of resentment, you begin to bump people back. And, let me confess, you feel that way most of the time. You ache with the need to convince yourself that you do exist in the real world, that you're a part of all the sound and anguish, and you strike out with your fists, you curse and you swear to make them recognize you. And, alas, it's seldom successful.

One night I accidentally bumped into a man, and perhaps because of the near darkness he saw me and called me an insulting name. I sprang at him, seized his coat lapels and demanded that he apologize. He was a tall blond man, and as my face came close to his he looked insolently out of his blue eyes and cursed me, his breath hot in my face as he struggled. I pulled his chin down sharp upon the crown of my head, butting him as I had seen the West Indians do, and I felt his flesh tear and the blood gush out, and I yelled, "Apologize! Apologize!" But he continued to curse and struggle, and I butted him again and again until he went down heavily, on his knees, profusely bleeding. I kicked him repeatedly, in a frenzy because he still uttered insults though his lips were frothy with blood. Oh yes, I kicked him! And in my outrage I got out my knife and prepared to slit his throat, right there beneath the lamplight in the deserted street, holding him by the collar with one hand, and opening the knife with my teeth—when it occurred to me that the man had not *seen* me, actually; that he, as far as he knew, was in the midst of a walking nightmare! And I stopped the blade, slicing the air as I pushed him away, letting him fall back to the street. I stared at him hard as the lights of a car stabbed through the darkness. He lay there, moaning on the asphalt; a man almost killed by a phantom. It unnerved me. I was both disgusted and ashamed. I was like a drunken man myself, wavering about on weakened legs. Then I was amused. Something in this man's thick head had sprung out and beaten him within an inch of his life. I began to laugh at this crazy discovery. Would he have awakened at the point of death? Would Death himself have freed him for wakeful living? But I didn't linger. I ran away into the dark, laughing so hard I feared I might rupture myself. The next day I saw his picture in the *Daily News*, beneath a caption stating that he had been "mugged." Poor fool, poor blind fool, I thought with sincere compassion, mugged by an invisible man!

Most of the time (although I do not choose as I once did to deny the violence of my days by ignoring it) I am not so overtly violent. I remember that I am invisible and walk softly so as not to awaken the sleeping ones. Sometimes it is best not to awaken them; there are few things in the world as dangerous as sleepwalkers. I learned in time though that it is possible to carry on a fight against them without their realizing it. For instance, I have been carrying on a fight with Monopolated Light & Power for some time now. I use their service and pay them nothing at all, and they don't know it. Oh, they suspect that power is being drained off, but they don't know where. All they know is that according to the master meter back there in their power station a hell of a lot of free current is disappearing somewhere into the jungle of Harlem. The joke, of course, is that I don't live in Harlem but in a border area. Several years ago (before I discovered the advantage of being invisible) I went through the routine process of buying service and paying their outrageous rates. But no more. I gave up all that, along with my apartment, and my old way of life: That way based upon the fallacious assumption that I, like other men, was visible. Now, aware of my invisibility, I live rent-free in a building rented strictly to whites, in a section of the basement that was shut off and forgotten during the nineteenth century, which I discovered when I was trying to escape in the night from Ras the Destroyer. But that's getting too far ahead of the story, almost to the end, although the end is in the beginning and lies far ahead.

The point now is that I found a home—or a hole in the ground, as you will. Now don't jump to the conclusion that because I call my home a "hole" it is damp and cold like a grave; there are cold holes and warm holes. Mine is a warm hole. And remember, a bear retires to his hole for the winter and lives until spring; then he comes strolling out like the Easter chick breaking from its shell. I say all this to assure you that it is incorrect to assume that, because I'm invisible and live in a hole, I am dead. I am neither dead nor in a state of suspended animation. Call me Jack-the-Bear, for I am in a state of hibernation.

My hole is warm and full of light. Yes, *full* of light. I doubt if there is a brighter spot in all New York than this hole of mine, and I do not exclude Broadway. Or the Empire State Building on a photographer's dream night. But that is taking advantage of you. Those two spots are among the darkest of our whole civilization—pardon me, our whole *culture* (an important distinction, I've heard)—which might sound like a hoax, or a contradiction, but that (by contradiction, I mean) is how the world moves: Not like an arrow, but a boomerang. (Beware of those who speak of the *spiral* of history; they are preparing a boomerang. Keep a steel helmet handy.) I know; I have been boomeranged across my head so much that I now can see the darkness of lightness. And I love light. Perhaps you'll think it strange that an invisible man should need light, desire light, love light. But maybe it is exactly because I *am* invisible. Light confirms my reality, gives birth to my form. A beautiful girl once told me of a recurring nightmare in which she lay in the center of a large dark room and felt her face expand until it filled the whole room, becoming a formless mass while her eyes ran in bilious jelly up the chimney. And so it is with me. Without light I am not only invisible, but formless as well; and to be unaware of one's form is to live a death. I myself, after existing some twenty years, did not become alive until I discovered my invisibility.

That is why I fight my battle with Monopolated Light & Power. The deeper reason, I mean: It allows me to feel my vital aliveness. I also fight them for taking so much of my money before I learned to protect myself. In my hole in the basement there are exactly 1,369 lights. I've wired the entire ceiling, every inch of it. And not with fluorescent bulbs, but with the older, more-expensive-to-operate kind, the filament type. An act of sabotage, you know. I've already begun to wire the wall. A junk man I know, a man of vision, has supplied me with wire and sockets. Nothing, storm or flood, must get in the way of our need for light and ever more and brighter light. The truth is the light and light is the truth. When I finish all four walls, then I'll start on the floor. Just how that will go, I don't know. Yet when you have lived invisible as long as I have you develop a certain ingenuity. I'll solve the problem. And maybe I'll invent a gadget to place my coffeepot on the fire while I lie in bed, and even invent a gadget to warm my bed—like the fellow I saw in one of the picture magazines who made himself a gadget to warm his shoes! Though invisible, I am in the great American tradition of tinkers. That makes me kin to Ford, Edison and Franklin. Call me, since I have a theory and a concept, a "thinker-tinker." Yes, I'll warm my shoes; they need it, they're usually full of holes. I'll do that and more.

Now I have one radio-phonograph; I plan to have five. There is a certain acoustical deadness in my hole, and when I have music I want to *feel* its vibration, not only with my ear but with my whole body. I'd like to hear five recordings of Louis Armstrong playing and singing "What Did I Do to Be so Black and Blue"—all at the same time. Sometimes now I listen to Louis while I have my favorite dessert of vanilla ice cream and sloe gin. I pour the red liquid over the white mound, watching it glisten and the vapor rising as Louis bends that military instrument into a beam of lyrical sound. Perhaps I like Louis Armstrong because he's made poetry out of being invisible. I think it must be because he's unaware that he *is* invisible. And my own grasp of invisibility aids me to understand his music. Once when I asked for a cigarette, some jokers gave me a reefer, which I lighted when I got home and sat listening to my phonograph. It was a strange evening. Invisibility, let me explain, gives one a slightly different sense of time, you're never quite on the beat. Sometimes you're ahead and sometimes behind. Instead of the swift and imperceptible flowing of time, you are aware of its nodes, those points where time stands still or from which it leaps ahead. And you slip into the breaks and look around. That's what you hear vaguely in Louis' music.

Once I saw a prizefighter boxing a yokel. The fighter was swift and amazingly scientific. His body was one violent flow of rapid rhythmic action. He hit the yokel a hundred times while the yokel held up his arms in stunned surprise. But suddenly the yokel, rolling about in the gale of boxing gloves, struck one blow and knocked science, speed and footwork as cold as a well-digger's posterior. The smart money hit the canvas. The long shot got the nod. The yokel had simply stepped inside of his opponent's sense of time. So under the spell of the reefer I discovered a new analytical way of listening to music. The unheard sounds came through, and each melodic line existed of itself, stood out clearly from all the rest, said its piece, and waited patiently for the other voices to speak. That night I found myself hearing not only in time, but in space as well. I not only entered the music but descended, like Dante, into its depths. And *beneath the swiftness of the hot tempo there was a slower tempo and a cave and I entered it and looked around and heard an old woman singing a spiritual as full of Weltschmerz as flamenco, and beneath that lay a still lower level on which I saw a beautiful girl the color of ivory pleading in a voice like my mother's as she stood before a group of slave owners who bid for her naked body, and below that I found a lower level and a more rapid tempo and I heard someone shout:*

"Brothers and sisters, my text this morning is the 'Blackness of Blackness.'"

And a congregation of voices answered: "That blackness is most black, brother, most black . . ."

"In the beginning . . ."

"At the very start," they cried.

". . . there was blackness . . ."

"Preach it . . ."

". . . and the sun . . ."

"The sun, Lawd . . ."

". . . was bloody red . . ."

"Red . . ."

"Now black is . . ." the preacher shouted.

"Bloody . . ."

"I said black is . . ."

"Preach it, brother . . ."

". . . an' black ain't . . ."

"Red, Lawd, red: He said it's red!"

"Amen, brother . . ."

"Black will git you . . ."

"Yes, it will . . ."

". . . an' black won't . . ."

"Naw, it won't!"

"It do . . ."

"It do, Lawd . . ."

". . . an' it don't."

"Halleluiah . . ."

". . . it'll put you, glory, glory, Oh my Lawd, in the WHALE'S BELLY."

"Preach it, dear brother . . ."

". . . an' make you tempt . . ."

"Good God a-mighty!"

"Old Aunt Nelly!"

"Black will make you . . ."

"Black . . ."

". . . or black will un-make you."

"Ain't it the truth, Lawd?"

And at that point a voice of trombone timbre screamed at me, "Git out of here, you fool! Is you ready to commit treason?"

And I tore myself away, hearing the old singer of spirituals moaning, "Go curse your God, boy, and die."

I stopped and questioned her, asked her what was wrong.

"I dearly loved my master, son," she said.

"You should have hated him," I said.

"He gave me several sons," she said, "and because I loved my sons I learned to love their father though I hated him too."

"I too have become acquainted with ambivalence," I said. "That's why I'm here."

"What's that?"

"Nothing, a word that doesn't explain it. Why do you moan?"

"I moan this way 'cause he's dead," she said.

"Then tell me, who is that laughing upstairs?"

"Them's my sons. They glad."

"Yes, I can understand that too," I said.

"I laughs too, but I moans too. He promised to set us free but he never could bring hisself to do it. Still I loved him . . ."

"Loved him? You mean . . ."

"Oh yes, but I loved something else even more."

"What more?"

"Freedom."

"Freedom," I said. "Maybe freedom lies in hating."

"Naw, son, it's in loving. I loved him and give him the poison and he withered away like a frost-bit apple. Them boys woulda tore him to pieces with they homemake knives."

"A mistake was made somewhere," I said, "I'm confused." And I wished to say other things, but the laughter upstairs became too loud and moan-like for me and I tried to break out of it, but I couldn't. Just as I was leaving I felt an urgent desire to ask her what freedom was and went back. She sat with her head in her hands, moaning softly; her leather-brown face was filled with sadness.

"Old woman, what is this freedom you love so well?" I asked around a corner of my mind.

She looked surprised, then thoughtful, then baffled. "I done forgot, son. It's all mixed up. First I think it's one thing, then I think it's another. It gits my head to spinning. I guess now it ain't nothing but knowing how to say what I got up in my head. But it's a hard job, son. Too much is done happen to me in too short a time. Hit's like I have a fever. Ever' time I starts to walk my head gits to swirling and I falls down. Or if it ain't that, it's the boys; they gits to laughing and wants to kill up the white folks. They's bitter, that's what they is . . ."

"But what about freedom?"

Leave me 'lone, boy; my head aches!"

I left her, feeling dizzy myself. I didn't get far.

Suddenly one of the sons, a big fellow six feet tall, appeared out of nowhere and struck me with his fist.

"What's the matter, man?" I cried.

"You made Ma cry!"

"But how?" I said, dodging a blow.

"Askin' her them questions, that's how. Git outa here and stay, and next time you got questions like that, ask yourself!"

He held me in a grip like cold stone, his fingers fastening upon my windpipe until I thought I would suffocate before he finally allowed me to go. I stumbled about dazed, the music beating hysterically in my ears. It was dark. My head cleared and I wandered down a dark narrow passage, thinking I heard his footsteps hurrying behind me. I was sore, and into my being had come a profound craving for tranquillity, for peace and quiet, a state I felt I could never achieve. For one thing, the trumpet was blaring and the rhythm was too hectic. A tom-tom beating like heart-thuds began drowning out the trumpet, filling my ears. I longed for water and I heard it rushing through the cold mains my fingers touched as I felt my way, but I couldn't stop to search because of the footsteps behind me.

"Hey, Ras," I called. "Is it you, Destroyer? Rinehart?"

No answer, only the rhythmic footsteps behind me. Once I tried crossing the road, but a speeding machine struck me, scraping the skin from my leg as it roared past.

Then somehow I came out of it, ascending hastily from this underworld of sound to hear Louis Armstrong innocently asking,

> *What did I do*
> *To be so black*
> *And blue?*

At first I was afraid; this familiar music had demanded action, the kind of which I was incapable, and yet had I lingered there beneath the surface I might have attempted to act. Nevertheless, I know now that few really listen to this music. I sat on the chair's edge in a soaking sweat, as though each of my 1,369 bulbs had everyone become a klieg light in an individual setting for a third degree with Ras and Rinehart in charge. It was exhausting—as though I had held my breath continuously for an hour under the terrifying serenity that comes from days of intense hunger. And yet, it was a strangely satisfying experience for an invisible man to hear the silence of sound. I had discovered unrecognized compulsions of my being—even though I could not answer "yes" to their promptings. I haven't smoked a reefer since, however; not because they're illegal, but because to *see* around corners is enough (that is not unusual when you are invisible). But to hear around them is too much; it inhibits action. And despite Brother Jack and all that sad, lost period of the Brotherhood, I believe in nothing if not in action.

Please, a definition: A hibernation is a covert preparation for a more overt action.

Besides, the drug destroys one's sense of time completely. If that happened, I might forget to dodge some bright morning and some cluck would run me down with an orange and yellow street car, or a bilious bus! Or I might forget to leave my hole when the moment for action presents itself.

Meanwhile I enjoy my life with the compliments of Monopolated Light & Power. Since you never recognize me even when in closest contact with me, and since, no doubt, you'll hardly believe that I exist, it won't matter if you know that I tapped a power line leading into the building and ran it into my hole in the ground. Before that I lived in the darkness into which I was chased, but now I see. I've illuminated the blackness of my invisibility—and vice versa. And so I play the invisible music of my isolation. The last statement doesn't seem just right, does it? But it is; you hear this music simply because music is heard and seldom seen, except by musicians. Could this compulsion to put invisibility down in black and white be thus an urge to make music of invisibility? But I am an orator, a rabble rouser—Am? I *was*, and perhaps shall be again. Who knows? All sickness is not unto death, neither is invisibility.

I can hear you say, "What a horrible, irresponsible bastard!" And you're right. I leap to agree with you. I am one of the most irresponsible beings that ever lived. Irresponsibility is part of my invisibility; any way you face it, it is a denial. But to whom can I be responsible, and why should I be, when you refuse to see me? And wait until I reveal how truly irresponsible I am. Responsibility rests upon recognition, and recognition is a form of agreement. Take the man whom I almost killed: Who was responsible for that near murder —I? I don't think so, and I refuse it. I won't buy it. You can't give it to me. *He* bumped *me, he* insulted *me.* Shouldn't he, for his own personal safety, have recognized my hysteria, my "danger potential"? He, let us say, was lost in a dream world. But didn't *he* control that dream world—which, alas, is only too real!—and didn't *he* rule me out of it? And if he had yelled for a policeman, wouldn't *I* have been taken for the offending one? Yes, yes, yes! Let me agree with you, I was the irresponsible one; for I should have used my knife to protect the higher interests of society. Some day that kind of foolishness will cause us tragic trouble. All dreamers and sleepwalkers must pay the price, and even the invisible victim is responsible for the fate of all. But I shirked that responsibility; I became too snarled in the incompatible notions that buzzed within my brain. I was a coward. . . .

But what did *I* do to be so blue? Bear with me.

QUESTIONS FOR DISCUSSION AND WRITING

1. Why is the black man an invisible man?
2. In what sense must the black man become "acquainted with ambivalence"? How can this phrase be defined?
3. "Maybe freedom lies in hating," suggests the narrator. "Naw, son, it's in loving," says the old singer. How, and in what context, is "freedom" being defined?
4. Do whites, as Ellison suggests, live in a dream world? To what extent?
5. DuBois (p. 97) states that "above all, the better classes of the Negroes should recognize their duty toward the masses. They should not forget that the spirit of the twentieth century is to be the turning of the high toward the lowly. . . . This the Negro is far from recognizing for himself; his social evolution . . . is approaching a mediaeval stage. . . ." What is the relationship of this idea to Ellison's concept of invisibility?

ST. CLAIR DRAKE AND HORACE R. CAYTON, BLACK SOCIOLOGISTS, HAVE TAUGHT AT MANY MAJOR AMERICAN UNIVERSITIES. DR. DRAKE IS CURRENTLY PROFESSOR OF BLACK STUDIES AT STANFORD UNIVERSITY; DR. CAYTON, WHO DIED IN JANUARY 1970, WAS A MEMBER OF THE INSTITUTE FOR BUSINESS AND ECONOMIC RESEARCH AT THE UNIVERSITY OF CALIFORNIA, BERKELEY. THEIR BOOK *Black Metropolis: A Study of Negro Life in a Northern City* WON THE ROSENWALD PRIZE IN 1945.

ST. CLAIR DRAKE

HORACE R. CAYTON

BRONZEVILLE

Ezekiel saw a wheel—
Wheel in the middle of a wheel—
The big wheel run by faith,
An' the little wheel run by the grace of God—
Ezekiel saw a wheel.

Negro Spiritual

Stand in the center of the Black Belt—at Chicago's 47th St. and South Parkway. Around you swirls a continuous eddy of faces—black, brown, olive, yellow, and white. Soon you will realize that this is not "just another neighborhood" of Midwest Metropolis. Glance at the newsstand on the corner. You will see the Chicago dailies—the

BRONZEVILLE From *Black Metropolis* by St. Clair Drake and Horace R. Cayton, Chapter 14.

Tribune, the *Times*, the *Herald-American*, the *News*, the *Sun*. But you will also find a number of weeklies headlining the activities of Negroes —Chicago's *Defender*, *Bee*, *News-Ledger*, and *Metropolitan News*, the Pittsburgh *Courier*, and a number of others. In the nearby drugstore colored clerks are bustling about. (They are seldom seen in other neighborhoods.) In most of the other stores, too, there are colored salespeople, although a white proprietor or manager usually looms in the offing. In the offices around you, colored doctors, dentists, and lawyers go about their duties. And a brown-skinned policeman saunters along swinging his club and glaring sternly at the urchins who dodge in and out among the shoppers.

Two large theaters will catch your eye with their billboards featuring Negro orchestras and vaudeville troupes, and the Negro great and near-great of Hollywood—Lena Horne, Rochester, Hattie McDaniels.

On a spring or summer day this spot, "47th and South Park," is the urban equivalent of a village square. In fact, Black Metropolis has a saying, "If you're trying to find a certain Negro in Chicago, stand on the corner of 47th and South Park long enough and you're bound to see him." There is continuous and colorful movement here—shoppers streaming in and out of stores; insurance agents turning in their collections at a funeral parlor; club reporters rushing into a newspaper office with their social notes; irate tenants filing complaints with the Office of Price Administration; job-seekers moving in and out of the United States Employment Office. Today a picket line may be calling attention to the "unfair labor practices" of a merchant. Tomorrow a girl may be selling tags on the corner for a hospital or community house. The next day you will find a group of boys soliciting signatures to place a Negro on the All-Star football team. And always a beggar or two will be in the background—a blind man, cup in hand, tapping his way along, or a legless veteran propped up against the side of a building. This is Bronzeville's central shopping district, where rents are highest and Negro merchants compete fiercely with whites for the choicest commercial spots. A few steps away from the intersection is the "largest Negro-owned department store in America," attempting to challenge the older and more experienced white retail establishments across the street. At an exclusive "Eat Shoppe" just off the boulevard, you may find a Negro Congressman or ex-Congressman dining at your elbow, or former heavyweight champion Jack Johnson, beret pushed back on his head, chuckling at the next table; in the private dining-room there may be a party of civic leaders, black and white, planning reforms. A few doors away, behind the Venetian blinds of a well-appointed tavern, the "big shots" of the sporting world crowd the bar on one side of the house, while the respectable "élite" takes its beers and "sizzling steaks" in the booths on the other side.

Within a half-mile radius of "47th and South Park" are clustered the major community institutions: the Negro-staffed Provident Hospital; the George Cleveland Hall Library (named for a colored physician); the YWCA; the "largest colored Catholic church in the country"; the "largest Protestant congregation in America"; the Black Belt's Hotel Grand; Parkway Community House; and the imposing Michigan Boulevard Garden Apartments for middle-income families.

As important as any of these is the large four-square-mile green, Washington Park—playground of the South Side. Here in the summer thousands of Negroes of all ages congregate to play softball and tennis, to swim, or just lounge around. Here during the Depression, stormy crowds met to listen to leaders of the unemployed.

Within Black Metropolis, there are neighborhood centers of activity having their own drugstores, grocery stores, theaters, poolrooms, taverns, and churches, but "47th and South Park" overshadows all other business areas in size and importance.

If you wander about a bit in Black Metropolis you will note that one of the most striking features of the area is the prevalence of churches, numbering some 500. Many of these edifices still bear the marks of previous ownership—six-pointed Stars of David, Hebrew and Swedish inscriptions, or names chiseled on old cornerstones which do not tally with those on new bulletin boards. On many of the business streets in the more run-down areas there are scores of "storefront" churches. To the uninitiated, this plethora of churches is no less baffling than the bewildering variety and the colorful extravagance of the names. Nowhere else in Midwest Metropolis could one find, within a stone's throw of one another, a Hebrew Baptist Church, a Baptized Believers' Holiness Church, a Universal Union Independent, a Church of Love and Faith, Spiritual, a Holy Mt. Zion Methodist Episcopal Independent, and a United Pentecostal Holiness Church. Or a cluster such as St. John's Christian Spiritual, Park Mission African Methodist Episcopal, Philadelphia Baptist, Little Rock Baptist, and the Aryan Full Gospel Mission, Spiritualist.

Churches are conspicuous, but to those who have eyes to see

they are rivaled in number by another community institution, the policy station, which is to the Negro community what the race-horse bookie is to white neighborhoods. In these mysterious little shops, tucked away in basements or behind stores, one may place a dime bet and hope to win $20 if the numbers "fall right." Definitely illegal, but tolerated by the law, the policy station is a ubiquitous institution, absent only from the more exclusive residential neighborhoods.

In addition to these more or less legitimate institutions, "tea pads" and "reefer dens," "buffet flats" and "call houses" also flourish, known only to the habitués of the underworld and to those respectable patrons, white and colored, without whose faithful support they could not exist. (Since 1912, when Chicago's Red-light District was abolished, prostitution has become a clandestine affair, though open "street-walking" does occur in isolated areas.) An occasional feature story or news article in the daily press or in a Negro weekly throws a sudden light on one of these spots—a police raid or some unexpected tragedy; and then, as in all communities, it is forgotten.

In its thinking, Black Metropolis draws a clear line between the "shady" and the "respectable," the "sporting world" and the world of churches, clubs, and polite society. In practice, however, as we shall see, the line is a continuously shifting one and is hard to maintain, in the Black Metropolis as in other parts of Midwest Metropolis.

This is a community of stark contrasts, the facets of its life as varied as the colors of its people's skins. The tiny churches in deserted and dilapidated stores, with illiterately scrawled announcements on their painted windows, are marked off sharply from the fine edifices on the boulevards with stained-glass windows and electric bulletin boards. The rickety frame dwellings, sprawled along the railroad tracks, bespeak a way of life at an opposite pole from that of the quiet and well-groomed orderliness of middle-class neighborhoods. And many of the still stately-appearing old mansions, long since abandoned by Chicago's wealthy whites, conceal interiors that are foul and decayed.

The Anatomy of a Black Ghetto

. . . The Black Belt has higher rates of sickness and death than the rest of the city, and the lowest average incomes. But misery is not spread evenly over the Black Ghetto, for Black Metropolis, as a part of Midwest Metropolis, has followed the same general pattern of city growth. Those Negroes who through the years have become prosperous tend to gravitate to stable neighborhoods far from the center of the city.[1] They have slowly filtered southward within the Black Belt. Always, however, they hit the invisible barbed-wire fence of restrictive covenants. The fence may be moved back a little here and there, but never fast enough nor far enough.

Out of this moving about, this twenty-five-year-old search for "a better neighborhood," has arisen a spatial pattern *within* the Black Belt similar to that found in the city as a whole. E. Franklin Frazier, a Negro sociologist, was the first to demonstrate clearly this progressive differentiation statistically. His *Negro Family in Chicago* graphically portrayed the existence of "zones" based on socio-economic status within Black Metropolis. . . . The Cayton-Warner Research, some years later, revealed what happens in a ghetto when the successful and ambitious can't get out and when the city does not provide the poor and the vicious with enough living space, or enough incentive and opportunity to modify their style of life. . . . The "worst" areas begin to encroach upon the "more desirable areas," and large "mixed" areas result. These, in turn, become gradually "worst," and the "more desirable" areas begin to suffer from "blight" and become "mixed."[2]

A few people from time to time do manage to escape from the Black Ghetto into the city's residential and commuters' zones. . . . They are immediately encysted by restrictive covenants and "sealed off." . . . Such settlements—"satellite areas"—are unable to expand freely, although there is a tendency, in time, for the white people in immediate proximity to move away.

The Spirit of Bronzeville

"Ghetto" is a harsh term, carrying overtones of poverty and suffering, of exclusion and subordination. In Midwest Metropolis it is used

[1] Faris and Dunham describe Black Metropolis as ". . . in general, similar in character to the foreign-born slum area," but add: "In the parts farther to the South live the Negroes who have resided longer in the city and who have been more successful economically. These communities have much the same character as the nearby apartment house areas inhabited by native-born whites." (Robert E. L. Faris, and H. Warren Dunham, *Mental Disorders in Urban Areas*, University of Chicago, 1939, p. 20.)

[2] E. Franklin Frazier, *The Negro Family in Chicago* (University of Chicago, 1932), pp. 91–116.

by civic leaders when they want to shock complacency into action. Most of the ordinary people in the Black Belt refer to their community as "the South Side," but everybody is also familiar with another name for the area—Bronzeville. This name seems to have been used originally by an editor of the Chicago *Bee*, who, in 1930, sponsored a contest to elect a "Mayor of Bronzeville." A year or two later, when this newspaperman joined the *Defender* staff, he took his brain-child with him. The annual election of the "Mayor of Bronzeville" grew into a community event with a significance far beyond that of a circulation stunt. Each year a Board of Directors composed of outstanding citizens of the Black Belt takes charge of the mock-election. Ballots are cast at corner stores and in barbershops and poolrooms. The "Mayor," usually a businessman, is inaugurated with a colorful ceremony and a ball. Throughout his tenure he is expected to serve as a symbol of the community's aspirations. He visits churches, files protests with the Mayor of the city, and acts as official greeter of visitors to Bronzeville. Tens of thousands of people participate in the annual election of the "Mayor." In 1944–45, a physician was elected mayor.

Throughout the remainder of this book we shall use the term "Bronzeville" for Black Metropolis because it seems to express the feeling that the people have about their own community.[3] They *live* in the Black Belt and to them it is more than the "ghetto" revealed by statistical analysis.

THE AXES OF LIFE What are the dominating interests, the "centers of orientation," the lines of attention, which claim the time and money of Bronzeville—the "axes of life"[4] around which individual and community life revolves? The most important of these are: (1) Staying Alive; (2) Having a Good Time; (3) Praising God; (4) Getting Ahead; (5) Advancing The Race.

The majority of Bronzeville's people will insist that they came to

[3] The expression "Bronze" when counterposed to "Black" reveals a tendency on the part of Negroes to avoid referring to themselves as "black." And, of course, as a descriptive term, the former is even more accurate than the latter, for most Negroes *are* brown.

[4] The term "axes of life" has been used by Samuel M. Strong, of the Cayton-Warner Research, to describe the dominant interests of Bronzeville. It is used here with some modifications of the original list that Strong compiled. (Cf. Samuel M. Strong, "The Social Type Method: Social Types in the Negro Community of Chicago," unpublished Ph.D. Thesis, University of Chicago, 1940.)

Midwest Metropolis to "better their condition." Usually they mean that they were seeking an opportunity to sell their labor for a steady supply of money to expend on food, clothing, housing, recreation, and plans for the future. They were also searching for adequate leisure time in which to enjoy themselves. Such goals are a part of the general American Dream. But when a Negro talks about "bettering his condition" he means something more: he refers also to finding an environment where exclusion and subordination by white men are not rubbed in his face—as they are in the South.

Staying Alive

Before people can enjoy liberty or pursue happiness, they must maintain life. During the Fat Years the problem of earning a living was not an acute one for Negroes in Chicago. More than three-fourths of the Negro men and almost half of the women were gainfully employed, though their work tended to be heavy or menial. Wages were generally lower than for the bulk of the white working people, but they permitted a plane of living considerably higher than anything most parts of the South had to offer. Though the first few years of the Depression resulted in much actual suffering in Bronzeville, the WPA eventually provided a bedrock of subsistence which guaranteed food and clothing. The ministrations of social workers and wide education in the use of public health facilities seem to have actually raised the level of health in the Black Ghetto during the Depression years.[5] The Second World War once more incorporated Negroes into the productive economic life of Midwest Metropolis, and most of them had plenty of money to spend for the first time in a decade.

The high infant mortality and general death rates, the high incidence of disease, and the overcrowding and hazardous work, have all operated to keep the rate of natural increase for Negroes below that for whites. The man in the street is not aware of these statistical indices, but he does experience life in the Black Belt as a struggle for existence, a struggle which he consciously interprets as a

[5] Data concerning pre-Depression incomes assembled for this study indicate that in a significant number of cases even the bare subsistence level permitted by relief allowances and WPA wages constituted a definitely higher material standard of living for the lowest income group than did the wages earned in private industry during the Fat Years.

fight against white people who deny Negroes the opportunity to compete for—and hold—"good jobs." Civic leaders, who see the whole picture, are also acutely aware of the role played by inadequate health and recreational facilities and poor housing. They also recognize the need for widespread adult education which will teach recent migrants how to make use of public health facilities and to protect themselves against disease. The struggle for survival proceeds on an unconscious level, except when it is highlighted by a depression, a race riot, or an economic conflict between Negroes and whites.

Enjoying Life

Bronzeville's people have never let poverty, disease, and discrimination "get them down." The vigor with which they enjoy life seems to belie the gloomy observations of the statisticians and civic leaders who know the facts about the Black Ghetto. In the Lean Years as well as the Fat, Bronzeville has shared the general American interest in "having a good time." Its people like the movies and shows, athletic events, dancing, card-playing, and all the other recreational activities—commercial and noncommercial—which Midwest Metropolis offers. The recreations of an industrial society reflect the need for an escape from the monotony of machine-tending and the discipline of office and factory. For the people of Bronzeville, "having a good time" also serves another function—escape from the tensions of contact with white people. Absorption in "pleasure" is, in part at least, a kind of adjustment to their separate, subordinate status in American life.

If working as servants, Negroes must be properly deferential to the white people upon whom they depend for meager wages and tips. In fact, they often have to overdo their act in order to earn a living; as they phrase it, they have to "Uncle Tom" to "Mr. Charley" a bit to survive. If working in a factory, they must take orders from a white managerial personnel and associate with white workers who, they know, do not accept them as social equals. If self-employed, they are continually frustrated by the indirect restrictions imposed upon Negro business and professional men. If civil servants, they are in continuous contact with situations that emphasize their ghetto existence and subordinate status. But, when work is over, the pressure of the white world is lifted. Within Bronzeville Negroes are at home. They find rest from white folks as well as from labor, and they make the most of it. In their homes, in lodge rooms and clubhouses, pool parlors and taverns, cabarets and movies, they can temporarily shake off the incubus of the white world. Their recreational activities parallel those of white people, but with distinctive nuances and shadings of behavior. What Bronzeville considers a good time—the pattern for enjoying life—is intimately connected with economic status, education, and social standing. . . . Bronzeville's people treasure their inalienable right to pursue happiness.

Praising the Lord

It is a matter for continuous surprise that churches in America's large urban communities are able to compete with secular interests and to emerge even stronger than the church in rural areas.[6] Despite the fact that only about half of the adults in America claim church membership, the strong Protestant and Catholic tradition in the culture retains its hold upon the minds of the American people. The church and religion have been displaced from the center of the average man's life, but remain an important side-interest for many people. The general trend toward secularization of interests has affected men more strongly than women, but probably the majority of Americans pay some lip-service to religion and participate occasionally in the rites and ceremonies—at least upon occasions of birth, marriage, and death.

It has become customary in America to refer to Negroes as a "religious people." The movies and the radio, by their selection of incident and dialogue, tend to reinforce this prevalent conception. A walk through Bronzeville also seems to lend confirmation to this belief, for the evidences of an interest in "praising the Lord" are everywhere—churches are omnipresent. Negroes have slightly more than their expected share of churches and twice their share of preachers; a large proportion of the people seem to enjoy "praising the Lord." The spirit of Bronzeville is tinctured with religion, but like "having a good time" the real importance of the church can be understood

[6] "City churches, collectively speaking, are succeeding better than rural ones." (H. Paul Douglass and Edmund deS. Brunner, *The Protestant Church as a Social Institution*, Harper, New York, 1935, p. 44.)

only by relating it to the economic and social status of the various groups in Bronzeville.

Getting Ahead

The dominating individual drive in American life is not "staying alive," nor "enjoying life," nor "praising the Lord"—it is "getting ahead." In its simplest terms this means progressively moving from low-paid to higher-paid jobs, acquiring a more comfortable home, laying up something for sickness and old age, and trying to make sure that the children will start out at a higher economic and cultural level than the parents. Individuals symbolize their progress by the way they spend their money—for clothes, real estate, automobiles, donations, entertaining, and the individual's choice is dictated largely in terms of the circle of society in which he moves or which he wishes to impress. These circles or groupings are myriad and complex, for not all people set their goals at the same distance. Out of the differential estimates of the meaning of success arise various social classes and "centers of orientation."

There are, of course, some small groups in Midwest Metropolis, as elsewhere, who interpret success in noneconomic terms, who prize "morality," or "culture," or talent and technical competence. In general, however, Americans believe that if a man is *really* "getting ahead," if he is *really* successful, his accomplishments will become translated into an effective increase in income. People are expected to "cash in" on brains or talent or political power.

For thousands of Negro migrants from the South, merely arriving in Bronzeville represented "getting ahead." Yet Negroes, like other Americans, share the general interest in getting ahead in more conventional terms. The Job Ceiling and the Black Ghetto limit free competition for the money and for residential symbols of success. Partly because of these limitations (which are not peculiar to Chicago) it has become customary among the masses of Negroes in America to center their interest upon living in the immediate present or upon going to heaven—upon "having a good time" or "praising the Lord." Though some derive their prestige from the respect accorded them by the white world, or by the professional and business segments of the Negro world, most Negroes seem to adopt a pattern of conspicuous behavior and conspicuous consumption. Maintaining a "front" and "showing off" become very important substitutes for getting ahead in the economic sense. Leadership in various organizations often constitutes the evidence that a man has "arrived."

Leaders in Bronzeville, like Negro leaders everywhere since the Civil War, are constantly urging the community to raise its sights above "survival," "enjoying life," and "praising the Lord." They present "getting ahead" as a *racial* duty as well as a personal gain. When a Negro saves money, buys bonds, invests in a business or in property, he is automatically "advancing The Race."[7] When Negroes "waste their substance," they are "setting The Race back." This appraisal of their activity is widely accepted by the rank and file, but leaders sometimes press their shots too hard. When they do so, they often get a response like that of the domestic servant who resented the attempts of a civic leader to discourage elaborate social club dances during the Depression: "We [the social club] give to the Federated Home and about ten or fifteen other institutions. If we want to give a dance, I think that's our business. We poor colored people don't have much as it is, and if we sat around and thought about our sufferings we'd go crazy."

Advancing The Race

White people in Midwest Metropolis become aware of Negroes only occasionally and sporadically. Negroes, however, live in a state of intense and perpetual awareness that they are a black minority in a white man's world. The Job Ceiling and the Black Ghetto are an ever-present experience. Petty discriminations (or actions that might be interpreted as such) occur daily. Unpleasant memories of the racial and individual past are a part of every Negro's personality structure. News and rumors of injustice and terror in the South and elsewhere circulate freely through Negro communities at all times. "Race consciousness" is not the work of "agitators" or "subversive influences"—it is forced upon Negroes by the very fact of their separate-subordi-

[7] "Service" is a key word in American life, cherished alike by Rotarian and labor leader, politician and priest. All forms of intense individual competition are sanctified under the name of "service," and individual success is represented as "service" to the community. The struggle for prestige, too, is dressed up as "service." Bronzeville, like the rest of Midwest Metropolis, has its frequent money-raising drives for charitable institutions and its corps of enthusiastic volunteers who, under the auspices of churches, lodges, clubs, and social agencies, function as part-time civic leaders. "Service" in Bronzeville is usually interpreted as "advancing The Race."

nate status in American life. And it is tremendously reinforced by life in a compact community such as Black Metropolis, set within the framework of a large white community.

Negroes are ill at ease in the land of their birth. They are bombarded with the slogans of democracy, liberty, freedom, equality, but they are not allowed to participate freely in American life. They develop a tormenting ambivalence toward themselves and the larger society of which they are a part. America rejects them; so they tend to hate. But it is the only land they know; so they are sentimentally attached to it. Their skin color and social origins subject them to discrimination and contumely; so they often (consciously or unconsciously) despise The Race. The people they know most intimately, however, are colored, and men cannot totally hate themselves and their friends. Thus their moods fluctuate between shame and defiance. Their conversation becomes a bewildering mixture of expressions of "racial depreciation" and "race pride."

THE CULT OF RACE Negroes feel impelled to prove to themselves continually that they are not the inferior creatures which their minority status implies. Thus, ever since emancipation, Negro leaders have preached the necessity for cultivating "race pride." They have assiduously repeated the half-truth that "no other race has ever made the progress that Negroes have made in an equivalent length of time." They have patiently attempted to popularize an expanding roster of Race Heroes—individuals who have attained success or prominence. "Catching up with the white folks" has been developed as the dominating theme of inspirational exhortations, and the Negro "firsts" and "onlies" are set up as Race Heroes.[8] "Beating the white man at his own game" becomes a powerful motivation for achievement and explains the popularity of such personalities as Joe Louis or Jesse Owens, George Washington Carver or outstanding soldier-heroes. A myth of "special gifts" has also emerged, with Negroes (and whites also) believing that American Negroes have some inborn, unusual talent as dancers, musicians, artists and athletes.

[8] Among Bronzeville's "firsts" are: Dr. Daniel Williams, "first man to suture a human heart"; Dr. Julian Lewis, "first Negro to serve on the faculty of the University of Chicago's medical school"; and Robert R. Taylor, "first Negro to serve as the head of the Chicago Housing Authority." Among the "onlies" are the only Negro on the schoolboard of the city, and the only Negro on the library board.

In the period between the First and the Second World Wars, this emphasis upon race pride became a mass phenomenon among the Negroes in large urban communities. Race consciousness was transformed into a positive and aggressive defensive racialism. Negroes in Black Metropolis, as in other communities, feeling the strength of their economic and political power, have become increasingly aware of the achievements of individual Negroes, and have developed an absorbing interest in every scrap of evidence that "The Race is advancing," or is "catching up with white folks," or is "beating the white man at his own game." Unable to compete freely *as individuals,* the Negro masses take intense vicarious pleasure in watching Race Heroes vindicate them in the eyes of the white world.

Race pride is a defensive reaction that can become a mere verbal escape mechanism. Negro leaders are therefore perpetually involved in an effort to make race pride more than an end in itself: to utilize it as a morale builder, as the raw material of "racial solidarity." They seek to use it for "advancing The Race." They foster race pride in order to elicit support for collective action—the support of Negro business enterprises, the organization of petition and protest, the focusing of economic and political power. The most persistent theme of speeches and editorials in Bronzeville is: "Negroes must learn to stick together." The leaders use it also to encourage individual achievement, by interpreting the success of one Negro as the success of all. Out of this interplay between race consciousness, race pride, and race solidarity arise certain definite social types: the Race Hero, the Race Leader, the Race Man, the Race Woman.

The average person in Bronzeville is primarily interested in "staying alive," "getting ahead," "having a good time" and "praising the Lord." Conscious preoccupation with "racial advancement" is fitful and sporadic, though always latent. The masses leave "the burden of The Race" to those individuals who are oriented around "service"—the Race Leaders. Some of these are people who devote much of their leisure time to charitable organizations or associations for racial advancement. For others solving the race problem is a full-time job. For instance, a score or so of individuals in Bronzeville are elected and appointed politicians who "represent The Race." There are also a few civic leaders who earn their living by administering social agencies such as the Urban League, the YMCA, the YWCA, settlement houses, and similar organizations. In Bronzeville, too, there are numerous "self-appointed leaders"—men and women, often illiterate and poverty-stricken, who feel the call to "lead The Race out of bondage." They harangue their small groups of followers on the streets, in store-fronts, or in the public parks with a fanaticism that alienates them from the masses as well as from the affluent and educated.

Most of the people in Bronzeville do not hold membership in any of the organizations for "racial advancement," such as the National Association for the Advancement of Colored People (NAACP), the National Negro Congress, the Urban League, or the Council of Negro Organizations. They follow the activities of Race Leaders in the Negro press, they cheer and applaud an occasionally highly publicized victory over those who maintain the Job Ceiling and the Black Ghetto. They grumble persistently about "lack of leadership." They contribute an occasional nickel or dime to drives for funds. But when some inciting incident stirs them deeply, they close ranks and put up a scrap—for a community housing project, to remove a prejudiced policeman, to force a recalcitrant merchant to employ Negroes. And they periodically vote for Negroes to represent them in state, local, and national bodies. In general, "solving the race problem" is left in the hands of Race Leaders—the "racial watchdogs," as one Bronzeville preacher called them.

RACE LEADERSHIP Race Leaders are expected to put up some sort of aggressive fight against the exclusion and subordination of Negroes. They must also stress "catching up with white folks," and this involves the less dramatic activity of appeals for discipline within the Black Belt, and pleas for Negroes to take advantage of opportunities to "advance." A Race Leader has to fight the Job Ceiling and Black Ghetto and at the same time needle, cajole, and denounce Negroes themselves for inertia, diffidence, and lack of race pride; and the functions sometimes conflict.

There is rather widespread agreement in Bronzeville on what an ideal Race Leader should be. When the people are asked to describe a "real Race Leader" they always stress "sincerity" as a cardinal virtue: A Race Leader, they say,

> . . . knows the difficulties of the race and fights without a selfish reason;
>
> . . . is a sincere person with some moral principle;
>
> . . . is sincere and has a plan;
>
> . . . has a constant, sincere interest in the race;

. . . is sincere and people know he is not after some hidden personal interest;

. . . has the interest and well-being of the Negro race uppermost in his life.

"Everybody will tell you," a young stenographer observed, "that a real Race Leader is 'square'!"

Sincerity is prized, but, as one of the persons quoted above stated, a leader must have a plan. Theories about solving the race problem range all the way from amalgamation to emigration to Africa, from sympathy with Communism to the demand for a "49th Negro state." The "accepted leaders," however, tend to be people who stress the use of political and economic pressure (without violence) and gradual advancement by slowly raising the economic and educational level of the entire group.

"An ardent racialist without ability is not a race leader," comments a clerical worker; "he must have something to contribute." A leader must be able to formulate and present the Negroes' demands and aspirations to white people. Many people insist that a real leader must be "calm, well poised, well trained." Some think he should be "an educated person who has a great deal of influence with whites and prestige with Negroes." The more conservative people feel that he should also be a person who "believes strongly in caution and patience" and who is "adept in the arts of personal and political compromise."

Bronzeville knows that the powers of its leaders are limited, that in the final analysis the white majority can break any leader who is too aggressive. It is well aware that white America makes concessions to Negroes primarily from the imperatives of economic necessity and political expediency rather than from devotion to democratic ideals. Out of this knowledge arises a kind of cynical realism which does not expect too much from leaders.

Bronzeville knows, too, that "leaders are human," that they are motivated by the desire for power and prestige as well as by the "service" ideal. The whole business of "advancing The Race" offers wide opportunities for fraud, graft, and chicanery. There are opportunities for "selling out to the white folks," diverting funds from "the cause," or making a racket out of race. People try to draw a line between "sincere Race Leaders" and those Race Men who "are always clamoring everything for The Race, just for the glory of being known."

They will characterize some leaders as being "like the William Randolph Hearst variety of patriot whose Americanism means a chance to make more money." They are skeptical of those who, "when you see them, are always talking about The Race." Sincerity is hard to test, however, and Bronzeville seems to expect that its leaders will "cash in" on their positions, in terms of personal influence if not in terms of money.

THE RACE MAN Frustrated in their isolation from the main streams of American life, and in their impotence to control their fate decisively, Negroes tend to admire an aggressive Race Man even when his motives are suspect.[9] They will applaud him, because, in the face of the white world, he remains "proud of his race and always tries to uphold it whether it is good or bad, right or wrong," because he sees "only the good points of the race." One high school girl explained that "the Race Man is interested in the welfare of the people. Everybody says that they admire a Race Man, but behind the scenes they may not regard him as being sincere. The Race Man is usually a politician or a businessman. He sponsors movements for the benefit of the people. It is a way of securing honor and admiration from the people. Personally, I admire a Race Man even if he seeks his own advancement." A well-known minister interpreted the admiration for the Race Man as follows: "The people are emotionally enthusiastic about a Race Man. They know that a Race Man may not be quite as sincere as some of the more quiet leaders. Still, the very fact of his

[9] The term Race Man is used in a dual sense in Bronzeville. It refers to any person who has a reputation as an uncompromising fighter against attempts to subordinate Negroes. It is also used in a derogatory sense to refer to people who pay loud lip-service to "race pride." It is interesting to note that Bronzeville is somewhat suspicious, generally, of its Race Men, but tends to be more trustful of the Race Woman. "A Race Woman is sincere," commented a prominent businessman; "she can't capitalize on her activities like a Race Man." The Race Woman is sometimes described as "forceful, outspoken, and fearless, a great advocate of race pride" . . . "devoted to the race" . . . "studies the conditions of the people" . . . "the Race is uppermost in her activities" . . . "you know her by the speeches she makes" . . . "she champions the rights of Negroes" . . . "active in civic affairs." The Race Woman is idealized as a "fighter," but her associated role of "uplifter" seems to be accepted with less antagonism than in the case of the Race Man. She is sometimes described as "continually showing the Negro people why they should better their condition economically and educationally." Cynics are apt to add: "intelligent and forceful but has little influence with whites." Certain women were repeatedly named as "good Race Women"—one or two local Bronzeville women who were active in civic organizations, and such nationally known figures as Mrs. Mary McLeod Bethune.

working for the race gives him prestige in their eyes." A Race Man is one type of Race Hero.

THE RACE HERO If a man "fights for The Race," if he seems to be "all for The Race," if he is "fearless in his approach to white people," he becomes a Race Hero. Similarly any Negro becomes a hero if he beats the white man at his own game or forces the white world to recognize his talent or service or achievement. Racketeer or preacher, reactionary or Communist, ignoramus or savant—if a man is an aggressive, vocal, uncompromising Race Man he is everybody's hero. Even conservative Negroes admire colored radicals who buck the white world. Preachers may oppose sin, but they will also express a sneaking admiration for a Negro criminal who decisively outwits white people. Even the quiet, well-disciplined family man may get a thrill when a "bad Negro" blows his top and goes down with both guns blazing at the White Law. Such identification is usually covert and unconscious, and may even be feared and regretted by the very persons who experience it. Race pride sometimes verges upon the vindictive, but it is a direct result of the position to which white America has consigned the Negro group.

World Within a World

The people of Bronzeville have, through the years, crystallized certain distinctive patterns of thought and behavior. Their tenacious clinging to life, their struggle for liberty, their quest for happiness, have resulted in the proliferation of institutions. The customs and habits of Bronzeville's people are essentially American but carry overtones of subtle difference. Bronzeville has all the major institutions found in any other Chicago neighborhood—schools and churches, a wide range of stores and shops, varied commercial amusements, segments of the city political machine, and numerous voluntary associations. And besides, as a low-income community it has had more than its share of relief stations and never enough playgrounds, clinics, and similar social services.

While Bronzeville's institutions differ little in form from those in other Midwest Metropolis communities, they differ considerably in content. The dissimilarity springs primarily from two facts: Because the community is spiritually isolated from the larger world, the development of its families, churches, schools, and voluntary associations has proceeded quite differently from the course taken by analogous white institutions; and, second, Bronzeville's "culture" is but a part of a larger, national Negro culture, its people being tied to thirteen million other Negroes by innumerable bonds of kinship, associational and church membership, and a common minority status. The customs inherited by Bronzeville have been slowly growing up among American Negroes in the eighty years since slavery.

But Bronzeville is also a part of Midwest Metropolis, and Negro life is organically bound up with American life. Negroes attend the same movies, read the same daily papers, study the same textbooks, and participate in the same political and industrial activity as other Americans. They know white America far better than white America knows them. Negroes live in two worlds and they must adjust to both. Their institutions reflect the standards of both. In so far as Midwest Metropolis is a "wide-open town," in so far as it has a "sporting tradition," to the extent that it is young and rapidly changing, Bronzeville reflects these characteristics.

QUESTIONS FOR DISCUSSION AND WRITING

1. In what way does this article suggest that Booker T. Washington's Atlanta speech was prophetic?
2. Drake and Cayton state that the "axes of life" in Bronzeville are: "(1) Staying Alive; (2) Having a Good Time; (3) Praising God; (4) Getting Ahead; (5) Advancing The Race." How do these "axes of life" differ from those in the present-day white community? How are they similar?
3. What pressures are put upon the citizens of Bronzeville in their associations with whites?
4. Evaluate the Job Ceiling and the Black Ghetto as causes for the frustration of Bronzeville residents.
5. According to Drake and Cayton, the people of Bronzeville "know white America far better than white America knows them." Is this statement valid? How can it be supported?

THE PUBLICATION OF GUNNAR MYRDAL'S *An American Dilemma* IN 1942 MARKED AN IMPORTANT TURNING POINT IN THE STUDY OF AMERICAN RACIAL PROBLEMS: FOR THE FIRST TIME NEARLY EVERY PHASE OF RACIAL DISCRIMINATION WAS STUDIED IN DETAIL. DR. MYRDAL IS CURRENTLY PROFESSOR OF SOCIAL ECONOMY AT THE UNIVERSITY OF STOCKHOLM.

GUNNAR MYRDAL

FACETS OF THE NEGRO PROBLEM

American Minority Problems

For some decades there has been a tendency to incorporate the American Negro problem into the broader American minority problem.[1] In the United States, the term "minority people" has a connotation dif-

FACETS OF THE NEGRO PROBLEM From *An American Dilemma* by Gunnar Myrdal, Chapter 3 (Twentieth Anniversary Edition). Copyright 1944, 1962 by Harper & Row, Publishers, Incorporated. Reprinted by permission of the publishers. Some footnotes deleted.

[1] More recently, Donald R. Young has been most outstanding in arguing this restatement of the Negro problem. We quote from him:

"The view here presented is that the problems and principles of race relations are remarkably similar, regardless of what groups are involved; and that only by an integrated study of all minority peoples in the United States can a real understanding and sociological analysis of the involved social phenomena be achieved." (*American Minority Peoples* [1932], pp. xiii–I.)

ferent from that in other parts of the world and especially in Central and Eastern Europe, where minority problems have existed. This difference in problem is due to a difference in situation. The minority peoples of the United States are fighting for status in the larger society; the minorities of Europe are mainly fighting for independence from it. In the United States the so-called minority groups as they exist today—except the Indians and the Negroes—are mostly the result of a relatively recent immigration, which it was for a long time the established policy to welcome as a nationally advantageous means of populating and cultivating the country. The newcomers themselves were bent upon giving up their language and other cultural heritages and acquiring the ways and attitudes of the new nation. There have been degrees of friction and delay in this assimilation process, and even a partially conscious resistance by certain immigrant groups. But these elements of friction and resistance are really only of a character and magnitude to bring into relief the fundamental difference between the typical American minority problems and those in, say, the old Austrian Empire. Of greatest importance, finally, is the fact that the official political creed of America denounced, in general but vigorous terms, all forms of suppression and discrimination, and affirmed human equality.

In addition to a cultural difference between the native-born and the foreign-born in the United States, there was always a class difference. At every point of time many of those who were already established in the new country had acquired wealth and power, and were thus in a position to lay down the rules to late-comers. The immigrants, who left their native lands mainly because they had little wealth, had to fit themselves as best they could into the new situation. Their lack of familiarity with the English language and ways of life also made them an easy prey of economic exploitation. But as long as the West was open to expansion, immigrant groups could avoid be-

---

In explaining the similarities of the deprivations imposed upon different minority groups, Donald R. Young points out that:

"It is . . . to be expected that dominating majorities in various regions, when faced with the problem of what to think and do about minorities, will fail to be sufficiently inventive to create unique schemes of relationships and action. Variations in intensity of restriction and oppression, special techniques in maintaining superior status and other adaptations to the local scene will always be found, but the choice of fundamental patterns of dominance in majority-minority relations is limited by the nature of man and his circumstances." (*Research Memorandum on Minority Peoples in the Depression,* Social Science Research Council, Bulletin No. 31 [1937], pp. 9–10.)

coming a subordinate class by going to a place where they were the only class. Gradually the frontier filled up, and free land no longer offered the immigrants cultural independence and economic self-protection. Increasingly they tended to come from lands where the cultures were ever more distant from the established American standards. They became distinguished more markedly as half-digested isolates, set down in the slums of American cities, and the level of discrimination rose.

The first stage of their assimilation often took them through the worst slums of the nation. Group after group of immigrants from every part of the world had their first course in Americanization in the squalid and congested quarters of New York's East Side and similar surroundings. They found themselves placed in the midst of utter poverty, crime, prostitution, lawlessness, and other undesirable social conditions. The assimilation process brought the immigrants through totally uncontrolled labor conditions and often through personal misery and social pressures of all kinds. The American social scientist might direct his curiosity to the occasional failures of the assimilation process and the tension created in the entire structure of larger society during its course. To the outside observer, on the other hand, the relative success will forever remain the first and greatest riddle to solve, when he sees that the children and grandchildren of these unassimilated foreigners are well-adjusted Americans. He will have to account for the basic human power of resistance and the flexibility of people's minds and cultures. He will have to appreciate the tremendous force in the American educational system. But it will not suffice as an explanation. He will be tempted to infer the influence upon the immigrant of a great national *ethos*, in which optimism and carelessness, generosity and callousness, were so blended as to provide him with hope and endurance.

From the viewpoint of the struggling immigrant himself, the harsh class structure, which thrust him to the bottom of the social heap, did not seem to be a rigid social determinant. In two or three generations, if not in one, the immigrant and his descendants moved into, and identified themselves with, the dominant American group, and—with luck and ability—took their position in the higher strata. Only because of this continuous movement of former immigrants and their descendants up and into the established group could the so-called "Americans" remain the majority during a century which saw more than a score of millions of immigrants added to its population. The causal mechanism of this social process has been aptly described as a continuous "push upwards" by a steady stream of new masses of toiling immigrants filling the ranks of the lower social strata. The class structure remained, therefore, fairly stable, while millions of individuals were continuously climbing the social ladder which it constituted. The unceasing process of social mobility and the prospect of its continuation, and also the established Creed of America promising and sanctioning social mobility, together with many other factors of importance, kept the minority groups contented and bent on assimilation.

Religious differences, differences in fundamental attitudes, and "racial" differences entered early as elements of friction in the process of assimilation and as reasons for discrimination while the process was going on. With the growing importance of the new immigration from Southern and Eastern Europe in the decades before the War, these factors acquired increased importance. They are, in a considerable degree, responsible for the fact that even recent community surveys, undertaken decades after the end of the mass immigration, give a picture of American class stratification which closely corresponds to the differentiation in national groups. This type of differentiation is one of the most distinguishing characteristics of the American social order.

The split of the nation into a dominant "American" group and a large number of minority groups means that American civilization is permeated by animosities and prejudices attached to ethnic origin or what is popularly recognized as the "race" of a person.[2] These animosities or prejudices are commonly advanced in defense of various

[2] The popular term "race prejudice," as it is commonly used, embraces the whole complex of valuations and beliefs which are behind discriminatory behavior on the part of the majority group (or, sometimes, also on the part of the minority group) and which are contrary to the equalitarian ideals in the American Creed. In this very inclusive sense the term will be used in this inquiry. It should be noted that little is explained when we say that "discrimination is due to prejudice." The concept "race prejudice" unfortunately carries connotations that the intergroup situation is fairly stable and that the complex of attitudes behind discrimination is homogeneous and solid. . . .

We do not need to enter into a discussion of whether "anti-minority feelings" in general are different from the "race prejudices" as they are displayed against Negroes. On the other hand, people in general also refer the former attitude to what they usually perceive of as "race." As Donald Young points out, there is also something of a common pattern in all discriminations (see footnote 1 to this chapter). On the other hand, there is this significant difference which we shall stress, that in regard to the colored minorities, amalgamation is violently denied them, while in regard to all the other minorities, it is welcomed as a long-run process.

discriminations which tend to keep the minority groups in a disadvantaged economic and social status. They are contrary to the American Creed, which is emphatic in denouncing differences made on account of "race, creed or color." In regard to the Negro, as well as more generally to all the other minorities, this conflict is what constitutes the problem, and it also contains the main factors in the dynamic development. Taking a cross-sectional view at any point of time, there is thus revealed an inconsistency in practically every American's social orientation. The inconsistency is not dissolved, at least not in the short run. Race prejudice and discrimination persist. But neither will the American Creed be thrown out. It is a hasty conclusion from the actual facts of discrimination that the Creed will be without influence in the long run, even if it is suppressed for the moment, or even that it is uninfluential in the short run.

In trying to reconcile conflicting valuations the ordinary American apparently is inclined to believe that, as generations pass on, the remaining minority groups—with certain distinct exceptions which will presently be discussed—will be assimilated into a homogeneous nation.[3] The American Creed is at least partially responsible for this, as well as for the American's inclination to deem this assimilation desirable. Of course, this view is also based on the memories of previous absorption of minority groups into the dominant "American" population. Even the American Indians are now considered as ultimately assimilable. "The American Indian, once constituting an inferior caste in the social hierarchy, now constitutes little more than a social class, since today his inferior status may be sloughed off by the process of cultural assimilation."[4] This, incidentally, speaks against the doctrine that race prejudice under all circumstances is an unchangeable pattern of attitudes.

This long-range view of ultimate assimilation can be found to coexist with any degree of race prejudice in the actual present-day situation. In many parts of the country Mexicans are kept in a status

[3] Even a prominent leader of the Ku Klux Klan, whose conservative attitudes on "racial" questions cannot be doubted, expressed to the writer the considered opinion that, in time, not only the Poles, Italians, Russians, Greeks, and Armenians, but also the Turks, Hindus, Jews, and Mexicans would come to be engulfed in the great American nation and disappear as separate, socially visible population segments. But it would take a very, very long time. I have heard this view affirmed by Americans in all social classes and regions of the country.

[4] Young, *Research Memorandum on Minority Peoples in the Depression*, pp. 18–19.

similar to the Negro's or only a step above. Likewise, in most places anti-Semitism is strong and has apparently been growing for the last ten years.[5] Italians, Poles, Finns, are distrusted in some communities; Germans, Scandinavians, and the Irish are disliked in others, or sometimes the same communities. There are sections of the majority group which draw the circle exclusively and who hate all "foreigners." There are others who keep a somewhat distinct line only around the more exotic peoples. The individual, regional, and class differentials in anti-minority feeling are great.[6]

In spite of all race prejudice, few Americans seem to doubt that it is the ultimate fate of this nation to incorporate without distinction not only all the Northern European stocks, but also the people from Eastern and Southern Europe, the Near East and Mexico. They see obstacles; they emphasize the religious and "racial" differences; they believe it will take a long time. But they assume that it is going to happen, and do not have, on the whole, strong objections to it—provided it is located in a distant future.

The Anti-Amalgamation Doctrine

The Negroes, on the other hand, are commonly assumed to be unassimilable and this is the reason why the characterization of the Negro problem as a minority problem does not exhaust its true import. The Negroes are set apart, together with other colored peoples, principally the Chinese and the Japanese. America fears the segregation into distinctive isolated groups of all other elements of its population and looks upon the preservation of their separate national attributes and group loyalties as a hazard to American institutions. Considerable efforts are directed toward "Americanizing" all groups of alien origin. But in regard to the colored peoples, the American policy is the reverse. They are excluded from assimilation. Even by their best friends in the dominant white group and by the promoters of racial peace and good-will, they are usually advised to keep to themselves and develop a race pride of their own.

Among the groups commonly considered unassimilable, the

[5] It is the present writer's impression that anti-Semitism, as he observed it in America during the last years before the Second World War, probably was somewhat stronger than in Germany before the Nazi regime.

[6] See Eugene L. Horowitz, "Race Attitudes" in Otto Klineberg (editor), *Characteristics of the American Negro*, prepared for this study, to be published; manuscript pages 115–123 *et passim*.

Negro people is by far the largest. The Negroes do not, like the Japanese and the Chinese, have a politically organized nation and an accepted culture of their own outside of America to fall back upon. Unlike the Oriental, there attaches to the Negro an historical memory of slavery and inferiority. It is more difficult for them to answer prejudice with prejudice and, as the Orientals may do, to consider themselves and their history superior to the white Americans and their recent cultural achievements. The Negroes do not have these fortifications for self-respect. They are more helplessly imprisoned as a subordinate caste in America, a caste[7] of people deemed to be lacking a cultural past and assumed to be incapable of a cultural future.

To the ordinary white American the caste line between whites and Negroes is based upon, and defended by, the anti-amalgamation doctrine. This doctrine, more than anything else, gives the Negro problem its uniqueness among other problems of lower status groups, not only in terms of intensity of feelings but more fundamentally in the character of the problem. We follow a general methodological principle, presented previously, when we now start out from the ordinary white man's notion of what constitutes the heart of the Negro problem.

When the Negro people, unlike the white minority groups, is commonly characterized as unassimilable, it is not, of course, implied that amalgamation is not biologically possible. But crossbreeding is considered undesirable. Sometimes the view is expressed that the offspring of crossbreeding is inferior to both parental stocks. Usually it is only asserted that it is inferior to the "pure" white stock. The assumption evidently held is that the Negro stock is "inferior" to the white stock. On the inherited inferiority of the Negro people there exists among white Americans a whole folklore, which is remarkably similar throughout the country. . . .

Whether this concept of the inferiority of the Negro stock is psychologically basic to the doctrine that amalgamation should be prohibited, or is only a rationalization of this doctrine, may for the

[7] In this inquiry we shall use the term "caste" to denote the social status difference between Negroes and whites in America. . . . It should be emphasized that, although the *dividing line* between Negroes and whites is held fixed and rigid so that no Negro legitimately can pass over from his caste to the higher white caste, the *relations* between members of the two castes are different in different regions and social classes and changing in time. It is true that the term "caste" commonly connotes a static situation even in the latter respect. However, for a social phenomenon we prefer to use a social concept with too static connotations rather than the biological concept "race" which, of course, carries not only static but many much more erroneous connotations.

moment be left open. The two notions, at any rate, appear together. The fact that one is used as argument for the other does not necessarily prove such a causal psychic relation between them. In many cases one meets an unargued and not further dissolvable *primary* valuation, which is assumed to be self-evident even without support of the inferiority premise. Miscegenation[8] is said to be a threat to "racial purity." It is alleged to be contrary to "human instincts." It is "contrary to nature" and "detestable." Not only in the South but often also in the North the stereotyped and hypothetical question is regularly raised without any intermediary reasoning as to its applicability or relevance to the social problem discussed: "Would you like to have your sister or daughter marry a Negro?" This is an unargued appeal to "racial solidarity" as a primary valuation. It is corollary to this attitude that in America the offspring of miscegenation is relegated to the Negro race.

A remarkable and hardly expected peculiarity of this American doctrine, expounded so directly in biological and racial terms, is that it is applied with a vast discretion depending upon the purely social and legal circumstances under which miscegenation takes place. As far as lawful marriage is concerned, the racial doctrine is laden with emotion. Even in the Northern states where, for the most part, intermarriage is not barred by the force of law, the social sanctions blocking its way are serious. Mixed couples are punished by nearly complete social ostracism. On the other hand, in many regions, especially in the South where the prohibition against intermarriage and the general reprehension against miscegenation have the strongest moorings, illicit relations have been widespread and occasionally allowed to acquire a nearly institutional character. Even if . . . such relations are perhaps now on the decline, they are still not entirely stamped out.

Considering the biological emphasis on the anti-amalgamation doctrine and the strong social sanctions against intermarriage tied to that doctrine, the astonishing fact is the great indifference of most white Americans toward real but illicit miscegenation. In spite of the doctrine, in some regions with a large Negro population, cohabitation

[8] Miscegenation is mainly an American term and is in America almost always used to denote only relations between Negroes and whites. Although it literally implies only mixture of genes between members of different races, it has acquired a definite emotional connotation. We use it in its literal sense—without implying necessarily that it is undesirable—as a convenient synonym of amalgamation.

with a Negro woman is, apparently, considered a less serious breach of sexual morals than illicit intercourse with a white woman. The illicit relations freely allowed or only frowned upon are, however, restricted to those between white men and Negro women. A white woman's relation with a Negro man is met by the full fury of anti-amalgamation sanctions.

If we now turn to the American Negro people, we can hardly avoid the strong impression that what there is of reluctance in principle toward amalgamation is merely in the nature of a reaction or response to the white doctrine, which thus stands as primary in the causal sense and strategic in a practical sense. It is true that white people, when facing the Negro group, make an ideological application of the general Jim Crow principle—"equal but separate" treatment and accommodations for the two racial groups—and proceed from the assertion that both races are good to the explanation that there is a value in keeping them unmixed. They appeal also to the Negroes' "race pride" and their interest in keeping their own blood "pure." But this is a white, not a Negro, argument.

The Negro will be found to doubt the sincerity of the white folks' interest in the purity of the Negro race. It will sound to him too much like a rationalization, in strained equalitarian terms, of the white supremacy doctrine of race purity. "But the outstanding joke is to hear a white man talk about race integrity, though at this the Negro is in doubt whether to laugh or swear."[9] Even the Negro in the uneducated classes is sensitive to the nuances of sincerity, trained as he is both in slavery and afterwards to be a good dissembler himself. The Negro will, furthermore, encounter considerable intellectual difficulties inherent in the idea of keeping his blood pure, owing to the fact that the large majority of American Negroes actually are of mixed descent. They already have white and Indian ancestry as well as African Negro blood. And in general they are aware of this fact.

In spite of this, race pride, with this particular connotation of the undesirability of miscegenation, has been growing in the Negro group. This is, however, probably to be interpreted as a defense reaction, a derived *secondary* attitude as are so many other attitudes of the Negro people. After weighing all available evidence carefully, it seems frankly incredible that the Negro people in America should feel inclined to develop any particular race pride at all or have any dislike

[9] Robert R. Moton, *What the Negro Thinks* (1929), p. 219.

for amalgamation, were it not for the common white opinion of the racial inferiority of the Negro people and the whites' intense dislike for miscegenation. The fact that a large amount of exploitative sexual intercourse between white men and Negro women has always been, and still is, part of interracial relations, coupled with the further fact that the Negroes sense the disgrace of their women who are not accepted into matrimony, and the inferior status of their mixed offspring, is a strong practical reason for the Negro's preaching "race pride" in his own group. But it is almost certainly not based on any fundamental feeling condemning miscegenation on racial or biological grounds.

On this central point, as on so many others, the whites' attitudes are primary and decisive; the Negroes' are in the nature of accommodation or protest.

The White Man's Theory of Color Caste

We have attempted to present in compressed and abstract formulation the white supremacy doctrine as applied to amalgamation, sex relations and marriage. The difficulty inherent in this task is great. As no scientifically controlled nation-wide investigations have been made, the author has here, as in other sections, had to rely on his own observations.[10]

Every widening of the writer's experience of white Americans has only driven home to him more strongly that the opinion that the Negro is unassimilable, or, rather, that his amalgamation into the

[10] This is much to be regretted. Indeed, it is urgently desirable that such impressionistic generalizations be critically examined and replaced by statistically verified and precise knowledge. Meanwhile, because of the lack of such studies, the author has simply been compelled to proceed by building up a system of preliminary hypotheses. The defense is that otherwise intelligent questions cannot be raised in those sectors of the Negro problem where statistics or other kinds of substantiated knowledge are not available.

Some attitude studies and public opinion polls have been made which touch on some of the statements presented in hypothetical form in the text. But they were designed to answer other questions and are practically never comprehensive, and so they cannot be used as conclusive proof of our hypotheses. We shall cite some of the relevant ones in footnotes at certain points. For a summary of all the attitude studies (up to 1940) dealing with the Negro, see the monograph prepared for this study by Eugene L. Horowitz, "Race Attitudes" in Klineberg (editor), *Characteristics of the American Negro*.

American nation is undesirable, is held more commonly, absolutely, and intensely than would be assumed from a general knowledge of American thoughtways. Except for a handful of rational intellectual liberals—who also, in many cases, add to their acceptance in principle of amalgamation an admission that they personally feel an irrational emotional inhibition against it—it is a rare case to meet a white American who will confess that, if it were not for public opinion and social sanctions not removable by private choice, he would have no strong objection to intermarriage.

The intensity of the attitude seems to be markedly stronger in the South than in the North. Its strength seems generally to be inversely related to the economic and social status of the informant and his educational level. It is usually strong even in most of the non-colored minority groups, if they are above the lowest plane of indifference. To the poor and socially insecure, but struggling, white individual, a fixed opinion on this point seems an important matter of prestige and distinction.

But even a liberal-minded Northerner of cosmopolitan culture and with a minimum of conventional blinds will, in nine cases out of ten, express a definite feeling against amalgamation. He will not be willing usually to hinder intermarriage by law. Individual liberty is to him a higher principle and, what is more important, he actually invokes it. But he will regret the exceptional cases that occur. He may sometimes hold a philosophical view that in centuries to come amalgamation is bound to happen and might become the solution. But he will be inclined to look on it as an inevitable deterioration.[11]

This attitude of refusing to consider amalgamation—felt and expressed in the entire country—constitutes the center in the complex of

[11] The response is likely to be anything but pleasant if one jestingly argues that possibly a small fraction of Negro blood in the American people, if it were blended well with all the other good stock brought over to the new continent, might create a race of unsurpassed excellence: a people with just a little sunburn without extra trouble and even through the winter; with some curl in the hair without the cost of a permanent wave; with, perhaps, a little more emotional warmth in their souls; and a little more religion, music, laughter, and carefreeness in their lives. Amalgamation is, to the ordinary American, not a proper subject for jokes at all, unless it can be pulled down to the level of dirty stories, where, however, it enjoys a favored place. Referred to society as a whole and viewed as a principle, the anti-amalgamation maxim is held holy; it is a consecrated taboo. The maxim might, indeed, be a remnant of something really in the "mores." It is kept unproblematic, which is certainly not the case with all the rest of etiquette and segregation and discrimination patterns, for which this quality is sometimes erroneously claimed.

attitudes which can be described as the "common denominator" in the problem. It defines the Negro group in contradistinction to all the non-colored minority groups in America and all other lower class groups. The boundary between Negro and white is not simply a class line which can be successfully crossed by education, integration into the national culture, and individual economic advancement. The boundary is fixed. It is not a temporary expediency during an apprenticeship in the national culture. It is a bar erected with the intention of permanency. It is directed against the whole group. Actually, however, "passing" as a white person is possible when a Negro is white enough to conceal his Negro heritage. But the difference between "passing" and ordinary social climbing reveals the distinction between a class line, in the ordinary sense, and a caste line.

This brings us to the point where we shall attempt to sketch, only in an abstract and preliminary form, the social mechanism by which the anti-amalgamation maxim determines race relations. This mechanism is perceived by nearly everybody in America, but most clearly in the South. Almost unanimously white Americans have communicated to the author the following logic of the caste situation which we shall call the *"white man's theory of color caste."*

1. The concern for "race purity" is basic in the whole issue; the primary and essential command is to prevent amalgamation; the whites are determined to utilize every means to this end.
2. Rejection of "social equality" is to be understood as a precaution to hinder miscegenation and particularly intermarriage.
3. The danger of miscegenation is so tremendous that the segregation and discrimination inherent in the refusal of "social equality" must be extended to nearly all spheres of life. There must be segregation and discrimination in recreation, in religious service, in education, before the law, in politics, in housing, in stores and in breadwinning.

This popular theory of the American caste mechanism is, of course, open to criticism. It can be criticized from a valuational point of view by maintaining that hindering miscegenation is not a worthwhile end, or that as an end it is not sufficiently worthwhile to counterbalance the sufferings inflicted upon the suppressed caste and the general depression of productive efficiency, standards of living and human culture in the American society at large—costs appreciated by all parties concerned. This criticism does not, however, endanger the theory which assumes that white people actually are following another valuation of means and ends and are prepared to pay the costs for attaining the ends. A second criticism would point out that, assuming the desirability of the end, this end could be reached without the complicated and, in all respects, socially expensive caste apparatus now employed. This criticism, however adequate though it be on the practical or political plane of discussion, does not disprove that people believe otherwise, and that the popular theory is a true representation of their beliefs and actions.

To undermine the popular theory of the caste mechanism, as based on the anti-amalgamation maxim, it would, of course, be necessary to prove that people really are influenced by other motives than the ones pronounced. Much material has . . . been brought together indicating that, among other things, competitive economic interests, which do not figure at all in the popular rationalization referred to, play a decisive role. The announced concern about racial purity is, when this economic motive is taken into account, no longer awarded the exclusive role as the *basic* cause in the psychology of the race problem.

Though the popular theory of color caste turns out to be a rationalization, this does not destroy it. For among the forces in the minds of the white people are certainly not only economic interests (if these were the only ones, the popular theory would be utterly demolished), but also sexual urges, inhibitions, and jealousies, and social fears and cravings for prestige and security. When they come under the scrutiny of scientific research, both the sexual and the social complexes take on unexpected designs. We shall then also get a clue to understanding the remarkable tendency of this presumably biological doctrine, that it refers only to legal marriage and to relations between Negro men and white women, but not to extra-marital sex relations between white men and Negro women.

However these sexual and social complexes might turn out when analyzed, they will reveal the psychological nature of the anti-amalgamation doctrine and show its "meaning." They will also explain the compressed emotion attached to the Negro problem. It is inherent in our type of modern Western civilization that sex and social status are for most individuals the danger points, the directions whence he fears the sinister onslaughts on his personal security. These two factors are more likely than anything else to push a life problem deep down into the subconscious and load it with emotions. There is some probability that in America both complexes are particularly laden with emotions. The American puritan tradition gives everything connected with sex a higher emotional charge. The roads for social climbing have been kept more open in America than perhaps anywhere else in the world, but in this upward struggle the competition for social status has also become more absorbing. In a manner and to a degree most uncomfortable for the Negro people in America, both the sexual and the social complexes have become related to the Negro problem.

These complexes are most of the time kept concealed. In occasional groups of persons and situations they break into the open. Even when not consciously perceived or expressed, they ordinarily determine interracial behavior on the white side.

The "Rank Order of Discriminations"

The anti-amalgamation doctrine represents a strategic constellation of forces in race relations. Their charting will allow us a first general overview of the discrimination patterns and will have the advantage that white Americans themselves will recognize their own paths on the map we draw. When white Southerners are asked to rank, in order of importance, various types of discrimination,[12] they consistently present a list in which these types of discrimination are ranked according to the degree of closeness of their relation to the anti-amalgamation doctrine. This rank order—which will be referred to as *"the white man's rank order of discriminations"*—will serve as an organizing principle in this book. It appears, actually, only as an elaboration of the popular theory of color caste sketched above. Like that theory, it is most clearly and distinctly perceived in the South; in the North ideas are more vague but, on the whole, not greatly divergent. Neither the popular theory of caste nor the rank order of discriminations has been noted much in scientific literature on the Negro problem.

The rank order held nearly unanimously is the following:

[12] In this introductory sketch the distinction between "segregation" and "discrimination" is entirely disregarded. This distinction, signified by the popular theory and legal construct "separate but equal," is mainly to be regarded as an equalitarian rationalization on the part of the white Americans, indicating the fundamental conflict of valuations involved in the matter. "Segregation" means only separation and does not, in principle, imply "discrimination." In practice it almost always does. . . .

Rank 1. Highest in this order stands the bar against intermarriage and sexual intercourse involving white women.

Rank 2. Next come the several etiquettes and discriminations, which specifically concern behavior in personal relations. (These are the barriers against dancing, bathing, eating, drinking together, and social intercourse generally; peculiar rules as to handshaking, hat lifting, use of titles, house entrance to be used, social forms when meeting on streets and in work, and so forth. These patterns are sometimes referred to as the denial of "social equality" in the narrow meaning of the term.)

Rank 3. Thereafter follow the segregations and discriminations in use of public facilities such as schools, churches and means of conveyance.

Rank 4. Next comes political disfranchisement.

Rank 5. Thereafter come discriminations in law courts, by the police, and by other public servants.

Rank 6. Finally come the discriminations in securing land, credit, jobs, or other means of earning a living, and discriminations in public relief and other social welfare activities.

It is unfortunate that this cornerstone in our edifice of basic hypotheses, like many of our other generalizations, has to be constructed upon the author's observations.[13] It is desirable that scientifically controlled, quantitative knowledge be substituted for impressionistic judgments as soon as possible.[14] It should be noted that the rank order is very apparently determined by the factors of sex and

[13] There are some studies, however, which provide evidence for the hypothesis of the "rank order of discriminations," even if they are not comprehensive enough to serve as conclusive proof. There are a host of attitude studies showing how whites have different attitudes toward Negroes in different spheres of life. Probably the earliest of these studies was that of Emory S. Bogardus, "Race Friendliness and Social Distance," *Journal of Applied Sociology* (1927), pp. 272–287. As an example of such studies which apply solely to Negro issues, we may cite the study by Euri Relle Bolton, "Measuring Specific Attitudes towards the Social Rights of the Negro," *The Journal of Abnormal and Social Psychology* (January–March, 1937), pp. 384–397. For a summary of other such studies, see Horowitz, *op. cit.*, pp. 123–148.

[14] Such studies should not only break the rank order into finer distinctions, but also develop a measure of the distance between the ranks in the order. It would, further, be desirable to ascertain individual differences in the apprehension of this rank order, and to relate these differences to age, sex, social class, educational level and region.

social status, so that the closer the association of a type of interracial behavior is to sexual and social intercourse on an equalitarian basis, the higher it ranks among the forbidden things.

Next in importance to the fact of the white man's rank order of discriminations is the fact that *the Negro's own rank order is just about parallel, but inverse, to that of the white man.* The Negro resists least the discrimination on the ranks placed highest in the white man's evaluation and resents most any discrimination on the lowest level. This is in accord with the Negro's immediate interests. Negroes are in desperate need of jobs and bread, even more so than of justice in the courts, and of the vote. These latter needs are, in their turn, more urgent even than better schools and playgrounds, or, rather, they are primary means of reaching equality in the use of community facilities. Such facilities are, in turn, more important than civil courtesies. The marriage matter, finally, is of rather distant and doubtful interest.

Such reflections are obvious; and most Negroes have them in their minds. It is another matter, however, whether the white man is prepared to stick honestly to the rank order which he is so explicit and emphatic in announcing. The question is whether he is really prepared to give the Negro a good job, or even the vote, rather than to allow him entrance to his front door or to ride beside him in the street car.

Upon the assumption that this question is given an affirmative answer, that the white man is actually prepared to carry out in practice the implications of his theories, this inverse relationship between the Negro's and the white man's rank orders becomes of strategical importance in the practical and political sphere of the Negro problem. Although not formulated in this way, such a relationship, or such a minimum moral demand on the ordinary white man, has always been the basis of all attempts to compromise and come to a better understanding between leaders of the two groups. It has been the basis for all interracial policy and also for most of the practical work actually carried out by Negro betterment organizations. Followed to its logical end, it should fundamentally change the race situation in America.

It has thus always been a primary requirement upon every Negro leader—who aspires to get any hearing at all from the white majority group, and who does not want to appear dangerously radical to the Negro group and at the same time hurt the "race pride" it has built up as a defense—that he shall explicitly condone the anti-amalgamation maxim, which is the keystone in the white man's structure of race prejudice, and forbear to express any desire on the part of the Negro people to aspire to intermarriage with the whites. The request for intermarriage is easy for the Negro leader to give up. Intermarriage cannot possibly be a practical object of Negro public policy. Independent of the Negroes' wishes, the opportunity for intermarriage is not favorable as long as the great majority of the white population dislikes the very idea. As a defense reaction a strong attitude against intermarriage has developed in the Negro people itself.[15] And the Negro people have no interest in defending the exploitative illicit relations between white men and Negro women. This race mingling is, on the contrary, commonly felt among Negroes to be disgraceful. And it often arouses the jealousy of Negro men.

The required soothing gesture toward the anti-amalgamation doctrine is, therefore, readily delivered. It is iterated at every convenient opportunity and belongs to the established routine of Negro leadership. For example, Robert R. Moton writes:

> As for amalgamation, very few expect it; still fewer want it; no one advocates it; and only a constantly diminishing minority practise it, and that surreptitiously. It is generally accepted on both sides of the colour line that it is best for the two races to remain ethnologically distinct.[16]

There seems thus to be unanimity among Negro leaders on the point deemed crucial by white Americans. If we attend carefully, we shall, however, detect some important differences in formulation. The Negro spokesman will never, to begin with, accept the common white premise of racial inferiority of the Negro stock. To quote Moton again:

[15] This goes far back. Frederick Douglass nearly endangered his position among Negroes by marrying a white woman. About Douglass, Kelly Miller observed: ". . . he has a hold upon the affection of his race, not on account of his second marriage but in spite of it. He seriously affected his standing with his people by that marriage." (Kelly Miller, *Race Adjustment—Essays on the Negro in America* [1908], p. 50.) And W. E. B. DuBois tells us in his autobiography: "I resented the assumption that we desired it [racial amalgamation]. I frankly refused the possibility while in Germany and even in America gave up courtship with one 'colored' girl because she looked quite white, and I should resent the inference on the street that I had married outside my race." (*Dusk of Dawn* [1940], p. 101.) . . .

[16] *Op. cit.*, p. 241.

> . . . even in the matter of the mingling of racial strains, however undesirable it might seem to be from a social point of view, he [the Negro] would never admit that his blood carries any taint of physiological, mental, or spiritual inferiority.[17]

A doctrine of equal natural endowments—a doctrine contrary to the white man's assumption of Negro inferiority, which is at the basis of the anti-amalgamation theory—has been consistently upheld. If a Negro leader publicly even hinted at the possibility of inherent racial inferiority, he would immediately lose his following. The entire Negro press watches the Negro leaders on this point.

Even Booker T. Washington, the supreme diplomat of the Negro people through a generation filled with severe trials, who was able by studied unobtrusiveness to wring so many favors from the white majority, never dared to allude to such a possibility, though he sometimes criticized most severely his own people for lack of thrift, skill, perseverance and general culture. In fact, there is no reason to think that he did not firmly believe in the fundamental equality of inherent capacities. Privately, local Negro leaders might find it advisable to admit Negro inferiority and, particularly earlier, many individual Negroes might have shared the white man's view. But it will not be expressed by national leaders and, in fact, never when they are under public scrutiny.[18] An emphatic assertion of equal endowments is article number one in the growing Negro "race pride."

Another deviation of the Negro faith in the anti-amalgamation doctrine is the stress that they, for natural reasons, lay on condemning exploitative illicit amalgamation. They turn the tables and accuse white men of debasing Negro womanhood, and the entire white culture for not rising up against this practice as their expressed antagonism against miscegenation should demand. Here they have a strong point, and they know how to press it.[19]

A third qualification in the Negro's acceptance of the anti-amal-

[17] *Ibid.*, p. 239.

[18] An exception, which by its uniqueness, and by the angry reception it received from the Negroes, rather proves our thesis, is the remarkable book by William H. Thomas, *The American Negro* (1901). The fact that Negroes privately often enjoy indulging in derogatory statements about Negroes in general is not overlooked. It is, however, a suppression phenomenon of quite another order. . . .

[19] "The rape which your gentlemen have done against helpless black women in defiance of your own laws is written on the foreheads of two millions of mulattoes, and written in ineffaceable blood." (W. E. B. DuBois, *The Souls of Black Folk* [1924; first edition, 1903], p. 106.)

gamation doctrine, expressed not only by the more "radical" and outspoken Negro leaders, is the assertion that intermarriage should not be barred by law. The respect for individual liberty is invoked as an argument. But, in addition, it is pointed out that this barrier, by releasing the white man from the consequences of intimacy with a Negro woman, actually has the effect of inducing such intimacy and thus tends to increase miscegenation. Moton makes this point:

> The Negro woman suffers not only from the handicap of economic and social discriminations imposed upon the race as a whole, but is in addition the victim of unfavourable legislation incorporated in the marriage laws of twenty-nine states, which forbid the intermarriage of black and white. The disadvantage of these statutes lies, not as is generally represented, in the legal obstacle they present to social equality, but rather in the fact that such laws specifically deny to the Negro woman and her offspring that safeguard from abuse and exploitation with which the women of the white race are abundantly surrounded. On the other side, the effect of such legislation leaves the white man, who is so inclined, free of any responsibility attending his amatory excursions across the colour line and leaves the coloured woman without redress for any of the consequences of her defencelessness; whereas white women have every protection, from fine and imprisonment under the law to enforced marriage and lynching outside the law.[20]

But even with all these qualifications, the anti-amalgamation doctrine, the necessity of assenting to which is understood by nearly everybody, obviously encounters some difficulties in the minds of intellectual Negroes. They can hardly be expected to accept it as a just rule of conduct. They tend to accept it merely as a temporary expedient necessitated by human weakness. Kelly Miller thus wrote:

> . . . you would hardly expect the Negro, in derogation of his common human qualities, to proclaim that he is so diverse from God's other human creatures as to make the blending of the races contrary to the law of nature. The Negro refuses to become excited or share in your frenzy on this subject. The amalgamation of the races is an ultimate possibility, though not an immediate probability. But what have you and I to do with ultimate questions, anyway? [21]

[20] *Op. cit.*, pp. 208–209.

[21] *Race Adjustment*, p. 48.

And a few years later, he said:

> It must be taken for granted in the final outcome of things that the color line will be wholly obliterated. While blood may be thicker than water, it does not possess the spissitude or inherency of everlasting principle. The brotherhood of man is more fundamental than the fellowship of race. A physical and spiritual identity of all peoples occupying common territory is a logical necessity of thought. The clear seeing mind refuses to yield or give its assent to any other ultimate conclusion. This consummation, however, is far too removed from the sphere of present probability to have decisive influence upon practical procedure.[22]

This problem is, of course, tied up with the freedom of the individual. "Theoretically Negroes would all subscribe to the right of freedom of choice in marriage even between the two races,"[23] wrote Moton. And DuBois formulates it in stronger terms:

> . . . a woman may say, I do not want to marry this black man, or this red man, or this white man. . . . But the impudent and vicious demand that all colored folk shall write themselves down as brutes by a general assertion of their unfitness to marry other decent folk is a nightmare.[24]

Negroes have always pointed out that the white man must not be very certain of his woman's lack of interest when he rises to such frenzy on behalf of the danger to her and feels compelled to build up such formidable fences to prevent her from marrying a Negro.

With these reservations both Negro leadership and the Negro masses acquiesce in the white anti-amalgamation doctrine. This attitude is noted with satisfaction in the white camp. The writer has observed, however, that the average white man, particularly in the South, does not feel quite convinced of the Negro's acquiescence. In several conversations, the same white person, in the same breath, has assured me, on the one hand, that the Negroes are perfectly satisfied in their position and would not like to be treated as equals, and on

[22] *Out of the House of Bondage* (1914), p. 45.

[23] *Op. cit.*, p. 241.

[24] Editorial, *The Crisis* (January, 1920), p. 106.

the other hand, that the only thing these Negroes long for is to be like white people and to marry their daughters.

Whereas the Negro spokesman finds it possible to assent to the first rank of discrimination, namely, that involving miscegenation, it is more difficult for him to give his approval to the second rank of discrimination, namely, that involving "etiquette" and consisting in the white man's refusal to extend the ordinary courtesies to Negroes in daily life and his expectation of receiving certain symbolic signs of submissiveness from the Negro. The Negro leader could not do so without serious risk of censorship by his own people and rebuke by the Negro press. In all articulate groups of Negroes there is a demand to have white men call them by their titles of Mr., Mrs., and Miss; to have white men take off their hats on entering a Negro's house; to be able to enter a white man's house through the front door rather than the back door, and so on. But on the whole, and in spite of the rule that they stand up for "social equality" in this sense, most Negroes in the South obey the white man's rules.

Booker T. Washington went a long way, it is true, in his Atlanta speech in 1895 where he explained that: "In all things that are purely social we [the two races] can be as separate as the fingers, yet one as the hand in all things essential to mutual progress."[25] He there seemed to condone not only these rules of "etiquette" but also the denial of "social equality" in a broader sense, including some of the further categories in the white man's rank order of discrimination. He himself was always most eager to observe the rules. But Washington was bitterly rebuked for this capitulation, particularly by Negroes in the North. And a long time has passed since then; the whole spirit in the Negro world has changed considerably in three decades.

The modern Negro leader will try to solve this dilemma by iterating that no Negroes want to intrude upon white people's private lives. But this is not what Southern white opinion asks for. It is not satisfied with the natural rules of polite conduct that no individual, of whatever race, shall push his presence on a society where he is not wanted. It asks for a general order according to which *all* Negroes are placed under *all* white people and excluded from not only the white man's society but also from the ordinary symbols of respect. No Negro shall ever aspire to them, and no white shall be allowed to offer them.

[25] *Up from Slavery* (1915; first edition, 1900), pp. 221–222.

Thus, on this second rank of discrimination there is a wide gap between the ideologies of the two groups. As we then continue downward in our rank order and arrive at the ordinary Jim Crow practices, the segregation in schools, the disfranchisement, and the discrimination in employment, we find, on the one hand, that increasingly larger groups of white people are prepared to take a stand against these discriminations. Many a liberal white professor in the South who, for his own welfare, would not dare to entertain a Negro in his home and perhaps not even speak to him in a friendly manner on the street, will be found prepared publicly to condemn disfranchisement, lynching, and the forcing of the Negro out of employment. Also, on the other hand, Negro spokesmen are becoming increasingly firm in their opposition to discrimination on these lower levels. It is principally on these lower levels of the white man's rank order of discriminations that the race struggle goes on. The struggle will widen to embrace all the thousand problems of education, politics, economic standards, and so forth, and the frontier will shift from day to day according to varying events.

Even a superficial view of discrimination in America will reveal to the observer: first, that there are great differences, not only between larger regions, but between neighboring communities; and, second, that even in the same community, changes occur from one time to another. There is also, contrary to the rule that all Negroes are to be treated alike, a certain amount of discretion depending upon the class and social status of the Negro in question. A white person, especially if he has high status in the community, is, furthermore, supposed to be free, within limits, to overstep the rules. The rules are primarily to govern the Negro's behavior.

Some of these differences and changes can be explained. But the need for their interpretation is perhaps less than has sometimes been assumed. The variations in discrimination between local communities or from one time to another are often not of primary consequence. All of these thousand and one precepts, etiquettes, taboos, and disabilities inflicted upon the Negro have a common purpose: to express the subordinate status of the Negro people and the exalted position of the whites. They have their meaning and chief function as symbols. As symbols they are, however, interchangeable to an extent: one can serve in place of another without causing material difference in the essential social relations in the community.

The differences in patterns of discrimination between the larger regions of the country and the temporal changes of patterns within one region, which reveal a definite trend, have, on the contrary, more material import. These differences and changes imply, in fact, a considerable margin of variation within the very notion of American caste, which is not true of all the other minor differences between the changes in localities within a single region—hence the reason for a clear distinction. For exemplification it may suffice here to refer only to the differentials in space. As one moves from the Deep South through the Upper South and the Border states to the North, the manifestations of discrimination decrease in extent and intensity; at the same time the rules become more uncertain and capricious. The "color line" becomes a broad ribbon of arbitrariness. The old New England states stand, on the whole, as the antipode to the Deep South. This generalization requires important qualifications, and the relations are in process of change.

The decreasing discrimination as we go from South to North in the United States is apparently related to a weaker basic prejudice. In the North the Negroes have fair justice and are not disfranchised; they are not Jim-Crowed in public means of conveyance; educational institutions are less segregated. The interesting thing is that the decrease of discrimination does *not* regularly follow the white man's rank order. Thus intermarriage, placed on the top of the rank order, is legally permitted in all but one of the Northern states east of the Mississippi. The racial etiquette, being the most conspicuous element in the second rank, is, practically speaking, absent from the North. On the other hand, employment discriminations, placed at the bottom of the rank order, at times are equally severe, or more so, in some Northern communities than in the South, even if it is true that Negroes have been able to press themselves into many more new avenues of employment during the last generation in the North than in the South.

There is plenty of discrimination in the North. But it is—or rather its rationalization is—kept hidden. We can, in the North, witness the legislators' obedience to the American Creed when they solemnly pass laws and regulations to condemn and punish such acts of discrimination which, as a matter of routine, are committed daily by the great majority of the white citizens and by the legislators themselves. In the North, as indeed often in the South, public speakers frequently pronounce principles of human and civic equality. We see here revealed in relief the Negro problem as an American Dilemma.

Relationships Between Lower Class Groups

It was important to compare the Negro problem with American minority problems in general because both the similarities and the dissimilarities are instructive. Comparisons give leads, and they furnish perspective.

This same reason permits us to point out that the consideration of the Negro problem as one minority problem among others is far too narrow. The Negro has usually the same disadvantages and some extra ones in addition. To these other disadvantaged groups in America belong not only the groups recognized as minorities, but all economically weak classes in the nation, the bulk of the Southern people, women, and others. This country is a "white man's country," but, in addition, it is a country belonging primarily to the elderly, male, upper class, Protestant Northerner. Viewed in this setting the Negro problem in America is but one local and temporary facet of that eternal problem of world dimension—how to regulate the conflicting interests of groups in the best interest of justice and fairness. The latter ideals are vague and conflicting, and their meaning is changing in the course of the struggle.

There seems to be a general structure of social relations between groups on different levels of power and advantage. From a consideration of our exaggeratedly "typical" case—the Negro—we may hope to reach some suggestions toward a more satisfactory general theory about this social power structure in general. Our hypothesis is that in a society where there are broad social classes and, in addition, more minute distinctions and splits in the lower strata, *the lower class groups will, to a great extent, take care of keeping each other subdued*, thus relieving, to that extent, the higher classes of this otherwise painful task necessary to the monopolization of the power and the advantages.

It will be observed that this hypothesis is contrary to the Marxian theory of class society, which in the period between the two World Wars has been so powerful, directly and indirectly, consciously and unconsciously, in American social science thinking generally. The Marxian scheme assumes that there is an actual solidarity between the several lower class groups against the higher classes, or, in any case, a potential solidarity which as a matter of natural development is bound to emerge. The inevitable result is a "class struggle" where all poor and disadvantaged groups are united behind the barricades.

Such a construction has had a considerable vogue in all discussions on the American Negro problem since the First World War. We are not here taking issue with the political desirability of a common front between the poorer classes of whites and the Negro people who, for the most part, belong to the proletariat. In fact, we can well see that such a practical judgment is motivated as a conclusion from certain value premises in line with the American Creed. But the thesis has also been given a theoretical content as describing actual trends in reality and not only political *desiderata*. A solidarity between poor whites and Negroes has been said to be "natural" and the conflicts to be due to "illusions." This thesis . . . has been a leading one in the field and much has been made of even the faintest demonstration of such solidarity.

In partial anticipation of what is to follow later in this volume, we might be permitted to make a few general, and perhaps rather dogmatic, remarks in criticism of this theory. Everything we know about human frustration and aggression, and the displacement of aggression, speaks against it. For an individual to feel interest solidarity with a group assumes his psychological identification with the group. This identification must be of considerable strength, as the very meaning of solidarity is that he is prepared to set aside and even sacrifice his own short-range private interests for the long-range interests of his group. Every vertical split within the lower class aggregate will stand as an obstacle to the feeling of solidarity. Even within the white working class itself, as within the entire American nation, the feeling of solidarity and loyalty is relatively low. Despite the considerable mobility, especially in the North, the Negroes are held apart from the whites by caste, which furnishes a formidable bar to mutual identification and solidarity.

It has often occurred to me, when reflecting upon the responses I get from white laboring people on this strategic question, that my friends among the younger Negro intellectuals, whose judgment I otherwise have learned to admire greatly, have perhaps, and for natural reasons, not had enough occasion to find out for themselves what a bitter, spiteful, and relentless feeling often prevails against the Negroes among lower class white people in America. Again relying upon my own observations, I have become convinced that the laboring Negroes do not resent whites in any degree comparable with the resentment shown in the opposite direction by the laboring whites. The competitive situation is, and is likely to remain, highly unstable.

It must be admitted that, in the midst of harsh caste resentment, signs of newborn working class solidarity are not entirely lacking; we shall have to discuss these recent tendencies in some detail in order to evaluate the resultant trend and the prospects for the future. On this point there seems, however, to be a danger of wishful thinking present in most writings on the subject. The Marxian solidarity between the toilers of all the earth will, indeed, have a long way to go as far as concerns solidarity of the poor white Americans with the toiling Negro. This is particularly true of the South but true also of the communities in the North where the Negroes are numerous and competing with the whites for employment.

Our hypothesis is similar to the view taken by an older group of Negro writers and by most white writers who have touched this crucial question: that the Negro's friend—or the one who is least unfriendly—is still rather the upper class of white people, the people with economic and social security who are truly a "noncompeting group." There are many things in the economic, political, and social history of the Negro which are simply inexplicable by the Marxian theory of class solidarity but which fit into our hypothesis of the predominance of internal lower class struggle. DuBois, in *Black Reconstruction*, argues that it would have been desirable if after the Civil War the landless Negroes and the poor whites had joined hands to retain political power and carry out a land reform and a progressive government in the Southern states; one sometimes feels that he thinks it would have been a possibility.[26] From our point of view such a possibility did not exist at all, and the negative outcome was neither an accident nor a result of simple deception or delusion. These two groups, illiterate and insecure in an impoverished South, placed in an intensified competition with each other, lacking every trace of primary solidarity, and marked off from each other by color and tradi-

[26] "The South, after the war, presented the greatest opportunity for a real national labor movement which the nation ever saw or is likely to see for many decades." (*Black Reconstruction* [1935], p. 353 *passim.*)

tion, could not possibly be expected to clasp hands. There is a Swedish proverb: "When the feed-box is empty, the horses will bite each other."

That part of the country where, even today, the Negro is dealt with most severely, the South, is also a disadvantaged and, in most respects, backward region in the nation. The Negro lives there in the midst of other relatively subordinated groups. Like the Negro, the entire South is a problem. We do not want to minimize other obvious explanations of the harsher treatment of the Negro in the South: his concentration there in large numbers, the tradition of subordination retained from slavery, and the traumatic effect of the Civil War and Reconstruction; but we do want to stress the fact that the masses of white Southerners are poor and to keep in mind the tendency of lower class groups to struggle against each other.[27]

[27] The great similarity in cultural situation—on a different level—between the Negro people in all America and the white South should not be overlooked. Many of the general things which can be said about the Negroes hold true, in large measure, of the white Southerners, or something quite similar can be asserted. Thus, just as the Negro sees himself economically excluded and exploited, so the Southern white man has been trained to think of his economy as a colony for Yankee exploitation. As the Negro has been compelled to develop race pride and a "protective" community, so the white South has also a strong group feeling. The white South is also something of a nation within a nation. It is certainly no accident that a "regional approach" in social science has been stressed in the South. The Southerner, like the Negro, is apt to be sensitive and to take any personal remark or observation as a rebuke, and a rebuke not only against himself but against the whole South. In analyzing himself, he finds the same general traits of extreme individualism and romanticism which are ascribed to the Negro. His educators and intellectual leaders find it necessary to complain of the same shortcomings in him as he finds in the Negro: violence, laziness, lack of thrift, lack of rational efficiency and respect for law and social order, lack of punctuality and respect for deadlines. The rickety rocking-chair on the porch has a symbolic meaning in the South not entirely different from that of the Negro's watermelon, although there is more an association of gloom and dreariness around the former stereotype, and happy-go-lucky carefreeness around the latter. The expression "C.P.T."—colored people's time—is often referred to in the South, but nearly as frequently it is jestingly suggested that it fits the folkways also of the white Southerners. The casual carrying of weapons, which is so associated in the Northerners' minds with the Negro, is commonplace among white Southerners. Both groups are on the average more religious than the rest of America, and the preacher is, or has been, more powerful in society. In both groups there is also a tendency toward fundamentalism and emotionalism, the former characteristic more important for the whites, the latter for the Negroes. The general educational level in the South has, for lack of school facilities, been lower than the national norm, and as a result an obvious double standard in favor of Southerners is actually being applied by higher educational institutions and by

A few remarks are now relevant on the internal social stratification of the Negro group itself. The stratification of the Negro caste into classes is well developed and the significance attached to class distinctions is great. This is not surprising in view of the fact that caste barriers, which prevent individuals of the lower group from rising out of it, force all social climbing to occur within the caste and encourage an increase in internal social competition for the symbols of prestige and power. Caste consigns the overwhelming majority of Negroes to the lower class. But at the same time as it makes higher class status rarer, it accentuates the desire for prestige and social distance within the Negro caste. In fact it sometimes causes a more minute class division than the ordinary one, and always invests it with more subjective importance. The social distinctions within a disadvantaged group for this reason become a fairly adequate index of the group's social isolation from the larger society.

Caste produces, on the one hand, a strong feeling of mutuality of fate, of in-group fellowship—much stronger than a general low class position can develop. The Negro community is a protective community, and we shall, in the following chapters, see this trait reflected in practically all aspects of the Negro problem. But, on the other hand, the interclass strivings, often heightened to vigorous mutual repulsion and resentment, are equally conspicuous.

Negro writers, especially newspapermen, particularly when directing themselves to a Negro audience, have always pointed out, as the great fault of the race, its lack of solidarity. The same note is struck in practically every public address and often in sermons when the preacher for a moment leaves his other-worldliness. It is the campaign cry of the organizations for Negro business. Everywhere one meets the same endless complaints: that the Negroes won't stick together, that they don't trust each other but rather the white man, that they can't plan and act in common, that they don't back their

---

such organizations as foundations awarding fellowships and encouraging research projects. The Yankee prejudice against the South often takes the form of a paternalistic favoring of a weaker group. The white writers of the South, like the Negro writers, are accustomed to work mainly for a "foreign" public of readers. And they have, for the benefit of the out-group, exploited the in-group's romance and oddness. During the 'twenties both groups had a literary renaissance, commonly described in both cases as an emancipation from outside determinants and as a new earthbound realism. This list could be continued to a considerable length, but it has already been made understandable both why the Negro in a way feels so much at home in the South and why his lot there sometimes becomes so sad and even tragic.

leaders, that the leaders can't agree, or that they deceive the people and sell out their interests to the whites.

In order not to be dogmatic in a direction opposite to the one criticized, we should point out that the principle of internal struggle in the lower classes is only one social force among many. Other forces are making for solidarity in the lower classes. In both of the two problems raised—the solidarity *between* lower class whites and Negroes and the internal solidarity *within* the Negro group—there can be any degree of solidarity, ranging between utter mistrust and complete trustfulness. The scientific problem is to find out and measure the degree of solidarity and the social forces determining it, not just to assume that solidarity will come about "naturally" and "inevitably." The factors making for solidarity are both irrational and rational. Among the irrational factors are tradition, fear, charisma, brute force, propaganda. The main rational factors are economic and social security and a planned program of civic education.

While visiting in Southern Negro communities, the writer was forced to the observation that often the most effective Negro leaders—those with a rational balance of courage and restraint, a realistic understanding of the power situation, and an unfailing loyalty to the Negro cause—were federal employees (for example, postal clerks), petty railway officials, or other persons with their economic basis outside the local white or Negro community and who had consequently a measure of economic security and some leisure time for thinking and studying. They were, unfortunately, few. Generally speaking, whenever the masses, in any part of the world, have permanently improved their social, economic, and political status through orderly organizations founded upon solidarity, these masses have not been a semi-illiterate proletariat, but have already achieved a measure of economic security and education. The vanguards of such mass reform movements have always belonged to the upper fringe of the lower classes concerned.

If this hypothesis is correct and if the lower classes have interests in common, the steady trend in this country toward improved educational facilities and toward widened social security for the masses of the people will work for increased solidarity between the lower class groups. But changes in this direction will probably be slow, both because of some general factors impeding broad democratic mass movements in America, and—in our special problems, solidarity between whites and Negroes—because of the existence of caste.

In this connection we must not forget the influence of ideological forces. And we must guard against the common mistake of reducing them solely to secondary expressions of economic interests. Independent (that is, independent of the economic interests involved in the Negro problem) ideological forces of a liberal character are particularly strong in America because of the central and influential position of the American Creed in people's valuations.

It may be suggested as an hypothesis, already fairly well substantiated by research and by common observation, that those liberal ideological forces tend to create a tie between the problems of all disadvantaged groups in society, and that they work for solidarity between these groups. A study of opinions in the Negro problem will reveal, we believe, that persons who are inclined to favor measures to help the underdog generally, are also, and as a part of this attitude, usually inclined to give the Negro a lift. There is a correlation between political opinions in different issues, which probably rests upon a basis of temperamental personality traits and has its deeper roots in all the cultural influences working upon a personality. If this correlation is represented by a composite scale running from radicalism, through liberalism and conservatism, to reactionism, it is suggested that it will be found that all subordinate groups—Negroes, women, minorities in general, poor people, prisoners, and so forth—will find their interests more favored in political opinion as we move toward the left of the scale. This hypothesis of a system of opinion correlation will, however, have to be taken with a grain of salt, since this correlation is obviously far from complete.

In general, poor people are not radical and not even liberal, though to have such political opinions would often be in their interest. Liberalism is not characteristic of Negroes either, except, of course, that they take a radical position in the Negro problem. We must guard against a superficial bias (probably of Marxian origin) which makes us believe that the lower classes are naturally prepared to take a broad point of view and a friendly attitude toward all disadvantaged groups. A liberal outlook is much more likely to emerge among people in a somewhat secure social and economic situation and with a background of education. The problem for political liberalism—if, for example, we might be allowed to pose the problem in the practical, instead of the theoretical mode—appears to be first to lift the masses to security and education and then to work to make them liberal.

The South, compared to the other regions of America, has the least economic security, the lowest educational level, and is most conservative. The South's conservatism is manifested not only with respect to the Negro problem but also with respect to all the other important problems of the last decades—woman suffrage, trade unionism, labor legislation, social security reforms, penal reforms, civil liberties—and with respect to broad philosophical matters, such as the character of religious beliefs and practices. Even at present the South does not have a full spectrum of political opinions represented within its public discussion. There are relatively few liberals in the South and practically no radicals.

The recent economic stagnation (which for the rural South has lasted much more than ten years), the flood of social reforms thrust upon the South by the federal government, and the fact that the rate of industrialization in the South is higher than in the rest of the nation, may well come to cause an upheaval in the South's entire opinion structure. The importance of this for the Negro problem may be considerable.

The Manifoldness and the Unity of the Negro Problem

The Negro problem has the manifoldness of human life. Like the women's problem, it touches every other social issue, or rather, it represents an angle of them all . . . : race, culture, population, breadwinning, economic and social policy, law, crime, class, family, recreation, school, church, press, organizations, politics, attitudes.

The perplexities and manifoldness of the Negro problem have even increased considerably during the last generation. One reason is migration and industrialization. The Negro has left his seclusion. A much smaller portion of the Negro people of today lives in the static, rather inarticulate folk society of the old plantation economy. The Negro people have increasingly stepped into the midst of America's high-geared metropolitan life, and they have by their coming added to the complication of these already tremendously complicated communities. This mass movement of Negroes from farms to cities and from the South to the North has, contrary to expectation, kept up in bad times as in good, and is likely to continue.

Another and equally important reason why the Negro problem

shows an increasing involvement with all sorts of other special problems is the fact that America, especially during the last ten years, has started to use the state as an instrument for induced social change. The New Deal has actually changed the whole configuration of the Negro problem. Particularly when looked upon from the practical and political viewpoints, the contrast between the present situation and the one prior to the New Deal is striking.

Until then the practical Negro problem involved civil rights, education, charity, and little more. Now it has widened, in pace with public policy in the new "welfare state," and involves housing, nutrition, medicine, education, relief and social security, wages and hours, working conditions, child and woman labor, and, lately, the armed forces and the war industries. The Negro's share may be meager in all this new state activity, but he has been given a share. He has been given a broader and more variegated front to defend and from which to push forward. This is the great import of the New Deal to the Negro. For almost the first time in the history of the nation the state has done something substantial in a social way without excluding the Negro.

In this situation it has sometimes appeared as if there were no longer a Negro problem distinct from all the other social problems in the United States. In popular periodicals, articles on the general Negro problem gave way to much more specific subjects during the 'thirties. Even on the theoretical level it has occurred to many that it was time to stop studying the Negro problem in itself. The younger generation of Negro intellectuals have become tired of all the talk about the Negro problem on which they were brought up, and which sometimes seemed to them so barren of real deliveries. They started to criticize the older generation of Negroes for their obsession with the Negro problem. In many ways this was a movement which could be considered as the continuation, during the 'thirties, of the "New Negro Movement" of the 'twenties.

We hear it said nowadays that there is no "race problem," but only a "class problem." The Negro sharecropper is alleged to be destitute not because of his color but because of his class position—and it is pointed out that there are white people who are equally poor. From a practical angle there is a point in this reasoning. But from a theoretical angle it contains escapism in new form. It also draws too heavily on the idealistic Marxian doctrine of the "class struggle." And it tends to conceal the whole system of special deprivations visited upon the Negro only because he is not white. We find also that as soon as the Negro scholar, ideologist, or reformer leaves these general ideas about how the Negro should think, he finds himself discussing nothing but Negro rights, the Negro's share, injustices against Negroes, discrimination against Negroes, Negro interests—nothing, indeed, but the old familiar Negro problem, though in some new political relations. He is back again in the "race issue." And there is substantial reason for it.

The reason, of course, is that there is really a common tie and, therefore, a unity in all the special angles of the Negro problem. All these specific problems are only outcroppings of one fundamental complex of human valuations—that of American caste. This fundamental complex derives its emotional charge from the equally common race prejudice, from its manifestations in a general tendency toward discrimination, and from its political potentialities through its very inconsistency with the American Creed.

The Theory of the Vicious Circle

A deeper reason for the unity of the Negro problem will be apparent when we now try to formulate our hypothesis concerning its dynamic causation. The mechanism that operates here is the "principle of cumulation," also commonly called the "vicious circle."[28] This principle has a much wider application in social relations. It is, or should be developed into, a main theoretical tool in studying social change.

Throughout this inquiry, we shall assume a general interdependence between all the factors in the Negro problem. White prejudice and discrimination keep the Negro low in standards of living, health, education, manners and morals. This, in its turn, gives support to white prejudice. White prejudice and Negro standards thus mutually "cause" each other. If things remain about as they are and have been, this means that the two forces happen to balance each other. Such a static "accommodation" is, however, entirely accidental. If either of the factors changes, this will cause a change in the other factor, too, and start a process of interaction where the change in one factor will continuously be supported by the reac-

28 . . . We call the principle the "principle of cumulation" rather than "vicious circle" because it can work in an "upward" desirable direction as well as in a "downward" undesirable direction.

tion of the other factor. The whole system will be moving in the direction of the primary change, but much further. This is what we mean by cumulative causation.

If, for example, we assume that for some reason white prejudice could be decreased and discrimination mitigated, this is likely to cause a rise in Negro standards, which may decrease white prejudice still a little more, which would again allow Negro standards to rise, and so on through mutual interaction. If, instead, discrimination should become intensified, we should see the vicious circle spiraling downward. The original change can as easily be a change of *Negro standards* upward or downward. The effects would, in a similar manner, run back and forth in the interlocking system of interdependent causation. In any case, the initial change would be supported by consecutive waves of back-effects from the reactions of the other factor.

The same principle holds true if we split one of our two variables into component factors. A rise in Negro employment, for instance, will raise family incomes, standards of nutrition, housing, and health, the possibilities of giving the Negro youth more education, and so forth, and all these effects of the initial change, will, in their turn, improve the Negroes' possibilities of getting employment and earning a living. The original push could have been on some other factor than employment, say, for example, an improvement of health or educational facilities for Negroes. Through action and interaction the whole system of the Negro's "status" would have been set in motion in the direction indicated by the first push. Much the same thing holds true of the development of white prejudice. Even assuming no changes in Negro standards, white prejudice can change, for example, as a result of an increased general knowledge about biology, eradicating some of the false beliefs among whites concerning Negro racial inferiority. If this is accomplished, it will in some degree censor the hostile and derogatory valuations which fortify the false beliefs, and education will then be able to fight racial beliefs with more success.

By this we have only wanted to give a hint of an explanatory scheme of dynamic causation which we are going to utilize throughout this inquiry. . . . The interrelations are in reality much more complicated than in our abstract illustrations, and there are all sorts of irregularities in the reaction of various factors. But the complications should not force us to give up our main hypothesis that a cumulative principle is working in social change. It is actually the hypothesis which gives a theoretical meaning to the Negro problem as a special phase of all other social problems in America. Behind the barrier of common discrimination, there is unity and close interrelation between the Negro's political power; his civil rights; his employment opportunities; his standards of housing, nutrition and clothing; his health, manners, and law observance; his ideals and ideologies. The unity is largely the result of cumulative causation binding them all together in a system and tying them to white discrimination. It is useful, therefore, to interpret all the separate factors from a central vantage point—the point of view of the Negro problem.

Another corollary from our hypothesis is practical. In the field of Negro politics any push upward directed on any one of those factors—if our main hypothesis is correct—moves all other factors in the same direction and has, through them, a cumulative effect upon general Negro status. An upward trend of Negro status in general can be effected by any number of measures, rather independent of where the initial push is localized. By the process of cumulation it will be transferred through the whole system.

But, as in the field of economic anti-depression policy, it matters a lot how the measures are proportioned and applied. The directing and proportioning of the measures is the task of social engineering. This engineering should be based on a knowledge of how all the factors are actually interrelated: what effect a primary change upon each factor will have on all other factors. It can be generally stated, however, that it is likely that *a rational policy will never work by changing only one factor*, least of all if attempted suddenly and with great force. In most cases that would either throw the system entirely out of gear or else prove to be a wasteful expenditure of effort which could reach much further by being spread strategically over various factors in the system and over a period of time.

This—and the impracticability of getting political support for a great and sudden change of just one factor—is the rational refutation of so-called panaceas. Panaceas are now generally repudiated in the literature on the Negro problem, though usually without much rational motivation. There still exists, however, another theoretical idea which is similar to the idea of panacea: the idea that there is *one* predominant factor, a "basic factor." Usually the so-called "economic factor" is assumed to be this basic factor. A vague conception of economic determinism has, in fact, come to color most of the modern writings on the Negro problem far outside the Marxist school. Such a view has unwarrantedly acquired the prestige of being a particularly "hard-boiled" scientific approach.

As we look upon the problem of dynamic social causation, this approach is unrealistic and narrow. We do not, of course, deny that the conditions under which Negroes are allowed to earn a living are tremendously important for their welfare. But these conditions are closely interrelated to all other conditions of Negro life. When studying the variegated causes of discrimination in the labor market, it is, indeed, difficult to perceive what precisely is meant by "the economic factor." The Negro's legal and political status and all the causes behind this, considerations by whites of social prestige, and everything else in the Negro problem belong to the causation of discrimination in the labor market, in exactly the same way as the Negro's low economic status is influential in keeping down his health, his educational level, his political power, and his status in other respects. Neither from a theoretical point of view—in seeking to explain the Negro's caste status in American society—nor from a practical point of view—in attempting to assign the strategic points which can most effectively be attacked in order to raise his status—is there any reason, or, indeed, any possibility of singling out "the economic factor" as basic. In an interdependent system of dynamic causation there is no "primary cause" but everything is cause *to* everything else.

If this theoretical approach is bound to do away in the practical sphere with all panaceas, it is, on the other hand, equally bound to encourage the reformer. The principle of cumulation—in so far as it holds true—promises final effects of greater magnitude than the efforts and costs of the reforms themselves. The low status of the Negro is tremendously wasteful all around—the low educational standard causes low earnings and health deficiencies, for example. The cumulatively magnified effect of a push upward on any one of the relevant factors is, in one sense, a demonstration and a measure of the earlier existing waste. In the end, the cost of raising the status of the Negro may not involve any "real costs" at all for society, but instead may result in great "social gains" and actual savings for society. A movement downward will, for the same reason, increase "social waste" out of proportion to the original saving involved in the push downward of one factor or another.

These dynamic concepts of "social waste," "social gain," and "real costs" are mental tools originated in the practical man's workshop. To give them a clearer meaning—which implies expressing also the underlying social value premises—and to measure them in quantitative terms represents from a practical viewpoint a main task of social science. Fulfilling that task in a truly comprehensive way is a stage of dynamic social theory still to be reached but definitely within vision.

A Theory of Democracy

The factors working on the white side in our system of dynamic causation were brought together under the heading "race prejudice." For our present purpose, it is defined as discrimination by whites against Negroes. One viewpoint on race prejudice needs to be presented at this point, chiefly because of its close relation to our hypothesis of cumulative causation.

The chemists talk about "irreversible processes," meaning a trait of a chemical process to go in one direction with ease but, for all practical purposes, to be unchangeable back to its original state (as when a house burns down). When we observe race prejudice as it appears in American daily life, it is difficult to avoid the reflection that it seems so much easier to increase than to decrease race prejudice. One is reminded of the old saying that nineteen fresh apples do not make a single rotten apple fresh, but that one rotten apple rapidly turns the fresh ones rotten. When we come to consider the various causative factors underlying race prejudice—economic competition; urges and fears for social status; and sexual drives, fears, jealousies, and inhibitions—this view will come to be understandable. It is a common observation that the white Northerner who settles in the South will rapidly take on the stronger race prejudice of the new surroundings; while the Southerner going North is likely to keep his race prejudice rather unchanged and perhaps even to communicate it to those he meets. The Northerner in the South will find the whole community intent upon his conforming to local patterns. The Southerner in the North will not meet such concerted action, but will feel, rather, that others are adjusting toward him wherever he goes. If the local hotel in a New England town has accommodated a few Negro guests without much worry one way or the other, the appearance one evening of a single white guest who makes an angry protest against it might permanently change the policy of the hotel.

If we assume that a decrease in race prejudice is desirable—on grounds of the value premise of the American Creed and of the mechanism of cumulative wastage just discussed—such a general tendency, inherent in the psychology of race prejudice, would be likely to force us to a pessimistic outlook. One would expect a constant tendency toward increased race prejudice, and the interlocking causation with the several factors on the Negro side would be expected to reinforce the movement. Aside from all valuations, the question must be raised: Why is race prejudice, in spite of this tendency to continued intensification which we have observed, nevertheless, on the whole not increasing but decreasing?

This question is, in fact, only a special variant of the enigma of philosophers for several thousands of years: the problem of Good and Evil in the world. One is reminded of that cynical but wise old man, Thomas Hobbes, who proved rather conclusively that, while any person's actual possibilities to improve the lot of his fellow creatures amounted to almost nothing, everyone's opportunity to do damage was always immense. The wisest and most virtuous man will hardly leave a print in the sand behind him, meant Hobbes, but an imbecile crank can set fire to a whole town. Why is the world, then, not steadily and rapidly deteriorating, but rather, at least over long periods, progressing? Hobbes raised this question. His answer was, as we know: the State, *Leviathan*. Our own tentative answer to the more specific but still overwhelmingly general question we have raised above will have something in common with that of the post-Elizabethan materialist and hedonist, but it will have its stress placed differently, as we shall subsequently see.

Two principal points will be made by way of a preliminary and hypothetical answer, as they influence greatly our general approach to the Negro problem. The first point is the American Creed, the relation of which to the Negro problem will become apparent as our inquiry proceeds. The Creed of progress, liberty, equality, and humanitarianism is not so uninfluential on everyday life as might sometimes appear.

The second point is the existence in society of huge institutional structures like the church, the school, the university, the foundation, the trade union, the association generally, and, of course, the state.

It is true, as we shall find, that these institutional structures in their operation show an accommodation to local and temporary interests and prejudices—they could not be expected to do otherwise as they are made up of individuals with all their local and temporary characteristics. As institutions they are, however, devoted to certain broad ideals. It is in these institutions that the American Creed has its instruments: it plays upon them as on mighty organs. In adhering to these ideals, the institutions show a pertinacity, matched only by their great flexibility in local and temporary accommodation.

The school, in every community, is likely to be a degree more broad-minded than local opinion. So is the sermon in church. The national labor assembly is prone to decide slightly above the prejudice of the median member. Legislation will, on the whole, be more equitable than the legislators are themselves as private individuals. When the man in the street acts through his orderly collective bodies, he acts more as an American, as a Christian, and as a humanitarian than if he were acting independently. He thus shapes social controls which are going to condition even himself.

Through these huge institutional structures, a constant pressure is brought to bear on race prejudice, counteracting the natural tendency for it to spread and become more intense. The same people are acting in the institutions as when manifesting personal prejudice. But they obey different moral valuations on different planes of life. In their institutions they have invested more than their everyday ideas which parallel their actual behavior. They have placed in them their ideals of how the world rightly ought to be. The ideals thereby gain fortifications of power and influence in society. This is a theory of social self-healing that applies to the type of society we call democracy.

QUESTIONS FOR DISCUSSION AND WRITING

1. What factors of the "American Creed" work toward eliminating racial segregation? How?
2. According to Myrdal, why will the "amalgamation theory" not work for blacks?

3. Alteration of the factors in the "principle of cumulation" is necessary in order to provide for black progress. What factors require the greatest change? What factors have already changed since the publication of Myrdal's book (1942)?
4. Is the Marxian theory of economics and history a valid means of examining black economics? Why?
5. According to Myrdal, sexual fears play a large role in "the white man's rank order of discriminations." Compare this point of view with that of DuBois (p. 98) and Allport (p. 207).

MOST OFTEN REFERRED TO AS THE 1954 "SCHOOL DESEGREGATION DECISION," *Brown v. Board of Education of Topeka* HAD WIDE IMPLICATIONS IN THE AREA OF CIVIL RIGHTS. IT REVERSED THE SUPREME COURT DOCTRINE IN FORCE SINCE THE *Plessy v. Ferguson* DECISION OF 1896, WHICH ENDORSED "SEPARATE BUT EQUAL" FACILITIES FOR THE RACES. IN *Brown v. Board of Education* THE DOCTRINE OF "SEPARATE BUT EQUAL" WAS DECLARED ILLEGAL. THE COURT'S OPINION WAS READ BY CHIEF JUSTICE EARL WARREN.

UNITED STATES

SUPREME COURT

BROWN v. BOARD OF EDUCATION OF TOPEKA

These cases come to us from the States of Kansas, South Carolina, Virginia, and Delaware. They are premised on different facts and different local conditions, but a common legal question justifies their consideration together in this consolidated opinion.

In each of the cases, minors of the Negro race, through their legal representatives, seek the aid of the courts in obtaining admission to the public schools of their community on a nonsegregated basis. In each instance, they have been denied admission to schools attended by white children under laws requiring or permitting segregation according to race. This segregation was alleged to deprive the plaintiffs of the equal protection of the laws under the Fourteenth Amendment. In each of the cases other than the Delaware case, a

BROWN V. BOARD OF EDUCATION OF TOPEKA 347 U.S. 483 (1954).

three-judge federal district court denied relief to the plaintiffs on the so-called "separate but equal" doctrine announced by this Court in Plessy v. Ferguson, 163 U. S. 537. Under that doctrine, equality of treatment is accorded when the races are provided substantially equal facilities, even though these facilities be separate. In the Delaware case, the Supreme Court of Delaware adhered to that doctrine, but ordered that the plaintiffs be admitted to the white schools because of their superiority to the Negro schools.

The plaintiffs contend that segregated public schools are not "equal" and cannot be made "equal," and that hence they are deprived of the equal protection of the laws. Because of the obvious importance of the question presented, the Court took jurisdiction. Argument was heard in the 1952 Term, and reargument was heard this Term on certain questions propounded by the Court.

Reargument was largely devoted to the circumstances surrounding the adoption of the Fourteenth Amendment in 1868. It covered exhaustively consideration of the Amendment in Congress, ratification by the states, then existing practices in racial segregation, and the views of proponents and opponents of the Amendment. This discussion and our own investigation convince us that, although these sources cast some light, it is not enough to resolve the problem with which we are faced. At best, they are inconclusive. The most avid proponents of the post-War Amendments undoubtedly intended them to remove all legal distinctions among "all persons born or naturalized in the United States." Their opponents, just as certainly, were antagonistic to both the letter and the spirit of the Amendments and wished them to have the most limited effect. What others in Congress and the state legislatures had in mind cannot be determined with any degree of certainty.

An additional reason for the inconclusive nature of the Amendment's history, with respect to segregated schools, is the status of public education at that time. In the South, the movement toward free common schools, supported by general taxation, had not yet taken hold. Education of white children was largely in the hands of private groups. Education of Negroes was almost nonexistent, and practically all of the race were illiterate. In fact, any education of Negroes was forbidden by law in some states. Today, in contrast, many Negroes have achieved outstanding success in the arts and sciences as well as in the business and professional world. It is true that public education had already advanced further in the North, but the effect of the Amendment on Northern States was generally ignored in the congressional debates. Even in the North, the conditions of public education did not approximate those existing today. The curriculum was usually rudimentary; ungraded schools were common in rural areas; the school term was but three months a year in many states; and compulsory school attendance was virtually unknown. As a consequence, it is not surprising that there should be so little in the history of the Fourteenth Amendment relating to its intended effect on public education.

In the first cases in this Court construing the Fourteenth Amendment, decided shortly after its adoption, the Court interpreted it as proscribing all state-imposed discriminations against the Negro race. The doctrine of "separate but equal" did not make its appearance in this Court until 1896 in the case of Plessy v. Ferguson, supra, involving not education but transportation. American courts have since labored with the doctrine for over half a century. In this Court, there have been six cases involving the "separate but equal" doctrine in the field of public education. In Cumming v. Board of Education of Richmond County, 175 U. S. 528, and Gong Lum v. Rice, 275 U. S. 78, the validity of the doctrine itself was not challenged. In more recent cases, all on the graduate school level, inequality was found in that specific benefits enjoyed by white students were denied to Negro students of the same educational qualifications. State of Missouri ex rel. Gaines v. Canada, 305 U. S. 337; Sipuel v. Board of Regents of University of Oklahoma, 332 U. S. 631; Sweatt v. Painter, 339 U. S. 629; McLaurin v. Oklahoma State Regents, 339 U. S. 637. In none of these cases was it necessary to reexamine the doctrine to grant relief to the Negro plaintiff. And in Sweatt v. Painter, supra, the Court expressly reserved decision on the question whether Plessy v. Ferguson should be held inapplicable to public education.

In the instant cases, that question is directly presented. Here, unlike Sweatt v. Painter, there are findings below that the Negro and white schools involved have been equalized, or are being equalized, with respect to buildings, curricula, qualifications and salaries of teachers, and other "tangible" factors. Our decision, therefore, cannot turn on merely a comparison of these tangible factors in the Negro and white schools involved in each of the cases. We must look instead to the effect of segregation itself on public education.

In approaching this problem, we cannot turn the clock back to 1868 when the Amendment was adopted, or even to 1896 when Plessy v. Ferguson was written. We must consider public education in the light of its full development and its present place in American life throughout the Nation. Only in this way can it be determined if segregation in public schools deprives these plaintiffs of the equal protection of the laws.

Today, education is perhaps the most important function of state and local governments. Compulsory school attendance laws and the great expenditures for education both demonstrate our recognition of the importance of education to our democratic society. It is required in the performance of our most basic public responsibilities, even service in the armed forces. It is the very foundation of good citizenship. Today it is a principal instrument in awakening the child to cultural values, in preparing him for later professional training, and in helping him to adjust normally to his environment. In these days, it is doubtful that any child may reasonably be expected to succeed in life if he is denied the opportunity of an education. Such an opportunity, where the state has undertaken to provide it, is a right which must be made available to all on equal terms.

We come then to the question presented: Does segregation of children in public schools solely on the basis of race, even though the physical facilities and other "tangible" factors may be equal, deprive the children of the minority group of equal educational opportunities? We believe that it does.

In Sweatt v. Painter, supra (339 U. S. 629, 70 S.Ct. 850), in finding that a segregated law school for Negroes could not provide them equal educational opportunities, this Court relied in large part on "those qualities which are incapable of objective measurement but which make for greatness in a law school." In McLaurin v. Oklahoma State Regents, supra (339 U. S. 637, 70 S.Ct. 853), the Court, in requiring that a Negro admitted to a white graduate school be treated like all other students, again resorted to intangible considerations: ". . . his ability to study, to engage in discussions and exchange views with other students, and, in general, to learn his profession." Such considerations apply with added force to children in grade and high schools. To separate them from others of similar age and qualifications solely because of their race generates a feeling of inferiority as to their status in the community that may affect their hearts and minds in a way unlikely ever to be undone. The effect of this separation on their educational opportunities was well stated by a finding in the Kansas case by a court which nevertheless felt compelled to rule against the Negro plaintiffs:

> Segregation of white and colored children in public schools has a detrimental effect upon the colored children. The impact is greater when it has the sanction of the law; for the policy of separating the races is usually interpreted as denoting the inferiority of the Negro group. A sense of inferiority affects the motivation of a child to learn. Segregation with the sanction of the law, therefore, has a tendency to retard the educational and mental development of Negro children and to deprive them of some of the benefits they would receive in a racially integrated school system.

Whatever may have been the extent of psychological knowledge at the time of Plessy v. Ferguson, this finding is amply supported by modern authority. Any language in Plessy v. Ferguson contrary to this finding is rejected.

We conclude that in the field of public education the doctrine of "separate but equal" has no place. Separate educational facilities are inherently unequal. Therefore, we hold that the plaintiffs and others similarly situated for whom the actions have been brought are, by reason of the segregation complained of, deprived of the equal protection of the laws guaranteed by the Fourteenth Amendment. This disposition makes unnecessary any discussion whether such segregation also violates the Due Process Clause of the Fourteenth Amendment.

Because these are class actions, because of the wide applicability of this decision, and because of the great variety of local conditions, the formulation of decrees in these cases presents problems of considerable complexity. On reargument, the consideration of appropriate relief was necessarily subordinated to the primary question—the constitutionality of segregation in public education. We have now announced that such segregation is a denial of the equal protection of the laws. In order that we may have the full assistance of the parties in formulating decrees, the cases will be restored to the docket, and the parties are requested to present further argument. . . . The Attorney General of the United States is again invited to participate. The Attorneys General of the states requiring or permitting segregation in public education will also be permitted to appear as *amici curiae* upon request to do so by September 15, 1954, and submission of briefs by October 1, 1954.

It is so ordered.

QUESTIONS FOR DISCUSSION AND WRITING

1. What is the Court's principal argument in reversing its previous decisions on segregation?
2. The Court's definition of "equal" differs from earlier definitions relating to facilities. What kind of definition did the Court follow in its 1954 interpretation?
3. In what ways is "equal protection under law" related to "equal educational opportunities"?
4. An opportunity for an education is a right that must "be made available to all on equal terms." In the Court's view "equal terms" applies not only to the right to school entrance but to matters of curriculum as well. What changes in curriculum are needed in order to meet the Court's definition of "equal terms"?
5. According to the Supreme Court, education is of major value to the nation. Nearly all the writers in this anthology assign education a major role. How is the Court's reasoning similar to DuBois' (p. 83) and King's (p. 341)? In what major ways does it differ from Barnett's (p. 217)?

E. FRANKLIN FRAZIER'S *Black Bourgeoisie: The Rise of a New Middle Class* WAS PUBLISHED IN 1957, WHILE FRAZIER WAS PROFESSOR OF SOCIOLOGY AT HOWARD UNIVERSITY. HIS OTHER STUDIES OF AMERICAN BLACKS INCLUDE *The Negro Family in the United States* AND *The Negro in the United States.* DR. FRAZIER DIED IN 1962, AT THE AGE OF SIXTY-EIGHT.

E. FRANKLIN FRAZIER

BEHIND THE MASKS

Since the black bourgeoisie live largely in a world of make-believe, the masks which they wear to play their sorry roles conceal the feelings of inferiority and of insecurity and the frustrations that haunt their inner lives. Despite their attempt to escape from real identification with the masses of Negroes, they can not escape the mark of oppression any more than their less favored kinsmen. In attempting to escape identification with the black masses, they have developed a self-hatred that reveals itself in their depreciation of the physical and social characteristics of Negroes. Likewise, their feelings of inferiority and insecurity are revealed in their pathological struggle for status within the isolated Negro world and craving for recognition in the white world. Their escape into a world of make-believe with its sham "society" leaves them with a feeling of emptiness and futility which causes them to constantly seek an escape in new delusions.

The Mark of Oppression

There is an attempt on the part of the parents in middle-class families to shield their children against racial discrimination and the contempt of whites for colored people. Sometimes the parents go to fantastic extremes, such as prohibiting the use of the words "Negro" or "colored" in the presence of their children.[1] They sometimes try to prevent their children from knowing that they can not enter restaurants or other public places because they are Negroes, or even that the schools they attend are segregated schools for Negroes. Despite such efforts to insulate their children against a hostile white world, the children of the black bourgeoisie can not escape the mark of oppression. This is strikingly revealed in the statement of a seventeen-year-old middle-class Negro youth. When asked if he felt inferior in the presence of white people, he gave the following answer—which was somewhat unusual for its frankness but typical of the attitude of the black bourgeoisie:

> Off-hand, I'd say no, but actually knowing all these things that are thrown up to you about white people being superior—that they look more or less down upon all Negroes—that we have to look to them for everything we get—that they'd rather think of us as mice than men—I don't believe I or any other Negro can help but feel inferior. My father says that it isn't so—that we feel only inferior to those whom we feel are superior. But I don't believe we can feel otherwise. Around white people until I know them a while I feel definitely out of place. Once I played a ping-pong match with a white boy whose play I know wasn't as good as mine, and boys he managed to beat I beat with ease, but I just couldn't get it out of my mind that I was playing a white boy. Sort of an Indian sign on me, you know.[2]

The statement of this youth reveals how deep-seated is the feeling of inferiority, from which even the most favored elements

[1] E. Franklin Frazier, *Negro Youth at the Crossways* (Washington, D.C.: American Council on Education, 1940), p. 62.

[2] *Ibid.*, p. 67.

among Negroes can not escape. However much some middle-class Negroes may seek to soothe their feeling of inferiority in an attitude which they often express in the adage, "it is better to reign in hell than serve in heaven," they are still conscious of their inferior status in American society. They may say, as did a bewildered middle-class youth, that they are proud of being a Negro or proud of being a member of the upper stratum in the Negro community and feel sorry for the Negro masses "stuck in the mud," but they often confess, as did this youth:

> However, knowing that there are difficulties that confront us all as Negroes, if I could be born again and had my choice I'd really want to be a white boy—I mean white or my same color, providing I could occupy the same racial and economic level I now enjoy. I am glad I am this color—I'm frequently taken for a foreigner. I wouldn't care to be lighter or darker and be a Negro. I am the darkest one in the family due to my constant outdoor activities. I realize of course that there are places where I can't go despite my family or money just because I happen to be a Negro. With my present education, family background, and so forth, if I was only white I could go places in life. A white face holds supreme over a black one despite its economic and social status. Frankly, it leaves me bewildered.[3]

Not all middle-class Negroes consciously desire, as this youth, to be white in order to escape from their feelings of inferiority. In fact, the majority of middle-class Negroes would deny having the desire to be white, since this would be an admission of their feeling of inferiority. Within an intimate circle of friends some middle-class Negroes may admit that they desire to be white, but publicly they would deny any such wish. The black bourgeoisie constantly boast of their pride in their identification as Negroes. But when one studies the attitude of this class in regard to the physical traits or the social characteristics of Negroes, it becomes clear that the black bourgeoisie do not really wish to be identified with Negroes.

Insecurities and Frustrations

Since the black bourgeoisie can not escape identification with Negroes, they experience certain feelings of insecurity because of their

[3] *Ibid.*, p. 66.

feeling of inferiority. Their feeling of inferiority is revealed in their fear of competition with whites. There is first a fear of competition with whites for jobs. Notwithstanding the fact that middle-class Negroes are the most vociferous in demanding the right to compete on equal terms with whites, many of them still fear such competition. They prefer the security afforded by their monopoly of certain occupations within the segregated Negro community. For example, middle-class Negroes demand that the two Negro medical schools be reserved for Negro students and that a quota be set for white students, though Negro students are admitted to "white" medical schools. Since the Supreme Court of the United States has ruled against segregated public schools, many Negro teachers, even those who are well-prepared, fear that they can not compete with whites for teaching positions. Although this fear stems principally from a feeling of inferiority which is experienced generally by Negroes, it has other causes.

The majority of the black bourgeoisie fear competition with whites partly because such competition would mean that whites were taking them seriously, and consequently they would have to assume a more serious and responsible attitude towards their work. Middle-class Negroes, who are notorious for their inefficiency in the management of various Negro institutions, excuse their inefficiency on the grounds that Negroes are a "young race" and, therefore, will require time to attain the efficiency of the white man. The writer has heard a Negro college president, who has constantly demanded that Negroes have equality in American life, declare before white people in extenuation of the shortcomings of his own administration, that Negroes were a "child race" and that they had "to crawl before they could walk." Such declarations, while flattering to the whites, are revealing in that they manifest the black bourgeoisie's contempt for the Negro masses, while excusing its own deficiencies by attributing them to the latter. Yet it is clear that the black worker who must gain a living in a white man's mill or factory and in competition with white workers can not offer any such excuse for his inefficiency.

The fear of competition with whites is probably responsible for the black bourgeoisie's fear of competence and first-rate performance within its own ranks. When a Negro is competent and insists upon first-rate work it appears to this class that he is trying to be a white man, or that he is insisting that Negroes measure up to white standards. This is especially true where the approval of whites is taken as a mark of competence and first-rate performance. In such cases the black bourgeoisie reveal their ambivalent attitudes toward the white world. They slavishly accept the estimate which almost any white man places upon a Negro or his work, but at the same time they fear and reject white standards. For example, when a group of Negro doctors were being shown the modern equipment and techniques of a white clinic, one of them remarked to a Negro professor in a medical school, "This is the white man's medicine. I never bother with it and still I make $30,000 a year." Negroes who adopt the standards of the white world create among the black bourgeoisie a feeling of insecurity and often become the object of both the envy and hatred of this class.

Among the women of the black bourgeoisie there is an intense fear of the competition of white women for Negro men. They often attempt to rationalize their fear by saying that the Negro man always occupies an inferior position in relation to the white woman or that he marries much below his "social" status. They come nearer to the source of their fear when they confess that there are not many eligible Negro men and that these few should marry Negro women. That such rationalizations conceal deep-seated feelings of insecurity is revealed by the fact that generally they have no objection to the marriage of white men to Negro women, especially if the white man is reputed to be wealthy. In fact, they take pride in the fact and attribute these marriages to the "peculiar" charms of Negro women. In fact, the middle-class Negro woman's fear of the competition of white women is based often upon the fact that she senses her own inadequacies and shortcomings. Her position in Negro "society" and in the larger Negro community is often due to some adventitious factor, such as a light complexion or a meager education, which has pushed her to the top of the social pyramid. The middle-class white woman not only has a white skin and straight hair, but she is generally more sophisticated and interesting because she has read more widely and has a larger view of the world. The middle-class Negro woman may make fun of the "plainness" of her white competitor and the latter's lack of "wealth" and interest in "society"; nevertheless she still feels insecure when white women appear as even potential competitors.

Both men and women among the black bourgeoisie have a feeling of insecurity because of their constant fear of the loss of status. Since they have no status in the larger American society, the intense struggle for status among middle-class Negroes is, as we have seen, an attempt to compensate for the contempt and low esteem of the whites. Great value is, therefore, placed upon all kinds of status symbols. Academic degrees, both real and honorary, are sought in order to secure status. Usually the symbols are of a material nature implying wealth and conspicuous consumption. Sometimes Negro doctors do not attend what are supposedly scientific meetings because they do not have a Cadillac or some other expensive automobile. School teachers wear mink coats and maintain homes beyond their income for fear that they may lose status. The extravagance in "social" life generally is due to an effort not to lose status. But in attempting to overcome their fear of loss of status they are often beset by new feelings of insecurity. In spite of their pretended wealth, they are aware that their incomes are insignificant and that they must struggle to maintain their mortgaged homes and the show of "wealth" in lavish "social" affairs. Moreover, they are beset by a feeling of insecurity because of their struggles to maintain a show of wealth through illegal means. From time to time "wealthy" Negro doctors are arrested for selling narcotics and performing abortions. The life of many a "wealthy" Negro doctor is shortened by the struggle to provide diamonds, minks, and an expensive home for his wife.

There is much frustration among the black bourgeoisie despite their privileged position within the segregated Negro world. Their "wealth" and "social" position can not erase the fact that they are generally segregated and rejected by the white world. Their incomes and occupations may enable them to escape the cruder manifestations of racial prejudice, but they can not insulate themselves against the more subtle forms of racial discrimination. These discriminations cause frustrations in Negro men because they are not allowed to play the "masculine role" as defined by American culture. They can not assert themselves or exercise power as white men do. When they protest against racial discrimination there is always the threat that they will be punished by the white world. In spite of the movement toward the wider integration of the Negro into the general stream of American life, middle-class Negroes are still threatened with the loss of positions and earning power if they insist upon their rights.[4] After the Supreme Court of the United States ruled that segregation in public education was illegal, Negro teachers in some parts of the

[4] See, for example, the article "YMCA Secretary in Virginia Fired for Equality Fight," *Washington Afro-American* (August, 1954), p. 20.

South were dismissed because they would not sign statements supporting racial segregation in education.

As one of the results of not being able to play the "masculine role," middle-class Negro males have tended to cultivate their "personalities"[5] which enable them to exercise considerable influence among whites and achieve distinction in the Negro world. Among Negroes they have been noted for their glamour.[6] In this respect they resemble women who use their "personalities" to compensate for their inferior status in relation to men. This fact would seem to support the observation of an American sociologist that the Negro was "the lady among the races," if he had restricted his observation to middle-class males among American Negroes.[7]

In the South the middle-class Negro male is not only prevented from playing a masculine role, but generally he must let Negro women assume leadership in any show of militancy. This reacts upon his status in the home where the tradition of female dominance, which is widely established among Negroes, has tended to assign a subordinate role to the male. In fact, in middle-class families, especially if the husband has risen in social status through his own efforts and married a member of an "old" family or a "society" woman, the husband is likely to play a pitiful role. The greatest compliment that can be paid such a husband is that he "worships his wife," which means that he is her slave and supports all her extravagances and vanities. But, of course, many husbands in such positions escape from their frustrations by having extra-marital sex relations. Yet the conservative and conventional middle-class husband presents a pathetic picture. He often sits at home alone, impotent physically and socially, and complains that his wife has gone crazy about poker and "society" and constantly demands money for gambling and expenditures which he can not afford. Sometimes he enjoys the sympathy of a son or daughter who has not become a "socialite." Such children often say that they had a happy family life until "mamma took to poker."

Preoccupation with poker on the part of the middle-class woman

[5] One can not determine to what extent homosexuality among Negro males is due to the fact that they can not play a "masculine role."

[6] See *Ebony* (July, 1949), where it is claimed that a poll on the most exciting Negro men in the United States reveals that the heyday of the "glamour boy" is gone and achievement rather than a handsome face and husky physique is the chief factor in making Negro men exciting to women.

[7] See Robert E. Park and Ernest W. Burgess, *Introduction to the Science of Sociology* (Chicago: University of Chicago Press, 1924), p. 139.

is often an attempt to escape from a frustrated life. Her frustration may be bound up with her unsatisfactory sexual life. She may be married to a "glamorous" male who neglects her for other women. For among the black bourgeoisie, the glamour of the male is often associated with his sexual activities. The frustration of many Negro women has a sexual origin.[8] Even those who have sought an escape from frustration in sexual promiscuity may, because of satiety or deep psychological reasons, become obsessed with poker in order to escape from their frustrations. One "society" woman, in justification of her obsession with poker, remarked that it had taken the place of her former preoccupation with sex. Another said that to win at poker was similar to a sexual orgasm.

The frustration of the majority of the women among the black bourgeoisie is probably due to the idle or ineffectual lives which they lead. Those who do not work devote their time to the frivolities of Negro "society." When they devote their time to "charity" or worthwhile causes, it is generally a form of play or striving for "social" recognition. They are constantly forming clubs which ostensibly have a serious purpose, but in reality are formed in order to consolidate their position in "society" or to provide additional occasions for playing poker. The idle, overfed women among the black bourgeoisie are generally, to use their language, "dripping with diamonds." They are forever dieting and reducing only to put on more weight (which is usually the result of the food that they consume at their club meetings). Even the women among the black bourgeoisie who work exhibit the same frustrations. Generally, they have no real interest in their work and only engage in it in order to be able to provide the conspicuous consumption demanded by "society." As we have indicated, the women as well as the men among the black bourgeoisie read very little and have no interest in music, art or the theater. They are constantly restless and do not know how to relax. They are generally dull people and only become animated when "social" matters are discussed, especially poker games. They are afraid to be alone and constantly seek to be surrounded by their friends, who enable them to escape from their boredom.

The frustrated lives of the black bourgeoisie are reflected in the attitudes of parents towards their children. Middle-class Negro families as a whole have few children, while among the families that con-

[8] See Kardiner and Ovesey, *The Mark of Oppression* (New York: Norton, 1951) pp. 312 ff., concerning this point.

stitute Negro "society" there are many childless couples.[9] One finds today, as an American observed over forty years ago, that "where the children are few, they are usually spoiled" in middle-class Negro families.[10] There is often not only a deep devotion to their one or two children, but a subservience to them. It is not uncommon for the only son to be called and treated as the "boss" in the family. Parents cater to the transient wishes of their children and often rationalize their behavior towards them on the grounds that children should not be "inhibited." They spend large sums of money on their children for toys and especially for clothes. They provide their children with automobiles when they go to college. All of this is done in order that the children may maintain the status of the parents and be eligible to enter the "social" set in Negro colleges. When they send their children to northern "white" colleges they often spend more time in preparing them for what they imagine will be their "social" life than in preparing them for the academic requirements of these institutions.

In their fierce devotion to their children, which generally results in spoiling them, middle-class Negro parents are seemingly striving at times to establish a human relationship that will compensate for their own frustrations in the realm of human relationships. Devotion to their children often becomes the one human tie that is sincere and free from the competition and artificiality of the make-believe world in which they live. Sometimes they may project upon their children their own frustrated professional ambitions. But usually, even when they send their children to northern "white" universities as a part of their "social" striving within the Negro community, they seem to hope that their children will have an acceptance in the white world which has been denied them.

Self-Hatred and Guilt Feelings

One of the chief frustrations of the middle-class Negro is that he can not escape identification with the Negro race and consequently is sub-

[9] See Frazier, *The Negro Family in the United States*, pp. 440–43.

[10] Robert E. Parks, "Negro Home Life and Standards of Living," in *The Negro's Progress in Fifty Years* (Philadelphia: American Academy of Political and Social Science, 1913), p. 163.

ject to the contempt of whites.[11] Despite his "wealth" in which he has placed so much faith as a solvent of racial discrimination, he is still subject to daily insults and is excluded from participation in white American society. Middle-class Negroes do not express their resentment against discrimination and insults in violent outbreaks, as lower-class Negroes often do. They constantly repress their hostility towards whites and seek to soothe their hurt self-esteem in all kinds of rationalizations. They may boast of their wealth and culture as compared with the condition of the poor whites. Most often they will resort to any kind of subterfuge in order to avoid contact with whites. For example, in the South they often pay their bills by mail rather than risk unpleasant contacts with representatives of white firms.[12] The daily repression of resentment and the constant resort to means of avoiding contacts with whites do not relieve them of their hostility toward whites. Even middle-class Negroes who gain a reputation for exhibiting "objectivity" and a "statesmanlike" attitude on racial discrimination harbor deep-seated hostilities toward whites. A Negro college president who has been considered such an inter-racial "statesman" once confessed to the writer that some day he was going to "break loose" and tell white people what he really thought. However, it is unlikely that a middle-class Negro of his standing will ever "break loose." Middle-class Negroes generally express their aggressions against whites by other means, such as deceiving whites and utilizing them for their own advantage.

[11] A middle-class mulatto woman, a former school teacher, who was fearful of the impact of this book on European readers and southern detractors of "The Race," concluded her review of the original French edition with these words:

> Isn't it about time our sociologists and specialists on the "race problem" in America, began to discuss and consider middle class Negroes as middle class Americans, or better, *all* U.S. Negroes as *Americans* with three hundred unbroken years of American tradition, way of life, cultural and spiritual contacts behind them—influences which have moulded them as they have moulded all others who are considered, even when not treated completely so, as members of the American community? Isn't it time to stop thinking of and talking about Negroes as a separate and distinct entity in the general scheme of things? And above all, isn't it time to realize that the melting pot has melted truly and fused together all the myriad (albeit conflicting) racial, cultural, educational, spiritual and social elements which have combined in such peculiar fashion to produce the American Negro of our time? (*Journal of Negro Education*, Vol. XXV, p. 141.)

[12] See Charles S. Johnson, *Patterns of Negro Segregation* (New York: Harper, 1943), Chapters XII, XIII, and XIV, which describe the ways in which Negroes in various classes deal with racial discrimination.

Because middle-class Negroes are unable to indulge in aggressions against whites as such, they will sometimes make other minority groups the object of their hostilities. For example, they may show hostility against Italians, who are also subject to discrimination. But more often middle-class Negroes, especially those who are engaged in a mad scramble to accumulate money, will direct their hostilities against Jews. They are constantly expressing their anti-Semitism within Negro circles, while pretending publicly to be free from prejudice. They blame the Jew for the poverty of Negroes and for their own failures and inefficiencies in their business undertakings. In expressing their hostility towards Jews, they are attempting at the same time to identify with the white American majority.

The repressed hostilities of middle-class Negroes to whites are not only directed towards other minority groups but inward toward themselves. This results in self-hatred, which may appear from their behavior to be directed towards the Negro masses but which in reality is directed against themselves.[13] While pretending to be proud of being a Negro, they ridicule Negroid physical characteristics and seek to modify or efface them as much as possible. Within their own groups they constantly proclaim that "niggers" make them sick. The very use of the term "nigger," which they claim to resent, indicates that they want to disassociate themselves from the Negro masses. They talk condescendingly of Africans and of African culture, often even objecting to African sculpture in their homes. They are insulted if they are identified with Africans. They refuse to join organizations that are interested in Africa. If they are of mixed ancestry, they may boast of the fact that they have Indian ancestry. When making compliments concerning the beauty of Negroes of mixed ancestry, they generally say, for example, "She is beautiful; she looks like an Indian." On the other hand, if a black woman has European features, they will remark condescendingly, "Although she is black, you must admit that she is good looking." Some middle-class Negroes of mixed ancestry like to wear Hindu costumes—while they laugh at the idea of wearing an African costume. When middle-class Negroes travel, they studiously avoid association with other Negroes, especially if they themselves have received the slightest recognition by whites. Even when they can not "pass" for white they fear that they will lose this recognition if they are identified as Negroes. Therefore, nothing pleases them

[13] See Kardiner and Ovesey, *op. cit.*, pp. 190, 282, 297.

more than to be mistaken for a Puerto Rican, Philippino, Egyptian or Arab or any ethnic group other than Negro.

The self-hatred of middle-class Negroes is often revealed in the keen competition which exists among them for status and recognition. This keen competition is the result of the frustrations which they experience in attempting to obtain acceptance and recognition by whites. Middle-class Negroes are constantly criticizing and belittling Negroes who achieve some recognition or who acquire a status above them. They prefer to submit to the authority of whites than to be subordinate to other Negroes. For example, Negro scholars generally refuse to seek the advice and criticism of competent Negro scholars and prefer to turn to white scholars for such co-operation. In fact, it is difficult for middle-class Negroes to co-operate in any field of endeavor. This failure in social relations is, as indicated in an important study, because "in every Negro he encounters his own self-contempt."[14] It is as if he said, "You are only a Negro like myself; so why should you be in a position above me?"

This self-hatred often results in guilt feelings on the part of the Negro who succeeds in elevating himself above his fellows.[15] He feels unconsciously that in rising above other Negroes he is committing an act of aggression which will result in hatred and revenge on their part. The act of aggression may be imagined, but very often it is real. This is the case when middle-class Negroes oppose the economic and social welfare of Negroes because of their own interests. In some American cities, it has been the black bourgeoisie and not the whites who have opposed the building of low-cost public housing for Negro workers. In one city two wealthy Negro doctors, who have successfully opposed public housing projects for Negro workers, own some of the worst slums in the United States. While their wives, who wear mink coats, "drip with diamonds" and are written up in the "society" columns of Negro newspapers, ride in Cadillacs, their Negro tenants sleep on the dirt floors of hovels unfit for human habitation. The guilt feelings of the middle-class Negro are not always unconscious. For example, take the case of the Negro leader who proclaimed over the radio in a national broadcast that the Negro did not want social equity. He was conscious of his guilt feelings and his self-hatred in playing such a role, for he sent word privately to the writer that he

[14] *Ibid.*, p. 177.

[15] *Ibid.*, p. 203.

never hated so much to do anything in his life, but that it was necessary because of his position as head of a state college which was under white supervision. The self-hatred of the middle-class Negro arises, then, not only from the fact that he does not want to be a Negro but also because of his sorry role in American society.

Escape into Delusions

The black bourgeoisie, as we have seen, has created a world of make-believe to shield itself from the harsh economic and social realities of American life. This world of make-believe is created out of the myth of Negro business, the reports of the Negro press on the achievements and wealth of Negroes, the recognition accorded them by whites, and the fabulous life of Negro "society." Some of the middle-class Negro intellectuals are not deceived by the world of make-believe. They will have nothing to do with Negro "society" and refuse to waste their time in frivolities. They take their work seriously and live in relative obscurity so far as the Negro world is concerned. Others seek an escape from their frustrations by developing, for example, a serious interest in Negro music—which the respectable black bourgeoisie often pretend to despise. In this way these intellectuals achieve some identification with the Negro masses and with the traditions of Negro life. But many more middle-class Negroes, who are satisfied to live in the world of make-believe but must find a solution to the real economic and social problems which they face, seek an escape in delusions.

They seek an escape in delusions involving wealth. This is facilitated by the fact that they have had little experience with the real meaning of wealth and that they lack a tradition of saving and accumulation. Wealth to them means spending money without any reference to its source. Hence, their behavior generally reflects the worst qualities of the gentleman and peasant from whom their only vital traditions spring. Therefore, their small accumulations of capital and the income which they receive from professional services within the Negro community make them appear wealthy in comparison with the low economic status of the majority of Negroes. The delusion of wealth is supported by the myth of Negro business. Moreover, the attraction of the delusion of wealth is enhanced by the belief that wealth will gain them acceptance in American life. In seeking an escape in the delusion of wealth, middle-class Negroes make a fetish of material things or physical possessions. They are constantly buying things—houses, automobiles, furniture and all sorts of gadgets, not to mention clothes. Many of the furnishings and gadgets which they acquire are never used; nevertheless they continue to accumulate things. The homes of many middle-class Negroes have the appearance of museums for the exhibition of American manufactures and spurious art objects. The objects which they are constantly buying are always on display. Negro school teachers who devote their lives to "society" like to display twenty to thirty pairs of shoes, the majority of which they never wear. Negro professional men proudly speak of the two automobiles which they have acquired when they need only one. The acquisition of objects which are not used or needed seems to be an attempt to fill some void in their lives.

The delusion of power also appears to provide an escape for middle-class Negroes from the world of reality which pierces through the world of make-believe of the black bourgeoisie. The positions of power which they occupy in the Negro world often enable them to act autocratically towards other Negroes, especially when they have the support of the white community. In such cases the delusion of power may provide an escape from their frustrations. It is generally, however, when middle-class Negroes hold positions enabling them to participate in the white community that they seek in the delusion of power an escape from their frustrations. Although their position may be only a "token" of the integration of the Negro into American life, they will speak and act as if they were a part of the power structure of American society. Negro advisers who are called into counsel by whites to give advice about Negroes are especially likely to find an escape from their feelings of inferiority in the delusion of power. Negro social workers, who are dependent upon white philanthropy, have often gained the reputation, with the support of the Negro press, of being powerful persons in American communities.

However, the majority of the black bourgeoisie who seek an escape from their frustrations in delusions seemingly have not been able to find it in the delusion of wealth or power. They have found it in magic or chance, and in sex and alcohol. Excessive drinking and sex seem to provide a means for narcotizing the middle-class Negro against a frustrating existence. A "social" function is hardly ever considered a success unless a goodly number of the participants "pass out." But gambling, especially poker, which has become an obsession among many middle-class Negroes, offers the chief escape into delusion. Among the black bourgeoisie it is not simply a device for winning money. It appears to be a magical device for enhancing their self-esteem through overcoming fate.[16] Although it often involves a waste of money which many middle-class Negroes can not afford, it has an irresistible attraction which they often confess they can not overcome.

Despite the tinsel, glitter and gaiety of the world of make-believe in which middle-class Negroes take refuge, they are still beset by feelings of insecurity, frustration and guilt. As a consequence, the free and easy life which they appear to lead is a mask for their unhappy existence.

QUESTIONS FOR DISCUSSION AND WRITING

1. Frazier suggests that middle-class blacks do not really want to be black at all. What kinds of escape are open to them? What causes their feelings of "self-hatred"?
2. Psychological factors weigh heavily in Frazier's discussion of "black capitalism." Why are these factors generally overlooked by the white community? Why are they so important to the black community?
3. What values does the black bourgeoisie share with white middle-class citizens? In what ways do their values differ?
4. According to Frazier, frustration haunts the inner lives of black middle-class citizens. What are the causes of this frustration? What do they reveal about the nature of the black middle class?
5. The role of the Negro male is the topic of many essays in this book. Compare Frazier's discussion of the problems of being a black male with that presented by Ellison (p. 113) and by Myrdal (p. 141). What assumptions do these writers have in common? What solutions do they offer? Is the frustration of black manhood unique to the middle-class black?

[16] *Ibid.*, pp. 313 ff.

GORDON W. ALLPORT WAS PROFESSOR OF PSYCHOLOGY AT HARVARD UNIVERSITY AND SERVED AS THE EDITOR OF THE *Journal of Abnormal and Social Psychology*. DR. ALLPORT DIED IN 1967. HE WAS THE AUTHOR OF SEVERAL WORKS, INCLUDING *The Nature of Prejudice* (1954), FROM WHICH THE FOLLOWING SELECTION IS TAKEN.

GORDON W. ALLPORT

ANXIETY, SEX, GUILT

> We are now in a position to understand the anti-Semite. He is a man who is afraid. Not of the Jews, to be sure, but of himself, of his own consciousness, of his liberty, of his instincts, of his responsibilities, of solitariness, of change, of society, and of the world—of everything except the Jews.
>
> *Jean-Paul Sartre*

What we have to say about the relation of fear, sexuality, and guilt to prejudice is in many respects similar to our analysis of the psychodynamics of aggression.

Fear and Anxiety

Rational and adaptive fear entails the accurate perception of the source of danger. An illness, an approaching fire or flood, a highwayman are among the conditions that make for realistic fear. When we perceive the source of the threat accurately, we ordinarily strike back at it or withdraw to safety.

Sometimes the source of the fear is correctly perceived, but the person can do nothing to control it. A workman fearful of losing his job or citizens living in a vague apprehension of atomic warfare are swayed by fear, but they are powerless. Under such circumstances, the fear becomes chronic—and we speak of *anxiety.*

Chronic anxiety puts us on the alert and predisposes us to see all sorts of stimuli as menacing. A man who lives in constant dread of losing his job feels surrounded by danger. He is sensitized to perceive the Negro or the foreigner as trying to take his job away from him. Here is a displacement of a realistic fear.

Sometimes the source of the fear is not known, or has been forgotten or repressed. The fear may be merely a mounting residue of inner feelings of weakness in dealing with the hazards of the outer world. Time and again the sufferer may have failed to win in his encounters with life. He thus develops a generalized feeling of inadequacy. He is fearful of life itself. He is afraid of his own ineffectiveness and grows suspicious of other people whose greater competence he regards as a threat.

Anxiety then is a diffuse, irrational fear, not directed at an appropriate target and not controlled by self-insight. Like a grease spot, it has spread throughout the life and stains the individual's social relationships.

Existentialists tell us that anxiety is basic in every life. It is more prominent than aggression because the very conditions of human existence are mysterious and dreadful, though they are not always frustrating. It is for this reason that fear becomes even more readily diffused and character-conditioned than does aggression.

Anxiety, however, is like aggression in that people tend to be ashamed of it. Our ethical codes place a premium on courage and self-reliance. Pride and self-respect lead us to mask our anxiety. While we repress it in part, we also give it a displaced outlet—upon socially sanctioned sources of fear. Some people suffer an almost hysterical fear of "communists" in our midst. It is a socially allowable phobia. The same people would not be respected if they admitted the real source of much of their anxiety, which lies in personal inadequacy and dread of life.

So far as our knowledge now extends, it seems probable that the principal source of character-conditioned anxiety comes from a bad start in early life. In previous chapters we have several times noted the peculiarities of child training that may arouse lasting anxiety. The male child, in particular, strives against odds to achieve a masculine role, and may carry lasting anxiety with him concerning the degree of his success. The rejective parent creates a condition of profound apprehension that we know may underlie nervous disorders, delinquency, and hostility.

Economic Insecurity

While much anxiety has its origin in childhood, the adult years are also potent sources, especially in connection with economic insufficiency. . . . Downward mobility, periods of unemployment and depression, and general economic dissatisfaction are all positively correlated with prejudice.

Sometimes, as we have likewise seen, there may be a realistic conflict involved, as when the upgrading of Negro workmen creates more competitors for certain jobs. It is not inconceivable, too, that members of one ethnic group may actually conspire to gain a monopoly of a business, a factory, or an occupation. But ordinarily, the "threat" that is felt is not geared to realities in that situation. The apprehensive and marginal man is vaguely terrified at any signs of ambition or progress on the part of any member of the out-group, whether or not it may constitute a realistic danger.

In most countries, people grow fiercely possessive of their property. It is a bastion of conservatism. Any threat, real or imagined, will invoke anxiety and anger (this blend is particularly suited to the growth of hatred). A grim reflection of this relationship is found in the experience of many Jews who were sent to concentration camps in central Europe during the Nazi control. These Jews often entrusted their property to some gentile friend. Most of the Jews were killed, and the property automatically became that of the friend.

But occasionally a Jew returned, and found that he was cordially hated for claiming his property, which perhaps had been used up by the trustee, sometimes to buy food. One Jew, foreseeing this outcome, refused to ask gentile friends to guard his goods, saying, "Isn't it enough for my enemies to want me to die? I don't want my friends also to want me dead."

Outright greed is certainly a cause of prejudice. If we took a historical over-view of feelings against colonial people, Jews, and aborigines (including the American Indian), we should probably find that rationalization of greed is a principal source. The formula is simple enough: greed → grabbing → justifying.

The role of economic apprehension in anti-Semitism has often been commented on. In the United States it seems that the well-to-do are especially prone to anti-Semitism.[1] The reason may be that the Jew is seen as a symbolic competitor. To keep him down is to avoid symbolically all potential threat. Hence he is excluded not only from occupations, but also from schools, clubs, neighborhoods. In this way a specious feeling of security and superiority results. McWilliams characterizes the total process as a "mask for privilege."[2]

Self-Esteem

Economic worries have their origins in hunger and the need to survive. But they continue to exist long after this rational function has been fulfilled. They ramify into the need for status, prestige, self-esteem. Food is no longer the issue, nor is money—excepting so far as it can buy that one thing in life that is always short in supply: *differential status.*

Not everyone can be "on top." Not everyone wants to be. But most people want to be higher on the status ladder than they are. "This hunger," writes Murphy, "operates like a vitamin deficiency." He regards it as the primary root of ethnic prejudice.[3]

The hunger for status is matched by a haunting fear that one's status may not be secure. The effort to maintain a precarious position

[1] H. H. Harlan. Some factors affecting attitudes toward Jews. *American Sociological Review,* 1942, 7, pp. 816–827.

[2] C. McWilliams. *A Mask for Privilege* (Boston: Little, Brown, 1948).

[3] G. Murphy. Preface to E. Hartley, *Problems in Prejudice* (New York: Kings Crown) 1946, p. viii.

can bring with it an almost reflex disparagement of others. Asch gives one instance:

> We observe this in the racial pride of Southerners, in the preoccupation with face-saving and self-justification, which are probably born of deep, mostly not conscious but also not bearable, doubts of their position. Sectional pride in the face of the North, the pride of a decaying landed group in the face of a newly arising industrial order, the pride of the new industrialist in the face of the old aristocracy, of the wretched poor white in the face of the precariously inferior Negro—these are the reactions of a people unsure whether their failures are not their own fault.[4]

The easiest idea to sell anyone is that he is better than someone else. The appeal of the Ku Klux Klan and racist agitators rests on this type of salesmanship. Snobbery is a way of clutching at one's status, and it is as common, perhaps more common, among those who are low in the ladder. By turning their attention to unfavored out-groups, they are able to derive from the comparison a modicum of self-esteem. Out-groups, as status builders, have the special advantage of being near at hand, visible (or at least nameable), and occupying a lower position by common agreement, thus providing social support for one's own sense of status enhancement.

The theme of egoism (status) has run through many of our chapters. Perhaps Murphy is right in regarding it as the "primary root" of prejudice. Our purpose in the present discussion is to bring this theme into proper relation with the factors of fear and anxiety. High status, we feel, would abolish our basic apprehensions, and for this reason we struggle to achieve a secure position for ourselves—often at the expense of our fellows.

Sexuality

Sex, like anger or fear, may ramify throughout the life, and may affect social attitudes in devious ways. Like these other emotions, it is less diffuse when it is rationally and adaptively directed. But in sexual maladjustment, frustration, and conflict, a tenseness spreads outward from the erotic area of the life into many by-paths. Some maintain

[4] S. Asch. *Social Psychology* (New York: Prentice-Hall, 1952), p. 605.

that it is impossible to understand group prejudice in the United States, particularly the prejudice of whites toward Negroes, without reference to sex maladjustment. Dingwall, a British anthropologist, writes:

> Sex dominates life in the United States in a manner and in a way which is found nowhere else in the world. Without a full appreciation of its influence and its results, no elucidation of the Negro problem is possible.[5]

We may overlook the unproved assertion that Americans are more sex-ridden than people in other countries, while at the same time admitting that an important issue has been raised.

A housewife in a Northern city was asked whether she would object to Negroes living on the same street. She replied,

> I wouldn't want to live with Negroes. They smell too much. They're of a different race. That's what creates racial hatreds. When I sleep with a Negro in the same bed, I'll live with them. But you know we can't.

Here the sexual barricade intrudes itself into a logically unrelated issue—the simple question of residence on the same street.

It is by no means only anti-Negro prejudice that reveals sex interest and sex accusations. An advertisement for an anti-Catholic pamphlet reads as follows:

> See the nun bound hand and foot, gagged, lying in a dungeon because she refused to obey a priest. . . . Read about [the] nun locked in a room stark naked with three drunken priests. . . . Poison, Murder, Rapine, Torturing and smothering babies. . . . If you want to know what goes on behind convent walls read this book *House of Death* or *Convent Brutality*.

The linking of lechery with the Roman Catholic Church (known also as "the mother of harlots") is an old and familiar trick of Catholic-haters. Dark tales of sexual debauchery were common a century ago, and were part of the whispering campaign of the Know-Nothing political party that flourished at that time.

The fierce persecution of the Mormons in the Nineteenth Cen-

[5] E. J. Dingwall. *Racial Pride and Prejudice* (London: Watts, 1946), p. 69.

tury was related to their doctrine, and occasional practice, of polygamy. Granted that plural marriage, ended by law in 1896, was an unsound social policy, a prurience of interest and licentiousness of fantasies were revealed in the anti-Mormon tracts of the time. The opposition to the sect drew nourishment from the conflict that many people had within their own sex lives. Why should others be allowed a wider choice of sex partners than they? And during the 1920's perhaps the commonest accusation against communist Russia was that it "nationalized" its women.

In Europe it is common to accuse the Jews of gross sexual immorality. They are said to be given to overindulgence, rape, perversion. Hitler, whose own sex life was far from normal, contrived over and over again to accuse the Jews of perversion, of having syphilis, and of other disorders suspiciously akin to Hitler's own phobias. Streicher, the Number One Nazi Jew-baiter, at least in private conversation, mentioned circumcision about as often as he mentioned Jew.[6]

In America one seldom hears sex accusations against the Jew. Is it because there is less anti-Semitism? Is it that American Jews are more moral than European Jews? Neither explanation seems right. The reason, more probably, . . . is that in America we have in the Negro a preferred target for our sexual complexes.

There is a subtle psychological reason why Negroid characteristics favor an association of ideas with sex. The Negro seems dark, mysterious, distant—yet at the same time warm, human, and potentially accessible. Sex is forbidden; colored people are forbidden; the ideas begin to fuse. It is no accident that prejudiced people call tolerant people "nigger-lovers." The very choice of the word suggests that they are fighting the feeling of attraction in themselves.

The fact that interracial sex attraction exists is proved by the millions of mixed breeds in the country. Differences in color and social status seem to be sexually exciting rather than repelling. It has often been noted that liaisons with members of lower classes seem particularly attractive to people with higher status. The daughter of the patrician family who runs away with the coachman is almost as familiar a theme in literature as is the prodigal son who wastes his substance in riotous living with lower-class women. Both reveal the same truth.

[6] G. M. Gilbert. *Nüremberg Diary* (New York: Farrar, Straus, 1947), *passim.*

We note that sun-bathing is for the purpose of darkening the skin—and is a pastime indulged in by male and female alike to enhance their attractiveness. There is intrigue in contrasting complexions. Moreno has reported that homosexual crushes between white and Negro adolescent girls were common in a reformatory, for difference in skin color in many instances seemed to serve as a functional substitute for difference in sex.[7]

The attraction is further enhanced by the fact (or legend) that Negroes have an open and unashamed way of looking at life. Many people with suppressed sex lives would like the same freedom. They grow jealous and irritated at the openness and directness of sex life among others. They accuse the males of extreme sexual potency, and the females of shamelessness. Even the size of the genitalia becomes a subject of jealous exaggeration. Fantasies easily get mixed with fact.

This illicit fascination may become obsessional in some localities where life is otherwise intolerably dull. In her novel *Strange Fruit*, Lillian Smith has described the emotional aridness of a small Southern town. Escape is sought in religious orgies, or in the excitement of race conflict. Or people may see in the Negro the lusty qualities they lack, and may alternately ridicule, desire, and persecute them. Forbidden fruit arouses contrasting emotional reactions. Helen McLean writes:

> In calling the Negro a child of nature, simple, lovable, without ambition, a person who gives way to his every impulse, white men have made a symbol which gives a secret gratification to those who are inhibited and crippled in their instinctual satisfactions. Indeed, white men are very loath to relinquish such a symbol.[8]

Now this common cross-race sexual fascination seldom expresses itself normally. The mixed dating of adolescents is virtually a social impossibility. Legal intermarriage, where possible at all, is rare and is bedeviled by social complications that create grave problems even for the most devoted couples. Hence sexual liaisons are clandestine, illicit, and accompanied by feelings of guilt. Yet the fascination is so strong that this most rigid of taboos is frequently broken, more often by the white male, however, than by the white female.

The psychodynamic process that relates this sexual situation to

[7] J. L. Moreno. *Who Shall Survive?* (Washington: Nervous and Mental Disease Publishing), 1934, p. 229.

[8] Helen V. McLean. Psychodynamic factors in racial relations. *The Annals of the American Academy of Political and Social Science*, 1946, 244, pp. 159–166.

prejudice may be described separately for the white female and white male.

Suppose a white woman is fascinated by the taboo against the Negro male. She is unlikely to admit, even to herself, that she finds his color and lower status attractive. She may, however, "project" her feelings, and accordingly imagine that the desire exists on the *other* side—that Negro males have sexually aggressive tendencies toward her. What is an inner temptation is perceived as an outer threat. Overgeneralizing her conflict, she develops an anxiety and hostility respecting the whole Negro race.

In the case of the white male the process may be even more complex. Suppose he is anxious concerning his own sexual adequacy and attractiveness. One study of adult prisoners discovered a close relationship between this condition and high prejudice. Men who were antagonistic toward minority groups, on the whole, showed more fierce protest against their own sexual passivity, semi-impotence, or homosexual trends. The protest took the form of exaggerated toughness and hostility. These individuals committed more crimes of a sexual nature than did those who were sexually more secure. And the pseudo-masculinity of the former group made them more hostile toward minorities.[9]

Again, a male who is dissatisfied with his own marriage may grow envious when he hears rumors of Negro sexual prowess and license. He may also resent and fear the approach Negroes might make to white women who are potentially his. A state of rivalry may thus result, based on the same type of reasoning that says the supply of jobs is limited and if Negroes have them, whites will be deprived.

Or suppose the white male has taken his pleasure with Negro women. Such liaisons, being illicit, give rise to guilt. A wry sense of justice forces him to see that the Negro males, in principle, should have equal access to white women. Jealousy plus guilt create a disagreeable conflict. He, too, finds a way out by "projecting." It is the lecherous Negro male that is the real menace. He would deflower white womanhood. The deflowering of Negro womanhood is conveniently forgotten in the outburst of righteous indignation. The indignation is guilt-evading and restorative of self-respect.

For this reason the penalties visited upon male Negroes for sex transgressions (with white women) are disproportionately heavy. (Al-

[9] W. R. Morrow. A psychodynamic analysis of the crimes of prejudiced and unprejudiced male prisoners. *Bulletin of the Menninger Clinic,* 1949, 13, pp. 204–212.

though in fact, of course, the bulk of transgression is on the white side.) During the years 1938–1948, in thirteen Southern states, 15 whites and 187 Negroes were executed for rape. In these same states Negroes made up only 23.8 percent of the population. Unless we assume that Negroes commit rape fifty-three times as often as white men (in proportion to their numbers in the population), we are forced to conclude that bias is largely responsible for the unequal number of executions for this crime.[10]

There is no doubt that lifting the sexual ban would reduce the glamor and the conflict. But the ban is a stubborn composite of several factors. It rests, in the first instance, upon a Puritanical view of sex activity of any sort. Sex itself is taboo. But since normal social intercourse and intermarriage are scarcely ever possible between Negroes and whites, any intimate relationships seem to take on an adulterous flavor.[11]

The central question allegedly is intermarriage. Since this sounds like a legal, and therefore respectable, issue, it becomes the pivot of nearly all discussion. The fact that miscegenation between two healthy people has no weakening effect on the offspring is overlooked. Intermarriage cannot rationally be opposed on biological grounds. It can, however, be rationally opposed on the grounds of the handicap and conflict it could cause both parents and offspring in the present state of society. But the opposition is seldom stated in these mild terms, for to do so would imply that the present state of society should be improved so that miscegenation can safely take place.

For the most part the marriage issue is not rational. It comprises a fierce fusion of sex attraction, sex repression, guilt, status superiority, occupational advantage, and anxiety. It is because intermarriage would symbolize the abolition of prejudice that it is so strenuously fought.

Perhaps the most interesting feature of the whole situation is the way in which the issue of intermarriage has come to dominate

[10] J. A. Dombrowski. Execution for rape is a race penalty. *The Southern Patriot*, 1950, 8, 1–2.

[11] Our account in these pages has said nothing about the Negro's point of view. It may be that color difference and the taboo add glamor to interracial mating for the Negro as well as for the white. It may be that hostility and resentment are released along with sex desire and occasionally lead to brutal rape. But it seems unlikely that potency and impulsiveness are greater among Negro males than among whites. In fact, certain studies suggest that fear, dependency, and broken homes create a passivity and impotence in Negro males to a surprisingly large extent. *Cf.* A. Kardiner and L. Ovesey. *The Mark of Oppression* (New York: W. W. Norton), 1951.

discussion. When a Negro obtains a good pair of shoes and learns to write a literate letter, some whites think he wants to marry their sister. Perhaps most discussions of discrimination end with the fatal question, "But would *you* want a Negro to marry your sister?" The reasoning seems to be that unless all forms of discrimination are maintained, intermarriage will result. The same argument was used to defend slavery. Nearly a hundred years ago Abraham Lincoln was forced to protest against "that counterfeit logic which presumes that, if I do not want a Negro woman for a slave, I do necessarily want her for a wife."[12]

Why the prejudiced person almost invariably hides behind the issue of marriage is itself a lesson in rationalization. He takes what is admittedly the argument most likely to confuse his opponent. Even the most tolerant person may not welcome intermarriage—because of the practical unwisdom in a prejudiced society. He may therefore say, "No, I wouldn't." The bigot then has the advantage, and replies in effect, "Now, see, there is ultimately an unbridgeable chasm, and I am therefore right in maintaining that we must look on Negroes as a different and undesirable group. All my strictures against them are justified. We had better not let down the barriers because it will raise their expectations and hopes of intermarriage." Thus, the intermarriage question (actually so irrelevant to most phases of the Negro question) is forcibly introduced to protect and justify prejudice.[13]

Guilt

A non-Catholic boy had a broken romance with a Catholic girl, and this affair was preceded by a rather free infatuation with another Catholic girl. He wrote:

> Both girls begged me to come back and marry them. They promised anything if I would do so. Their groveling disgusted me. But I realized that the Catholic Church has only an ignorant, bigoted following to draw from.

Not he, but the Church, was somehow to blame for the unpleasant situation. A gentile businessman was guilty of unethical practices

[12] Reply to Judge Stephen A. Douglas at Chicago, July 10, 1858.

[13] How the tolerant person should respond to the fatal question, "Would you want your sister to marry a Negro?" has caused some inventive speculation. One suggestion is to reply, "Perhaps not, but I shouldn't want her to marry you either."

that forced a Jewish competitor into bankruptcy. He, too, consoled himself, saying:

> Well, they are always trying to run Christians out of business, and so I had to get him first.

The student was a cad; the gentile a cheat. But subjectively each evaded his sense of guilt by projection; others were guilty, not he.

Somewhat more subtle is the evidence that comes from clinical studies. . . . The California studies[14] . . . show among prejudiced people a marked tendency to regard others (but not oneself) as blameworthy. Interesting confirmation comes from comparable studies in India, where the psychologist, Mitra, discovered in Hindu boys having greatest prejudice against Muslims a high tendency to unconscious guilt reactions in the Rorschach test.[15]

Some of the ways in which people handle guilt-feelings are benign and wholesome; some lead almost unavoidably to prejudice against out-groups. Let us list the principal modes of dealing with guilt. . . .

1. REMORSE AND RESTITUTION This is the response that receives highest ethical approval. It is wholly intropunitive and avoids all temptation to shift blame to other shoulders. A person who is normally penitent and contrite for his own failings is not likely to find much in others, specifically in out-groups, to criticize.

Sometimes, though not often, we find among persecutors of out-groups converts who repent and devote themselves ever after to supporting the cause of those they at first hated. St. Paul's conversion represented such a shift. Somewhat more often we find a sensitive person who feels a *collective* guilt. It is likely that some white workers who devote themselves to the improvement of conditions for Negroes may have some such motivation. Being intropunitive to a high degree, they feel that their own group is at fault, and work hard to make amends.

2. PARTIAL AND SPORADIC RESTITUTION Some people who themselves hold firmly the doctrine of white supremacy will, up to a point,

[14] [In a series of tests conducted by the University of California, strong evidence was found for the argument that prejudice is a basic personality trait; the specific object of prejudice is more or less immaterial—G. M.]

[15] Cited by G. Murphy. *In the Minds of Men* (New York: Basic Books), 1953, p. 228.

work for the betterment of the Negro. They feel that they can hold to a basic prejudice if only they act now and then as if it were nonexistent. "We frequently do good," wrote La Rochefoucauld, "to enable us with impunity to do evil." In one community the woman who was most active in keeping Negroes out of the neighborhood and "in their place," was found at the same time to be the most active in devoting herself to Negro charities. Here is a case of "alternation" and "compromise." . . .

3. DENIAL OF GUILT A common escape from feelings of guilt is to assert that there is no reason to have them. A familiar justification for discrimination against the Negroes is, "They are happier by themselves." A common Southern conceit is that Negroes prefer Southern to Northern employers because the former "understand" them better. During the Second World War, it was often said that Negroes, for this reason, preferred to serve under Southern rather than under Northern white officers. Also, it was maintained that they greatly preferred white to colored officers. The facts are entirely contradictory. When asked in a poll whether they would prefer to serve under white or Negro lieutenants, only four percent of the Northern and six percent of the Southern Negroes preferred white. Further, only one percent of the Northern Negroes preferred a white officer from the South, and only four percent of the Southern Negroes did so.[16]

4. DISCREDITING THE ACCUSER No one likes another person to blame him for misconduct. A common defense against facing the justice of an accusation is to declare the accuser to be somehow off base. Hamlet confronted his mother with her faithlessness in marrying her husband's murderer. Rather than face her own guilt, his mother reproves Hamlet for "the coinage" of his brain, laying his charges to his madness. In the realm of ethnic relations those who would rouse the voice of conscience are called "agitators," "troublemakers," "communists."

5. JUSTIFICATION OF CONDITIONS The simplest evasion of all is to say that the hated person is wholly to blame. . . . Many people who are prejudiced take this path. This is prejudice without compunction. "Who could tolerate them? Look, they are dirty, lazy, sexually liber-

[16] S. A. Stouffer, *et al. The American Soldier: Adjustment During Army Life* (Princeton: Princeton Univ. Press, 1949), Vol. I, p. 581.

tine." The fact that these qualities may be the very ones we have to fight in ourselves, makes it all the easier to see them in others.

6. PROJECTION The sense of guilt, by definition, means that I blame myself for some misdeed. But only Item 1 in this list (remorse and restitution) is strictly appropriate to this definition. It alone is a rationally adaptive mode of response. All others are devices for *guilt evasion*. Guilt-evading processes have one feature in common: the self-referred perception is repressed in favor of some external (extropunitive) perception. There is guilt somewhere, yet, but it is not *my* guilt.

Thus in all guilt evasion there is some projective mechanism at work. . . .

QUESTIONS FOR DISCUSSION AND WRITING

1. According to Allport's principles, which groups of whites are characteristically "anxious" about blacks? On what do they base their fears?
2. Sexual mythology—the attribution to "out-groups" of a large degree of sexual prowess and sexual interest—is commonly a part of racist practices. What particular sexual myths are associated with blacks? How are these myths relevant to state policy matters like welfare and birth control?
3. Allport suggests that an analogy exists between the experience of Jews in Nazi Germany and that of the blacks in modern America. To what extent is the analogy valid? Is property ownership the major parallel between the two situations?
4. The Kerner Commission findings (p. 279) suggest that "white racism" is the major cause of current racial problems. Is "white racism" also a factor in American reactions to other minority groups of color? Do Americans manifest the same degree of "anxiety, guilt, and sexual tension" toward other-than-black racial minority groups? How?
5. "Negrophobia" is not openly sanctioned in the United States, yet coded names for the same prejudice are socially sanctioned. What coded names are frequently used to allude to blacks? What explanation for this disparity does Allport use? Compare his point of view with Bennett's (p. 273).

ROSS R. BARNETT WORKED HIS WAY THROUGH LAW SCHOOL IN HIS NATIVE STATE OF MISSISSIPPI AND BECAME ITS GOVERNOR IN 1960. HE IS NOW SENIOR MEMBER OF ONE OF MISSISSIPPI'S LARGEST LAW FIRMS.

ROSS R. BARNETT

ADDRESS TO THE HARVARD LAW SCHOOL FORUM

It is a pleasure to be with you tonight. I would like to tell you a little about Mississippi, our opportunities, our economic development and our progress.

I hope all of you will visit our great state. I would like for you to see our beautiful new football stadium seating 46,000; our coliseum which will seat 10,000; I wish you could see the 40,000 acres of water known as the Ross Barnett Reservoir, which will be completed within the next year, and see the beautiful, scenic, historic Gulf Coast where we have the longest man-made beach in the world—a twenty-eight-mile sand beach.

Our tourist business is at an all-time high as thousands of people from every state in the nation come and enjoy our wide assortment

ADDRESS TO THE HARVARD LAW SCHOOL FORUM Originally appeared in the *Harvard Law Review*. Reprinted by permission of the author.

of outdoor sports, our recreation facilities, visit our historic shrines and ante-bellum homes, fish, boat and ski on our many lakes and rivers, play year 'round golf in the warm sunshine throughout various sections of our state.

In 1960, the Mississippi Legislature passed thirty-nine separate acts to make Mississippi more than competitive in our fight to secure industry and payrolls. We voted a right-to-work law into our state constitution by more than 2½ to 1. We reduced our state income taxes in 1960. We created a climate highly favorable to business and industry. Ninety-eight per cent of our people voted to give industry a ten-year ad valorem tax exemption.

Mississipi has secured over 400 substantial new industries and expansions in the last two and a half years. When these new industries and expansions get into full production, they will provide over 31,000 new industrial jobs for our people.

The United States Department of Commerce, in a December, 1962, report, showed that Mississippi's rate of progress was 25 per cent greater than the national average in manufacturing gains, 105 per cent greater in expenditures for new plants and equipment, and 13 per cent greater in new wholesale establishments.

Mississippi, in the last two years, has staged a reversal in population. Instead of losing, Mississippi has gained more than 73,000 since the 1960 census—a rate exceeding that of 22 other states. Every economic indicator points to the fact that Mississippi is moving forward at a record pace, and indications are that 1963 will surpass all previous records in economic gains.

The Standard Oil Company of Kentucky will complete a 125 million dollar oil refinery in Mississippi this year which will refine 100,000 barrels of crude oil per day and which will open the way for a great petro-chemical complex on the Mississippi Gulf Coast. In discussing the location of this major refinery in Mississippi, Mr. W. C. Smith, president of Standard of Kentucky, said:

> There is little room left on the old frontier. Mississippi is one of the last resorts for industry. Look at the other states that are broke or nearly broke as the result of the New Deal and the Fair Deal and you will see why we are glad to be in Mississippi where there is a friendly and healthy industrial and political climate.

The president of the great W. W. Sly Manufacturing Company said, in October, 1961:

> We, like you, still believe in the dignity of man, in a state's sovereign rights, that the Christian principles should be put ahead of material ones, that people have the right to work, that private property should be protected and that the Constitution of the United States should be interpreted in the same spirit in which it was written and not altered to suit expediency. Many people have asked why we built this plant in Mississippi. I'll tell you why. The attitudes, the spirit of the people of this state and this town came closer to our own beliefs than any other spot we could find.

Another industrialist said:

> We chose Mississippi because we felt that it possessed the healthiest political and industrial climate in the nation—the best potential for production workers, as well as all other necessary requisites for sound logical plant location.

Another said:

> Mississippi's understanding of industry problems in creating and maintaining a favorable climate for business is outstanding.

This is conclusive evidence that all areas of this nation are aware of the peace, harmony and opportunities that exist in Mississippi.

Another yardstick is the fact that, educationally, there is not a city in this nation that equals Mississippi's capital city of some 150,000 population. The citizens of Jackson have covered an average of 12.1 grades, unsurpassed in the nation. I would like to ask—what are the best-educated cities in the United States? What cities have the largest proportion of college graduates among their citizenry? You would be right if you answered Cambridge, Massachusetts... Madison, Wisconsin... Pasadena and Berkeley, California... and Jackson, Mississippi.

Mississippi is the greatest states' rights state in the nation. Mississippians, as far back as 1944, took a firm stand against the socialistic platforms that were then shaping up. For twenty years, we have stood upon the sound foundation of constitutional government and states' rights. In the last presidential election, our people voted unpledged and we gave our electoral votes to that great conservative, Senator Harry Byrd of Virginia.

Massachusetts was the Queen Mother of states' rights and constitutional government. For almost one hundred years of the history of the states under the Constitution, her statesmen were the most conservative and pronounced proponents and sticklers for preserving the faith embodied in her Declaration of Rights and in resisting the encroachments, potential or actual, of the federal government. These included many of your famous men such as Samuel and John Adams, John Hancock, George Cabot, and many, many others, equally as great.

The political ideas and principles of these men found eloquent expression in the Declaration of Rights prefacing the first Constitution of Massachusetts and in all future constitutions of this state, including the present one. Some of those political ideas merit repeating on this occasion. A few of them are:

> (1) The people inhabiting the territory formerly called the Province of Massachusetts Bay, do hereby solemnly and mutually agree with each other to form themselves into a free, sovereign and independent body politic, or state, by the name of the Commonwealth of Massachusetts. (Paragraph 32, present Constitution.)
>
> (2) The people of this commonwealth have the sole and exclusive right of governing themselves as a free, sovereign and independent state; and do and forever hereafter shall exercise and enjoy every power, jurisdiction and right, which is not, or may not hereafter be, by them expressly delegated to the United States of America and Congress assessed. (Paragraph 5, Article 4, present Constitution.)
>
> (3) All power residing originally in the people, and being derived from them, the several magistrates and officers of the government vested with authority, either Legislative, Executive or Judicial, are their substitutes and agents, and are at all times accountable to them. (Paragraph 6, Article 5, present Constitution.)

In 1809, during the controversy over Jefferson's Embargo, the Legislature of Massachusetts resolved as follows: "That the people of this state as one of the parties to the federal compact, have a right to express their sense of any violation of its provisions, and that it is the duty of this General Assembly to interfere for the purpose of protecting them from the ruinous infliction usurped by an unconstitutional power."

Later, the General Court of Massachusetts resolved again, respecting the Embargo, that "we spurn the idea that the free, sovereign and independent state of Massachusetts is reduced to a mere municipal corporation, without power to protect its people and defend them from oppression, from whatever quarter it comes. Whenever the national compact is violated, this Legislature is bound to interpose its power." (February 22, 1814.)

We have heard much here of late with reference to the rights of the states being sacrificed and ruthlessly destroyed by an all-consuming federal government. The federal government is constantly making a whipping boy of the states and is overstepping its constitutional powers. The federal government is assuming to exercise powers it does not have under the Constitution and that, by the Constitution, were expressly reserved in the states and the people thereof by the Tenth Amendment.

Today, more than at any time in this century, men and women, North and South, East and West, are rallying in defense of fundamental principles. In recent months, I have had thousands of letters and telegrams from people in every state in the nation calling for a return to constitutional government.

These Americans hold, with me, that the preservation or maintenance of state sovereignty is indispensable to the preservation of human rights. We are convinced that once the right of a state to exercise exclusive jurisdiction over a local problem is lost, human rights, liberty and freedom will perish.

A year ago, in February of 1962, Mississippi had the pleasure of having an official visit from Senator John E. Powers, president of the Massachusetts State Senate, accompanied by several leaders of the Massachusetts Senate and other state officials. In his address before a joint session of the Mississippi Legislature, Senator Powers told Mississippians that the time had come to reverse trends and put the legislative branch of government in first place, because it is closest to the people. He said that usurpation of authority by the executive and subsequently the judiciary is a lamentable trend that must be halted. He said that the state level government is lulled to impotency and that he, in his capacity as president of the Senate, "will not in my state preside over the liquidation of legislative powers or a legislative body."

I recently received a letter from the president of a bar association in Florida, from which I quote:

> We in this area are greatly interested in the position of your sovereign state. . . . Some of our association feel that our states

> are presently being reduced to the position of a province, much along the lines of some other countries. This is a matter of wide general interest.

In September, 1962, the National Legislative Conference, at its fifteenth annual meeting in Phoenix, Arizona, adopted a resolution in an effort to strengthen and uphold the Tenth Amendment to the United States Constitution. The Council of State Governments at its biennial general assembly of the states, held in Chicago, Illinois, in December, 1962, endorsed the resolution and recommended its adoption by all the states.

The people of the states are extremely conscious of this usurpation of the constitutional rights of the states, but much needs to be done to awaken the states to their perilous condition. There is a crying need for the states to organize into a compact, expressing the feeling of the states with reference to these usurpations, the consequent destruction of our constitutional form of government, and presenting a common front against such unconstitutional encroachment by the federal government.

Not only the Southern states, but all of the states in the union must be and are conscious of the present peril to state sovereignty. All of the states have a common interest in their own survival and the restoration of their respective constitutional powers.

Surely, the states are conscious of their peril and of the peril to their people. We must no longer remain idle or complacent. The clarion call must be sounded for the states to come to their own defense and obtain a restoration of constitutional government.

States' rights and constitutional government are inseparable. The Tenth Amendment to the Constitution of the United States very clearly states the position of the states as related to the federal government, and here is what it says:

> The powers not delegated to the United States by the Constitution nor prohibited by it to the states are reserved to the states respectively, or to the people.

Any high school student can understand what those twenty-eight words mean. It is indeed regrettable that many decrees, orders and edicts have been issued wholly contrary to the meaning of the Tenth Amendment.

The courts adhered to the meaning and fundamental principles of the Tenth Amendment for nearly a hundred years, and further held that state sovereignty could not be bartered away or surrendered by legislative action. Then suddenly, they reversed decisions handed down by such great and eminent scholars and jurists as Oliver Wendell Holmes, Chief Justice Taft, Chief Justice Hughes, McReynolds, Stone, Cardozo and other eminent jurists and began to enter orders, decrees and edicts based on sociological ideas as advanced and advocated by Gunnar Myrdal and others, thereby whittling away, year by year, the rights that are reserved to the states by the Tenth Amendment. These decisions are in conformity with the wishes of left-wing and communist front organizations.

We must not fall into the trap of world-wide communism. The basic tactic of world-wide communism is to divide and to conquer. It is to set free nation against free nation, and within the nation, to set brother against brother. Its objective in the United States is to promote tension, turmoil, strife, and to bring about misunderstanding and mistrust.

States' rights and local self-government are older than the Constitution. They existed before the nation was formed and were recognized and protected by Thomas Jefferson and the other founding fathers when they wrote the Constitution itself.

The preservation of the prerogatives of people of a sovereign state, their right to deal exclusively with domestic problems and the absolute and unqualified denial of a totalitarian state in the United States—these principles are just as vital as, and more intimately affect, the welfare of every man, woman and child in America than even such important questions as foreign policy and all other serious questions which we face today, important as those issues are. May God forbid that your respective states and mine, our counties, our cities, our farms and our businesses shall ever be subjected to Washington bureaucratic police rule.

If we lose states' rights which safeguard the most precious of all human rights—the right to control and govern ourselves at home—the right of life, liberty and the pursuit of happiness—then may we ask, "For what is a man profiteth if he shall gain the whole world and lose his own soul?"

A state that loses the right to exercise exclusive jurisdiction over its own local affairs loses its political soul and its citizens have lost their most valuable freedom.

I wish to emphasize that the term "States' Rights" means much more to the people of this nation than simple theory. It means the preservation of democracy and freedom itself.

The oldest form of government in the world is the highly centralized one, with all power concentrated. It is only with the founding of this country that democracy developed, and it came, and this country grew great, because the centralization of power was curtailed.

Every section of this nation favors human rights. Everybody favors human rights. But it is a fraud upon the American people to pretend that human rights can long endure without constitutional restrictions on the power of government. Many people living today have seen this truth written in blood in recent human history.

Hitler offered the people of Germany a short cut to human progress. He gained power by advocating human rights for minority groups. Under his plan, the constitutional rights of the people were destroyed. The proposal to take from you the right to deal with your local problems in a way that is satisfactory to you and to invest the right to deal with those problems in Washington in a way that is wholly unsatisfactory to you is so antagonistic to our form of government and so contrary to everything that we have stood for since 1776 that it is obliged to be un-American in principle and undemocratic in execution.

The moment that government becomes remote, distant, mysterious and beyond the comprehension of the people themselves, danger arises and we subject ourselves to the possibility of abuse of power and ultimate dictatorship. When the United States of America was formed and the Constitution was written, the people were insistent in demanding that local government be forever preserved in all of its dignity and all of its safeguards. In the drafting of the Constitution, it was specifically provided that the right and authority of the states to conduct their own affairs should be preserved inviolate and there was conferred upon the federal government only so much power and authority as was necessary to control and regulate the relationships of the states one with another and the conduct of this nation's foreign affairs and unified defense.

Ratification of the Constitution by the original states—of which Massachusetts was one—was obtained only after the citizens in each state received definite and positive assurances that this fundamental concept of government was recognized by the Constitution. Is this principle of states' rights an archaic doctrine, as insisted by those who seek the concentration of power in Washington? I say to you that it is a living principle, as vital and essential today as it was in the foundation days of the Republic—the doctrine of free society and free men, as opposed to regimentation of thought and action.

Democracy is not a thing of Washington. Democracy is a thing of the crossroads. It is at the crossroads of America that the children of this nation live. It is at the crossroads that their children are born—that they go to church on Sunday—that the schools are placed—that the average American citizen lives his life and is finally taken to his reward. It is at the crossroads that the life of America takes place—not in Washington.

That is where I stand tonight. I am convinced that our schools are local affairs, as is the police, the fire department, the city and county governments, the habits of the people, the conduct of local business and all the hundreds of affairs of daily life. The right to work, loaf or play, to choose our vocation and to change our job, to guide the education of our children, to attend the church of our choice, to work with whom we please, to go where we choose, are not inherent and divine rights. These rights are ours solely because the federal government, by the Constitution, was denied the power to interfere with them. Also, the fields of education, housing, employment, apportionment of state legislatures, voting qualifications, police powers, tidelands oil rights, and other sundry situations, are reserve powers under the Tenth Amendment.

Government, if not properly restricted, is essentially a dangerous thing. There is no truth more fundamental than that power seeks always to increase. I believe that the maintenance of states' rights is indispensable to the preservation of human rights—that once the right of a sovereign state to exercise exclusive jurisdiction over a local problem is lost, human rights, liberty and freedom will perish in the catastrophe. The people of all communities, cities, counties and states must either rule or they will be ruled.

There is no such thing as a vacuum in politics or government. If the rights of a sovereign state and local units of government are taken away, they will be replaced by a totalitarian government—a police state. Only our Constitution stands between the people and a dictatorship. If politicians are allowed to circumvent, misconstrue, cripple or disobey the Constitution, then constitutional government is in jeopardy and the liberty and freedom and right of every American citizen to the pursuit of happiness are menaced.

This republic is an indestructible union of indestructible states.

But a historical fact that many seem to have forgotten is that the states of this union are the fundamental sources of all sovereignty and all power. The Constitution merely states, in the form of a written contract, the degree of sovereignty that the states transfer to the federal government. This sovereignty was principally in the field of defense and operating highways and post offices. The sovereignty of the states flows both upward and downward—upward to the federal government and downward to the counties and municipalities. Some theorists try to reduce the principle of states' rights to an absurdity by saying that if states have a right to disagree with matters of national policy affecting their interest, then counties and municipalities likewise have a right to disagree with policies of the state affecting their interests. These people are simply not familiar with the facts of history.

Counties and municipalities are creatures of the state, even as the federal government is the creature of the states. The Constitution was not ratified by the people of the United States or by the people of the thirteen colonies voting in a mass referendum. It was ratified by the legislatures of the thirteen states, acting as the duly constituted officers of the people. In other words, the states ratified the Constitution in their capacities as sovereign political communities.

This dual sovereignty feature of our government is what sets it apart as an economic creation of the political genius of man. It sets it apart from all other governments in that it puts the powers which matter most to the people—namely, the police powers and the administration of local affairs—it places these close to the people where they can exercise vigilance on their adopted servants.

Not a single word of the Constitution can be changed by judicial decree or Congressional act. Any change is the prerogative of the legislatures of the states. They are the only ones who can change the wording—either by adding to or taking from—this is clearly stated in the Constitution.

A lot of people outside the South have the impression that states' rights is only concerned with segregation. This is far from the truth. Just to mention a couple of examples—the states of the West are deeply concerned about the federal government's encroachments of their water rights and I have heard a distinguished Republican senator say that if the federal government did not stay out of this field, they were going to find out what a scrap really was. (Water rights there have always gone with the land—it is an established principle in the West that when you buy a piece of land, whatever stream goes through it, you own the water rights, and the federal government is now trying to establish a principle that this is not true—that it belongs to the federal government and they have no right to use it.)

Other examples to illustrate the point are Nevada and Indiana. Nevada has legalized gambling on a large scale. Very few people in Mississippi believe in this, but we just don't think it is our place to try to tell the State of Nevada what to do about its internal affairs.

You might recall that a few years ago, the State of Indiana flatly refused to permit the federal government to inspect its old-age assistance rolls. The officials were very successful in preserving the right of their state to handle this matter as it saw fit.

Mississippians know we do not have the right to say what the people in Ohio or in any other state should do towards solving their problems. We certainly would not want to be discourteous in projecting our ignorance of conditions in other states because we could not contribute anything worthwhile to their solution—this is the American way—and all the South asks is the same simple courtesy from those who are not familiar with our problems.

Daniel Webster said in his *Eulogy of George Washington:*

> If disastrous war should sweep our commerce from the ocean, another generation may renew it; if it exhausts our treasury, future industry may replenish it; if it desolates and lays waste all our fields, still, under a new cultivation, they will grow green and ripen to future harvests.
>
> It were but a trifle even if the walls of yonder capitol were to crumble, if its lofty pillars should fall and its gorgeous decorations be all covered by the dust of the valley. All these may be rebuilt.
>
> But who shall reconstruct the fabric of demolished government? Who shall rear again the well-proportioned columns of constitutional liberty? Who shall frame together the skillful architecture which unites national sovereignty with states' rights, individual security and public prosperity?
>
> No, if these columns fall, they will be raised not again. Like the Colosseum and the Parthenon, they will be destined to mournful immortality. Bitterer tears, however, will flow over them than were ever shed over the monuments of Roman or Grecian art; and they will be the monuments of a more glorious edifice than Greece or Rome ever saw—the edifice of constitutional liberty.

It is time to identify the traitors throughout America. It is time to take the cowards out of the front lines. It is time for true Americans to become awakened.

QUESTIONS FOR DISCUSSION AND WRITING

1. What is Barnett's main argument? How does he support his assertions?
2. From Barnett's point of view, who are the "traitors throughout America"? What characteristics do they have? At what points do they depart so much from Barnett's point of view that he can characterize them as "traitors"?
3. Why does Governor Barnett open his speech with a recitation of vital statistics about Mississippi? Of what significance is the information that he offers? What statistics—ones that would be of undoubted interest to the Harvard Law School Forum—does he omit?
4. Drawing upon his personal view of recent history, Barnett suggests an analogy between the United States and Nazi Germany. What are the connections between Barnett's use of this analogy and Allport's (p. 205)? And Elkins' (p. 234)? Does the analogy reveal the purpose of Barnett's address?
5. Why should the "sociological ideas as advanced and advocated by Gunnar Myrdal [p. 141] and others" influence Supreme Court decisions? How does sociology threaten the Tenth Amendment? Can Supreme Court decisions be attacked on their alleged conformity to either sociological ideas or communism?

STANLEY M. ELKINS IS PROFESSOR OF HISTORY AT SMITH COLLEGE. HIS BOOK *Slavery: A Problem in American Institutional and Intellectual Life* WAS PUBLISHED IN 1959.

STANLEY M. ELKINS

SLAVERY AND PERSONALITY

An examination of American slavery, checked at certain critical points against a very different slave system, that of Latin America, reveals that a major key to many of the contrasts between them was an institutional key: The presence or absence of other powerful institutions in society made an immense difference in the character of slavery itself. In Latin America, the very tension and balance among three kinds of organizational concerns—church, crown, and plantation agriculture—prevented slavery from being carried by the planting class to its ultimate logic. For the slave, in terms of the space thus allowed for the development of men and women as moral beings, the result was an "open system": a system of contacts with free society through which ultimate absorption into that society could and did occur with great frequency. The rights of personality implicit in the ancient traditions of slavery and in the church's most venerable assumptions on the nature of the human soul were thus in a vital sense conserved, whereas to a staggering extent the very opposite was true in North American slavery. The latter system had developed virtually unchecked by institutions having anything like the power of their Latin counterparts; the legal structure which supported it, shaped only by the demands of a staple-raising capitalism, had defined with such nicety the slave's character as chattel that his character as a moral individual was left in the vaguest of legal obscurity. In this sense American slavery operated as a "closed" system—one in which, for the generality of slaves in their nature as men and women, *sub specie aeternitatis*, contacts with free society could occur only on the most narrowly circumscribed of terms. The next question is whether living within such a "closed system" might not have produced noticeable effects upon the slave's very personality.

The name "Sambo" has come to be synonymous with "race stereotype." Here is an automatic danger signal, warning that the analytical difficulties of asking questions about slave personality may not be nearly so great as the moral difficulties. The one inhibits the other; the morality of the matter has had a clogging effect on its theoretical development that may not be to the best interests of either. And yet theory on group personality is still in a stage rudimentary enough that this particular body of material—potentially illuminating—ought not to remain morally impounded any longer.

Is it possible to deal with "Sambo" as a type? The characteristics that have been claimed for the type come principally from Southern lore. Sambo, the typical plantation slave, was docile but irresponsible, loyal but lazy, humble but chronically given to lying and stealing; his behavior was full of infantile silliness and his talk inflated with childish exaggeration. His relationship with his master was one of utter dependence and childlike attachment: it was indeed this childlike quality that was the very key to his being. Although the merest hint of Sambo's "manhood" might fill the Southern breast with scorn, the child, "in his place," could be both exasperating and lovable.

Was he real or unreal? What order of existence, what rank of legitimacy, should be accorded him? Is there a "scientific" way to talk about this problem? For most Southerners in 1860 it went without saying not only that Sambo was real—that he was a dominant plantation type—but also that his characteristics were the clear product of racial inheritance. That was one way to deal with Sambo, a way that persisted a good many years after 1860. But in recent times, the discrediting, as unscientific, of racial explanations for any feature of plantation slavery has tended in the case of Sambo to discredit not simply the explanation itself but also the thing it was supposed to explain. Sambo is a mere stereotype—"stereotype" is itself a bad word, insinuating racial inferiority and invidious discrimination.[1] This modern approach to Sambo had a strong counterpart in the way Northern reformers thought about slavery in ante-bellum times: they thought that nothing could actually be said about the Negro's "true" nature because that nature was veiled by the institution of slavery. It could only be revealed by tearing away the veil. In short, no order of reality could be given to assertions about slave character, because those assertions were illegitimately grounded on race, whereas their only basis was a corrupt and "unreal" institution. "To be sure," a recent writer concedes, "there were plenty of opportunists among the Negroes who played the role assigned to them, acted the clown, and curried the favor of their masters in order to win the maximum re-

[1] The historian Samuel Eliot Morison was taken to task a few years ago by students of Queens College, Long Island, for his use of the name "Sambo" (in Volume I of his and H. S. Commager's text *The Growth of the American Republic*) and for referring to the pre-Civil War Negroes as "a race with exasperating habits" and to the typical slave as "childlike, improvident, humorous, prevaricating, and superstitious." As a result, the use of the text at Queens was discontinued. See *Time*, February 26, 1951, pp. 48–49.

The following is from the "Concluding Summary" of one of the series of studies begun in the late 1930's under the inspiration of Gunnar Myrdal: "The description of the stereotypes held concerning the American Negro indicates the widespread tendency to look upon the Negro as inferior, and to ascribe to him qualities of intellect and personality which mark him off with some definiteness from the surrounding white American population . . . [;] not all these alleged characteristics of the Negro are uncomplimentary, but even those which may be regarded as favorable have the flavor of inferiority about them. When the Negro is praised, he is praised for his childlike qualities of happiness and good nature or for his artistic and musical gifts. . . . Negro writers do express much more frequently, as one would expect, the belief that whites and Negroes have essentially equal potentialities, and that it is only the accidents of training and economic opportunity which have produced temporary differences; even among Negro writers, however, some have accepted the prevailing stereotype." Otto Klineberg (ed.), *Characteristics of the American Negro* (New York: Harper, 1944). Instead of proposing an actual program of inquiry, the intentions of this line of thought appear to be primarily moral and its objectives to be of a normative sort: desistance from the use of stereotypes.

wards within the system. . . ."[2] To impeach Sambo's legitimacy in this way is the next thing to talking him out of existence.

There ought, however, to be still a third way of dealing with the Sambo picture, some formula for taking it seriously. The picture has far too many circumstantial details, its hues have been stroked in by too many different brushes, for it to be denounced as counterfeit. Too much folk-knowledge, too much plantation literature, too much of the Negro's own lore, have gone into its making to entitle one in good conscience to condemn it as "conspiracy." One searches in vain through the literature of the Latin-American slave systems for the "Sambo" of our tradition—the perpetual child incapable of maturity. How is this to be explained?[3] If Sambo is not a product of race (that "explanation" can be consigned to oblivion) and not simply a product of "slavery" in the abstract (other societies have had slavery),[4] then he must be related to our own peculiar variety of it. And

[2] Kenneth Stampp, "The Historian and Southern Negro Slavery," *American Historical Review*, LVII (April, 1952), 617.

[3] There is such a word as "Zambo" in Latin America, but its meaning has no relation to our "Sambo." "A Zambo or Sambo (Spanish, *Zambo,* 'bandy-legged') is a cross between a *Negro* and an Amerindian (sometimes this name is given to the cross between a pure Negro and a mulatto, which the French called 'griffe')." Sir Harry Johnston, *The Negro in the New World* (London: Methuen, 1910), p. 3. I am not implying that racial stigma of some kind did not exist in South America . . . ; indeed, anthropological research has shown that the Latin-Americans were, and are, a good deal more conscious of "race" than such writers as Gilberto Freyre have been willing to admit. Even in Brazil, derogatory Negro stereotypes are common, and are apparently of long standing. On this point see Charles Wagley, *Race and Class in Rural Brazil* (Paris: UNESCO, 1952). On the other hand, it would be very difficult to find evidence in the literature of Brazil, or anywhere else in Latin America, of responsible men seriously maintaining that the Negro slave was constitutionally incapable of freedom. The views of a man like James H. Hammond, or for that matter the views of any average Southerner during the ante-bellum period, would have had little meaning in nineteenth-century Latin America. One is even inclined to think that these Latin-American stereotypes would compare more closely with the stereotypes of eastern and southern European immigrants that were held by certain classes in this country early in the twentieth century. See, e.g., Madison Grant's *Passing of the Great Race* (New York: Scribner, 1916). There are stereotypes and stereotypes: it would be quite safe to say that our "Sambo" far exceeds in tenacity and pervasiveness anything comparable in Latin America.

[4] It is, however, one thing to say that no longer are there any responsible men of science to be found advancing the racial argument, and quite another to assert that the argument is closed. In an odd sense we still find any number of statements indicating that the *other* side of the controversy is still being carried on, long after the bones of the enemy lie bleaching on the sands. For example, in the preface to a recent study on the American Negro by two distinguished psychologists, the authors define their "scientific position" by announcing that

if Sambo is uniquely an American product, then his existence, and the reasons for his character, must be recognized in order to appreciate the very scope of our slave problem and its aftermath. The absoluteness with which such a personality ("real" or "unreal") had been stamped upon the plantation slave does much to make plausible the ante-bellum Southerner's difficulty in imagining that blacks anywhere could be anything but a degraded race—and it goes far to explain his failure to see any sense at all in abolitionism. It even casts light on the peculiar quality of abolitionism itself; it was so all-enveloping a problem in human personality that our abolitionists could literally not afford to recognize it. Virtually without exception, they met this dilemma either by sidetracking it altogether (they explicitly refused to advance plans for solving it, arguing that this would rob their message of its moral force) or by countering it with theories of infinite human perfectibility. The question of personality, therefore, becomes a crucial phase of the entire problem of slavery in the United States, having conceivably something to do with the difference—already alluded to—between an "open" and a "closed" system of slavery.

. . . Several million people were detached with a peculiar effectiveness from a great variety of cultural backgrounds in Africa—a detachment operating with infinitely more effectiveness upon those brought to North America than upon those who came to Latin America. It was achieved partly by the shock experience inherent in the very mode of procurement but more specifically by the type of authority-system to which they were introduced and to which they had to adjust for physical and psychic survival. The new adjustment, to absolute power in a closed system, involved infantilization, and the detachment was so complete that little trace of prior (and thus alternative) cultural sanctions for behavior and personality remained

their book was "conceived and written on the premise that group characteristics are adaptive in nature and therefore not inborn, but acquired" and that "anyone who wishes to quote from [its] conclusions . . . to uphold any other thesis risks doing injustice to the material in the book, to the intentions of the authors, and to the Negro people." They then quote a kind of manifesto, signed by a group of prominent psychologists and social scientists, attesting that "as social scientists we know of no evidence that any ethnic group is inherently inferior." This is followed by a portion of the 1950 UNESCO "Statement on Race" which declares that "biological studies lend support to the ethic of universal brotherhood." From Abram Kardiner and Lionel Ovesey, *The Mark of Oppression: A Psychosocial Study of the American Negro* (New York: Norton, 1951), pp. v–vi. While these are sentiments which may (and must) be pronounced on any number of occasions among men of good will (the President regularly conceives it his duty to do this), their *scientific* content (which is the level at which they are here being offered) has long since ceased to be a matter of controversy.

for the descendants of the first generation. For them, adjustment to clear and omnipresent authority could be more or less automatic—as much so, or as little, as it is for anyone whose adjustment to a social system begins at birth and to whom that system represents normality. We do not know how generally a full adjustment was made by the first generation of fresh slaves from Africa. But we do know—from a modern experience [the German concentration camps]—that such an adjustment is possible, not only within the same generation but within two or three years.

. . .

Both [the concentration camp and the American plantation] were closed systems from which all standards based on prior connections had been effectively detached. A working adjustment to either system required a childlike conformity, a limited choice of "significant others." Cruelty per se cannot be considered the primary key to this; of far greater importance was the simple "closedness" of the system, in which all lines of authority descended from the master and in which alternative social bases that might have supported alternative standards were systematically suppressed.[5] The individual, consequently, for his very psychic security, had to picture his master in some way as the "good father,"[6] even when, as in the concentra-

[5] The experience of American prisoners taken by the Chinese during the Korean War seems to indicate that profound changes in behavior and values, if not in basic personality itself, can be effected without the use of physical torture or extreme deprivation. The Chinese were able to get large numbers of Americans to act as informers and to co-operate in numerous ways in the effort to indoctrinate all the prisoners with Communist propaganda. The technique contained two key elements. One was that all formal and informal authority structures within the group were systematically destroyed; this was done by isolating officers, non-commissioned officers, and any enlisted men who gave indications of leadership capacities. The other element involved the continual emphasizing of the captors' power and influence by judicious manipulation of petty rewards and punishments and by subtle hints of the greater rewards and more severe punishments (repatriation or non-repatriation) that rested with the pleasure of those in authority. See Edgar H. Schein, "Some Observations on Chinese Methods of Handling Prisoners of War," *Public Opinion Quarterly*, XX (Spring, 1956), 321–27.

[6] In a system as tightly closed as the plantation or the concentration camp, the slave's or prisoner's position of absolute dependency virtually compels him to see the authority-figure as somehow really "good." Indeed, all the evil in his life may flow from this man—but then so also must everything of any value. Here is the seat of the only "good" he knows, and to maintain his psychic balance he must persuade himself that the good is in some way dominant. A threat to this illusion is thus in a real sense a threat to his very existence. It is a common experience

tion camp, it made no sense at all.[7] But why should it not have made sense for many a simple plantation Negro whose master did exhibit, in all the ways that could be expected, the features of the good father who was really "good"? If the concentration camp could produce in two or three years the results that it did, one wonders how much more pervasive must have been those attitudes, expectations, and

---

among social workers dealing with neglected and maltreated children to have a child desperately insist on his love for a cruel and brutal parent and beg that he be allowed to remain with that parent. The most dramatic feature of this situation is the cruelty which it involves, but the mechanism which inspires the devotion is not the cruelty of the parent but rather the abnormal dependency of the child. A classic example of this mechanism in operation may be seen in the case of Varvara Petrovna, mother of Ivan Turgenev. Mme Turgenev "ruled over her serfs with a rod of iron." She demanded utter obedience and total submission. The slightest infraction of her rules brought the most severe punishment: "A maid who did not offer her a cup of tea in the proper manner was sent off to some remote village and perhaps separated from her family forever; gardeners who failed to prevent the plucking of a tulip in one of the flower beds before the house were ordered to be flogged; a servant whom she suspected of mutinous disposition was sent off to Siberia." Her family and her most devoted servants were treated in much the same manner. "Indeed," wrote Varvara Zhitova, the adopted daughter of Mme Turgenev, "those who loved her and were most devoted to her suffered most of all." Yet in spite of her brutality she was adored by the very people she tyrannized. David Magarshack describes how once when thrashing her eldest son she nearly fainted with sadistic excitement, whereupon "little Nicholas, forgetting his punishment, bawled at the top of his voice: 'Water! Water for mummy!' " Mme Zhitova, who knew Mme Turgenev's cruelty intimately and was herself the constant victim of her tyranny, wrote: "In spite of this, I loved her passionately, and when I was, though rarely, separated from her, I felt lonely and unhappy." Even Mme Turgenev's maid Agatha, whose children were sent to another village, when still infants so that Agatha might devote all her time to her mistress, could say years later, "Yes, she caused me much grief. I suffered much from her, but all the same I loved her! She was a real lady!" V. Zhitova, *The Turgenev Family*, trans. A. S. Mills (London: Havill Press, 1954), p. 25; David Magarshack, *Turgenev: A Life* (New York: Grove, 1954), pp. 14, 16, 22.

[7] Bruno Bettelheim tells us of the fantastic efforts of the old prisoners to believe in the benevolence of the officers of the SS. "They insisted that these officers [hid] behind their rough surface a feeling of justice and propriety; he, or they, were supposed to be genuinely interested in the prisoners and even trying, in a small way, to help them. Since nothing of these supposed feelings and efforts ever became apparent, it was explained that he hid them so effectively because otherwise he would not be able to help the prisoners. The eagerness of these prisoners to find reasons for their claims was pitiful. A whole legend was woven around the fact that of two officers inspecting a barrack one had cleaned his shoes from mud before entering. He probably did it automatically, but it was interpreted as a rebuff of the other officer and a clear demonstration of how he felt about the concentration camp." Bettelheim, "Individual and Mass Behavior," p. 451.

values which had, certainly, their benevolent side and which were accepted and transmitted over generations.

For the Negro child, in particular, the plantation offered no really satisfactory father-image other than the master. The "real" father was virtually without authority over his child, since discipline, parental responsibility, and control of rewards and punishments all rested in other hands; the slave father could not even protect the mother of his children except by appealing directly to the master. Indeed, the mother's own role loomed far larger for the slave child than did that of the father. She controlled those few activities—household care, preparation of food, and rearing of children—that were left to the slave family. For that matter, the very etiquette of plantation life removed even the honorific attributes of fatherhood from the Negro male, who was addressed as "boy"—until, when the vigorous years of his prime were past, he was allowed to assume the title of "uncle."

From the master's viewpoint, slaves had been defined in law as property, and the master's power over his property must be absolute. But then this property was still human property. These slaves might never be quite as human as *he* was, but still there were certain standards that could be laid down for their behavior: obedience, fidelity, humility, docility, cheerfulness, and so on. Industry and diligence would of course be demanded, but a final element in the master's situation would undoubtedly qualify that expectation. Absolute power for him meant absolute dependency for the slave—the dependency not of the developing child but of the perpetual child. For the master, the role most aptly fitting such a relationship would naturally be that of the father. As a father he could be either harsh or kind, as he chose, but as a *wise* father he would have, we may suspect, a sense of the limits of his situation. He must be ready to cope with *all* the qualities of the child, exasperating as well as ingratiating. He might conceivably have to expect in this child—besides his loyalty, docility, humility, cheerfulness, and (under supervision) his diligence—such additional qualities as irresponsibility, playfulness, silliness, laziness, and (quite possibly) tendencies to lying and stealing. Should the entire prediction prove accurate, the result would be something resembling "Sambo."

The social and psychological sanctions of role-playing may in the last analysis prove to be the most satisfactory of the several approaches to Sambo, for, without doubt, of all the roles in American life that of Sambo was by far the most pervasive. The outlines of the role might be sketched in by crude necessity, but what of the finer shades? The sanctions against overstepping it were bleak enough,[8] but the rewards—the sweet applause, as it were, for performing it with sincerity and feeling—were something to be appreciated on quite another level. The law, untuned to the deeper harmonies, could command the player to be present for the occasion, and the whip might even warn against his missing the grosser cues, but could those things really insure the performance that melted all hearts? Yet there was many and many a performance, and the audiences (whose standards were high) appear to have been for the most part well pleased. They were actually viewing their own masterpiece. Much labor had been lavished upon this *chef d'oeuvre,* the most genial resources of Southern society had been available for the work; touch after touch had been applied throughout the years, and the result—embodied not in the unfeeling law but in the richest layers of Southern lore—had been the product of an exquisitely rounded collective creativity. And indeed, in a sense that somehow transcended the merely ironic, it was a labor of love. "I love the simple and unadulterated slave, with his geniality, his mirth, his swagger, and his nonsense," wrote Edward Pollard. "I love to look upon his countenance shining with content and grease; I love to study his affectionate heart; I love to mark that peculiarity in him, which beneath all his buffoonery exhibits him as a creature of the tenderest sensibilities, mingling his joys and his sorrows with those of his master's home."[9] Love, even on those terms, was surely no inconsequential reward.

But what were the terms? The Negro was to be a child forever. "The Negro . . . in his true nature, is always a boy, let him be ever so old. . . ."[10] "He is . . . a dependent upon the white race; dependent for guidance and direction even to the procurement of his most indispensable necessaries. Apart from this protection he has the helplessness of a child—without foresight, without faculty of contrivance, without thrift of any kind."[11] Not only was he a child; he was a happy child. Few Southern writers failed to describe with obvious fondness

[8] Professor Stampp, in a chapter called "To Make Them Stand in Fear," describes the planter's resources for dealing with a recalcitrant slave. *Peculiar Institution,* pp. 141–91.

[9] Edward A. Pollard, *Black Diamonds Gathered in the Darkey Homes of the South* (New York: Pudney & Russel, 1859), p. 58.

[10] *Ibid.*, p. viii.

[11] John Pendleton Kennedy, *Swallow Barn* (Philadelphia: Carey & Lea, 1832).

the bubbling gaiety of a plantation holiday or the perpetual good humor that seemed to mark the Negro character, the good humor of an everlasting childhood.

The role, of course, must have been rather harder for the earliest generations of slaves to learn. "Accommodation," according to John Dollard, "involves the renunciation of protest or aggression against undesirable conditions of life and the organization of the character so that protest does not appear, but acceptance does. It may come to pass in the end that the unwelcome force is idealized, that one identifies with it and takes it into the personality; it sometimes even happens that what is at first resented and feared is finally loved."[12]

Might the process, on the other hand, be reversed? It is hard to imagine its being reversed overnight. The same role might still be played in the years after slavery—we are told that it was[13]—and yet it was played to more vulgar audiences with cruder standards, who paid much less for what they saw. The lines might be repeated more and more mechanically, with less and less conviction; the incentives

[12] John Dollard, *Caste and Class in a Southern Town* (2d ed.; New York: Harper, 1949), p. 255. The lore of "accommodation," taken just in itself, is very rich and is, needless to say, morally very complex. It suggests a delicate psychological balance. On the one hand, as the Dollard citation above implies, accommodation is fraught with dangers for the personalities of those who engage in it. On the other hand, as Bruno Bettelheim has reminded me, this involves a principle that goes well beyond American Negro society and is to be found deeply imbedded in European traditions: the principle of how the powerless can manipulate the powerful through aggressive stupidity, literal-mindedness, servile fawning, and irresponsibility. In this sense the immovably stupid "Good Soldier Schweik" and the fawning Negro in Richard Wright's *Black Boy* who allowed the white man to kick him for a quarter partake of the same tradition. Each has a technique whereby he can in a real sense exploit his powerful superiors, feel contempt for them, and suffer in the process no great damage to his own pride. Jewish lore, as is well known, teems with this sort of thing. There was much of it also in the traditional relationships between peasants and nobles in central Europe.

Still, all this required the existence of some sort of alternative forces for moral and psychological orientation. The problem of the Negro in slavery times involved the virtual absence of such forces. It was with the end of slavery, presumably, that they would first begin to present themselves in generally usable form—a man's neighbors, the Loyal Leagues, white politicians, and so on. It would be in these circumstances that the essentially intermediate technique of accommodation could be used as a protective device beneath which a more independent personality might develop.

[13] Even Negro officeholders during Reconstruction, according to Francis B. Simkins, "were known to observe carefully the etiquette of the Southern caste system." "New Viewpoints of Southern Reconstruction," *Journal of Southern History*, V (February, 1939), 52.

to perfection could become hazy and blurred, and the excellent old piece could degenerate over time into low farce. There could come a point, conceivably, with the old zest gone, that it was no longer worth the candle. The day might come at last when it dawned on a man's full waking consciousness that he had really grown up, that he was, after all, only playing a part.

QUESTIONS FOR DISCUSSION AND WRITING

1. Elkins asserts that "fifty years ago, if the American Negro was congratulated for anything, it was for his remarkable advancement from a state of primitive ignorance." Is this attitude still present in American thought? How does it manifest itself?
2. What effect has the loss of his past had on the American Negro? What efforts are being made to restore that past to him? Why?
3. What were the effects of the "closed system"? To what extent is the "closed system" present in contemporary American life? How is it shown?
4. Elkins suggests that an analysis of stereotypes helps us to understand the small degree of truth they contain. Analyze the present-day stereotype of the black man. Why does it have so much meaning to so many whites? What white attitudes does the black stereotype reflect?
5. According to Elkins, the experience of slavery brought about a Sambo-like childishness among slaves. To what extent has the experience of "freedom" undone this childlike attitude? How do Douglass (p. 47), Grier and Cobbs (p. 309), Carmichael (p. 336), Jones (p. 257), and Clorox (p. 399) feel about the idea of black childishness?

ROBERT M. COLES IS A RESEARCH PSYCHIATRIST CURRENTLY ASSOCIATED WITH THE HARVARD UNIVERSITY HEALTH SERVICES. HIS BOOK *Children of Crisis*, FIRST PUBLISHED IN 1964, IS BASED UPON HIS EXPERIENCES AS A PSYCHIATRIST IN THE SOUTH. A FREQUENTLY PUBLISHED WRITER, COLES IS A MEMBER OF THE EDITORIAL BOARD OF *The New Republic*.

ROBERT M. COLES

THE MEANING OF RACE

Sally, one of the Negro children I knew in New Orleans, drew heavily upon her grandmother's spirit when confronted with the hate and violence of mobs and the forced, pointed loneliness brought on by the boycott of "her" desegregated school. Like the other three girls selected, Sally (and her parents) had no idea that she would face exposure to mobs as the price for entering a once all-white elementary school. Her parents had submitted her application because many of their neighbors were doing likewise. Having arrived only recently in New Orleans, they had assumed that its attitudes were not those of the state's rural areas. So much else was different in New Orleans—

THE MEANING OF RACE From *Children of Crisis* by Robert M. Coles, Chapter 10. Originally appeared in *Daedalus*, Journal of the American Academy of Arts and Sciences.

its buildings that anyone could enter, its streetcars where anyone could sit anywhere, its sidewalks where Negroes could walk on the "inside" without interruption instead of retiring to the road at the approach of a white person, its stores serving *all* customers by proper turn—that school desegregation seemed another miracle to be accepted quickly as part of living in the city.

Sally and her parents were eventually to realize they were fated to challenge their city rather than quietly enjoy some of its advantages. There came a point in my observations of how they managed such a fate when I was puzzled at their continuing calm in the midst of danger. I frankly wondered—at first to myself, then aloud to them—why they did not gather themselves together and leave. Sally's grandmother gave the following explanation: "If we run away, we'll fool ourselves; you can't run away from being a colored man. It don't make any difference where you go—you has the same problem, one way or another." I asked her whether she thought those problems in any way comparable to those faced by white people—for example the few white families who were resisting the mob's will, defying its boycott to keep their children at school with Sally. "Yes," she replied firmly, "we is all the same under God, so we has the same problems; but colored folk has special ones, too. It's the same being colored as white, but it's different being colored, too." Then she repeated the words, nodding her agreement with them, "It's the same, but it's different."

It may seem a bit obvious and simple-minded to insist upon putting the Negro's problems in the context of those shared by all of us as human beings; moreover, it hardly seems surprising to learn that the Negro has problems that are all his own. Still, I think research into what it means to be a Negro will sooner or later meet up with the methodological hazards involved in abstracting people on racial grounds (on religious, social, economic or geographical ones as well) and then talking about "their" feeling (in contrast to any individual's or, for that matter, those found in *all* individuals). I do not think either Sally, her parents or her grandmother established any new record of courage and endurance in the face of threats. In many ways the crowds were angrier at the few white parents who defied them by keeping their children in school. Each family—confronting similar daily odds—stood fast for its own reasons, even as they all had some purposes in common. We lose when we dwell exclusively on either the private or the shared experience or intention.

What interested me about the remarks of Sally's grandmother was that she gave me an essentially matter-of-fact explanation for her steadfastness: there was simply no alternative. A Negro cannot flee danger, try though he might. Danger is everywhere, a never-ending consequence of his social and economic condition. Danger is written into history with his blood, into everyday customs by laws, into living itself by the size of his wages, the nature of his neighborhood. In contrast, every white parent I knew fell back upon another kind of reason for his actions. One father was a minister; he called upon his religious faith. Another parent was especially devoted to the education of her children; she could not stand idle while a school was destroyed, her children untaught. One family had only recently come to New Orleans; they did not "believe" in segregation—and they were stubborn and plucky enough to want to stand up for their beliefs, or, in this case, the absence of them. (Of course, I met a few others who put their ideals more positively; they were very much "for" integration; yet they were also "for" the safety of their children, enough so that they yielded to the prevailing storm and sought out other schools for their children.)

What all these white families revealed together was a willingness to "choose" danger in the pursuit of an ideal or goal. Each one of them would mention the possibility open to them of rejecting a role in school desegregation. One father mentioned travel, just as Sally's grandmother did: "When I saw those people acting that way, I became ashamed of the city. We even talked of moving away, to Texas or California; but then we thought we just couldn't rest easy, running away." Each one of them rejected flight from the mobs, or indifference to them. Many others, very much like them, could rationalize their disinterest in desegregation, or defend their unwillingness to oppose segregationist street violence, by pointing to the fact that even the police—let alone the majority of the white parents in the school district—were disinclined to disperse the mob.

I do not think that situation in New Orleans was unlike the general situation in our country, as it confronts Negro and white people. The stakes may usually be less grim, less distinctly defined, less dangerously at issue; but the Negro has his skin to help him establish the nature of his problems and his beliefs, while white people must grapple for other mainstays of self-awareness or faith. Children who grow up and experience the Negro's lot in our society—no matter how various its expressions—achieve at least some measure of self-definition. It may be insufficient, it may lead to ruin, yet it cannot be seen only as a burden. To quote again from Sally's grandmother: "We may not have anything; but at least we know why." She was telling me about the whites of her region, whose ability to look down upon her did little to elevate their material or spiritual welfare. Oppressors, they knew little about the reasons for their own impoverishment.

What can be said about how Sally feels being a Negro, about how her grandmother feels, or any of the other children, the other adults we have met in this book? All that has been said about the meaning of skin color to Negro children[1] surely holds for Sally—and has always held for her parents and grandparents. Sally at six could tell me rather openly that she wished she were white. Other Negro children her age deny and conceal similar wishes with great vehemence—that they, in fact, have such wishes is all too clear from their drawings, games and "innocent" or "unintended" remarks.

Still, as we grow, or live, we all want occasionally to be what we are not, or cannot really ever become. What must be done is to establish the relevance, the importance of Sally's fantasies about her skin for the rest of her life. To do so requires placing discrete psychological events (and the observations made by psychiatrists of those events) in the context of the general growth and development of the child, including, of course, the influence of society upon how he is reared and taught to regard himself.

My clinical impression—slowly consolidated over these past years of working with Negro children—is that most of the "usual" problems and struggles of growing up find an additional dimension in the racial context. In a very real sense being Negro serves to organize

[1] See Mary Ellen Goodman, *Race Awareness in Young Children* (Cambridge, Mass., 1952); K. B. Clark and M. Clark, "The Development of Consciousness of Self and the Emergence of Racial Identification in Negro Preschool Children," *Journal of Social Psychology*, Vol. 10, No. 4 (November 1939), pp. 591–599. K. B. Clark and M. Clark, "Skin Color as a Factor in Racial Identification of Negro Preschool Children," *Journal of Social Psychology*, Vol. 11, No. 1 (February 1940), pp. 159–169; K. B. Clark and M. Clark, "Emotional Factors in Racial Identification and Preference in Negro Children," *Journal of Negro Education*, Vol. 19 (1950), pp. 341–350. Eugene B. Brody, "Color and Identity Conflict in Young Boys," *Psychiatry*, Vol. 26, No. 2 (May 1963), pp. 188–201; Eugene B. Brody, "Color and Identity Conflict in Young Boys, II," *Archives of General Psychiatry*, Vol. 10 (April 1964), pp. 354–360; R. Coles, "Southern Children Under Desegregation," *American Journal of Psychiatry*, Vol. 120, No. 4 (October 1963), pp. 332–344; R. Coles, "Racial Conflict and a Child's Question," *Journal of Nervous and Mental Disease*, Vol. 140, No. 2 (February 1965), pp. 162–170.

and render coherent many of the experiences, warnings, punishments and prohibitions that Negro children face. The feelings of inferiority or worthlessness they acquire, the longing to be white they harbor and conceal, the anger at what they find to be their relatively confined and moneyless condition, these do not fully account for the range of emotions in many Negro children as they come to terms with the "meaning" of their skin color. Sally's grandmother said more concisely what I am struggling to say: "They can scream at our Sally, but she knows why, and she's not surprised. She knows that even when they stop screaming, she'll have whispers, and after them the stares. It'll be with her for life. . . . We tell our children that, so by the time they have children, they'll know how to prepare them. . . . It takes a lot of preparing before you can let a child loose in a white world. If you're black in Louisiana it's like cloudy weather; you just don't see the sun much."

The "preparation" for such a climate of living begins in the first year of life. At birth the shade of the child's skin may be very important to his parents—so important that it determines in large measure how he is accepted, particularly in the many Negro marriages which bring together a range of genes which, when combined, offer the possibility of almost *any* color. What is often said about color-consciousness in Negroes (their legendary pursuit of skin bleaches and hair-straightening lotions) must be seen in its relentless effect upon the life of the mind, upon babies and upon child-rearing. A Negro sociologist—involved in, rather than studying, the sit-in movement—insisted to me that "when a Negro child is shown to his mother and father, the first thing they look at is his color, and then they check for fingers and toes." I thought such a remark extreme indeed, until two years later when I made a point of asking many parents what they thought of it—and found them unashamedly in agreement.

As infants become children, they begin to form some idea of how they look, and how their appearance compares with that of others. They watch television, accompany their mothers to the local market or stores downtown. They play on the street and ride in cars which move through cities or small towns. They hear talk, at the table or in Sunday school, or from other children while playing. By the time they enter school, at five or six, to "begin" to learn, they have already learned some lessons of self-respect (or its absence) quite well.

I have been continually astonished to discover just how intricately children come to examine the social system, the political and economic facts of life in our society. I had always imagined myself rather sensible and untouched by those romantic nineteenth-century notions of childhood "innocence." As a child psychiatrist I had even committed myself to a professional life based on the faith that young children see and feel what is happening in their family life—and if properly heard will tell much of it to the doctor, whether by words, in games or with crayons. Yet I had never quite realized that children so quickly learn to estimate who can vote, or who has the money to frequent this kind of restaurant or that kind of theater, or what groups of people contribute to our police force—and why. Children, after all, have other matters on their minds—and so do many adults.

I do not think Negro children are, by definition, budding sociologists or political scientists, but I have been struck by how specifically aware they become of those forces in our society which, reciprocally, are specifically sensitive to *them*. They remark upon the scarcity of colored faces on television, and I have heard them cheer the sight of a Negro on that screen. In the South they ask their parents why few if any policemen or bus drivers are colored. In the ghettos of the North they soon enough come to regard the Negro policeman or bus driver as specially privileged—as indeed he is, with his steady pay, with his uniform that calls for respect and signifies authority—and perhaps as an enemy in the inevitable clash with "whitey."

"The first thing a colored mother has to do when her kids get old enough to leave the house and play in the street is teach them about the white man and what he expects. I've done it with seven kids, and I've got two more to go; and then I hope I'll be through." She was talking about her earnest desire to "be done with" bringing children into the world, but she had slipped into a recital of how Negro mothers must be loyal to the segregationist customs of Southern towns. Still, she preferred them to the North; and so did her son, a youth I had watched defy sheriffs (and his mother's early admonitions) in Alabama and Mississippi for several years. "In the North," her son added, "I'd have learned the same thing, only it's worse, because there a mother can't just lay it on the line. It takes time for the boy to get the full pitch, and realize it's really the same show, just a little dressed up; and until he makes that discovery, he's liable to be confused. The thing we're not down here is confused."

The Negro child growing up is thus likely to be quite rigidly and fearfully certain about what he may do, where he may go and who he eventually will be. In the desegregated schools of the South, where

Southern whites have had a fresh opportunity and reason to watch Negro children closely, teachers have been especially impressed by what one of them called the "worldliness" of the colored child. She did not mean the jaded, tough indifference of the delinquent—perhaps a later stage of "development." She simply was referring to the shrewd, calculating awareness in children who have been taught—worried about, screamed at, slapped and flogged in the process—the rules of the game as they apply to Negroes. She had come to realize that growing up as a Negro child had its special coherence and orderliness as well as its chaos. The children she was teaching were lonely, isolated and afraid—a few of them in a large, only recently desegregated white elementary school in Tennessee—but they also knew exactly what they feared, and exactly how to be as safe as possible in the face of what they feared.

For that matter, it is not simply that Negro children learn the bounds of their fate, the limits of the kinds of work allowed to them, the extent of their future disenfranchisement, the confines of their social freedom, the edge of the residential elbowroom permitted them, the margin of free play, whim or sport available to them now or within their grasp when they are grown. They learn how to make use of such knowledge, and in so doing gain quite gradually and informally an abiding, often tough sense of what is about them in the world, and what must be in them to survive. In the words of Sally's grandmother, "Sally can get through those mobs; she was born to, and one way or another she'll have to do it for the rest of her life."

So it is not all disorder and terror for these children. As they grow older, go to school, think of a life for themselves, they can envision a life which is quiet, pleasant and uneventful for long stretches of time, or at least as much so as for any "other" children. That is, the Negro child will play and frolic, eat and sleep like all other children; and, though this may seem no great discovery, it is essential that it be mentioned in a discussion which necessarily singles out special pains or hazards for analysis. Sometimes when I read descriptions of "what it is like to be a Negro" I have to turn away in disbelief: the children I have been working with—in sharecropper cabins and migrant camps as well as in cities—simply do not resemble the ones portrayed. Perhaps it is impossible in *any* description to do justice to the continuity and contradiction of life, but we can at least try by qualifying our assumptions, by acknowledging that they do not encompass the entire range of human experience.

"It's like being two people: when I'm around here I'm just me;

when I leave and go to school or go downtown I'm just another person." A high school student in Atlanta is speaking, a Negro youth who is trying to integrate those two facets of his personality as well as himself into a white school. Yet, not even his sharp, clear-cut statement can account for the range of sensibilities which develop in Negro children as a result of their race's history and present condition.

As in all matters of human behavior, each Negro child or adult I have met has developed or is developing his or her own style of dealing with what is essentially a social experience that becomes for the individual a series of psychological ones capable of giving "significant" structure or form to a life. Some of the styles are well established in folklore and in the daily expectations of both whites and Negroes: subservience, calculated humiliation, sly ingratiation, self-mockery; or, changing the tone somewhat, aloof indifference, suspicious withdrawal, sullen passivity or grim, reluctant compliance. Again, in areas of diminished repression, where outright submission has been replaced by the possibility of social and racial disengagement or "co-existence," one sees impatience, or ill-tempered, measured distrust; indeed, in evidence is everything from irritability and barely concealed resentment to an almost numbing hatred and fury.

What most Negro children of ten or twelve have learned is a tendency, stimulated by the white man's presence or appearance, for one or (more likely) a mixture of several of these or other adaptive modes of dealing with him. The choice, of course, depends on the private life of the child, his general development of personality—there are reasons other than racial ones for being prone to good-humored supplication or to anger, despair, resignation, sulkiness, insensibility or inertia. The manner of adjustment also varies, as I mentioned, by region and by class or occupation, too.

Even though Negroes in general grow to be especially sensitive to—and on their guard with—whites, the quality and quantity of experience, hence of feeling, between Negroes and whites is not all of a kind. Some Negroes are constantly in contact with whites: taking care of their homes, waiting on them, carrying out their orders in offices and stores or working alongside them, even of late giving them orders or directions. Others live in the shadow of the white world, but really have very little direct encounter with white individuals. "They touches on us, but we don't much see them, to tell the truth." The wife of a sharecropper, she worked the land of a white farmer, lived in his house, saw him or his deputies drive by; yet, her actual, person-to-person meetings with white people were few. She and her family carried on their daily lives with that mixture of freedom and restraint characteristic of poor rural folk. Though their "inheritance" as Negroes—their social and cultural traditions—set a different atmosphere for them than, say, white sharecroppers or small farmers in the same county, the similarities of living in that county are by far more striking. Negroes tend to discount the importance of "legal" marriage, are often much more open and relaxed about breast-feeding or toilet training, and tend to keep less orderly house-holds. On the other hand, white parents tend to be more attentive to their children as they become of school age, their individual preferences indulged where reasonable or possible. However, what both races share are similar routines, similar worlds with which they must contend. These common experiences fashion a common attitude toward education, food, clothing and other people in contrast to those of one's own family.[2]

In the ghettos, or the all-Negro middle-class areas of our cities, a somewhat similar pattern holds, of random association with whites in the midst of an ordinarily exclusive relationship with one's own people. Naturally, class differences obtain, it being one thing to try to imitate the white middle-class world (and to have the means to do it) and quite another to live the uncertain, hand-to-mouth existence characteristic of any slum. Yet even in Atlanta, where there is a Negro residential district of matchless elegance (if compared only with other Negro districts), the experience of crossing into contiguous white areas demands its recognition, a recognition not unlike that in the Negro who leaves the same city's ample slums on a shopping trip or to look for a job downtown.

The word "caste" only partially explains such shared feelings, which persist in the North regardless of class, even among those Negroes—their number is obviously increasing now—who live predominantly in the white world. For that matter, in the psychotherapeutic or psychoanalytic relationship—where presumably troubled *individuals* are consulting *doctors*—psychiatrists have commented on certain general problems which arise out of the difference between

[2] I tried to illustrate the development of such attitudes among the rural poor in "The Lives of Migrant Farmers," *American Journal of Psychiatry*, Vol. 122, No. 3 (September 1965), and *The Migrant Worker*, a pamphlet issued by the Southern Regional Council (Atlanta, Georgia, Fall 1965).

the patient's skin color and the doctor's.[3] Regardless of their particular symptoms, Negroes and whites in the psychiatric office have a special problem to face, not necessarily difficult, by no means insurmountable, but nonetheless real and rather commonly present. There is a likelihood of more distrust, more fearful hesitation, than is usually the case; and the mind of both the Negro and white person—whether doctor or patient—will find it difficult to refrain from noticing and responding to the various symbolic and emotional meanings of color.[4] They are, after all, part of our entire culture, and certainly significant in the childhood and adulthood of Negroes in America.

When I lived in Mississippi I had a home in a small town. The people I knew were intelligent and kindly—all of them white, middle-class people who were born in the state, brought up from their first days by Negro "mammies." I recall their weekly trips to "nigger town"—they were adults now, and there was laundry to take there, or a favorite servant's birthday to remember. After I became interested in how young Negroes lived and got along with whites, I went with a doctor and his wife one day to the colored section of our town. They had always ignored laundromats, would not think of buying a washing machine; Louisa had been washing and ironing their sheets and shirts for years. Louisa and her mother had taken care of the doctor's wife when she was a child: "She fed me as a baby. I was the first baby she cared for; she learned from her mother how to do it—I don't remember much of it; I just remember Louisa smiling and helping me choose a dress to wear for a party at school, and maybe a game or two she played with us." Later that day this very sensitive woman told me of an experience she *did* remember, and quite clearly: "I think I was seven or eight, and I went with my mother to a five-and-dime store. It was one of those old ones; I can still see the counters, and the fans going. They hung in rows from the ceilings. . . . Any-

[3] For example, H. R. St. Claire, "Psychiatric Interview Experiences with Negroes," *American Journal of Psychiatry*, Vol. 108, No. 2 (August 1951), pp. 113–119; Viola W. Bernard, "Psychoanalysis and Members of Minority Groups," *Journal of the American Psychoanalytic Association*, Vol. 1, No. 2 (April 1953), pp. 256–267; Walter A. Adams, "The Negro Patient in Psychiatric Treatment," *American Journal of Orthopsychiatry*, Vol. 20, No. 2 (April 1950), pp. 305–310.

[4] See Harold R. Isaacs, *The New World of Negro Americans* (New York, 1963), pp. 62–96, for an excellent discussion, with references, of the symbolic meaning of color to Negroes. See also A. Kardiner and L. Ovesey, *The Mark of Oppression* (New York, 1951). An interesting paper on this subject is Janet Kennedy's "Problems Posed in the Analysis of Negro Patients," *Psychiatry*, Vol. 15, No. 3 (August 1952), pp. 313–327.

way, we were walking down the aisle, and I bumped right into a nigra woman. I said, 'Excuse me, ma'am,' and right in front of her my mother told me never to use 'ma'am' with the colored. It was okay to say 'excuse me,' because that showed I was a well-mannered girl; but 'ma'am' was different. . . . I had trouble making sense of that, and I asked my mother her reasons for being so against using 'ma'am' with the nigra. She tried to tell me that it was the way we did things in the world, but it never made sense to me. . . . I think what *did* make sense to me was that I had to obey my mother's wish. Then you grow older, and you stop trying to make sense of things like that. You just know that there are things you can do, and things you can't, and that's it. My brother once tried to get my parents to explain to him why he had to wear a tie one place, and not another. It was the same thing. My daddy just said, 'Jimmie, that's the way it is, and that's the way we have to do it.' "

Looking back at all the conversations I have had with individuals like this lady since that day, it has been a rare person—even a rare "poor white"—who has not mentioned similar memories. The confused and tortured intimacy of white and Negro people in the South has been described by writer after writer.[5] Yet to be confronted by it comes as a challenge to anyone interested in just how the human mind deals with the inconsistencies and contradictions of social existence. That woman today—in spite of her ordinary civility and even graciousness—is grimly opposed to any change in the way Negroes and whites get along with one another. She feels that others, "outsiders," are imposing strange and unsettling demands upon her. The strangeness of her own childhood, of her own relationship to Negroes as a child, no longer troubles her. Yes, there are memories, and if she is not pressed, not questioned with any intent to argue or even interpret but simply to learn, she will reveal them to herself as well as her listener. All in all, though, her present anger at Negroes and her long-standing sense of them as beyond the bounds of her politesse combine to exact a price: she cannot really feel comfortable with some of the best moments in her own childhood; she must work hard

[5] Lillian Smith, *Killers of the Dream* (New York, 1949); W. J. Cash, *Mind of the South* (New York, 1941); C. Vann Woodward, *The Strange Career of Jim Crow* (New York, 1955). Southern writers like Faulkner, Eudora Welty, Shirley Ann Grau and Flannery O'Connor constantly return to the themes of savage hate and sly or desperate love between whites and Negroes. William Taylor's *Cavalier and Yankee* (New York, 1961) illustrates how the racial problem similarly touched and influenced writers in earlier times.

at denying them in order to keep her present attitudes properly charged and effective in her daily life. There is no romantic indulgence in Faulkner's descriptions of the passion that fuels the hate of white Southerners for Negroes, particularly those white yeomen hard-pressed by hunger, self-doubt and loneliness, whether in comparison to other Southerners or (as even well-to-do Southerners often feel) in relation to their countrymen in other regions.

If the white man must often deny his early, increasingly confusing friendliness with Negroes, the Negro has little choice but to come to terms with his early, equally confusing awe, envy and hate of whites, and his friendliness with them. "Keep your fear of the white man, I has to tell it to every child all the time until they knows it for themselves." I asked this poor, uneducated wife of a former sharecropper whether her children had *only* fear of whites. She shook her head. "They be jealous of them. Sometimes they might want to see how they live; so my husband drives them over and picks me up from work." (She worked as a maid in a comfortable Atlanta suburb, and her daughter was now at school with children who lived in that suburb.) "I told her, we can have all the rights they have, but you can't feel easy with them so fast. . . . I just make sure my kids know to be afraid."

The "ma'am" that the white child learns to drop the Negro child learns to say—say fearfully, say anxiously, say reluctantly, say eagerly, say out of habit, say with conviction, say and mean, or say with reservations that surely include a wide range of bitterness and resentment. Doubtless the experience of a Negro growing up in Boston is different from that of a Negro in the Black Belt of Alabama, but I think the common need persists everywhere in America for Negro youth to gauge their relationships to white people warily. While the white man loses part of his own life history, his own kindness or good will when he isolates his present self from his past feelings, the Negro loses part of his own life history, his natural self-protective assertiveness, his confidence with others and ease about himself, when he learns to separate his past experience of surprised indignation from his present sense of what the world expects and will demand. Just as we can compare white people by how easily they submit the occasions or psychological moments in their "private" lives to the judgment of social and cultural imperatives, so I should imagine Negroes differ in their willingness to deny and surrender themselves in order to curry the favor of the white man.

One of the most thoughtful and careful investigators of how Negroes endure their lot in American society has asked in one of his papers:[6] "Why do not all Negro men become schizophrenic?" The very fact that such a question can be formulated suggests at once some of the problems facing both Negroes and social scientists. We do not know for certain the cause (or causes) of schizophrenia; but we do feel that consistently disorganized, brittle, tense, fearful parents in some way influence its development in their children. It does not seem fatuous, therefore, to inquire why *all* Negro men are not schizophrenic. A number of observers, from several disciplines,[7] have remarked upon the serious psychological problems facing large numbers of Negroes who live impoverished lives, in a social and cultural climate which commonly rejects them, and in families often enough unstable, disturbed and split apart.

Of course, it is obvious that millions of Negroes survive such special strains—if not handily, then at least with no crippling mental disease. As a matter of fact, what is puzzling to those of us who have worked with the more penniless, "backward," rural Negroes is our continuing sense of the remarkable sturdiness and poise in many of them. Many others, of course, are tired, apathetic, almost lifeless; though even people in this latter group show a striking capacity to come alive when exposed to the momentum of social and political change.

The privation, the domination and oppression of the Negro in this country have been all of a special kind. It is futile to compare it to the intermittent excesses of colonial powers, or to the sadistic regressions to bestiality characteristic of totalitarian regimes; for that matter, I am not sure there isn't a real difference between the way persecuted minorities once lived with their oppressors in the various European countries and the way Negroes and whites have lived in the South. Likewise, the caste systems in Asia are not quite like ours. Despite our flaws, we claim ourselves a democracy, and have almost torn ourselves apart for a century working to justify the assertion.

[6] Eugene B. Brody, "Social Conflict and Schizophrenic Behavior in Young Adult Negro Males," *Psychiatry*, Vol. 24 (November 1961), pp. 337–346.

[7] For example, Allison Davis and John Dollard, *The Children of Bondage* (Washington, D.C., 1940); Gunnar Myrdal, *An American Dilemma* (New York, 1944 and 1962); Kenneth B. Clark, *Prejudice and Your Child* (Boston, 1955); Marie Jahoda, *Race Relations and Mental Health* (Paris, 1960); Group for the Advancement of Psychiatry, "Psychiatric Aspects of Desegregation," Report No. 37, 1957; Kardiner and Ovesey, *op. cit.*

In addition to holding the Negro first a slave, then isolated legally and socially, we have also lived side by side with him, blended our blood and skin with his, shared our homes and names with him, entrusted our children to him, and in the South, scene of his longest and most dismal affliction, nevertheless and coincidentally joined him in poverty and suffering, given him food and clothing and even affection. It may not be very easy these days to consider the kindness and warmth over the generations of many white Southerners toward Negroes[8] as anything but condescension, or a peculiar refinement of an exploitative social and economic system. Nevertheless, for many years such living habits, and particularly the emotional climate that accompanied them, have constituted a very definite psychological inheritance for millions of Negro people—setting standards for their behavior, giving form to their individual feelings. I don't know where else in the world, when else in history, two groups of people have had quite so wide a range of relationships—spread over time, involving all the complicated and often conflicting social, economic, political and psychological influences at play in our nation, our South.

When I first started interviewing Negro children and their parents my chief concern was with the hard life they faced, the special stresses they met when seeking entrance into a society often only grudgingly willing to greet and welcome them. My chief task—as I saw it for a long time—was to document carefully and precisely the specific psychiatric toll such personal hardship, such social repudiation exacted from these individuals.

Though in no way do I deny what Kardiner and Ovesey[9] have called the "mark of oppression" (in fact, I have ample evidence to add further confirmation of just how cruel, enfeebling and unsettling a brand it can be), it remains equally true that alongside suffering I have encountered resilience and an incredible capacity for survival. To travel about with migrant workers, to stop with them as they visit their sharecropper brothers or cousins, is to realize how tenaciously and sternly they persist, as well as how unequipped they are for our white, middle-class world. Moreover, I will risk being called

[8] John Dollard, in *Caste and Class in a Southern Town* (Garden City, N.Y., 1957), gives a close analysis to the roots of such emotions. Less analytical than descriptive and autobiographical are such books as Hodding Carter's *Southern Legacy* (Baton Rouge, La., 1950); or William A. Percy's *Lanterns on the Levee* (New York, 1959).

[9] Kardiner and Ovesey, *op. cit.*

anything from a fool to a sentimental apologist for a dying order by insisting upon the fun, good times and frolic I daily saw in these people. Of course, they have downcast and sour moments, too—often brought on by the presence of white people. Yet, as one man reminded me, "We can always forget them when they're gone, and most of the time they're just not here to bother us—we know they're always on our back, but it's when they get in front of us and try tripping us up that we get upset." I watched his angry petulance, his artful self-abasement with the white foreman on the farm he helped cultivate; I also saw how very pleasant and even sprightly he could be at home with his wife and children. "We has it rough, but we knows how to live with it, and we learned it so long ago it's second nature; so most of the time it's not so bad; tell the truth, it's only once in a while things get bad . . . so long as you keeps your wits and doesn't ask for but your rights." Even in segregated, impoverished rural areas there are "rights" in the sense that the social system is not erratic, chaotic or inconsistent with its own (if peculiar and arbitrary) traditions.

I have, for instance, seen migrant farmers cut a farmer to the quick, refuse to appear on his land, because he has gone "too far," screamed too loudly at a worker. Sheriffs can use electric prods and shout to a pitch of frenzy at Negroes demonstrating for the right to vote, but they will often hardly so much as raise their voices with other Negroes "going about their business," even if they are thoroughly annoyed at how badly or ineffectively that business is being done.

In general, I have been trying to indicate that I find the task of talking about "the Negro" difficult indeed, the more so because of how many individual Negro men, women and children I know. Even their common suffering, a suffering that has cursed all Americans since the beginning of this country and has yet to be ended, fails to bind them together sufficiently to cause them to lose their individuality, a fact that may be sad for zealous social scientists but is ultimately hopeful for America.

There is undeniably a concrete reality in being an American Negro; millions of people are tied down to it; some of them are driven mad by it; others are frightfully torn by its prospects; the spectacle of what its consequences have been for this nation is not yet completed; in its grip people have faltered, cowered and pretended; from its grip people have fled and battled their way; and finally, the worst and best in mankind have emerged.

I hear talk about the Negro's childlike behavior in the face of a culture that so regards him. I hear that he is a symbol of this or that to nervous, sexually troubled whites; or that he is himself foolishly, childishly wanton and bold, or fearfully thwarted and stunted. I hear that he has his special black soul, mysterious and wonderful, defying description—the very attempt to describe it being a characteristic of the white soul.

Who can limit by any list of attributes the nature of any person, the possibilities in any group of people? We cannot forsake our informed attempts to do just that, particularly in the case of those kept so long outside us while so deeply and sacrificially within us. I would only hope that someday soon the Negro will achieve an order of freedom that will make our descriptions and categories no longer so relevant—indeed, not only out of date, but out of order. It may not now be impertinent for a psychiatrist to talk about "*the* problems" of "*the* Negro," but I surely hope it soon will be.

QUESTIONS FOR DISCUSSION AND WRITING

1. "The Negro has his skin color to help him establish the nature of his problems and his beliefs, while white people must grapple for other mainstays of self-awareness or faith." In what ways do blacks have an advantage over whites? How does the advantage manifest itself?
2. What are the psychological effects of living in a racially segregated environment? For blacks? For whites?
3. Coles quotes from a black mother speaking about whites: "We can have all the rights they have, but you can't feel easy with them so fast. . . . I just make sure my kids know to be afraid." Why should blacks fear whites? In what ways do whites fear blacks?
4. Coles avoids making generalizations about blacks and whites. Why?
5. Would Coles favor the ideas of Garvey (p. 103), Carmichael (p. 329), and Malcolm X (p. 317)? How might he respond to the "Back to Africa" movement and the concepts of "black power" and "the black revolution"?

LEROI JONES HAS EARNED NATIONWIDE FAME AS A PLAYWRIGHT (*Dutchman, The Slave, Toilet*) AND AS AN ESSAYIST. HE IS CURRENTLY ONE OF THE MAJOR LEADERS OF BCD (BLACK COMMUNITY DEVELOPMENT) IN NEWARK, NEW JERSEY, AND GOES BY THE NAME AMEER BARAKA. THE FOLLOWING ESSAY WAS PUBLISHED IN 1962, WHEN JONES WAS TWENTY-EIGHT.

LEROI JONES

TOKENISM: 300 YEARS FOR FIVE CENTS

In Marietta, Georgia, the Lockheed Airplane people maintain a plant that employs more than 10,000 people, only a few of whom are black people. As is customary in the South, all the black people who work in that Lockheed plant work at menial jobs such as porters, messengers, haulers, etc. Recently, however, the national office of the NAACP and the Federal Government have been chiding the Lockheed people to hire Negroes in capacities other than the traditional porter-messenger syndrome. And I suppose it is a credit to those organizations that they finally did get Lockheed to concur with their wishes; in fact, the Marietta plant promoted one of their Negro porters to a clerical position. This move was hailed by the Federal Government, the

NAACP, and similar secret societies as "a huge step forward in race relations" (to quote from *The New York Times*). The Negro who received the promotion, thus becoming "a symbol of American determination to rid itself of the stigma of racial discrimination" (*op. cit.*), was shown smiling broadly (without his broom) and looking generally symbolic. *The Times* added that this promotion and this symbolic move toward "racial understanding" also gives the ex-porter a five-cents-an-hour increase, or two dollars more a week. This means that instead of forty-five dollars a week (if, indeed, the porter made that much) this blazing symbol of social progress now makes forty-seven dollars a week.

There are almost 20,000,000 Negroes in the United States. One of these 20 million has been given a two-dollar raise and promoted to a clerical job that my two-year-old daughter could probably work out without too much trouble. And we are told that this act is *symbolic* of the "gigantic strides the Negro has taken since slavery."

In 1954, the Supreme Court ruled that segregated schools were illegal, and that, indeed, segregation in public schools should be wiped out "with all deliberate speed." Since 1954, this ruling has affected about 6.9 per cent of the nearly 4,000,000 Negro students in Southern segregated schools, and there are four states, Mississippi, South Carolina, Georgia, and Alabama, who have ignored the ruling entirely. And yet, here again, we are asked to accept the ruling itself (with its hypocritical double-talk—what is "all deliberate speed"?) as yet another example of "the gigantic strides," etc. The fact that the ruling affects only 6.9 per cent of 4,000,000 Negro students in the South (and this percentage stands greatly boosted by the inclusion of figures from the "liberal" border states such as Maryland, Missouri, and the District of Columbia—in fact Maryland and the District account for *more than half* of the total percentage) apparently does not matter to the liberals and other eager humanists who claim huge victories in their "ceaseless war on inequality."

Negroes have been in this country since the early part of the seventeenth century. And they have only "legally" been free human beings since the middle of the nineteenth. So we have two hundred years of complete slavery and now for the last one hundred years a "legal" freedom that has so many ands, ifs, or buts that I, for one, cannot accept it as freedom at all but see it as a legal fiction that has been perpetuated to assuage the occasional loud rumbles of moral conscience that must at times smite all American white men.

These last hundred years, according to our official social chiropractors, have been for American Negroes years of progress and advancement. As *Time* magazine said, "Never has the Negro been able to purchase so much and never has he owned so much, free and clear." That is, everything but his own soul. It is not "progress" that the majority of Negroes want, but Freedom. And I apologize if that word, Freedom, sounds a little too unsophisticated or a little too much like 1930's social renascence for some people; the fact remains that it is the one thing that has been most consistently denied the Negro in America (as well as black men all over the world).

Self-determination is the term used when referring to some would-be nation's desire for freedom. The right to choose one's own path. The right to become exactly what one thinks himself capable of. And it strikes me as monstrous that a nation or, for that matter, a civilization like our Western civilization, reared for the last five hundred years exclusively in the humanistic bombast of the Renaissance, should find it almost impossible to understand the strivings of enslaved peoples to free themselves. It is this kind of paradox that has caused the word "Nationalism" to be despised and/or feared in the West, or shrugged off in official circles as "just another Communist plot." Even here in the United States the relatively mild attempts at "integration" in the South are met by accusations of being Communist-inspired. (And I would add as, say, a note of warning to the various Southern congressmen whose sole qualification for office is that they are more vociferous in their disparagement of Negroes than their opponents, that if they persist in crediting the Communists with every attempt at delivering the black American out of his real and constant bondage, someone's going to believe them . . . namely the new or aspirant nations of Asia, Latin America, and Africa.)

Actual slavery in the United States was supposed to have been brought to an end by the Civil War. There is rather bitter insistence in the point that it was *Americans* who were supposedly being freed; the African slaves had long since become American slaves. But it is by now almost a truism to point out that there was much more at stake in that war than the emancipation of the slaves. The Civil War, or at least the result of the Civil War, was undoubtedly the triumph of the Northern industrial classes over the Southern agricultural classes. As so many writers have termed it, "the triumph of American capitalism." The small oligarchy of American industrial capital had overcome its last great enemy, the rich Southern planter, and was now more or less free to bring the very processes of American government under its control.

But on the surface the Civil War looked like a great moral struggle out of which the side of right and justice had emerged victorious. The emancipation of Negroes, the passage, by the Republican Congress, of the 13th, 14th and 15th amendments (to give a "legal basis" for black citizenship), and the setting up of the Reconstruction governments in the South, all gave promise that a new era had arrived for Negroes. And in fact it had, but was of a complexion which was not immediately apparent, and was certainly not the new era most Negroes would have looked forward to.

The Reconstruction governments fell because the Northern industrialists joined with the planter classes of the South to disfranchise the Negro once again, frightened that a "coalition" of the poor and disfranchised Southern whites—the agrarian interests—and the newly freed Negroes might prove too strong a threat to their designs of absolute political and economic control of the South. As E. Franklin Frazier points out in *Black Bourgeoisie,*

> When agrarian unrest among the "poor whites" of the South joined forces with the Populist movement, which represented the general unrest among American farmers, the question of race was used to defeat the co-operation of "poor whites" and Negroes. It was then that the demagogues assumed leadership of the "poor whites" and provided a solution of the class conflict among whites that offered no challenge to the political power and economic privileges of the industrialists and the planter class. The program, which made the Negro the scapegoat, contained the following provisions: (1) The Negro was completely disfranchised by all sorts of legal subterfuges, with the threat of force in the background; (2) the funds which were appropriated on a per capita basis for Negro school children were diverted to white schools; and (3) a legal system of segregation in all phases of public life was instituted. In order to justify this program, the demagogues, who were supported by the white propertied classes, engaged for twenty-five years in a campaign to prove that the Negro was subhuman, morally degenerated and intellectually incapable of being educated.

Tokenism, or what I define as the setting up of social stalemates or the extension of meager privilege to some few "selected" Negroes in order that a semblance of compromise or "progress," or a lessening in racial repression might seem to be achieved, while actually helping to maintain the status quo just as rigidly, could not, of course, really come into being until after the emancipation. Before that, there was no real need to extend even a few tokens to the slave. There was, indeed, no reason why anyone had to create the illusion for the slave that he was "making progress," or governing himself, or any other such untruth. In a sense, however, the extension of "special privileges" to Negro house servants ("house niggers") did early help to create a new *class* of Negro, within the slave system. The "house nigger" not only assimilated "massa's" ideas and attitudes at a rapid rate, but his children were sometimes allowed to learn trades and become artisans and craftsmen. And it was these artisans and craftsmen who made up the bulk of the 500,000 black "freedmen" extant at the beginning of the Civil War.

The Reconstruction governments are the first actual example of the kind of crumb-dropping that was to characterize the Federal Government's attitude regarding the status of the "free" Negro. The Reconstruction governments were nothing but symbols, since no real lands were ever given to the Negroes, and even any political influence which had come to the ex-slaves as part of the Reconstruction was nullified by 1876, (the so-called redemption of the South).

Another aspect of tokenism is the setting apart or appointing of "leaders" among Negroes who in effect glorify whatever petty symbol the white ruling classes think is necessary for Negroes to have at that particular time. So, at the fall of the Reconstruction governments, the industrialist-financier-planter oligarchy found an able "leader" in Booker T. Washington, a Negro through whom these interests could make their wishes known to the great masses of Negroes. After the North had more or less washed its hands of the whole "Southern mess," and it was a generally accepted idea that the Negroes had ruined the Reconstruction simply because they were incapable of governing themselves, Booker T. Washington came into great prominence and influence as a Negro leader because he accepted the idea of segregation as a "solution" to the race problem, and also because he advocated that Negroes learn trades rather than go into any of the more ambitious professions.

> Coming from Booker T. Washington, who enjoyed entré into the society of Standard Oil executives, railroad magnates, and Andrew Carnegie, the strategy was persuasive. Washington avowed

> his loyalty to laissez faire, took his stand in the South as a southerner, and accepted social inequality for the foreseeable future. Blocked by the power of the whites and told by their own spokesman that "white leadership is preferable," most Negroes followed . . . (from *The Contours of American History*, W. A. Williams).

The wealth and influence of the great industrialists backed the Washington solution and as Williams points out, "Washington's position was made almost impregnable through the generosity of northern white philanthropists who liked his ideology (which included a code of labor quietism and even strikebreaking)." "Negro intellectuals like W. E. B. DuBois who attacked Washington's position had little chance to shake it, opposed by such formidable opponents as the monied interests and the philanthropists, who replaced the "radical republican" idea of actually redistributing land to the freed Negroes with ineffective philanthropies such as Howard University or Tuskeegee (which was Booker T.'s pet—a college for Negroes that taught trades, *e.g.*, carpentry, masonry). And of course, as it was intended, the tokens did very little to improve the general conditions of Negroes anywhere. The Sumner-Stevens plan of redistributing land among the freedmen, in fact even breaking up the large plantations and making small farms for both white and black would have changed the entire history of this country had it been implemented in good faith. But such an idea definitely proved a threat to the hold of the planters and industrialists over the politics and economy of the South. So it was defeated.

Radicals like DuBois (who left Atlanta University so he would not embarrass them with his opinions) helped set up the National Association for the Advancement of Colored People in 1909. At that time the organization was considered extremely radical, and it was merely asking—but for the first time—for "complete equality." Most of the financiers and philanthropists who made a sometime hobby out of extending stale crumbs to Negroes denounced the organization. Also, most of the so-called Negro middle class could not abide by the radicalism of the organization's program, and some of them (the Negro educators in particular, who depended on the philanthropists for their bread, butter, and prestige) brought as much pressure as they could on the fledgling NAACP to modify its policies. (And I think it is not too violent a digression to ask just what kind of men or what kind of desperation would have to be inflicted upon a man's soul in order for him to say that giving him equal rights in his own country is "too radical"? E. Franklin Frazier does a very good job in *Black Bourgeoisie* of describing the type of man who would be capable of such social pathology.) But radicalism or no, when the First World War ended and the great exodus of Negroes from the South began, membership in the NAACP grew tremendously. Yet despite the great support the NAACP received from the Negro masses in its incunabula, the organization was more and more influenced by its white liberal supporters and gradually modified its program and position to that of the white middle class, thereby swiftly limiting its appeal to the middle-class Negro. Today, the NAACP is almost completely out of touch with the great masses of blacks and bases its programs on a "liberal" middle-class line, which affects only a very tiny portion of the 20,000,000 Negroes living in the United States. It has, in fact, become little more than a token itself.

A rich man told me recently that a liberal is a man who tells other people what to do with their money. I told him that that was right from the side of the telescope he looked through, but that as far as I was concerned a liberal was a man who told other people what to do with their poverty.

I mention this peculiarly American phenomenon, *i.e.*, American Liberalism, because it is just this group of amateur social theorists, American Liberals, who have done most throughout American history to insure the success of tokenism. Whoever has proposed whatever particular social evasion or dilution—to whatever ignominious end—it is usually the liberal who gives that lie the greatest lip service. They, liberals, are people with extremely heavy consciences and almost nonexistent courage. Too little is always enough. And it is always the *symbol* that appeals to them most. The single futile housing project in the jungle of slums and disease eases the liberals' conscience, so they are loudest in praising it—even though it might not solve any problems at all. The single black student in the Southern university, the promoted porter in Marietta, Georgia—all ease the liberals' conscience like a benevolent but highly addictive drug. And, for them, "moderation" is a kind of religious catch phrase that they are wont to mumble on street corners even alone late at night.

Is it an excess for a man to ask to be free? To declare, even vehemently, that no man has the right to dictate the life of another man? Is it so radical and untoward for nations to claim the right of self-determination? Freedom *now!* has become the cry of a great many American Negroes and colonial nations. Not freedom "when you get ready to give it," as some spurious privilege or shabby act of charity; but *now!* The liberal says, "You are a radical." So be it.

Liberals, as good post-Renaissance men, believe wholeheartedly in *progress*. There are even those people who speak knowingly about "progress in the arts." But progress is not, and never has been the question as far as the enslaving of men is concerned. Africans never asked to be escorted to the New World. They never had any idea that learning "good English" and wearing shoes had anything to do with the validity of their lives on earth. Slavery was not anything but an unnecessarily cruel and repressive method of making money for the Western white man. Colonialism was a more subtle, but equally repressive method of accomplishing the same end. The liberal is in a strange position because his conscience, unlike the conscience of his richer or less intelligent brothers, has always bothered him about these acts, but never sufficiently to move him to any concrete action except the setting up of palliatives and symbols to remind him of his own good faith. In fact, even though the slave trade, for instance, was entered into for purely commercial reasons, after a few years the more liberal-minded Americans began to try to justify it as a method of converting heathens to Christianity. And, again, you can see how perfect Christianity was for the slave then; a great number of slave uprisings were dictated by the African's gods or the new slaves' desire to return to the land of their gods. As I put it in a recent essay on the sociological development of blues: "You can see how necessary, how perfect, it was that Christianity came first, that the African was given something 'to take his mind off Africa,' that he was forced, if he still wished to escape the filthy paternalism and cruelty of slavery, to wait at least until he died, when he could be transported peacefully and majestically to 'the promised land.'" I'm certain the first Negro spirituals must have soothed a lot of consciences as well as enabling a little more relaxation among the overseers. It almost tempts me toward another essay tentatively titled *Christianity as a Deterrent to Slave Uprisings*. More tokens.

A Negro who is told that the "desegregation" of a bus terminal in Georgia somehow represents "progress" is definitely being lied to. Progress to where? The bare minimum of intelligent life is what any man wants. This was true in 1600 when the first slaves were hauled off the boats, and it has not changed. Perhaps the trappings and the external manifestations that time and the lessons of history have proposed make some things seem different or changed in the world, but the basic necessities of useful life are the same. If a tractor has replaced a mule, the need to have the field produce has not changed. And if a black man can speak English now, or read a newspaper, whereas (ask any liberal) he could not in 18 so-and-so, he is no better off now than he was then if he still cannot receive the basic privileges of manhood. In fact, he is perhaps worse off than in 18 so-and-so since he is now being constantly persuaded that he *is* receiving these basic privileges (or, at least, he is told that he soon will, *e.g.*, R. Kennedy's high comic avowal that perhaps in forty years a Negro might be president).

But, for me, the idea of "progress" is a huge fallacy. An absurd Western egoism that has been foisted on the rest of the world as an excuse for slavery and colonialism. An excuse for making money. Because this progress the Western slavemaster is always talking about means simply the mass acquisition of all the dubious fruits of the industrial revolution. And the acquisition of material wealth has, in my mind, only very slightly to do with self-determination or freedom. Somehow, and most especially in the United States, the fact that more Negroes can buy new Fords this year than they could in 1931 is supposed to represent some great stride *forward*. To where? How many new Fords will Negroes have to own before police in Mississippi stop using police dogs on them. How many television sets and refrigerators will these same Negroes have to own before they are allowed to vote without being made to live in tents, or their children allowed decent educations? And even if a bus station in Anniston, Alabama, is "integrated," how much does this help reduce the 25 per cent unemployment figure that besets Negroes in Harlem.

If, right this minute, I were, in some strange fit of irrationality, to declare that "I am a free man and have the right of complete self-determination," chances are that I would be dead or in jail by nightfall. But being an American Negro, I am supposed to be conditioned to certain "unfortunate" aspects of American democracy. And all my reactions are supposedly based on this conditioning, which is, in effect, that even as a native born American, etc., etc., there are certain things I cannot do because I have a black skin. Tokenism is that philosophy (of psychological exploitation) which is supposed to assuage my natural inclinations toward complete freedom. For the middle-class Negro this assuagement can take the form it takes in the mainstream of American life, *i.e.*, material acquisition, or the elevating of one "select" coon to some position that seems heaped in "prestige," *e.g.*, Special Delegate to the United Nations, Director of Public Housing, Assistant Press Secretary to the President of the United States, Vice President In Charge Of Personnel for Chock Full 'O Nuts, Borough President of Manhattan, etc. The "Speaking Of People" column in *Ebony* magazine is the banal chronicler of such "advances," *e.g.*, the first Negro sheriff of Banwood, Utah, or the first Negro Asst. Film Editor for BRRR films. But the lower class Negro cannot use this kind of tokenism, so he is pretty much left in the lurch. But so effective is this kind of crumb-dropping among the *soi-disant* black middle class that these people become the actual tokens themselves, or worse. Thus when an issue like the treacherous relief cuts in Newburgh, New York, presents itself, the black middle class is actually likely to side with reactionaries, even though, as in the Newburgh case, such a situation harms a great many poorer Negroes. This kind of process reaches perhaps its most absurd, albeit horrible, manifestation when a man like George Schuyler, in the Negro paper *The Pittsburgh Courier*, can write editorials *defending the Portuguese* in Angola, even after the United States Government itself had been pressured into censuring this NATO ally. It is also a man like Schuyler who is willing to support one of the great aphorisms of tokenism (this one begun by the worst elements of racist neo-colonialism) that somehow a man, usually a black man, must "make progress to freedom." That somehow, a man must show he is "*ready* for independence or self-determination." A man is either free or he is not. There cannot be any apprenticeship for freedom. My God, what makes a black man, in America or Africa, or any of the other oppressed colonial peoples of the world, less ready for freedom than the average *Daily News* reading American white man?

But again, while it is true that there is a gulf of tokens seemingly separating the middle-class Negro from the great masses of Negroes (just as there is seemingly a great gulf of tokens separating the "select cadre" of a great many colonial countries from their oppressed people), I insist that it is only an artificial separation, and that the black bourgeoisie (and their foreign cousins) are no better off than the poorest Negro in this country. But how to tell the *first* Negro Asst. Film Editor of BRRR films that he is just as bad off as the poorest and most oppressed of his black brothers? Tokenism is no abstract philosophy; it was put into action by hardheaded realists.

But realists or no, there is in the world now among most of its oppressed peoples, a growing disaffection with meaningless platitudes, and a reluctance to be had by the same shallow phrases that have characterized the hypocritical attitude of the West toward the plight of the American black man and all colonial peoples. There will be fewer and fewer tragedies like the murder of Patrice Lumumba. The new nations will no longer allow themselves to be sucked in by these same hackneyed sirens of tokenism or malevolent liberalism. The world, my friends, is definitely changing.

QUESTIONS FOR DISCUSSION AND WRITING

1. According to Jones, what is revealed by the philosophy of tokenism?
2. "A man is either free or he is not. There cannot be any apprenticeship for freedom." What evidence does Jones use to support his assertion that the black man is free and that he must have self-determination? In what ways would American society have to change in order for the black man's freedom and self-determination to be acknowledged?
3. What groups of Americans have played a major role in bringing about black "freedom"? How do their commitments differ from those of the "white liberal" as seen by Jones?
4. Why are "mild attempts at integration" labeled "communist"?
5. Compare and contrast Jones' definition of "progress" with those of Washington (p. 65), Frazier (p. 187), and King (p. 341). To what extent is Jones' view of black progress a valid one? Why?

LERONE BENNETT, JR., IS SENIOR EDITOR OF *Ebony* MAGAZINE AND CURRENTLY TEACHES AT NORTHWESTERN UNIVERSITY. HIS WRITINGS INCLUDE *Before the Mayflower: A History of the Negro in America, 1619–1964* AND *What Manner of Man: A Biography of Martin Luther King, Jr.* THE FOLLOWING ESSAY FIRST APPEARED IN A SPECIAL ISSUE OF *Ebony*.

LERONE BENNETT, JR.

THE WHITE PROBLEM IN AMERICA

There is no Negro problem in America.

The problem of race in America, insofar as that problem is related to packets of melanin in men's skins, is a white problem. And in order to solve that problem we must seek its source, not in the Negro but in the white American (in the process by which he was educated, in the needs and complexes he expresses through racism) and in the structure of the white community (in the power arrangements and the illicit uses of racism in the scramble for scarce values: power, prestige, income).

The depth and intensity of the race problem in America is, in part, a result of a 100-year flight from that unpalatable truth. It was a stroke of genius really for white Americans to give Negro Americans the name of their problem, thereby focusing attention on symptoms (the Negro and the Negro community) instead of causes (the white man and the white community).

When we say that the causes of the race problem are rooted in the white American and the white community, we mean that the power is the white American's and so is the responsibility. We mean that the white American created, *invented* the race problem and that his fears and frailties are responsible for the urgency of the problem.

When we say that the fears of white Americans are at the root of the problem, we mean that the white American is a problem to himself and that because he is a problem to himself he has made others problems to themselves.

When we say that the white American is a problem to himself, we mean that racism is a reflection of personal and collective anxieties lodged deep in the hearts and minds of white Americans.

By all this, we must understand that Harlem is a white-made thing and that in order to understand Harlem we must go not to Harlem but to the conscience of white Americans and we must ask not what is Harlem but what have you made of Harlem. Why did you create it? And why do you need it?

The validity of this approach has been underlined by many experts, including Gunnar Myrdal, who began his massive work on the Negro (*An American Dilemma*) by admitting, in so many words, that he had studied the wrong people. "Although the Negro problem is a moral issue both to Negroes and to whites in America," he wrote, "we shall in this book have to give *primary* attention to what goes on in the minds of white Americans. . . . When the present investigator started his inquiry, his preconception was that it had to be focused on the Negro people and their peculiarities. . . . But as he proceeded in his studies into the Negro problem, it became increasingly evident that little, if anything, could be scientifically explained in terms of the peculiarities of the Negroes themselves. . . . It is thus the white majority group that naturally determines the Negro's 'place.' All our attempts to reach scientific explanations of why the Negroes are what they are and why they live as they do have regularly led to determinants on the white side of the racial line. In the practical and political struggles of affecting changes, the views and attitudes of the white Americans are likewise strategic. The Negro's entire life, and, consequently, also his opinions on the Negro problem, are, in the main, to be considered as secondary reactions to more primary pressures from the side of the dominant white majority."

Scores of investigators have reached the same conclusions: namely, that the peculiarities of white folk are the primary determinants of the American social problem.

Consider, for example, the testimony of James Weldon Johnson, the great Negro leader:

". . . the main difficulty of the race question does not lie so much in the actual condition of the blacks as it does in the mental attitude of the whites."

Johnson also said:

"The race question involves the saving of black America's body and white America's soul."

White Americans have perceived the same truth. Author Ray Stannard Baker wrote:

"It keeps coming to me that this is more a white man's problem than it is a Negro problem."

So it seemed also to Thomas P. Bailey, a Southern white.

"The real problem," he wrote, "is not the Negro but the white man's attitude toward the Negro."

And again:

"Yes, we Southerners need a freedom from suspicion, fear, anxiety, doubt, unrest, hate, contempt, disgust, and all the rest of the race-feeling-begotten brood of vituperation."

Ralph McGill, another Southerner, made a similar observation.

"We do not have a minority problem," he said, "but a majority problem."

Of like tone and tenor was the perceptive statement of Thomas Merton, the Trappist monk.

"The purpose of non-violent protest, in its deepest and most spiritual dimension is then to awaken the conscience of the white man to the awful responsibility of his injustice and sin, so that he will be able to see that the Negro problem is really a *White* problem: that the cancer of injustice and hate which is eating white society and is only partly manifested in racial segregation with its consequences, *is rooted in the heart of the white man himself*." [Merton's emphasis.]

It is there, "in the heart of the white man himself," in his peculiarities, in his mental attitudes, in his need for "a freedom from suspicion, fear, anxiety, doubt, unrest, hate, contempt, disgust," that we must situate the racial problem. For here, as elsewhere, the proper statement of the problem, though not a solution, is at least a strong step in the right direction. For too long now, we have focused attention on the Negro, forgetting that the Negro is who he is because white people are what they are. In our innocence—and in our guile—we have spoken of Negro crime, when the problem is white crime; we have spoken of the need for educating Negroes, when the problem is the education of whites; we have spoken of the lack of responsible Negro leadership, when the problem is the lack of responsible white leadership.

The premise of this special issue is that America can no longer afford the luxury of ignoring its real problem: the white problem. To be sure, Negroes are not blameless. It takes two to tango and the Negro, at the very least, is responsible for accepting the grapes of degradation. But that, you see, has nothing to do with the man who is responsible for the degradation. The prisoner is always free to try to escape. What the jailer must decide is whether he will help escaping prisoners over the wall or shoot them in the back. And the lesson of American life is that no Negro—no matter how much money he accumulated, no matter how many degrees he earned—has ever crossed completely the wall of color-caste, except by adopting the expedient of passing. Let us come to that point and stand on it: Negroes are condemned in America, not because they are poor, not because they are uneducated, not because they are brown or black—Negroes are condemned in America because they are Negroes, i.e., because of an idea of the Negro and of the Negro's place in the white American's mind.

When we say that the race problem in America is a white problem, we mean that the real problem is an irrational and antiscientific idea of race in the minds of white Americans. Let us not be put off by recitations of "social facts." Social facts do not make Negroes; on the contrary, it is the idea of the Negro which organizes and distorts social facts in order to make "Negroes." Hitler, who had some experience in the matter, said social facts are sustainers and not creators of prejudice. In other words: If we assume that Negroes are inferior and if we use that assumption as a rationale for giving Negroes poor schools, poor jobs, and poor housing, we will sooner or later create a condition which "confirms" our assumption and "justifies" additional discrimination.

No: social facts are not at the heart of the problem. In fact, social facts tell us more about whites, about their needs, insecurities, and immaturities, than about Negroes. Many Negroes are poor, but so are forty to fifty million American whites. Some Negro women have babies out of wedlock, but so do millions of middle-class American white women. Racists and millions of "normal" white Americans know this; but they are not and cannot be convinced *for their knowledge precedes facts*. Because the *idea of race* intervenes between the concrete Negro and the social fact, Negro intellectuals and white racists rarely, if ever, understand each other. What the white racist means by social facts is that there are "Negro social facts," that Negroes, by virtue of their birth, have within them a magical substance that gives facts a certain quality. He means by that that there is a Negro and a white way of being poor, that there is a Negro and white way of being immoral, that, in his mind, white people and black people are criminals in different ways. As a result of this magical thinking, millions on millions of white Americans are unable to understand that slums, family disorganization and illiteracy are not the causes of the racial problem, but the end product of the problem.

That problem, in essence, is racism. But we misunderstand racism completely if we do not understand that racism is a mask for a much deeper problem involving not the victims of racism but the perpetrators. We must come to see that racism in America is the poor man's way out and the powerful man's way in: *a way in* for the powerful who derive enormous profits from the divisions in our society; *a way out* for the frustrated and frightened who excuse economic, social, and sexual failure by convincing themselves that no matter how low they fall they are still higher and better than Harry Belafonte, Ralph Bunche, Cassius Clay and Martin Luther King, Jr., all rolled up into one.

We must realize also that prejudice on all levels reflects a high level of personal and social disorganization in the white community. On a personal level, particularly among lower-income and middle-income whites, prejudice is an avenue of flight, a cry for help from desperate men stifling in the prisons of their skins. Growing up in a culture permeated with prejudice, imbibing it, so to speak, with their milk, millions of white Americans find that Negroes are useful screens to hide themselves from themselves. Repeated studies have shown that Negro hate is, in part, a socially-sanctioned outlet for personal and social anxieties and frustrations. From this standpoint, racism is a flight from the self, a flight from freedom, a flight from the intolerable burdens of being a man in a menacing world.

Not all white Americans are biased, of course, but all white Americans and all Americans have been affected by bias. This issue suggests that we need to know a great deal more about how white Americans exist with their whiteness, and how some white Americans, to a certain extent, rise above early conditioning through non-Communist radicalism or liberalism.

The racist impulse, which white Americans express in different ways but which almost all do express, either by rebelling against it or by accepting it, reflects deep forces in the dominant community. There is considerable evidence, for example, that the culture's stress on success and status induces exaggerated anxieties and fears which are displaced onto the area of race relations. The fear of failure, the fear of competitors, the fear of losing status, of not living in the "right" neighborhood, of not having the "right" friends or the "right" gadgets: these fears weigh heavily on the minds of millions of white Americans and lead to a search for avenues of escape. And so the second- or third-generation factory worker or the poor white farmer who finds himself at a dead end with a nagging wife, a problem child, and a past-due bill may take out his aggressive feelings and his frustrations in race hatred.

The concept of the Negro problem as a white problem suggests that there is a need for additional research to determine to what extent Negro hate is a defense against self-hate. It also suggests that attention should be directed to the power gains of highly-placed politicians and businessmen who derive direct power gains from the division of our population into mutually hostile groups. By using racism, consciously or unconsciously, to divert public discontent and to boost the shaky egos of white groups on or near the bottom, men of power in America have played a key role in making racism a permanent structure of our society.

It is fashionable nowadays to think of racism as a vast impersonal system for which no one is responsible. But this is still another evasion. Racism did not fall from the sky; it was not secreted by insects. No: racism in America was made by men, neighborhood by neighborhood, law by law, restrictive covenant by restrictive covenant, deed by deed.

It is not remembered often enough today that the color-caste vise, which constricts both Negroes and whites, was created by men of power who artificially separated Negroes and whites who got on famously in Colonial America. This is a fact of capital importance in considering the white problem. The first black immigrants in America were not slaves; nor, for the most part, were the first white immigrants free. Most of the English colonists, in the beginning, were white indentured servants possessing remarkably little racial prejudice.

Back there, in the beginning, Negro and white indentured servants worked together in the same fields, lived together in the same huts and played together after working hours. And, of course, they also mated and married. So widespread was intermingling during this period that Peter Fontaine and other writers said the land "swarmed with mulatto" children.

From 1619 to about 1660, a period of primary importance in the history of America, America was not ruled by color. Some, perhaps all, of the first group of African-Americans worked out their terms of servitude and were freed. Within a few years, Negroes were accumulating property, pounds, and indentured servants. One Negro immigrant, Richard Johnson, even imported a white man and held him in servitude.

The breaking of the developing bonds of community between Negro and white Americans began with a conscious decision by the power structures of Colonial America. In the 1660's, men of power in the colonies decided that human slavery, based on skin color, was to be the linchpin of the new society. Having made this decision, they were forced to take another, more ominous step. Nature does not prepare men for the roles of master or racist. It requires rigid training, long persisted in, to make men and women deny other men and women and themselves. Men must be carefully taught to hate, and the lessons learned by one generation must be relearned by the next.

The Negro and white working class of the 1660's, the bulk of the population, had not been prepared for the roles outlined in the new script of statutes. It was necessary, therefore, to teach them that they could not deal with each other as fellow human beings.

How was this done?

It was done by an assault on the Negro's body and the white man's soul.

Legislatures ground out laws of every imaginable description and vigilantes whipped the doubtful into line. Behind the nightriders, of course, stood God himself in the person of parsons who blessed the rupture in human relations with words from the Bible.

Who was responsible for this policy?

The planters, the aristocrats, the parsons, the lawyers, the Founding Fathers—*the good people:* they created the white problem.

Men would say later that there is a natural antipathy between Negro and white Americans. But the record belies them. Negro and white Americans were taught to hate and fear each other by words, sermons, whips, and signed papers. The process continued over a period of more than 100 years, a period which saw the destruction of the Negro family and the exclusion of Negro workers from one skilled trade after another. Nor did white men escape. They saw, dimly, what they were doing to themselves and to others and they drew back from themselves, afraid. But they did not stop; perhaps they could not stop. For, by now, racism had become central to their needs and to their identity. Moreover, they were moved by dark and turbulent forces within. The evidence of their deeds bred fear and guilt which, in turn, led to more anxiety and guilt and additional demands for exclusion and aggression. Propelled by this dynamic, the whole process of excluding and fearing reached something of a peak in the first decade of the Twentieth Century with a carnival of Jim Crow in the South and a genteel movement which blanketed the North with restrictive covenants. The net result was a system of color-caste which divided communities, North and South, into mutually hostile groups.

Since that time, investigators have focused almost all of their attention on the Negro community, with the resulting neglect of primary determinants on the white side of the racial line. By asserting that the Negro problem is predominantly a white problem, this issue summons us to a new beginning and suggests that anything that hides the white American from a confrontation with himself and with the fact that he must change before the Negro can change is a major part of the problem.

QUESTIONS FOR DISCUSSION AND WRITING

1. What does Bennett mean by his assertion that there is no Negro problem, only a white one?
2. How does Bennett define "racism"? Do you agree with his definition?

3. According to Bennett, in racial relations "knowledge precedes facts." How is this perception related to racial discrimination?
4. The "self-fulfilling prophecy" dictates that perceptions and attitudes shape outcomes. For instance, if a teacher treats students as if they were incapable, they become incapable. To what extent is this concept relevant to "the white problem in America"? To Bennett's essay?
5. What does the white man's willingness to prejudge Negroes reveal about the white man's needs? Does Bennett agree with Jones' view of the white man (p. 257)?

THE FOLLOWING SUMMARY OF THE KERNER COMMISSION REPORT (SEE P. 1) ASSERTS THAT IF SOME AMERICAN ATTITUDES ABOUT RACE ARE NOT CHANGED, FUNDAMENTAL DEMOCRATIC VALUES MAY BE DESTROYED. THE COMMISSION CALLS FOR CONCERTED ACTION TO PRESERVE DEMOCRACY AND TO AVOID VIOLENCE.

KERNER COMMISSION

SUMMARY OF THE KERNER REPORT

Introduction

The summer of 1967 again brought racial disorders to American cities, and with them shock, fear and bewilderment to the nation.

The worst came during a two-week period in July, first in Newark and then in Detroit. Each set off a chain reaction in neighboring communities.

On July 28, 1967, the President of the United States established this Commission and directed us to answer three basic questions:

What happened?

Why did it happen?

What can be done to prevent it from happening again?

SUMMARY OF THE KERNER REPORT From *The Report of the National Advisory Commission on Civil Disorders* (1968).

To respond to these questions, we have undertaken a broad range of studies and investigations. We have visited the riot cities; we have heard many witnesses; we have sought the counsel of experts across the country.

This is our basic conclusion: Our nation is moving toward two societies, one black, one white—separate and unequal.

Reaction to last summer's disorders has quickened the movement and deepened the division. Discrimination and segregation have long permeated much of American life; they now threaten the future of every American.

This deepening racial division is not inevitable. The movement apart can be reversed. Choice is still possible. Our principal task is to define that choice and to press for a national resolution.

To pursue our present course will involve the continuing polarization of the American community and, ultimately, the destruction of basic democratic values.

The alternative is not blind repression or capitulation to lawlessness. It is the realization of common opportunities for all within a single society.

This alternative will require a commitment to national action—compassionate, massive and sustained, backed by the resources of the most powerful and the richest nation on this earth. From every American it will require new attitudes, new understanding, and, above all, new will.

The vital needs of the nation must be met; hard choices must be made, and, if necessary, new taxes enacted.

Violence cannot build a better society. Disruption and disorder nourish repression, not justice. They strike at the freedom of every citizen. The community cannot—it will not—tolerate coercion and mob rule.

Violence and destruction must be ended—in the streets of the ghetto and in the lives of people.

Segregation and poverty have created in the racial ghetto a destructive environment totally unknown to most white Americans.

What white Americans have never fully understood—but what the Negro can never forget—is that white society is deeply implicated in the ghetto. White institutions created it, white institutions maintain it, and white society condones it.

It is time now to turn with all the purpose at our command to the major unfinished business of this nation. It is time to adopt strategies for action that will produce quick and visible progress. It is time to make good the promises of American democracy to all citizens—urban and rural, white and black, Spanish-surname, American Indian, and every minority group.

Our recommendations embrace three basic principles:

To mount programs on a scale equal to the dimension of the problems.

To aim these programs for high impact in the immediate future in order to close the gap between promise and performance.

To undertake new initiatives and experiments that can change the system of failure and frustration that now dominates the ghetto and weakens our society.

These programs will require unprecedented levels of funding and performance, but they neither probe deeper nor demand more than the problems which called them forth. There can be no higher priority for national action and no higher claim on the nation's conscience.

We issue this Report now, four months before the date called for by the President. Much remains that can be learned. Continued study is essential.

As Commissioners we have worked together with a sense of the greatest urgency and have sought to compose whatever differences exist among us. Some differences remain. But the gravity of the problem and the pressing need for action are too clear to allow further delay in the issuance of this Report.

QUESTIONS FOR DISCUSSION AND WRITING

1. "Discrimination and segregation have long permeated much of American life; they now threaten the future of every American." Why does the Kerner Commission emphasize the future? What projections, in general terms, does it make for that future?
2. The Commission warns against the destruction of basic democratic values. What relationship exists between American racial policy and democratic values?
3. What changes will be necessary in order to "make good the promises of American democracy to all citizens"?

4. The Kerner report, published in early 1968, created headlines throughout America. What specific steps have been taken to arrest the movement "toward two societies, one black, one white—separate and unequal"?
5. "Segregation and poverty have created in the racial ghetto a destructive environment totally unknown to most white Americans." Relate this statement to Ellison's view of invisibility (p. 113). Is there a relationship between the white man's lack of knowledge about Negroes and the "destructive environment"?

ELDRIDGE CLEAVER WROTE HIS WELL-KNOWN BOOK *Soul on Ice* WHILE SERVING A SENTENCE IN CALIFORNIA'S FOLSOM PRISON. THE BOOK WAS PUBLISHED IN 1968. UPON HIS RELEASE FROM PRISON, CLEAVER SERVED AS MINISTER OF INFORMATION FOR THE BLACK PANTHER PARTY. HE IS CURRENTLY LIVING IN EXILE FROM THE UNITED STATES.

ELDRIDGE CLEAVER

THE WHITE RACE AND ITS HEROES

> White people cannot, in the generality, be taken as models of how to live. Rather, the white man is himself in sore need of new standards, which will release him from his confusion and place him once again in fruitful communion with the depths of his own being.
>
> *James Baldwin,* THE FIRE NEXT TIME

Right from the go, let me make one thing absolutely clear: I am not now, nor have I ever been, a white man. Nor, I hasten to add, am I now a Black Muslim—although I used to be. But I *am* an Ofay

THE WHITE RACE AND ITS HEROES From *Soul on Ice* by Eldridge Cleaver. Copyright © 1968 by Eldridge Cleaver. Used with permission of McGraw-Hill Book Company. The quote from James Baldwin's *The Fire Next Time* is reprinted by permission of the publisher, The Dial Press, Inc.

Watcher, a member of that unchartered, amorphous league which has members on all continents and the islands of the seas. Ofay Watchers Anonymous, we might be called, because we exist concealed in the shadows wherever colored people have known oppression by whites, by white enslavers, colonizers, imperialists, and neo-colonialists.

Did it irritate you, compatriot, for me to string those epithets out like that? Tolerate me. My intention was not necessarily to sprinkle salt over anyone's wounds. I did it primarily to relieve a certain pressure on my brain. Do you cop that? If not, then we're in trouble, because we Ofay Watchers have a pronounced tendency to slip into that mood. If it is bothersome to you, it is quite a task for me because not too long ago it was my way of life to preach, as ardently as I could, that the white race is a race of devils, created by their maker to do evil, and make evil appear as good; that the white race is the natural, unchangeable enemy of the black man, who is the original man, owner, maker, cream of the planet Earth; that the white race was soon to be destroyed by Allah, and that the black man would then inherit the earth, which has always, in fact, been his.

I have, so to speak, washed my hands in the blood of the martyr, Malcolm X, whose retreat from the precipice of madness created new room for others to turn about in, and I am now caught up in that tiny space, attempting a maneuver of my own. Having renounced the teachings of Elijah Muhammad, I find that a rebirth does not follow automatically, of its own accord, that a void is left in one's vision, and this void seeks constantly to obliterate itself by pulling one back to one's former outlook. I have tried a tentative compromise by adopting a select vocabulary, so that now when I see the whites of *their* eyes, instead of saying "devil" or "beast" I say "imperialist" or "colonialist," and everyone seems to be happier.

In silence, we have spent our years watching the ofays, trying to understand them, on the principle that you have a better chance coping with the known than with the unknown. Some of us have been, and some still are, interested in learning whether it is *ultimately* possible to live in the same territory with people who seem so disagreeable to live with; still others want to get as far away from ofays as possible. What we share in common is the desire to break the ofays' power over us.

At times of fundamental social change, such as the era in which we live, it is easy to be deceived by the onrush of events, beguiled by the craving for social stability into mistaking transitory phenomena for enduring reality. The strength and permanence of "white backlash" in America is just such an illusion. However much this rear-guard action might seem to grow in strength, the initiative, and the future, rest with those whites and blacks who have liberated themselves from the master/slave syndrome. And these are to be found mainly among the youth.

Over the past twelve years there has surfaced a political conflict between the generations that is deeper, even, than the struggle between the races. Its first dramatic manifestation was within the ranks of the Negro people, when college students in the South, fed up with Uncle Tom's hat-in-hand approach to revolution, threw off the yoke of the NAACP. When these students initiated the first sit-ins, their spirit spread like a raging fire across the nation, and the technique of non-violent direct action, constantly refined and honed into a sharp cutting tool, swiftly matured. The older Negro "leaders," who are now all die-hard advocates of this tactic, scolded the students for sitting-in. The students rained down contempt upon their hoary heads. In the pre-sit-in days, these conservative leaders had always succeeded in putting down insurgent elements among the Negro people. (A measure of their power, prior to the students' rebellion, is shown by their success in isolating such great black men as the late W. E. B. DuBois and Paul Robeson, when these stalwarts, refusing to bite their tongues, lost favor with the U.S. government by their unstinting efforts to link up the Negro revolution with national liberation movements around the world.)

The "Negro leaders," and the whites who depended upon them to control their people, were outraged by the impudence of the students. Calling for a moratorium on student initiative, they were greeted instead by an encore of sit-ins, and retired to their ivory towers to contemplate the new phenomenon. Others, less prudent because held on a tighter leash by the whites, had their careers brought to an abrupt end because they thought they could lead a black/white backlash against the students, only to find themselves in a kind of Bay of Pigs. Negro college presidents, who expelled students from all-Negro colleges in an attempt to quash the demonstrations, ended up losing their jobs; the victorious students would no longer allow them to preside over the campuses. The spontaneous protests on southern campuses over the repressive measures of their college administrations were an earnest of the Free Speech upheaval which years later was to shake the UC campus at Berkeley. In countless ways, the rebellion of the black students served as catalyst for the brewing revolt of the whites.

What has suddenly happened is that the white race has lost its heroes. Worse, its heroes have been revealed as villains and its greatest heroes as the arch-villains. The new generations of whites, appalled by the sanguine and despicable record carved over the face of the globe by their race in the last five hundred years, are rejecting the panoply of white heroes, whose heroism consisted in erecting the inglorious edifice of colonialism and imperialism; heroes whose careers rested on a system of foreign and domestic exploitation, rooted in the myth of white supremacy and the manifest destiny of the white race. The emerging shape of a new world order, and the requisites for survival in such a world, are fostering in your whites a new outlook. They recoil in shame from the spectacle of cowboys and pioneers—their heroic forefathers whose exploits filled earlier generations with pride—galloping across a movie screen shooting down Indians like Coke bottles. Even Winston Churchill, who is looked upon by older whites as perhaps the greatest hero of the twentieth century—even he, because of the system of which he was a creature and which he served, is an arch-villain in the eyes of the young white rebels.

At the close of World War Two, national liberation movements in the colonized world picked up new momentum and audacity, seeking to cash in on the democratic promises made by the Allies during the war. The Atlantic Charter, signed by President Roosevelt and Prime Minister Churchill in 1941, affirming "the right of all people to choose the form of government under which they may live," established the principle, although it took years of postwar struggle to give this piece of rhetoric even the appearance of reality. And just as world revolution has prompted the oppressed to re-evaluate their self-image in terms of the changing conditions, to slough off the servile attitudes inculcated by long years of subordination, the same dynamics of change have prompted the white people of the world to re-evaluate their self-image as well, to disabuse themselves of the Master Race psychology developed over centuries of imperial hegemony.

It is among the white youth of the world that the greatest change is taking place. It is they who are experiencing the great psychic pain of waking into consciousness to find their inherited heroes turned by events into villains. Communication and understanding between the older and younger generations of whites has entered a crisis. The elders, who, in the tradition of privileged classes or races, genuinely do not understand the youth, trapped by old ways of thinking and blind to the future, have only just begun to be vexed—because the youth have only just begun to rebel. So thoroughgoing is the revolution in the psyches of white youth that the traditional tolerance which every older generation has found it necessary to display is quickly exhausted, leaving a gulf of fear, hostility, mutual misunderstanding, and contempt.

The rebellion of the oppressed peoples of the world, along with the Negro revolution in America, have opened the way to a new evaluation of history, a re-examination of the role played by the white race since the beginning of European expansion. The positive achievements are also there in the record, and future generations will applaud them. But there can be no applause now, not while the master still holds the whip in his hand! Not even the master's own children can find it possible to applaud him—he cannot even applaud himself! The negative rings too loudly. Slave-catchers, slaveowners, murderers, butchers, invaders, oppressors—the white heroes have acquired new names. The great white statesmen whom school children are taught to revere are revealed as the architects of systems of human exploitation and slavery. Religious leaders are exposed as condoners and justifiers of all these evil deeds. Schoolteachers and college professors are seen as a clique of brainwashers and whitewashers.

The white youth of today are coming to see, intuitively, that to escape the onus of the history their fathers made they must face and admit the moral truth concerning the works of their fathers. That such venerated figures as George Washington and Thomas Jefferson owned hundreds of black slaves, that all of the Presidents up to Lincoln presided over a slave state, and that every President since Lincoln connived politically and cynically with the issues affecting the human rights and general welfare of the broad masses of the American people—these facts weigh heavily upon the hearts of these young people.

The elders do not like to give these youngsters credit for being able to understand what is going on and what has gone on. When speaking of juvenile delinquency, or the rebellious attitude of today's youth, the elders employ a glib rhetoric. They speak of the "alienation of youth," the desire of the young to be independent, the problems of "the father image" and "the mother image" and their effect upon growing children who lack sound models upon which to pattern themselves. But they consider it bad form to connect the problems of the youth with the central event of our era—the national liberation movements abroad and the Negro revolution at home. The foundations of authority have been blasted to bits in America because the whole society has been indicted, tried, and convicted of injustice. To the youth, the elders are Ugly Americans; to the elders, the youth have gone mad.

The rebellion of the white youth has gone through four broadly discernible stages. First there was an initial recoiling away, a rejection of the conformity which America expected, and had always received, sooner or later, from its youth. The disaffected youth were refusing to participate in the system, having discovered that America, far from helping the underdog, was up to its ears in the mud trying to hold the dog down. Because of the publicity and self-advertisements of the more vocal rebels, this period has come to be known as the beatnik era, although not all of the youth affected by these changes thought of themselves as beatniks. The howl of the beatniks and their scathing, outraged denunciation of the system—characterized by Ginsberg as Moloch, a bloodthirsty Semitic deity to which the ancient tribes sacrificed their firstborn children—was a serious, irrevocable declaration of war. It is revealing that the elders looked upon the beatniks as mere obscene misfits who were too lazy to take baths and too stingy to buy a haircut. The elders had eyes but couldn't see, ears but couldn't hear—not even when the message came through as clearly as in this remarkable passage from Jack Kerouac's *On the Road:*

> At lilac evening I walked with every muscle aching among the lights of the 27th and Welton in the Denver colored section, wishing I were a Negro, feeling that the best the white world had offered was not enough ecstasy for me, not enough life, joy, kicks, darkness, music, not enough night. I wished I were a Denver Mexican, or even a poor overworked Jap, anything but what I so drearily was, a "white man" disillusioned. All my life I'd had white ambitions. . . . I passed the dark porches of Mexican and Negro homes; soft voices were there, occasionally the dusky knee of some mysterious sensuous gal; the dark faces of the men behind rose arbors. Little children sat like sages in ancient rocking chairs.

The second stage arrived when these young people, having decided emphatically that the world, and particularly the U.S.A., was unacceptable to them in its present form, began an active search for roles they could play in changing the society. If many of these young people were content to lay up in their cool beat pads, smoking pot and listening to jazz in a perpetual orgy of esoteric bliss, there were others, less crushed by the system, who recognized the need for positive action. Moloch could not ask for anything more than to have its disaffected victims withdraw into safe, passive, apolitical little non-participatory islands, in an economy less and less able to provide jobs for the growing pool of unemployed. If all the unemployed had followed the lead of the beatniks, Moloch would gladly have legalized the use of euphoric drugs and marijuana, passed out free jazz albums and sleeping bags, to all those willing to sign affidavits promising to remain "beat." The non-beat disenchanted white youth were attracted magnetically to the Negro revolution, which had begun to take on a mass, insurrectionary tone. But they had difficulty understanding their relationship to the Negro, and what role "whites" could play in a "Negro revolution." For the time being they watched the Negro activists from afar.

The third stage, which is rapidly drawing to a close, emerged when white youth started joining Negro demonstrations in large numbers. The presence of whites among the demonstrators emboldened the Negro leaders and allowed them to use tactics they never would have been able to employ with all-black troops. The racist conscience of America is such that murder does not register as murder, really, unless the victim is white. And it was only when the newspapers and magazines started carrying pictures and stories of white demonstrators being beaten and maimed by mobs and police that the public began to protest. Negroes have become so used to this double standard that they, too, react differently to the death of a white. When white freedom riders were brutalized along with blacks, a sigh of relief went up from the black masses, because the blacks knew that white blood is the coin of freedom in a land where for four hundred years black blood has been shed unremarked and with impunity. America has never truly been outraged by the murder of a black man, woman, or child. White politicians may, if Negroes are aroused by a particular murder, say with their lips what they know with their minds they should feel with their hearts—but don't.

It is a measure of what the Negro feels that when the two white and one black civil rights workers were murdered in Mississippi in 1964, the event was welcomed by Negroes on a level of understanding beyond and deeper than the grief they felt for the victims and their families. This welcoming of violence and death to whites can almost be heard—indeed it can be heard—in the inevitable words, oft repeated by Negroes, that those whites, and blacks, do not die in vain. So it was with Mrs. Viola Liuzzo. And much of the anger which Negroes felt toward Martin Luther King during the Battle of Selma stemmed from the fact that he denied history a great moment, never to be recaptured, when he turned tail on the Edmund Pettus Bridge and refused to all those whites behind him what they had traveled thousands of miles to receive. If the police had turned them back by force, all those nuns, priests, rabbis, preachers, and distinguished ladies and gentlemen old and young—as they had done the Negroes a week earlier—the violence and brutality of the system would have been ruthlessly exposed. Or if, seeing King determined to lead them on to Montgomery, the troopers had stepped aside to avoid precisely the confrontation that Washington would not have tolerated, it would have signaled the capitulation of the militant white South. As it turned out, the March on Montgomery was a show of somewhat dim luster, stage-managed by the Establishment. But by this time the young whites were already active participants in the Negro revolution. In fact they had begun to transform it into something broader, with the potential of encompassing the whole of America in a radical reordering of society.

The fourth stage, now in its infancy, sees these white youth taking the initiative, using techniques learned in the Negro struggle to attack problems in the general society. The classic example of this new energy in action was the student battle on the UC campus at Berkeley, California—the Free Speech Movement. Leading the revolt were veterans of the civil rights movement, some of whom spent time on the firing line in the wilderness of Mississippi/Alabama. Flowing from the same momentum were student demonstrations against U.S. interference in the internal affairs of Vietnam, Cuba, the Dominican Republic, and the Congo and U.S. aid to apartheid in South Africa. The students even aroused the intellectual community to actions and positions unthinkable a few years ago: witness the teach-ins. But their revolt is deeper than single-issue protest. The characteristics of the white rebels which most alarm their elders—the long hair, the new dances, their love for Negro music, their use of marijuana, their mystical attitude toward sex—are all tools of their rebellion. They have turned these tools against the totalitarian fabric of American society—and they mean to change it.

From the beginning, America has been a schizophrenic nation. Its two conflicting images of itself were never reconciled, because never before has the survival of its most cherished myths made a reconciliation mandatory. Once before, during the bitter struggle between North and South climaxed by the Civil War, the two images of America came into conflict, although whites North and South scarcely understood it. The image of America held by its most alienated citizens was advanced neither by the North nor by the South; it was perhaps best expressed by Frederick Douglass, who was born into slavery in 1817, escaped to the North, and became the greatest leader-spokesman for the blacks of his era. In words that can still, years later, arouse an audience of black Americans, Frederick Douglass delivered, in 1852, a scorching indictment in his Fourth of July oration in Rochester:

> What to the American slave is your Fourth of July? I answer: a day that reveals to him, more than all other days in the year, the gross injustice and cruelty to which he is the constant victim. To him your celebration is a sham; your boasted liberty, an unholy license; your national greatness, swelling vanity; your sounds of rejoicing are empty and heartless; your denunciation of tyrants, brass-fronted impudence; your shouts of liberty and equality, hollow mockery; your prayers and hymns, your sermons and thanksgivings, with all your religious parade and solemnity, are, to him, more bombast, fraud, deception, impiety and hypocrisy —a thin veil to cover up crimes which would disgrace a nation of savages. . . .
>
> You boast of your love of liberty, your superior civilization, and your pure Christianity, while the whole political power of the nation (as embodied in the two great political parties) is solemnly pledged to support and perpetuate the enslavement of three millions of your countrymen. You hurl your anathemas at the crown-headed tyrants of Russia and Austria and pride yourselves on your democratic institutions, while you yourselves consent to be the mere *tools* and *bodyguards* of the tyrants of Virginia and Carolina.
>
> You invite to your shores fugitives of oppression from abroad, honor them with banquets, greet them with ovations, cheer them, toast them, salute them, protect them, and pour out your money to them like water; but the fugitive from your own land you advertise, hunt, arrest, shoot, and kill. You glory in your refinement and your universal education; yet you maintain a system as barbarous and dreadful as ever stained the character of a nation—a system

> begun in avarice, supported in pride, and perpetuated in cruelty.
> You shed tears over fallen Hungary, and make the sad story of her wrongs the theme of your poets, statesmen and orators, till your gallant sons are ready to fly to arms to vindicate her cause against the oppressor; but, in regard to the ten thousand wrongs of the American slave, you would enforce the strictest silence, and would hail him as an enemy of the nation who dares to make these wrongs the subject of public discourse!

This most alienated view of America was preached by the Abolitionists, and by Harriet Beecher Stowe in her *Uncle Tom's Cabin.* But such a view of America was too distasteful to receive wide attention, and serious debate about America's image and her reality was engaged in only on the fringes of society. Even when confronted with overwhelming evidence to the contrary, most white Americans have found it possible, after steadying their rattled nerves, to settle comfortably back into their vaunted belief that America is dedicated to the proposition that all men are created equal and endowed by their creator with certain inalienable rights—life, liberty and the pursuit of happiness. With the Constitution for a rudder and the Declaration of Independence as its guiding star, the ship of state is sailing always toward a brighter vision of freedom and justice for all.

Because there is no common ground between these two contradictory images of America, they had to be kept apart. But the moment the blacks were let into the white world—let out of the voiceless and faceless cages of their ghettos, singing, walking, talking, dancing, writing, and orating *their* image of America and of Americans—the white world was suddenly challenged to match its practice to its preachments. And this is why those whites who abandon the *white* image of America and adopt the *black* are greeted with such unmitigated hostility by their elders.

For all these years whites have been taught to believe in the myth they preached, while Negroes have had to face the bitter reality of what America practiced. But without the lies and distortions, white Americans would not have been able to do the things they have done. When whites are forced to look honestly upon the objective proof of their deeds, the cement of mendacity holding white society together swiftly disintegrates. On the other hand, the core of the black world's vision remains intact, and in fact begins to expand and spread into the psychological territory vacated by the non-viable white lies, i.e., into the minds of young whites. It is remarkable how the system worked for so many years, how the majority of whites remained effectively unaware of any contradiction between their view of the world and that world itself. The mechanism by which this was rendered possible requires examination at this point.

Let us recall that the white man, in order to justify slavery and, later on, to justify segregation, elaborated a complex, all-pervasive myth which at one time classified the black man as a subhuman beast of burden. The myth was progressively modified, gradually elevating the blacks on the scale of evolution, following their slowly changing status, until the plateau of separate-but-equal was reached at the close of the nineteenth century. During slavery, the black was seen as a mindless Supermasculine Menial. Forced to do the backbreaking work, he was conceived in terms of his ability to do such work—"field niggers," etc. The white man administered the plantation, doing all the thinking, exercising omnipotent power over the slaves. He had little difficulty dissociating himself from the black slaves, and he could not conceive of their positions being reversed or even reversible.

Blacks and whites being conceived as mutually exclusive types, those attributes imputed to the blacks could not also be imputed to the whites—at least not in equal degree—without blurring the line separating the races. These images were based upon the social function of the two races, the work they performed. The ideal white man was one who knew how to use his head, who knew how to manage and control things and get things done. Those whites who were not in a position to perform these functions nevertheless aspired to them. The ideal black man was one who did exactly as he was told, and did it efficiently and cheerfully. "Slaves," said Frederick Douglass, "are generally expected to sing as well as to work." As the black man's position and function became more varied, the images of white and black, having become stereotypes, lagged behind.

The separate-but-equal doctrine was promulgated by the Supreme Court in 1896. It had the same purpose domestically as the Open Door Policy toward China in the international arena: to stabilize a situation and subordinate a non-white population so that racist exploiters could manipulate those people according to their own selfish interests. These doctrines were foisted off as *the epitome of enlightened justice, the highest expression of morality*. Sanctified by religion, justified by philosophy and legalized by the Supreme Court, separate-but-equal was enforced by day by agencies of the law, and by the KKK & Co. under cover of night. Booker T. Washington, the Martin Luther King of his day, accepted separate-but-equal in the name of all Negroes. W. E. B. DuBois denounced it.

Separate-but-equal marked the last stage of the white man's flight into cultural neurosis, and the beginning of the black man's frantic striving to assert his humanity and equalize his position with the white. Blacks ventured into all fields of endeavor to which they could gain entrance. Their goal was to present in all fields a performance that would equal or surpass that of the whites. It was long axiomatic among blacks that a black had to be twice as competent as a white in any field in order to win grudging recognition from the whites. This produced a pathological motivation in the blacks to equal or surpass the whites, and a pathological motivation in the whites to maintain a distance from the blacks. This is the rack on which black and white Americans receive their delicious torture! At first there was the color bar, flatly denying the blacks entrance to certain spheres of activity. When this no longer worked, and blacks invaded sector after sector of American life and economy, the whites evolved other methods of keeping their distance. The illusion of the Negro's inferior nature had to be maintained.

One device evolved by the whites was to tab whatever the blacks did with the prefix "Negro." We had *Negro* literature, *Negro* athletes, *Negro* music, *Negro* doctors, *Negro* politicians, *Negro* workers. The malignant ingeniousness of this device is that although it accurately describes an objective biological fact—or, at least, a sociological fact in America—it concealed the paramount psychological fact: that to the white mind, prefixing anything with "Negro" automatically consigned it to an inferior category. A well-known example of the white necessity to deny due credit to blacks is in the realm of music. White musicians were famous for going to Harlem and other Negro cultural centers literally to steal the black man's music, carrying it back across the color line into the Great White World and passing off the watered-down loot as their own original creations. Blacks, meanwhile, were ridiculed as *Negro* musicians playing inferior coon music.

The Negro revolution at home and national liberation movements abroad have unceremoniously shattered the world of fantasy in which the whites have been living. It is painful that many do not yet see that their fantasy world has been rendered uninhabitable in the last half of the twentieth century. But it is away from this world that the white youth of today are turning. The "paper tiger" hero, James Bond, offering the whites a triumphant image of themselves, is saying what many whites want desperately to hear reaffirmed: *I am still the White Man, lord of the land, licensed to kill, and the world is still an empire at my feet.* James Bond feeds on that secret little anxiety, the psychological white backlash, felt in some degree by most whites alive. It is exasperating to see little brown men and little yellow men from the mysterious Orient, and the opaque black men of Africa (to say nothing of these impudent American Negroes!) who come to the UN and talk smart to us, who are scurrying all over *our* globe in their strange modes of dress—much as if they were new, unpleasant arrivals from another planet. Many whites believe in their ulcers that it is only a matter of time before the Marines get the signal to round up these truants and put them back securely in their cages. But it is away from this fantasy world that the white youth of today are turning.

In the world revolution now under way, the initiative rests with people of color. That growing numbers of white youth are repudiating their heritage of blood and taking people of color as their heroes and models is a tribute not only to their insight but to the resilience of the human spirit. For today the heroes of the initiative are people not usually thought of as white: Fidel Castro, Che Guevara, Kwame Nkrumah, Mao Tse-tung, Gamal Abdel Nasser, Robert F. Williams, Malcolm X, Ben Bella, John Lewis, Martin Luther King, Jr., Robert Parris Moses, Ho Chi Minh, Stokely Carmichael, W. E. B. DuBois, James Forman, Chou En-lai.

The white youth of today have begun to react to the fact that the "American Way of Life" is a fossil of history. What do they care if their old baldheaded and crew-cut elders don't dig their caveman mops? They couldn't care less about the old, stiffassed honkies who don't like their new dances: Frug, Monkey, Jerk, Swim, Watusi. All they know is that it feels good to swing to way-out body-rhythms instead of dragassing across the dance floor like zombies to the dead beat of mind-smothered Mickey Mouse music. Is it any wonder that the youth have lost all respect for their elders, for law and order, when for as long as they can remember all they've witnessed is a monumental bickering over the Negro's place in American society and the right of people around the world to be left alone by outside powers? They have witnessed the law, both domestic and international, being spat upon by those who do not like its terms. Is it any wonder, then, that they feel justified, by sitting-in and freedom riding, in breaking laws made by lawless men? Old funny-styled, zipper-mouthed political night riders know nothing but to haul out an investigating committee *to look into the disturbance* to find the cause of the unrest among the youth. Look into a mirror! The cause is you, Mr. and Mrs. Yesterday, you with your forked tongues.

A young white today cannot help but recoil from the base deeds of his people. On every side, on every continent, he sees racial arrogance, savage brutality toward the conquered and subjugated people, genocide; he sees the human cargo of the slave trade; he sees the systematic extermination of American Indians; he sees the civilized nations of Europe fighting in imperial depravity over the lands of other people—and over possession of the very people themselves. There seems to be no end to the ghastly deeds of which his people are guilty. GUILTY. The slaughter of the Jews by the Germans, the dropping of atomic bombs on the Japanese people—these deeds weigh heavily upon the prostrate souls and tumultuous consciences of the white youth. The white heroes, their hands dripping with blood, are dead.

The young whites know that the colored people of the world, Afro-Americans included, do not seek revenge for their suffering. They seek the same things the white rebel wants: an end to war and exploitation. Black and white, the young rebels are free people, free in a way that Americans have never been before in the history of their country. And they are outraged.

There is in America today a generation of white youth that is truly worthy of a black man's respect, and this is a rare event in the foul annals of American history. From the beginning of the contact between blacks and whites, there has been very little reason for a black man to respect a white, with such exceptions as John Brown and others lesser known. But respect commands itself and it can neither be given nor withheld when it is due. If a man like Malcolm X could change and repudiate racism, if I myself and other former Muslims can change, if young whites can change, then there is hope for America. It was certainly strange to find myself, while steeped in the doctrine that all whites were devils by nature, commanded by the heart to applaud and acknowledge respect for these young whites—despite the fact that they are descendants of the masters and I the descendant of slave. The sins of the fathers are visited upon the heads of the children—but only if the children continue in the evil deeds of the fathers.

QUESTIONS FOR DISCUSSION AND WRITING

1. According to Cleaver, youth has liberated itself from the "master/slave" syndrome. What do you think the sydrome is? According to Cleaver, how is release possible?
2. Cleaver focuses attention on white youth. Why? Why have some white college students sought to ally themselves with the black movement?
3. Can an effective analogy be drawn between white youth movements on college campuses and the organization, strategy, and tactics of the black movement?
4. Marcus Garvey alludes to Woodrow Wilson (p. 109); Cleaver refers to Franklin Roosevelt and Winston Churchill (p. 286). Why? What is the effect of such references?
5. Cleaver refers to Booker T. Washington as "the Martin Luther King of his day." Why? What similarities can be found in the ideas of the two men? What are the major differences? Compare the ideas expressed by Washington (p. 65) and King (p. 341) with Cleaver's presentations of them.

QUESTIONS FOR DISCUSSION AND WRITING

[illegible]

WILLIAM H. GRIER AND PRICE M. COBBS ARE PSYCHIATRISTS IN SAN FRANCISCO AND PROFESSORS AT THE UNIVERSITY OF CALIFORNIA MEDICAL CENTER THERE. THE FOLLOWING SELECTION IS TAKEN FROM THEIR 1968 WORK *Black Rage*, WHICH DISCUSSES THE EFFECTS OF WHITE AMERICA ON THE BLACK MAN'S PSYCHE.

WILLIAM H. GRIER

PRICE M. COBBS

THE "PROMISE" OF EDUCATION

Weep for Our Children

A twelve-year-old boy, watching TV with his family, was engrossed in a dramatic work, which turned on a young man's discovery that he was color-blind. The younger watchers did not understand the concept "color-blindness." The twelve-year-old then, referring to the condition as "Daltonism" (the correct term), described how John Dalton had discovered the condition in himself and had first described it. He pointed out that it is sex-linked and differentiated congenital red-green color-blindness from other related conditions.

The boy's parents were pleased and surprised, but, aware that he was an omnivorous reader, they regarded this display of knowledge as just another example of his accumulation of incidental information. They all but dismissed it from their minds and only later paid much attention to it, when the boy's school counselor told him that he was not very bright and that he should abandon aspirations for college and "work with his hands."

All his life the boy had shown his parents evidence of his above-average intellectual gifts, but his *performance* in school was always mediocre and they found themselves treating him as if he were a dull child in need of coaching and tutoring. Only when they consciously set their child's discourse on Daltonism against his counselor's recommendation that he work with his hands were they able to break the spell woven by the teachers' and their own anxiety.

Children are responsive to the expectations of their environment. They read clearly both the conscious and the unconscious message. While it is clear that the counselor's expectations and preconceptions of how black boys functioned intellectually prevented him from seeing this child's true capabilities, what is less obvious, but more important, was the parents' excessive concern that their son not be stupid. If they muster so much energy to keep him from performing poorly, then with his own logic he must conclude that they feel he is very close to being stupid or is very likely to perform poorly and that it is this stupidity, this poor performance, which represents the great danger to them. They reveal in this way their own imperfectly disguised expectation of the child, which parallels that of the counselor.

The unfortunate child finds himself in a world where even his own parents can barely see beyond the color of his skin. It is as if he yells and waves his arms but no one notices *him*; everyone sees only his dark cloak. The process of learning, a uniquely personal event under any circumstances, becomes for this child a lonely task, in which his triumphs pass unnoticed and any idle act may bring down a rain of admonition to do better, along with poorly concealed contempt.

The child is in danger of being what both parents and counselor might have been: stupid, ignorant, contemptible—and black. The very ordinary process of learning has vaulted him into the center of everyone's conflict, namely: Will I be smart, clean, clever, obedient, loved, successful, important, rich (and white), or will I be stupid, dirty, awkward, defiant, despised, and an unimportant, impoverished failure (who is black)?

He finds himself at the center of a storm so violent that he stands little chance of moving beyond it unaffected. And there is even less chance that his capacity to learn will remain fresh and broad. For him the long process of education is something akin to the trial of a long-distance runner who is occasionally peppered with buckshot; he may complete the race but it will take something out of him.

One of the keystones in white America's justification of its exploitation of black people is the assumption that black men are stupid. It is assumed that they cannot learn as much as a white man and therefore cannot assume positions of power and responsibility. (The essence of the concept of white supremacy is that every white man is inherently superior to every black man.) It is a vital piece of the American self-concept, for it has allowed the nation to grow fat off black men's labor and to bar them from even the meanest participation in the wealth they have produced. South Africa is merely America with the pretty tinsel ripped off.

So our black child has been raised by parents who have lived all their lives in these brackish waters, who may have held on to a perception of their own intelligence and capability but at great psychological expense. It is more likely, however, that the parents absorbed some of the poison of white society and to some extent they felt about themselves as their country felt about them. They may have fought against this concept and set out to prove that it was not true, unaware that they were driven to disprove it because in part they believed it. They may have projected the idea onto other black men saying: "Aren't they stupid?" or "Aren't they dumb niggers?"—all the while comforting themselves with that sad, sad comment: "I'm glad I'm different."

Such parents would no doubt say to their child: "You must be different also." And the child hears that he must be like his parents, dreading some blackness in himself which, he further hears, is associated with all the negative things said about black men.

The whole conflict at this level between black and white carries strong overtones of filth and cleanliness for the child—not too far removed in time from his earliest years, when such matters were of fundamental concern to him. It easily gets mixed with the moral injunctions of a few years before, when his parents humiliated him for being dirty and praised him for being clean. And now he is asked to be clean (white), even though he is black. All the positive attributes, including cleverness, are associated with being good and clean, and his parents urge him in that direction. But they act as if they know he cannot be what they want him to be. His blackness carries so many implications which he must learn.

> A black child was approached by a white child who rubbed his dark skin with her fingers and asked: "But how do you ever get clean?"

The concepts of cleanliness and orderliness and the joyful acquisition of knowledge are all related. Black children go to school and rapidly come to perceive the formal learning process as different, strange, unnatural, not meant for them, and not really relevant for them. The air they breathe, the water they drink, and the words they read all tell them that white people are smart and black people are dumb. And they could blot it all out and fight their way to intellectual distinction were it not for their parents. All messages are filtered through the child-parent relationship—and all have relevance only as they relate to that union. The child looks with clear eyes into the parent's heart and says: "Forget the world beyond. Tell me how you are, and that is how I will be, in my love for you." And he dashes away happy, shouting for all the world to hear: "I am black, dumb, and dirty," and to himself saying: "My love for her is boundless."

Schools are designed to train children to participate in the work of the society and to impart to them a certain attitude about the nation. The earliest schools taught the children of nobility to wage war and to govern. Only in relatively recent times has the work of the common man reached such complexity as to acquire special training. It is more than coincidence that in this country the growth of universal education has run parallel with the growth of industrialization and its need for more skilled laborers. Since 1865, black people have occupied a truly anomalous position in this country—unskilled agricultural laborers in an economy which has had a rapidly decreasing use for them. Moreover, they were rigorously excluded from participation in the wave of industrialization and were left, like buggy-whip makers, high and dry with no salable skill.

In spite of the yammering of naive observers, education has never offered a significant solution to the black man's dilemma in

America. In the eyes of policy makers, education has always been meant to serve the pragmatic function of training people for work. If black men have not been allowed into the job markets, then the educational opportunities denied them by the nation generally have reflected that fact. The point is that they continue to be regarded as a class of illiterate laborers who are bothersome and underfoot because the nation now sees no way to profitably exploit them. Moreover, it has not decided what to do with them. There was something orderly and proper about blacks laboring in the cotton fields and America is loath to relinquish this idea. Although education may in the long run be an important instrument for black people, children may have clearer vision when they see the classroom as immediately irrelevant. Their vision is clearer than that of men who plead for black people to become educated in a land which views all blacks as bondsmen temporarily out of bondage.

These are the poisonous waters through which black children must find their way.

Having made it to school, the child encounters that reluctant instrument of the establishment, the teacher. In such an encounter one is at a loss to decide who is more deserving of pity, the children or the teacher, who may have nursed an idealism longer than most people, who sees it eroding in the face of hypocrisy, who slowly comes to view her task as the crushing of spirit and the dulling of eyes.

Teachers are in low repute in America in large measure because they have no independent atmosphere in which to exercise their calling. The rigid control of teachers, curriculum, and budget by generally small-minded governing bodies again reflects the essential purpose of the schools—which is to serve the immediate economic ends of those who control them. Out of the same pragmatic thinking which produced the trade school and the commercial school has lately come the tracking program, a system for selecting one of several programs for students based on the child's performance and test results. These programs have operated to launch white children into college and to provide mindless "busy work" for black children until they are seventeen.

A black educator, a specialist in instructional materials, insists that, in spite of all other factors, an imaginative approach to learning could keep the spark alive in black children. Since the cost of such materials and training is modest, he said, to deny the children these aids is to deny them the union card of a high school or college education, without which employment these days is a sometime thing.

No one is more aware of this bizarre state of affairs than the teacher. It makes no difference if the teacher is white in a white suburban school, manning the ramparts against black invaders, or in fact a dedicated white teacher in a black ghetto. The white teacher knows as well as her black counterpart that the general quality of education in this country is rather seedy and the training children get is geared to mediocrity. The teacher would doubtless welcome an opportunity to participate in the development of an enlightened and intellectually vigorous citizenry. But the slow disenchantment of teachers, as they see the true dimensions of their task, contributes heavily, we feel, to the profusion of "bad teachers"—bitter, resentful beings who arrive at school each day with a baggage of contempt, ridicule, and sometimes open hatred for their tender charges. Frustrated idealists make poor guardians of a nation's youth.

The black parent approaches the teacher with the great respect due a person of learning. The soaring expectations which are an important part of the parent's feelings find substance in the person of the teacher. Here is the person who can do for this precious child all the wonderful things a loving parent cannot. The child is admonished to obey the teacher as he would his parents and the teacher is urged to exercise parental prerogatives, including beating. In this the parent yields up his final unique responsibility, the protection of his child against another's aggression. The child is placed in the teacher's hands to do with as she sees fit, with the sole requirement that she teach him. The meaning of this gift is not lost on the teacher, who is alternately touched by the parent's trust and staggered by the responsibility, for the teacher knows best of all that much has gone on before she gets the child and knows that, even as the parent urges her not to spare the rod, that same parent is telling volumes about the life that child has led up to this moment. The parent tells of a child both beloved and beaten, of a child taught to look for pain from even those who cherish him most, of a child who has come to feel that beatings are right and proper for him, and of a child whose view of the world, however gently it persuades him to act toward others, decrees for him that he is to be driven by the infliction of pain.

Pity that child.

Beating in child-rearing actually has its psychological roots in slavery and even yet black parents will feel that, just as they have suffered beatings as children, so it is right that their children be so treated. This kind of physical subjugation of the weak forges early in the mind of the child a link with the past and, as he learns the details of history, with slavery per se.

Beyond these early years rise the fantastic promise of "higher education." When all is taken into account, the proliferation of educational institutions for Negroes, along with the large number of black people attending these schools, has been a remarkable phenomenon. In view of the fact that this development has occurred primarily in the South, where early education has been poor, the phenomenon takes on even more unusual dimensions. When finally one adds the sobering fact that even with education the fate of black people in the South has been dismal, eagerness for learning on the part of black people becomes a curiosity worthy of study.

Any explanation of this drive toward learning must take into account the dearth of alternative modes of expression. Black people have always had reason to be skeptical of success in other fields of endeavor, for, if success were measured in terms of goods acquired, those goods could easily be taken away. Education was said to be "something no one can ever take away from you." It was therefore one of the very few areas of accomplishment where a level of "success" could be attained within a special Jim Crow arena of competition.

Black merchants were nonexistent; black politicians floated in a curious nonexistence, representing merely a cluster of black people and far removed from the seats of power. Black men were left pretty much to the fields of entertainment and education as areas in which advancement was possible.

Education had an ennobling quality which set one apart from the more common people. Just as white garments distinguished an upper-class nineteenth-century Korean from his brethren of the soil, and as the bound feet of upper-class Chinese women indicated that they had no need to walk as did the common people—so did the possession of an education separate a learned black man from his less fortunate brothers. It was of special significance, too, because of the all-pervading notion that blacks were ignorant and stupid. The black man found himself isolated by society generally as one who was "different," an "exception"—which was to say that his accomplishment was set to one side and the prevailing view that all black people were ignorant continued in full force.

This view fostered his own alienation from his group as well, offering him rewards not for his scholarship but often on the basis of his being a curiosity, much as one pays to see a seal play the piano. If, then, he is to capitalize on his efforts, he must accept this role and affirm the general view that he is an exception and that in fact no blacks can learn. And this continues to be the dilemma of the black intellectual—fighting to maintain a tie with his people but paid for being so curiously different from the mass of them.

America, by virtue of its incredible rate of economic growth, has had a constant need for men in increasing numbers and with increasing skills to fully exploit its potential and realize its promise. As a result, it has been able to say to every man—learn, and your skills will take you further than you ever imagined in your wildest dreams. There is no ceiling for you; this is truly the land of opportunity. This was no illusion, but every thoughtful man must now ask himself why the vast reservoir of black manpower was excluded from these opportunities. Why were the burgeoning factories of the North peopled by immigrants from Europe brought to this country at some risk and expense? Why were the lands of the West opened to all men of the soil save the most accomplished lovers of land—black men? With education the magic key to all this land's riches, why were only those with fair skin allowed to have it?

We propose that it was the economic usefulness of slavery in the period when cotton was king which in turn gave rise to the moral, religious, and psychological justification of the enslavement of blacks. Moral justification followed economic necessity and black Americans were viewed as subhumans designed for laboring in the fields. The incidental freeing of blacks after the Civil War was followed by a "conservative" backlash in which the newly freed slaves were abandoned to the tender mercies of their former owners while the main commercial business of America moved ahead under a gathering impetus. Negroes drifted into a "nonexistence" which they still occupy.

To have maintained a fervent interest in education and a belief in the rewards of learning required a major act of faith. Black people in America have been nothing if not idealists and devotees of the American dream. It is a source of wonder where such unending faith had its origins.

Whatever its source, faith in education has been a disappearing commodity among the most fortunate black beneficiaries of the educational system. Black intellectuals are a disenchanted lot. They have overcome incredible odds and have performed the impossible. They have had to cling to their own view of themselves amid violent contrary winds, holding fast only to ties that feel familiar and right, however strange those ties may seem to others.

> A brilliant high school student was awarded a scholarship to a prestigious Eastern school. Despite the enthusiastic encouragement of friends and family, he chose rather a small Negro college of modest reputation located in the South. He finally explained:
>
> "If I go East, I can never come back."

"Back" was to home, family, friends, and a brotherhood of black people.

Black people feel bound to the concept of equality. It is a belief which allows them to live. It cannot have merely an occasional hortatory meaning for black Americans—it must be seen as a universal truth. No other conviction can sustain black people in this country. It is absorbed in childhood and built on the child's conception of fairness. Public pronouncements of every kind can find a responsive affirmation in black breasts if they only include the word "equality." The idea of all men's equality lies at the deepest level of the black man's conception of social organization. Slavery and the post-Civil War experience have made this concept dear indeed.

It extends from the broad social meanings to its implementation in everyday life. Black children are acutely sensitive to the undemocratic formation of "exclusive" groups and social bodies. This conviction finds support in the concept of brotherhood. We are not only brothers but brothers keenly aware of our equal status.

But the belief in equality produces conflict when the black child is introduced to intellectual striving, competition, and the evaluation of his innate abilities. Some youngsters are far brighter than their brethren. When their gifts allow them to soar beyond the modest accomplishments of the others, the binding requirement of equality is encountered and problems arise. One may feel that to outstrip one's brothers is a wicked thing. To announce oneself as an exception is to bring calumny down on one's head. To say that one is smarter is to say that one's brothers are dumber, and that is a difficult thing for a black student.

Those with great intellectual gifts develop the technique of denying or minimizing them. A striking example of this occurred in treatment.

> A young woman revealed her intellectual gifts only gradually. She told over a period of weeks, bit by bit, that she had achieved a distinguished academic record and finally that she had been given numerous intelligence tests and on all of them had "gone off the top," which is to say she was gifted to a degree that the tests were not calibrated to measure. Her intelligence could only be estimated.
>
> In one session this bright woman described a major Caribbean island as located in the Mediterranean. Questioned repeatedly, she stuck to her mistake. Finally the therapist suggested that she knew better and that she made the error for some other purpose. She laughed and said that her great dread during treatment was the prospect of finding that she was brighter than the therapist and that from her earliest school years she had tried to obscure her knowledge and to make herself appear less gifted than she was.
>
> She was a vigorous champion of the cause of black people and found the idea of an intellectual aristocracy repugnant to her. Although she welcomed the challenge to match wits with white opponents and in fact rose to magnificent heights in such intellectual combat, she laid down her arms when confronted by a black antagonist.

Her situation is typical of many bright black students. Intellectual achievement is regarded as elevating oneself to a higher plane and removing oneself from the black brotherhood. The tie to blackness here is rarely perceived as the militant self-conscious pride of being black but rather as the deeper, sweeter, more profound ties to beloved figures of childhood.

Such a conflict partly explains why so many gifted black students achieve academic distinction but fail to fulfill their vocational promise. Accomplishment in school can be seen as simply carrying out the wishes of the family, whereas accomplishment in a career may represent a major move beyond the family—a move to another level out of contact with those whose love is life itself.

The scholar finds himself especially torn, driven to excel academically by the ambitions of family, yet pulled to maintain an all-important equality with those same beloved ones. He yields most often to the stronger force—the leveling effect of love.

The unique quality of this conflict arises from the strength of the call for equality. All Americans feel committed to the principle of "all men, created equal," but it does not occupy a central position in their view of their place in America. It is a case of "All men are born equal, but white men are more equal than anyone else."

For black men the concept of equality functions as an ideological bulwark against the pervasive idea that Negroes are stupid. The black man clings to it as one of the nation's highest principles. By calling upon Americans to respond to a statement of national conscience and by reminding them of their declared ideals, he is defending himself against the institutionalized depreciation of black people in this country. This devotion to principles, ideals, and conscience marks all black [men] with a certain idealism which seems inappropriate in so atavistic a land.

There is a separate and curious effect that American attitudes have had on the academic aspirations of black children which is related to the sexual roles adopted by boys and girls. It has often been observed that black parents push girls in the family to remain in school and in many ways encourage them and make higher education more accessible to them. On the other hand, the same family may discourage its sons, urge them to drop out of school, and make it difficult for them to obtain an education. The reasons are not immediately obvious.

> Mrs. J., who lived in the South in the 1920's, had eight children. She prodded her four daughters to obtain higher education and in spite of the family's extremely low income she made sure that the girls had some college instruction. Mrs. J. was a domestic and earned a precarious living unaided by public assistance. Her sons, she felt, "could look out for themselves," and when they were very young she told them of her need for whatever money they could earn. As a result, the oldest son quit school at fourteen and the others by the age of sixteen. All contributed to help the girls continue their education.

Here the rationale is clearer than most. Living in the South, Mrs. J. was concerned about the physical safety and protection she could offer her children. She admonished her sons to avoid conflict with white people and it would be blessing enough for her if they avoided the hostile physical encounters which could place their lives in jeopardy.

With her daughters it was a different story. Her aim was to protect them from the sexual exploitation they might suffer if they were forced to work as domestics. She knew that in the South an attractive young black girl who worked in a white household was in considerable danger of being used sexually by the men of the house. She also knew that the weapon used to bend the girl to their will was the economic threat of being fired if she refused to submit. To free the girls from this certain development, the mother sought to give them economic freedom through the education which allowed them all to become schoolteachers. As teachers, the girls would possess a dignity and an autonomy they could never have as black domestics in the South.

But even this strategy did not always succeed. The story is heard from many lips of white school administrators threatening to fire black teachers if they spurned sexual advances. If this pressure could be applied at so elevated and public a level, it must have been common indeed in the narrow secret world of the domestic servant.

For the boys, the world was quite a different place. It was exceedingly dangerous, and the first task was to develop a style of life which allowed one to survive. Avoid fights with white boys, particularly avoid gangs of white toughs, and speak with deference to white men. If one learned what situations to *avoid*, one could achieve as much safety as the South could afford a black man. Those slow to learn might not live very long in any event. The lessons were swift and cruel.

> A boy lived with his uncle, whom he adored. Their particular pleasure was spending Saturdays in town together. One such afternoon while walking along a street, they met a white man with his son, who was larger than the dark child. Without ado the white man kicked the black child and ordered his son to beat him up. The white boy beat him thoroughly while the uncle stood aside and sadly watched the proceedings.

In later life the black boy, now a man, said it took many years to forgive his uncle and even more to understand how painful it must have been for him, how wretched a life he led which required him, probably under penalty of death, to watch a child he loved being beaten and to be unable to raise a hand in protest. That boy is now a man and there are no words to convey the depth of his hatred for white men. But he carries on his daily life without a hint of rage.

If the boys learned this lesson, they learned something about the male role as well. For black men in America, in the old South and the new North, masculinity carries overtones of violence. One must either deal with and placate a violent white man or as a man defend oneself with violence against murderous threats. To position oneself, then, in relation to aggression became a vital part of masculinity. The man who fought when threatened and lived to tell the tale became a man who had dealt successfully with truly manly things—a man among men, a man of violence, a man who held his manhood dear, and though his life was likely to be brief had laid hold of the essential task of men and particularly black men—survival and opposition to the foe. And although . . . they terrified the Negro community and in a sense provided a negative model for "nice families," such men (bad niggers) had profound importance for the Negro community. They provided the measure of manhood for all black men and stood in ultimate masculine opposition to the feminine counterpart who sought protection from the foe by turning to education.

Thus any man who turned from violent confrontation of the white enemy and instead followed academic pursuits would have to feel deep inside, in his heart of hearts, that he had retreated from the battle. It was his secret, this cowardice, and there was an emptiness where his manhood might have been.

This played a part in the division of roles in girls who went to school and boys who dropped out. For in one sense school was seen by black families in a very special way. Beset on all sides by a cruel enemy, school was often primarily a refuge—a place of safety for those who were to be protected—and in a sense it was a case of women and children first.

These attitudes do not complete the catalogue of black people's feelings about school and schooling but they are important. They continue to play an important part to this day because the violence to which blacks are exposed in this country is faced by no other group of people in America. If school is seen as a refuge from the white aggressor, and if the black family places its women and children within such safe confines, and if the men then turn to face the enemy —*pray show me that critic of the "weak" Negro family!*

If the critics do not understand, then one may say that such everyday heroics are not performed for the critics' sake; fortunately they are carried out for love of man for woman and both for child.

And if school is regarded as of secondary importance and as having little relevance in the heat of battle where men are called to war, pray tell us who wages war on black people? One can only feel dismay if a man lays deadly siege to your house and then criticizes you for not going about innocent daily chores.

Such are the profound influences of American racism on the black man's involvement in education. In his mind school is converted from an instrument of social mobility to a place of refuge. The roles of black boys and girls are changed from potential participants in the fullness of America to females to be protected and men to face the enemy. It is a greater source of wonder that black children choose to learn at all.

Such are the factors that make academic achievement difficult for dark students: loving but untrusting parents, discouraged teachers, institutional opposition to a learned black community, and a state of war that has both historical roots and a contemporary reality. When in spite of these barriers a student surfaces as an academician, the passage through these dark places has left its mark. He steps onstage to put his skill to work in a nation and an economy which has blocked his progress at every step and which yet offers him serious obstacles.

The systematic discrimination against black academicians and intellectuals is a dreary tale well told by many voices. Let us add only this: The paths beyond scholarly excellence may lead to positions of power in government, in industry, or in the administrative hierarchy of major educational institutions. But the black man who has breached so many barriers to achieve academic status must at this writing realize that further doors are open to all save him. His is a blind alley. His achievements are circumscribed by the same impediments of discrimination as are those of his less gifted brother.

If education truly freed the brother from this peculiarly American latter-day bondage, the transition from black to white might actually be approached by means of the refinement of skills. But there is no prospect of this and no one realizes it more keenly than the black intellectual.

A distinguished black educator was sent overseas to organize the educational system for a sizable population. The area in which he was billeted offered many scenic views and he took a walk one afternoon with his camera to take photographs. He came upon a small village and walked down the main road. A jeep with several American military policemen roared up and the occupants spoke impatiently: "Over there! Over there!" pointing to a side road which they meant he should take.

He asked why, and they answered: "Beloved soldiers go on that side!"

Furious, he went where they indicated and discovered that the village housed mainly prostitutes who had been neatly divided for blacks on one side and whites on the other. The military policemen had thought he was seeking prostitutes and made sure he realized that their wares were segregated. The same man, as it happened, did a commendable job of reorganization and on his return to the United States found himself in line for a promotion to a major administrative position, one carrying great power and prestige. His training and experience fitted him perfectly for the job. He was taken aside, however, and the explanation given was that the region was simply "not ready" for a Negro to occupy so sensitive and so powerful a position.

It may not be appropriate to feel pity for so gifted and so fortunate a man, but we know that he does not share the affection his colleagues feel for this social system. He must know that his area of function is sharply limited by his blackness. He knows that there is no substantial difference between him and the lowliest black laborer save the grandeur of the arena in which they play out their lives. Both are held in check, both are restricted, both are called upon to embrace a society which views them with contempt.

Within the space of a few months this man had heard the harsh voice of his country telling him first which whores were not for him and next what power he must not have. He would surely have been hard put to differentiate between the laborer and the intellectual, at least if they are black and live in America.

And this precisely is the dilemma of the black intellectual. Now most of all he sees no difference whatsoever between himself and his poorer brother as they both relate themselves to the nation. The crux of the issue is that he alone sees their common bond. Others see him as only incidentally black, as an intellectual who happens to be a Negro, as a white black man. His poorer brethren cheer him on and vicariously relish his triumphs, but if he is too long in their company they become uncomfortable and wonder what they should say. They sense that he has no home with them any longer. The white community sees him as "different" from his darker brothers and capable of being viewed as one of their own when such meets their convenience. The net effect is an alienation from his roots with no substitute available. He cannot go forward and cannot go back. He may try to bind himself to blackness and voice the spirit of dark people; he may attack the white man, taking up the sword for his people; he may try in a thousand ways to become engaged in the battle, but always he enters from the outside and his contribution is that of an outsider. As the giants move toward battle, his is the voice of the bystander begging for engagement.

The black intellectual must accept his exclusion from this battle. If he is called by his brothers, he will leap to their aid. If they fail to call, he will continue to pursue his version of truth. He cannot force himself on them. He must be primarily devoted to truth. If the white man challenges him, the black scholar must demolish him with truth. His sword is his science, and only when he has finally fashioned a formidable weapon can it be put to use for his people and only when he limits his thrust to his special view of the world.

Thus it would be a pity if black scholars were swept up in a tide of anti-intellectualism. It would be understandable, of course, since education has been yearned for by the masses and has proven a failure. We can understand their turning away as well as their mounting distrust of the complexities of modern affairs. Why shouldn't black masses look upon such complexities with a jaundiced eye? They have always meant exclusion. Moreover, if education is necessary for participation in national affairs and education is denied him, the black man sees accurately if he sees education as an arm of that depriving white majority. No, his attitude is justified.

Such an attitude cannot be justified, however, by the black scholar. He has made his way past the impediments and finds himself now armed with modern science. To turn away from this opportunity shared by so few of his brothers is to deprive them of an arm they need desperately.

Our thesis is that black people are locked in a life struggle, and the black mothers all over America who urge their children: "Get some knowledge in your head; that's something no one can take away from you," are telling them a great deal about a vicious social order which rapes and exploits them and in which only a black man's ideas are safe from the white predator. The message is not lost on the children.

QUESTIONS FOR DISCUSSION AND WRITING

1. What major changes must American education undergo in order to become relevant to the black child? Should American colleges and universities revise their entrance standards in order to achieve a greater enrollment of black students? In what ways must the college institution change if its education of blacks is to be made relevant to them?
2. Grier and Cobbs claim that the school shows the black child that he cannot learn. How, specifically, does the school get the message to the individual child? What is the result?
3. Grier and Cobbs state that "in spite of the yammering of naive observers, education has never offered a significant solution to the black man's dilemma in America." Evaluate this assertion.
4. What values do Americans have about education? In what ways do blacks share these values? In what ways do black expectations differ?
5. What is the dilemma of the black intellectual? What responsibility does he have toward his people?

MALCOLM X WAS MURDERED IN 1965, A SHORT TIME AFTER HE FOUNDED THE ORGANIZATION FOR AFRO-AMERICAN UNITY. *The Autobiography of Malcolm X* DETAILS HIS CONVERSION FROM "STREET LIFE" TO MEMBERSHIP IN THE BLACK MUSLIMS, WHICH HE QUIT IN 1964. HIS WRITINGS HAVE HAD A UNIFYING EFFECT ON YOUNG BLACKS. THE FOLLOWING SELECTION IS A SPEECH DELIVERED BY MALCOLM X BEFORE A RACIALLY MIXED AUDIENCE IN APRIL 1964.

MALCOLM X

THE BLACK REVOLUTION

Friends and enemies: Tonight I hope that we can have a little fireside chat with as few sparks as possible being tossed around. Especially because of the very explosive condition that the world is in today. Sometimes, when a person's house is on fire and someone comes in yelling fire, instead of the person who is awakened by the yell being thankful, he makes the mistake of charging the one who awakened him with having set the fire. I hope that this little conversation tonight about the black revolution won't cause many of you to accuse us of igniting it when you find it at your doorstep. . . .

During recent years there has been much talk about a population explosion. Whenever they are speaking of the population explosion, in my opinion they are referring primarily to the people in Asia or in Africa—the black, brown, red, and yellow people. It is seen by people of the West that, as soon as the standard of living is raised in Africa and Asia, automatically the people begin to reproduce abundantly. And there has been a great deal of fear engendered by this in the minds of the people of the West, who happen to be, on this earth, a very small minority.

In fact, in most of the thinking and planning of whites in the West today, it's easy to see the fear in their minds, conscious minds and subconscious minds, that the masses of dark people in the East, who already outnumber them, will continue to increase and multiply and grow until they eventually overrun the people of the West like a human sea, a human tide, a human flood. And the fear of this can be seen in the minds, in the actions, of most of the people here in the West in practically everything that they do. It governs their political views and it governs their economic views and it governs most of their attitudes toward the present society.

I was listening to Dirksen, the senator from Illinois, in Washington, D.C., filibustering the civil-rights bill; and one thing that he kept stressing over and over and over was that if this bill is passed, it will change the social structure of America. Well, I know what he's getting at, and I think that most other people today, and especially our people, know what is meant when these whites, who filibuster these bills, express fears of changes in the social structure. Our people are beginning to realize what they mean.

Just as we can see that all over the world one of the main problems facing the West is race, likewise here in America today, most of your Negro leaders as well as the whites agree that 1964 itself appears to be one of the most explosive years yet in the history of America on the racial front, on the racial scene. Not only is this racial explosion probably to take place in America, but all of the ingredients for this racial explosion in America to blossom into a world-wide racial explosion present themselves right here in front of us. America's racial powder keg, in short, can actually fuse or ignite a world-wide powder keg.

There are whites in this country who are still complacent when they see the possibilities of racial strife getting out of hand. You are complacent simply because you think you outnumber the racial minority in this country; what you have to bear in mind is wherein you might outnumber us in this country, you don't outnumber us all over the earth.

Any kind of racial explosion that takes place in this country today, in 1964, is not a racial explosion that can be confined to the shores of America. It is a racial explosion that can ignite the racial powder keg that exists all over the planet that we call earth. I think that nobody would disagree that the dark masses of Africa and Asia and Latin America are already seething with bitterness, animosity, hostility, unrest, and impatience with the racial intolerance that they themselves have experienced at the hands of the white West.

And just as they have the ingredients of hostility toward the West in general, here we also have 22 million African-Americans, black, brown, red, and yellow people, in this country who are also seething with bitterness and impatience and hostility and animosity at the racial intolerance not only of the white West but of white America in particular.

And by the hundreds of thousands today we find our own people have become impatient, turning away from your white nationalism, which you call democracy, toward the militant, uncompromising policy of black nationalism. I point out right here that as soon as we announced we were going to start a black nationalist party in this country, we received mail from coast to coast, especially from young people at the college level, the university level, who expressed complete sympathy and support and a desire to take an active part in any kind of political action based on black nationalism, designed to correct or eliminate immediately evils that our people have suffered here for 400 years.

The black nationalists to many of you may represent only a minority in the community. And therefore you might have a tendency to classify them as something insignificant. But just as the fuse is the smallest part or the smallest piece in the powder keg, it is yet that little fuse that ignites the entire powder keg. The black nationalists to you may represent a small minority in the so-called Negro community. But they just happen to be composed of the type of ingredient necessary to fuse or ignite the entire black community.

And this is one thing that whites—whether you call yourselves liberals or conservatives or racists or whatever else you might choose to be—one thing that you have to realize is, where the black community is concerned, although the large majority you come in contact with may impress you as being moderate and patient and loving and long-suffering and all that kind of stuff, the minority who you consider to be Muslims or nationalists happen to be made of the type of ingredient that can easily spark the black community. This should be understood. Because to me a powder keg is nothing without a fuse.

1964 will be America's hottest year; her hottest year yet; a year of much racial violence and much racial bloodshed. But it won't be blood that's going to flow only on one side. The new generation of black people that have grown up in this country during recent years are already forming the opinion, and it's a just opinion, that if there is to be bleeding, it should be reciprocal—bleeding on both sides.

It should also be understood that the racial sparks that are ignited here in America today could easily turn into a flaming fire abroad, which means it could engulf all the people of this earth into a giant race war. You cannot confine it to one little neighborhood, or one little community, or one little country. What happens to a black man in America today happens to the black man in Africa. What happens to a black man in America and Africa happens to the black man in Asia and to the man down in Latin America. What happens to one of us today happens to all of us. And when this is realized, I think that the whites—who are intelligent even if they aren't moral or aren't just or aren't impressed by legalities—those who are intelligent will realize that when they touch this one, they are touching all of them, and this in itself will have a tendency to be a checking factor.

The seriousness of this situation must be faced up to. I was in Cleveland last night, Cleveland, Ohio. In fact I was there Friday, Saturday and yesterday. Last Friday the warning was given that this is a year of bloodshed, that the black man has ceased to turn the other cheek, that he has ceased to be nonviolent, that he has ceased to feel that he must be confined by all these restraints that are put upon him by white society in struggling for what white society says he was supposed to have had a hundred years ago.

So today, when the black man starts reaching out for what America says are his rights, the black man feels that he is within his rights—when he becomes the victim of brutality by those who are depriving him of his rights—to do whatever is necessary to protect himself. An example of this was taking place last night at this same time in Cleveland, where the police were putting water hoses on our people there and also throwing tear gas at them—and they met a hail of stones, a hail of rocks, a hail of bricks. A couple of weeks ago in Jacksonville, Florida, a young teen-age Negro was throwing Molotov cocktails.

Well, Negroes didn't do this ten years ago. But what you should learn from this is that they are waking up. It was stones yesterday,

Molotov cocktails today; it will be hand grenades tomorrow and whatever else is available the next day. The seriousness of this situation must be faced up to. You should not feel that I am inciting someone to violence. I'm only warning of a powder-keg situation. You can take it or leave it. If you take the warning, perhaps you can still save yourself. But if you ignore it or ridicule it, well, death is already at your doorstep. There are 22 million African-Americans who are ready to fight for independence right here. When I say fight for independence right here, I don't mean any nonviolent fight, or turn-the-other-cheek fight. Those days are gone. Those days are over.

If George Washington didn't get independence for this country nonviolently, and if Patrick Henry didn't come up with a nonviolent statement, and you taught me to look upon them as patriots and heroes, then it's time for you to realize that I have studied your books well. . . .

1964 will see the Negro revolt evolve and merge into the world-wide black revolution that has been taking place on this earth since 1945. The so-called revolt will become a real black revolution. Now the black revolution has been taking place in Africa and Asia and Latin America; when I say black, I mean non-white—black, brown, red or yellow. Our brothers and sisters in Asia, who were colonized by the Europeans, our brothers and sisters in Africa, who were colonized by the Europeans, and in Latin America, the peasants, who were colonized by the Europeans, have been involved in a struggle since 1945 to get the colonialists, or the colonizing powers, the Europeans, off their land, out of their country.

This is a real revolution. Revolution is always based on land. Revolution is never based on begging somebody for an integrated cup of coffee. Revolutions are never fought by turning the other cheek. Revolutions are never based upon love-your-enemy and pray-for-those-who-spitefully-use-you. And revolutions are never waged singing "We Shall Overcome." Revolutions are based upon bloodshed. Revolutions are never compromising. Revolutions are never based upon negotiations. Revolutions are never based upon any kind of tokenism whatsoever. Revolutions are never even based upon that which is begging a corrupt society or a corrupt system to accept us into it. Revolutions overturn systems. And there is no system on this earth which has proven itself more corrupt, more criminal, than this system that in 1964 still colonizes 22 million African-Americans, still enslaves 22 million Afro-Americans.

There is no system more corrupt than a system that represents itself as the example of freedom, the example of democracy, and can go all over this earth telling other people how to straighten out their house, when you have citizens of this country who have to use bullets if they want to cast a ballot.

The greatest weapon the colonial powers have used in the past against our people has always been divide and conquer. America is a colonial power. She has colonized 22 million Afro-Americans by depriving us of first-class citizenship, by depriving us of civil rights, actually by depriving us of human rights. She has not only deprived us of the right to be a citizen, she has deprived us of the right to be human beings, the right to be recognized and respected as men and women. In this country the black can be fifty years old and he is still a "boy."

I grew up with white people. I was integrated before they even invented the word and I have never met white people yet—if you are around them long enough—who won't refer to you as a "boy" or a "gal," no matter how old you are or what school you came out of, no matter what your intellectual or professional level is. In this society we remain "boys."

So America's strategy is the same strategy as that which was used in the past by the colonial powers: divide and conquer. She plays one Negro leader against the other. She plays one Negro organization against the other. She makes us think we have different objectives, different goals. As soon as one Negro says something, she runs to this Negro and asks him, "What do you think about what he said?" Why, anybody can see through that today—except some of the Negro leaders.

All of our people have the same goals, the same objective. That objective is freedom, justice, equality. All of us want recognition and respect as human beings. We don't want to be integrationists. Nor do we want to be separationists. We want to be human beings. Integration is only a method that is used by some groups to obtain freedom, justice, equality and respect as human beings. Separation is only a method that is used by other groups to obtain freedom, justice, equality or human dignity.

Our people have made the mistake of confusing the methods with the objectives. As long as we agree on objectives, we should never fall out with each other just because we believe in different methods or tactics or strategy to reach a common objective.

We have to keep in mind at all times that we are not fighting for integration, nor are we fighting for separation. We are fighting for recognition as human beings. We are fighting for the right to live as free humans in this society. In fact, we are actually fighting for rights that are even greater than civil rights and that is human rights. . . .

Among the so-called Negroes in this country, as a rule the civil-rights groups, those who believe in civil rights, spend most of their time trying to prove they are Americans. Their thinking is usually domestic, confined to the boundaries of America, and they always look upon themselves as a minority. When they look upon themselves upon the American stage, the American stage is a white stage. So a black man standing on that stage in America automatically is in the minority. He is the underdog, and in his struggle he always uses an approach that is a begging, hat-in-hand, compromising approach.

Whereas the other segment or section in America, known as the black nationalists, are more interested in human rights than they are in civil rights. And they place more stress on human rights than they do on civil rights. The difference between the thinking and the scope of the Negroes who are involved in the human-rights struggle and those who are involved in the civil-rights struggle is that those so-called Negroes involved in the human-rights struggle don't look upon themselves as Americans.

They look upon themselves as a part of dark mankind. They see the whole struggle not within the confines of the American stage, but they look upon the struggle on the world stage. And, in the world context, they see that the dark man outnumbers the white man. On the world stage the white man is just a microscopic minority.

So in this country you find two different types of Afro-Americans —the type who looks upon himself as a minority and you as the majority, because his scope is limited to the American scene; and then you have the type who looks upon himself as part of the majority and you as part of a microscopic minority. And this one uses a different approach in trying to struggle for his rights. He doesn't beg. He doesn't thank you for what you give him, because you are only giving him what he should have had a hundred years ago. He doesn't think you are doing him any favors.

He doesn't see any progress that he has made since the Civil War. He sees not one iota of progress because, number one, if the Civil War had freed him, he wouldn't need civil-rights legislation today. If the Emancipation Proclamation, issued by that great shining liberal called Lincoln, had freed him, he wouldn't be singing "We Shall Overcome" today. If the amendments to the Constitution had solved his problem, his problem wouldn't still be here today. And if the Supreme Court desegregation decision of 1954 was genuinely and sincerely designed to solve his problem, his problem wouldn't be with us today.

So this kind of black man is thinking. He can see where every maneuver that America has made, supposedly to solve this problem, has been nothing but political trickery and treachery of the worst order. Today he doesn't have any confidence in these so-called liberals. (I know that all that have come in here tonight don't call yourselves liberals. Because that's a nasty name today. It represents hypocrisy.) So these two different types of black people exist in the so-called Negro community and they are beginning to wake up and their awakening is producing a very dangerous situation.

You have whites in the community who express sincerity when they say they want to help. Well, how can they help? How can a white person help the black man solve his problem? Number one, you can't solve it for him. You can help him solve it, but you can't solve it for him today. One of the best ways that you can help him solve it is to let the so-called Negro, who has been involved in the civil-rights struggle, see that the civil-rights struggle must be expanded beyond the level of civil rights to human rights. Once it is expanded beyond the level of civil rights to the level of human rights, it opens the door for all of our brothers and sisters in Africa and Asia, who have their independence, to come to our rescue.

When you go to Washington, D.C., expecting those crooks down there—and that's what they are—to pass some kind of civil-rights legislation to correct a very criminal situation, what you are doing is encouraging the black man, who is the victim, to take his case into the court that's controlled by the criminal that made him the victim. It will never be solved in that way. . . .

The civil-rights struggle involves the black man taking his case to the white man's court. But when he fights it at the human-rights level, it is a different situation. It opens the door to take Uncle Sam to the world court. The black man doesn't have to go to court to be free. Uncle Sam should be taken to court and made to tell why the black man is not free in a so-called free society. Uncle Sam should be taken into the United Nations and charged with violating the UN charter of human rights.

You can forget civil rights. How are you going to get civil rights with men like Eastland and men like Dirksen and men like Johnson? It has to be taken out of their hands and taken into the hands of those whose power and authority exceed theirs. Washington has become too corrupt. Uncle Sam has become bankrupt when it comes to a conscience—it is impossible for Uncle Sam to solve the problem of 22 million black people in this country. It is absolutely impossible to do it in Uncle Sam's courts—whether it is the Supreme Court or any other kind of court that comes under Uncle Sam's jurisdiction.

The only alternative that the black man has in America today is to take it out of Senator Dirksen's and Senator Eastland's and President Johnson's jurisdiction and take it downtown on the East River and place it before that body of men who represent international law, and let them know that the human rights of black people are being violated in a country that professes to be the moral leader of the free world.

Any time you have a filibuster in America, in the Senate, in 1964 over the rights of 22 million black people, over the citizenship of 22 million black people, or that will affect the freedom and justice and equality of 22 million black people, it's time for that government itself to be taken before a world court. How can you condemn South Africa? There are only 11 million of our people in South Africa, there are 22 million of them here. And we are receiving an injustice which is just as criminal as that which is being done to the black people of South Africa.

So today those whites who profess to be liberals—and as far as I am concerned it's just lip-profession—you understand why our people don't have civil rights. You're white. You can go and hang out with another white liberal and see how hypocritical they are. A lot of you sitting right here know that you've seen whites up in a Negro's face with flowery words, and as soon as that Negro walks away you listen to how your white friend talks. We have black people who can pass as white. We know how you talk.

We can see that it is nothing but a governmental conspiracy to continue to deprive the black people in this country of their rights. And the only way we will get these rights restored is by taking it out of Uncle Sam's hands. Take him to court and charge him with genocide, the mass murder of millions of black people in this country—political murder, economic murder, social murder, mental murder. This is the crime that this government has committed, and if you yourself don't do something about it in time, you are going to open the doors for something to be done about it from outside forces.

I read in the paper yesterday where one of the Supreme Court justices, Goldberg, was crying about the violation of human rights of three million Jews in the Soviet Union. Imagine this. I haven't got anything against Jews, but that's their problem. How in the world are you going to cry about problems on the other side of the world when you haven't got the problems straightened out here? How can the plight of three million Jews in Russia be qualified to be taken to the United Nations by a man who is a justice in this Supreme Court, and is supposed to be a liberal, supposed to be a friend of black people, and hasn't opened up his mouth one time about taking the plight of black people down here to the United Nations? . . .

If Negroes could vote south of the—yes, if Negroes could vote south of the Canadian border—south South, if Negroes could vote in the southern part of the South, Ellender wouldn't be the head of the Agricultural and Forestry Committee, Richard Russell wouldn't be head of the Armed Services Committee, Robertson of Virginia wouldn't be head of the Banking and Currency Committee. Imagine that, all of the banking and currency of the government is in the hands of a cracker.

In fact, when you see how many of these committee men are from the South, you can see that we have nothing but a cracker government in Washington, D.C. And their head is a cracker president. I said a cracker president. Texas is just as much a cracker state as Mississippi. . . .

The first thing this man did when he came in office was invite all the big Negroes down for coffee. James Farmer was one of the first ones, the head of CORE. I have nothing against him. He's all right—Farmer, that is. But could that same president have invited James Farmer to Texas for coffee? And if James Farmer went to Texas, could he have taken his white wife with him to have coffee with the president? Any time you have a man who can't straighten out Texas, how can he straighten out the country? No, you're barking up the wrong tree.

If Negroes in the South could vote, the Dixiecrats would lose power. When the Dixiecrats lost power, the Democrats would lose power. A Dixiecrat lost is a Democrat lost. Therefore the two of them have to conspire with each other to stay in power. The Northern Dixiecrat puts all the blame on the Southern Dixiecrat. It's a con game, a giant political con game. The job of the Northern Democrat is to make the Negro think that he is our friend. He is always smiling and wagging his tail and telling us how much he can do for us if we vote for him. But at the same time that he's out in front telling us what he's going to do, behind the door he's in cahoots with the Southern Democrat setting up the machinery to make sure he'll never have to keep his promise.

This is the conspiracy that our people have faced in this country for the past hundred years. And today you have a new generation of black people who have come on the scene, who have become disenchanted with the entire system, who have become disillusioned over the system, and who are ready now and willing to do something about it.

So, in my conclusion, in speaking about the black revolution, America today is at a time or in a day or at an hour where she is the first country on this earth that can actually have a bloodless revolution. In the past, revolutions have been bloody. Historically you just don't have a peaceful revolution. Revolutions are bloody, revolutions are violent, revolutions cause bloodshed and death follows in their paths. America is the only country in history in a position to bring about a revolution without violence and bloodshed. But America is not morally equipped to do so.

Why is America in a position to bring about a bloodless revolution? Because the Negro in this country holds the balance of power, and if the Negro in this country were given what the Constitution says he is supposed to have, the added power of the Negro in this country would sweep all of the racists and the segregationists out of office. It would change the entire political structure of the country. It would wipe out the Southern segregationism that now controls America's foreign policy, as well as America's domestic policy.

And the only way without bloodshed that this can be brought about is that the black man has to be given full use of the ballot in every one of the fifty states. But if the black man doesn't get the ballot, then you are going to be faced with another man who forgets the ballot and starts using the bullet.

Revolutions are fought to get control of land, to remove the absentee landlord and gain control of the land and the institutions that flow from that land. The black man has been in a very low condition because he has had no control whatsoever over any land. He has been a beggar economically, a beggar politically, a beggar socially, a beggar even when it comes to trying to get some education. The past type of mentality, that was developed in this colonial system among our people, today is being overcome. And as the young ones come up, they know what they want. And as they listen to your beautiful preaching about democracy and all those other flowery words, they know what they're supposed to have.

So you have a people today who not only know what they want, but also know what they are supposed to have. And they themselves are creating another generation that is coming up that not only will know what it wants and know what it should have, but also will be ready and willing to do whatever is necessary to see that what they should have materializes immediately. Thank you.

QUESTIONS FOR DISCUSSION AND WRITING

1. According to Malcolm X, what is the difference between civil rights and human rights? Why is the difference significant?
2. What connections does Malcolm X make between the point of view of the non-white peoples formerly colonized abroad and that of the blacks in America? How can "Third World" peoples unite?
3. How does Malcolm X's point of view differ from that of King (p. 341)? On what matters do they agree?
4. What does Malcolm X mean by "revolution"? Is his definition similar to Carmichael's (p. 336)? To Browne's (p. 389)?
5. What are Malcolm X's ideas about nationalism? Are his ideas similar to Garvey's (p. 103)? Does Malcolm X's definition of nationalism echo Douglass' (p. 47) and DuBois' (p. 86)?

STOKELY CARMICHAEL ATTENDED HOWARD UNIVERSITY AND IS THE CO-AUTHOR (WITH CHARLES HAMILTON) OF *Black Power.* HE IS CURRENTLY PRIME MINISTER OF SNCC, THE STUDENT NATIONAL COORDINATING COMMITTEE (FORMERLY THE STUDENT NONVIOLENT COORDINATING COMMITTEE). THE NEW NAME OF THE GROUP EXPRESSES ITS ADJUSTED POINT OF VIEW, WHICH IS EXPLAINED IN PART IN THE FOLLOWING ESSAY.

STOKELY CARMICHAEL

WHAT WE WANT

One of the tragedies of the struggle against racism is that up to now there has been no national organization which could speak to the growing militancy of young black people in the urban ghetto. There has been only a civil rights movement, whose tone of voice was adapted to an audience of liberal whites. It served as a sort of buffer zone between them and angry young blacks. None of its so-called leaders could go into a rioting community and be listened to. In a sense, I blame ourselves—together with the mass media—for what has happened in Watts, Harlem, Chicago, Cleveland, Omaha. Each time the people in those cities saw Martin Luther King get slapped, they became angry; when they saw four little black girls bombed to death, they were angrier; and when nothing happened, they were

WHAT WE WANT From *The New York Review of Books* (September 22, 1966). Reprinted with the permission of SNCC.

steaming. We had nothing to offer that they could see, except to go out and be beaten again. We helped to build their frustration.

For too many years, black Americans marched and had their heads broken and got shot. They were saying to the country, "Look, you guys are supposed to be nice guys and we are only going to do what we are supposed to do—why do you beat us up, why don't you give us what we ask, why don't you straighten yourselves out?" After years of this, we are at almost the same point—because we demonstrated from a position of weakness. We cannot be expected any longer to march and have our heads broken in order to say to whites: come on, you're nice guys. For you are not nice guys. We have found you out.

An organization which claims to speak for the needs of a community—as does the Student Nonviolent Coordinating Committee—must speak in the tone of that community, not as somebody else's buffer zone. This is the significance of black power as a slogan. For once, black people are going to use the words they want to use, not just the words whites want to hear. And they will do this no matter how often the press tries to stop the use of the slogan by equating it with racism or separatism.

An organization which claims to be working for the needs of a community—as SNCC does—must work to provide that community with a position of strength from which to make its voice heard. This is the significance of black power beyond the slogan.

Black power can be clearly defined for those who do not attach the fears of white America to their questions about it. We should begin with the basic fact that black Americans have two problems: they are poor and they are black. All other problems arise from this two-sided reality: lack of education, the so-called apathy of black men. Any program to end racism must address itself to that double reality.

Almost from its beginning, SNCC sought to address itself to both conditions with a program aimed at winning political power for impoverished Southern blacks. We had to begin with politics because black Americans are a propertyless people in a country where property is valued above all. We had to work for power, because this country does not function by morality, love, and nonviolence, but by power. Thus we determined to win political power, with the idea of moving on from there into activity that would have economic effects. With power, the masses could *make or participate in making* the decisions which govern their destinies, and thus create basic change in their day-to-day lives.

But if political power seemed to be the key to self-determination, it was also obvious that the key had been thrown down a deep well many years earlier. Disenfranchisement, maintained by racist terror, makes it impossible to talk about organizing for political power in 1960. The right to vote had to be won, and SNCC workers devoted their energies to this from 1961 to 1965. They set up voter registration drives in the Deep South. They created pressure for the vote by holding mock elections in Mississippi in 1963 and by helping to establish the Mississippi Freedom Democratic Party (MFDP) in 1964. That struggle was eased, though not won, with the passage of the 1965 Voting Rights Act. SNCC workers could then address themselves to the question: "Who can we vote for, to have our needs met—how do we make our vote meaningful?"

SNCC had already gone to Atlantic City for recognition of the Mississippi Freedom Democratic Party by the Democratic convention and been rejected; it had gone with the MFDP to Washington for recognition by Congress and been rejected. In Arkansas, SNCC helped thirty Negroes to run for school board elections; all but one were defeated, and there was evidence of fraud and intimidation sufficient to cause their defeat. In Atlanta, Julian Bond ran for the state legislature and was elected—twice—and unseated—twice. In several states, black farmers ran in elections for agricultural committees which make crucial decisions concerning land use, loans, etc. Although they won places on a number of committees, they never gained the majorities needed to control them.

All of the efforts were attempts to win black power. Then, in Alabama, the opportunity came to see how blacks could be organized on an independent party basis. An unusual Alabama law provides that any group of citizens can nominate candidates for county office and, if they win 20 per cent of the vote, may be recognized as a county political party. The same then applies on a state level. SNCC went to organize in several counties such as Lowndes, where black people—who form 80 per cent of the population and have an average annual income of $943—felt they could accomplish nothing within the framework of the Alabama Democratic Party because of its racism and because the qualifying fee for this year's elections was raised from $50 to $500 in order to prevent most Negroes from becoming candidates. On May 3, five new county "freedom organizations" convened and nominated candidates for the offices of sheriff, tax assessor, members of the school boards. These men and women are up for election in November—if they live until then. Their ballot symbol is the black panther: a bold, beautiful animal, representing the strength and dignity of black demands today. A man needs a black panther on his side when he and his family must endure—as hundreds of Alabamians have endured—loss of job, eviction, starvation, and sometimes death, for political activity. He may also need a gun and SNCC reaffirms the right of black men everywhere to defend themselves when threatened or attacked. As for initiating the use of violence, we hope that such programs as ours will make that unnecessary; but it is not for us to tell black communities whether they can or cannot use any particular form of action to resolve their problems. Responsibility for the use of violence by black men, whether in self defense or initiated by them, lies with the white community.

This is the specific historical experience from which SNCC's call for "black power" emerged on the Mississippi march last July. But the concept of "black power" is not a recent or isolated phenomenon: it has grown out of the ferment of agitation and activity by different people and organizations in many black communities over the years. Our last year of work in Alabama added a new concrete possibility. In Lowndes county, for example, black power will mean that if a Negro is elected sheriff, he can end police brutality. If a black man is elected tax assessor, he can collect and channel funds for the building of better roads and schools serving black people—thus advancing the move from political power into the economic arena. In such areas as Lowndes, where black men have a majority, they will attempt to use it to exercise control. This is what they seek: control. Where Negroes lack a majority, black power means proper representation and sharing of control. It means the creation of power bases from which black people can work to change statewide or nationwide patterns of oppression through pressure from strength—instead of weakness. Politically, black power means what it has always meant to SNCC: the coming-together of black people to elect representatives and *to force those representatives to speak to their needs.* It does not mean merely putting black faces into office. A man or woman who is black and from the slums cannot be automatically expected to speak to the needs of black people. Most of the black politicians we see around the country today are not what SNCC means by black power. The power must be that of a community, and emanate from there.

SNCC today is working in both North and South on programs of voter registration and independent political organizing. In some places, such as Alabama, Los Angeles, New York, Philadelphia, and New Jersey, independent organizing under the black panther symbol is in progress. The creation of a national "black panther party" must come about; it will take time to build, and it is much too early to predict its success. We have no infallible master plan and we make no claim to exclusive knowledge of how to end racism; different groups will work in their own different ways. SNCC cannot spell out the full logistics of self-determination but it can address itself to the problem by helping black communities define their needs, realize their strength, and go into action along a variety of lines which they must choose for themselves. Without knowing all the answers, it can address itself to the basic problem of poverty; to the fact that in Lowndes County, 86 white families own 90 per cent of the land. What are black people in that county going to do for jobs, where are they going to get money? There must be reallocation of land, of money.

Ultimately, the economic foundations of this country must be shaken if black people are to control their lives. The colonies of the United States—and this includes the black ghettoes within its borders, north and south—must be liberated. For a century, this nation has been like an octopus of exploitation, its tentacles stretching from Mississippi and Harlem to South America, the Middle East, southern Africa, and Vietnam; the form of exploitation varies from area to area but the essential result has been the same—a powerful few have been maintained and enriched at the expense of the poor and voiceless colored masses. This pattern must be broken. As its grip loosens here and there around the world, the hopes of black Americans become more realistic. For racism to die, a totally different America must be born.

This is what the white society does not wish to face; this is why that society prefers to talk about integration. But integration speaks not at all to the problem of poverty, only to the problem of blackness. Integration today means the man who "makes it," leaving his black brothers behind in the ghetto as fast as his new sports car will take him. It has no relevance to the Harlem wino or to the cotton-picker making three dollars a day. As a lady I know in Alabama once said, "The food that Ralph Bunche eats doesn't fill my stomach."

Integration, moreover, speaks to the problem of blackness in a despicable way. As a goal, it has been based on complete acceptance of the fact that *in order to have* a decent house or education, blacks must move into a white neighborhood or send their children to a white school. This reinforces, among both black and white, the idea that "white" is automatically better and "black" is by definition inferior. This is why integration is a subterfuge for the maintenance of white supremacy. It allows the nation to focus on a handful of Southern children who get into white schools, at great price, and to ignore the 94 per cent who are left behind in unimproved all-black schools. Such situations will not change until black people have power—to control their own school boards, in this case. Then Negroes become equal in a way that means something, and integration ceases to be a one-way street. Then integration doesn't mean draining skills and energies from the ghetto into white neighborhoods; then it can mean white people moving from Beverly Hills into Watts, white people joining the Lowndes County Freedom Organization. Then integration becomes relevant.

Last April, before the furor over black power, Christopher Jencks wrote in a *New Republic* article on white Mississippi's manipulation of the anti-poverty program:

> The war on poverty has been predicated on the notion that there is such a thing as *a community* which can be defined geographically and mobilized for a collective effort to help the poor. This theory has no relationship to reality in the Deep South. In every Mississippi county there are *two* communities. Despite all the pious platitudes of the moderates on both sides, these two communities habitually see their interests in terms of conflict rather than cooperation. Only when the Negro community can muster enough political, economic and professional strength to compete on somewhat equal terms, will Negroes believe in the possibility of true cooperation and whites accept its necessity. En route to integration, the Negro community needs to develop greater independence—a chance to run its own affairs and not cave in whenever "the man" barks. . . . Or so it seems to me, and to most of the knowledgeable people with whom I talked in Mississippi. To OEO, this judgment may sound like black nationalism. . . .

Mr. Jencks, a white reporter, perceived the reason why America's anti-poverty program has been a sick farce in both North and South. In the South, it is clearly racism which prevents the poor from running their own programs; in the North, it more often seems to be politicking and bureaucracy. But the results are not so different:

In the North, non-whites make up 42 per cent of all families in metropolitan "poverty areas" and only 6 per cent of families in areas classified as not poor. SNCC has been working with local residents in Arkansas, Alabama, and Mississippi to achieve control by the poor of the program and its funds; it has also been working with groups in the North, and the struggle is no less difficult. Behind it all is a federal government which cares far more about winning the war on the Vietnamese than the war on poverty; which has put the poverty program in the hands of self-serving politicians and bureaucrats rather than the poor themselves; which is unwilling to curb the misuse of white power but quick to condemn black power.

To most whites, black power seems to mean that the Mau Mau are coming to the suburbs at night. The Mau Mau are coming, and whites must stop them. Articles appear about plots to "get whitey," creating an atmosphere in which "law and order must be maintained." Once again, responsibility is shifted from the oppressor to the oppressed. Other whites chide, "Don't forget—you're only 10 per cent of the population; if you get too smart, we'll wipe you out." If they are liberals, they complain, "What about me?—don't you want my help any more?" These are people supposedly concerned about black Americans, but today they think first of themselves, of their feelings of rejection. Or they admonish, "You can't get anywhere without coalitions," when there is in fact no group at present with whom to form a coalition in which blacks will not be absorbed and betrayed. Or they accuse us of "polarizing the races" by our calls for black unity, when the true responsibility for polarization lies with whites who will not accept their responsibility as the majority power for making the democratic process work.

White America will not face the problem of color, the reality of it. The well-intended say: "We're all human, everybody is really decent, we must forget color." But color cannot be "forgotten" until its weight is recognized and dealt with. White America will not acknowledge that the ways in which this country sees itself are contradicted by being black—and always have been. Whereas most of the people who settled this country came here for freedom or for economic opportunity, blacks were brought here to be slaves. When the Lowndes County Freedom Organization chose the black panther as its symbol, it was christened by the press "the Black Panther Party"—but the Alabama Democratic Party, whose symbol is a rooster, has never been called the White Cock Party. No one ever talked about "white power" because power in this country *is* white.

All this adds up to more than merely identifying a group phenomenon by some catchy name or adjective. The furor over that black panther reveals the problems that white America has with color and sex; the furor over "black power" reveals how deep racism runs and the great fear which is attached to it.

Whites will not see that I, for example, as a person oppressed because of my blackness, have common cause with other blacks who are oppressed because of blackness. This is not to say that there are no white people who see things as I do, but that it is black people I must speak to first. It must be the oppressed to whom SNCC addresses itself primarily, not to friends from the oppressing group.

From birth, black people are told a set of lies about themselves. We are told that we are lazy—yet I drive through the Delta area of Mississippi and watch black people picking cotton in the hot sun for fourteen hours. We are told, "If you work hard, you'll succeed"—but if that were true, black people would own this country. We are oppressed because we are black—not because we are ignorant, not because we are lazy, not because we're stupid (and got good rhythm), but because we're black.

I remember that when I was a boy, I used to go to see Tarzan movies on Saturday. White Tarzan used to beat up the black natives. I would sit there yelling, "Kill the beasts, kill the savages, kill 'em!" I was saying: Kill *me*. It was as if a Jewish boy watched Nazis taking Jews off to concentration camps and cheered them on. Today, I want the chief to beat hell out of Tarzan and send him back to Europe. But it takes time to become free of the lies and their shaming effect on black minds. It takes time to reject the most important lie: that black people inherently can't do the same things white people can do, unless white people help them.

The need for psychological equality is the reason why SNCC today believes that blacks must organize in the black community. Only black people can convey the revolutionary idea that black people are able to do things themselves. Only they can help create in the community an aroused and continuing black consciousness that will provide the basis for political strength. In the past, white allies have furthered white supremacy without the whites involved realizing it—or wanting it, I think. Black people must do things for themselves; they must get poverty money they will control and spend themselves, they must conduct tutorial programs themselves so that black children can identify with black people. This is one reason Africa has such importance: The reality of black men ruling their own natives gives blacks elsewhere a sense of possibility, of power, which they do not now have.

This does not mean we don't welcome help, or friends. But we want the right to decide whether anyone is, in fact, our friend. In the past, black Americans have been almost the only people whom everybody and his momma could jump up and call their friends. We have been tokens, symbols, objects—as I was in high school to many young whites, who liked having "a Negro friend." We want to decide who is our friend, and we will not accept someone who comes to us and says: "If you do X, Y, and Z, then I'll help you." We will not be told whom we should choose as allies. We will not be isolated from any group or nation except by our own choice. We cannot have the oppressors telling the oppressed how to rid themselves of the oppressor.

I have said that most liberal whites react to "black power" with the question, What about me?, rather than saying: Tell me what you want me to do and I'll see if I can do it. There are answers to the right question. One of the most disturbing things about almost all white supporters of the movement has been that they are afraid to go into their own communities—which is where the racism exists—and work to get rid of it. They want to run from Berkeley to tell us what to do in Mississippi; let them look instead at Berkeley. They admonish blacks to be nonviolent; let them preach nonviolence in the white community. They come to teach me Negro history; let them go to the suburbs and open up freedom schools for whites. Let them work to stop America's racist foreign policy; let them press this government to cease supporting the economy of South Africa.

There is a vital job to be done among poor whites. We hope to see, eventually, a coalition between poor blacks and poor whites. That is the only coalition which seems acceptable to us, and we see such a coalition as the major internal instrument of change in American society. SNCC has tried several times to organize poor whites; we are trying again now, with an initial training program in Tennessee. It is purely academic today to talk about bringing poor blacks and whites together, but the job of creating a poor-white power bloc must be attempted. The main responsibility for it falls upon whites. Black and white can work together in the white community where possible; it is not possible, however, to go into a poor Southern town and talk about integration. Poor whites everywhere are becoming more hostile—not less—partly because they see the nation's attention focussed on black poverty and nobody coming to them. Too many young middle-class Americans, like some sort of Pepsi generation, have wanted to come alive through the black community; they've wanted to be where the action is—and the action has been in the black community.

Black people do not want to "take over" this country. They don't want to "get whitey"; they just want to get him off their backs, as the saying goes. It was for example the exploitation by Jewish landlords and merchants which first created black resentment toward Jews—not Judaism. The white man is irrelevant to blacks, except as an oppressive force. Blacks want to be in his place, yes, but not in order to terrorize and lynch and starve him. They want to be in his place because that is where a decent life can be had.

But our vision is not merely of a society in which all black men have enough to buy the good things of life. When we urge that black money go into black pockets, we mean the communal pocket. We want to see money go back into the community and used to benefit it. We want to see the cooperative concept applied in business and banking. We want to see black ghetto residents demand that an exploiting store keeper sell them, at minimal cost, a building or a shop that they will own and improve cooperatively; they can back their demand with a rent strike, or a boycott, and a community so unified behind them that no one else will move into the building or buy at the store. The society we seek to build among black people, then, is not a capitalist one. It is a society in which the spirit of community and humanistic love prevail. The word love is suspect; black expectations of what it might produce have been betrayed too often. But those were expectations of a response from the white community, which failed us. The love we seek to encourage is within the black community, the only American community where men call each other "brother" when they meet. We can build a community of love only where we have the ability and power to do so: among blacks.

As for white America, perhaps it can stop crying out against "black supremacy," "black nationalism," "racism in reverse," and begin facing reality. The reality is that this nation, from top to bottom, is racist; that racism is not primarily a problem of "human relations" but of an exploitation maintained—either actively or through silence—by the society as a whole. Camus and Sartre have asked, Can a man condemn himself? Can whites, particularly liberal whites, condemn themselves? Can they stop blaming us, and blame their own system? Are they capable of the shame which might become a revolutionary emotion?

We have found that they usually cannot condemn themselves, and so we have done it. But the rebuilding of this society, if at all possible, is basically the responsibility of whites—not blacks. We won't fight to save the present society, in Vietnam or anywhere else. We are just going to work, in the way *we* see fit, and on goals *we* define, not for civil rights but for all our human rights.

QUESTIONS FOR DISCUSSION AND WRITING

1. Carmichael's essay, published in 1966, introduced the term "black power" to the white community and sparked great controversy about what it "really" meant. According to Carmichael, what does black power mean? What implications does the black power movement have for American society? In what specific areas?
2. The term "black power" has raised fears in the white community. Why should the term frighten whites? What fearsome definitions might the white community give it? Do whites find "integration" as frightening a term? Does Carmichael?
3. Carmichael writes of "the colonies of the United States" and states that "ultimately, the economic foundations of this country must be shaken if black people are to control their lives." What connection does black power have to financial power? To exploitation?
4. In commenting on white liberal support, Carmichael states: "I have said that most liberal whites react to 'black power' with the question, What about me?, rather than saying: Tell me what you want me to do and I'll see if I can do it. There are answers to the right question. One of the most disturbing things about almost all white supporters of the movement has been that they are afraid to go into their own communities—which is where the racism exists—and work to get rid of it." To what extent does racism reside in the white community? Where?
5. Evaluate Carmichael's assertion that "the need for psychological equality is the reason why SNCC today believes that blacks must organize in the black community." How is this statement related to Grier and Cobbs' definition of "equality" (p. 301)? To the Supreme Court's definition (p. 185)?

MARTIN LUTHER KING, JR., ACHIEVED PROMINENCE FOR HIS LEADERSHIP IN CIVIL RIGHTS ACTIVITIES DURING THE 1950'S AND 1960'S. HE SERVED AS PRESIDENT OF THE SOUTHERN CHRISTIAN LEADERSHIP CONFERENCE AND WAS PASTOR OF THE DEXTER AVENUE BAPTIST CHURCH OF MONTGOMERY, ALABAMA. DR. KING RECEIVED THE NOBEL PEACE PRIZE IN 1964. HE WAS MURDERED IN APRIL 1968. *A Testament of Hope* IS HIS LAST PUBLISHED ESSAY.

MARTIN LUTHER KING, JR.

A TESTAMENT OF HOPE

Whenever I am asked my opinion of the current state of the civil rights movement, I am forced to pause: it is not easy to describe a crisis so profound that it has caused the most powerful nation in the world to stagger in confusion and bewilderment. Today's problems are so acute because the tragic evasions and defaults of several centuries have accumulated to disaster proportions. The luxury of a leisurely approach to urgent solutions—the ease of gradualism—was forfeited by ignoring the issues for too long. The nation waited until the black man was explosive with fury before stirring itself even to partial concern. Confronted now with the interrelated problems of war, inflation, urban decay, white backlash and a climate of violence, it is now *forced* to address itself to race relations and poverty, and it is tragically unprepared. What might once have been a series of separate problems now merge into a social crisis of almost stupefying complexity.

I am not sad that black Americans are rebelling: this was not only inevitable but eminently desirable. Without this magnificent ferment among Negroes, the old evasions and procrastinations would have continued indefinitely. Black men have slammed the door shut on a past of deadening passivity. Except for the Reconstruction years, they have never in their long history on American soil struggled with such creativity and courage for their freedom. These are our bright years of emergence; though they are painful ones, they cannot be avoided.

Yet despite the widening of our stride, history is racing forward so rapidly that the Negro's inherited and imposed disadvantages slow him down to an infuriating crawl. Lack of education, the dislocations of recent urbanization and the hardening of white resistance loom as such tormenting roadblocks that the goal sometimes appears not as a fixed point in the future but as a receding point never to be reached. Still, when doubts emerge, we can remember that only yesterday Negroes were not only grossly exploited but negated as human beings. They were invisible in their misery. But the sullen and silent slave of 110 years ago, an object of scorn at worst or of pity at best, is today's angry man. He is vibrantly on the move; he is forcing change, rather than waiting for it in pathetic futility. In less than two decades, he has roared out of slumber to change so many of his life's conditions that he may yet find the means to accelerate his march forward and overtake the racing locomotive of history.

These words may have an unexpectedly optimistic ring at a time when pessimism is the prevailing mood. People are often surprised to learn that I am an optimist. They know how often I have been jailed, how frequently the days and nights have been filled with frustration and sorrow, how bitter and dangerous are my adversaries. They expect these experiences to harden me into a grim and desperate man. They fail, however, to perceive the sense of affirmation generated by the challenge of embracing struggle and surmounting obstacles. They have no comprehension of the strength that comes from faith in God and man. It is possible for me to falter, but I am profoundly secure in my knowledge that God loves us; He has not worked out a design for our failure. Man has the capacity to do right as well as wrong, and his history is a path upward, not downward. The past is strewn with the ruins of the empires of tyranny, and each is a monument not merely to man's blunders but to his capacity to overcome them. While it is a bitter fact that in America in 1968, I am denied equality solely because I am black, yet I am not a chattel slave. Millions of people have fought thousands of battles to enlarge my freedom: restricted as it still is, progress has been made. This is why I remain an optimist, though I am also a realist about the barriers before us. Why is the issue of equality still so far from solution in America, a nation that professes itself to be democratic, inventive, hospitable to new ideas, rich, productive and awesomely powerful? The problem is so tenacious because, despite its virtues and attributes, America is deeply racist and its democracy is flawed both economically and socially. All too many Americans believe justice will unfold painlessly or that its absence for black people will be tolerated tranquilly.

Justice for black people will not flow into society merely from court decisions nor from fountains of political oratory. Nor will a few token changes quell all the tempestuous yearnings of millions of disadvantaged black people. White America must recognize that justice for black people cannot be achieved without radical changes in the structure of our society. The comfortable, the entrenched, the privileged cannot continue to tremble at the prospect of change in the *status quo*.

Stephen Vincent Benét had a message for both white and black Americans in the title of a story, *Freedom Is a Hard Bought Thing*. When millions of people have been cheated for centuries, restitution is a costly process. Inferior education, poor housing, unemployment, inadequate health care—each is a bitter component of the oppression that has been our heritage. Each will require billions of dollars to correct. Justice so long deferred has accumulated interest and its cost for this society will be substantial in financial as well as human terms. This fact has not been fully grasped, because most of the gains of the past decade were obtained at bargain rates. The desegregation of public facilities cost nothing; neither did the election and appointment of a few black public officials.

The price of progress would have been high enough at the best of times, but we are in an agonizing national crisis because a complex of profound problems has intersected in an explosive mixture. The black surge toward freedom has raised justifiable demands for racial justice in our major cities at a time when all the problems of city life have simultaneously erupted. Schools, transportation, water supply, traffic and crime would have been municipal agonies whether or not Negroes lived in our cities. The anarchy of unplanned city growth was destined to confound our confidence. What is unique to this period is our inability to arrange an order of priorities that promises solutions that are decent and just.

Millions of Americans are coming to see that we are fighting an immoral war that costs nearly 30 billion dollars a year, that we are perpetuating racism, that we are tolerating almost 40,000,000 poor during an overflowing material abundance. Yet they remain helpless to end the war, to feed the hungry, to make brotherhood a reality; this has to shake our faith in ourselves. If we look honestly at the realities of our national life, it is clear that we are not marching forward; we are groping and stumbling; we are divided and confused. Our moral values and our spiritual confidence sink, even as our material wealth ascends. In these trying circumstances, the black revolution is much more than a struggle for the rights of Negroes. It is forcing America to face all its interrelated flaws—racism, poverty, militarism and materialism. It is exposing evils that are rooted deeply in the whole structure of our society. It reveals systemic rather than superficial flaws and suggests that radical reconstruction of society itself is the real issue to be faced.

It is time that we stopped our blithe lip service to the guarantees of life, liberty and pursuit of happiness. These fine sentiments are embodied in the Declaration of Independence, but that document was always a declaration of intent rather than of reality. There were slaves when it was written; there were still slaves when it was adopted; and to this day, black Americans have not life, liberty nor the privilege of pursuing happiness, and millions of poor white Americans are in economic bondage that is scarcely less oppressive. Americans who genuinely treasure our national ideals, who know they are still elusive dreams for all too many, should welcome the stirring of Negro demands. They are shattering the complacency that allowed a multitude of social evils to accumulate. Negro agitation is requiring America to re-examine its comforting myths and may yet catalyze the drastic reforms that will save us from social catastrophe.

In indicting white America for its ingrained and tenacious racism, I am using the term "white" to describe the majority, not *all* who are white. We have found that there are many white people who clearly perceive the justice of the Negro struggle for human dignity. Many of them joined our struggle and displayed heroism no less inspiring than that of black people. More than a few died by our side; their memories are cherished and are undimmed by time.

Yet the largest part of white America is still poisoned by racism, which is as native to our soil as pine trees, sagebrush and buffalo grass. Equally native to us is the concept that gross exploitation of the Negro is acceptable, if not commendable. Many whites who concede that Negroes should have equal access to public facilities and the untrammeled right to vote cannot understand that we do not intend to remain in the basement of the economic structure; they cannot understand why a porter or a housemaid would dare dream of a day when his work will be more useful, more remunerative and a pathway to rising opportunity. This incomprehension is a heavy burden in our efforts to win white allies for the long struggle.

But the American Negro has in his nature the spiritual and worldly fortitude to eventually win his struggle for justice and freedom. It is a moral fortitude that has been forged by centuries of oppression. In their sorrow and their hardship, Negroes have become almost instinctively cohesive. We band together readily; and against white hostility, we have an intense and wholesome loyalty to one another. But we cannot win our struggle for justice all alone, nor do I think that most Negroes want to exclude well-intentioned whites from participation in the black revolution. I believe there is an important place in our struggle for white liberals and I hope that their present estrangement from our movement is only temporary. But many white people in the past joined our movement with a kind of messianic faith that they were going to save the Negro and solve all of his problems very quickly. They tended, in some instances, to be rather aggressive and insensitive to the opinions and abilities of the black people with whom they were working: this has been especially true of students. In many cases, they simply did not know how to work in a supporting, secondary role. I think this problem became most evident when young men and women from elite Northern universities came down to Mississippi to work with the black students at Tougaloo and Rust colleges, who were not quite as articulate, didn't type quite as fast and were not as sophisticated. Inevitably, feelings of white paternalism and black inferiority became exaggerated. The Negroes who rebelled against white liberals were trying to assert their own equality and to cast off the mantle of paternalism.

Fortunately, we haven't had this problem in the Southern Christian Leadership Conference. Most of the white people who were working with us in 1962 and 1963 are still with us. We have always enjoyed a relationship of mutual respect. But I think a great many white liberals outside SCLC also have learned this basic lesson in human relations, thanks largely to Jimmy Baldwin and others who have articulated some of the problems of being black in a multiracial society. And I am happy to report that relationships between whites and Negroes in the human rights movement are now on a much healthier basis.

In society at large, abrasion between the races is far more evident—but the hostility was always there. Relations today are different only in the sense that Negroes are expressing the feelings that were so long muted. The constructive achievements of the decade 1955 to 1965 deceived us. Everyone underestimated the amount of violence and rage Negroes were suppressing and the vast amount of bigotry the white majority was disguising. All-black organizations are a reflection of that alienation—but they are only a contemporary way-station on the road to freedom. They are a product of this period of identity crisis and directionless confusion. As the human rights movement becomes more confident and aggressive, more nonviolently active, many of these emotional and intellectual problems will be resolved in the heat of battle, and we will not ask what is our neighbor's color but whether he is a brother in the pursuit of racial justice. For much of the fervent idealism of the white liberals has been supplemented recently by a dispassionate recognition of some of the cold realities of the struggle for that justice.

One of the most basic of these realities was pointed out by the President's Riot Commission, which observed that the nature of the American economy in the late 19th and early 20th Centuries made it possible for the European immigrants of that time to escape from poverty. It was an economy that had room for—even a great need for—unskilled manual labor. Jobs were available for willing workers, even those with the educational and language liabilities they had brought with them. But the American economy today is radically different. There are fewer and fewer jobs for the culturally and educationally deprived; thus does present-day poverty feed upon and perpetuate itself. The Negro today cannot escape from his ghetto in the way that Irish, Italian, Jewish and Polish immigrants escaped from their ghettos 50 years ago. New methods of escape must be found. And one of these roads to escape will be a more equitable sharing of political power between Negroes and whites. Integration is meaningless without the sharing of power. When I speak of integration, I don't mean a romantic mixing of colors. I mean a real sharing of power and responsibility. We will eventually achieve this, but it is going to be much more difficult for us than for any other minority. After all, no other minority has been so constantly, brutally and deliberately exploited. But because of this very exploitation, Negroes bring a special spiritual and moral contribution to American life—a contribution without which America could not survive.

The implications of true racial integration are more than just national in scope. I don't believe we can have world peace until America has an "integrated" foreign policy. Our disastrous experiences in Vietnam and the Dominican Republic have been, in one sense, a result of racist decision making. Men of the white West, whether or not they like it, have grown up in a racist culture, and their thinking is colored by that fact. They have been fed on a false mythology and tradition that blinds them to the aspirations and talents of other men. They don't really respect anyone who is not white. But we simply cannot have peace in the world without mutual respect. I honestly feel that a man without racial blinders—or, even better, a man with personal experience of racial discrimination—would be in a much better position to make policy decisions and to conduct negotiations with the underprivileged and emerging nations of the world (or even with Castro, for that matter) than would an Eisenhower or a Dulles.

The American Marines might not even have been needed in Santo Domingo, had the American ambassador there been a man who was sensitive to the color dynamics that pervade the national life of the Dominican Republic. Black men in positions of power in the business world would not be so unconscionable as to trade or traffic with the Union of South Africa, nor would they be so insensitive to the problems and needs of Latin America that they would continue the patterns of American exploitation that now prevail there. When we replace the rabidly segregationist chairman of the Armed Services Committee with a man of good will, when our ambassadors reflect a creative and wholesome interracial background, rather than a cultural heritage that is a conglomeration of Texas and Georgia politics, then we will be able to bring about a qualitative difference in the nature of American foreign policy. This is what we mean when we talk about redeeming the soul of America. Let me make it clear that I don't think white men have a monopoly on sin or greed. But I think there has been a kind of collective experience—a kind of shared misery in the black community—that makes it a little harder for us to exploit other people.

I have come to hope that American Negroes can be a bridge between white civilization and the nonwhite nations of the world, because we have roots in both. Spiritually, Negroes identify understandably with Africa, an identification that is rooted largely in our color; but all of us are a part of the white-American world, too. Our education has been Western and our language, our attitudes—though we sometimes tend to deny it—are very much influenced by Western civilization. Even our emotional life has been disciplined and sometimes stifled and inhibited by an essentially European upbringing. So, although in one sense we are neither, in another sense we are both Americans and Africans. Our very bloodlines are a mixture. I hope and feel that out of the universality of our experience, we can help make peace and harmony in this world more possible.

Although American Negroes could, if they were in decision-making positions, give aid and encouragement to the underprivileged and disenfranchised people in other lands, I don't think it can work the other way around. I don't think the nonwhites in other parts of the world can really be of any concrete help to us, given their own problems of development and self-determination. In fact, American Negroes have greater collective buying power than Canada, greater than all four of the Scandinavian countries combined. American Negroes have greater economic potential than most of the nations—perhaps even more than *all* of the nations—of Africa. We don't *need* to look for help from some power outside the boundaries of our country, except in the sense of sympathy and identification. Our challenge, rather, is to organize the power we already have in our midst. The Newark riots, for example, could certainly have been prevented by a more aggressive political involvement on the part of that city's Negroes. There is utterly no reason Addonizio should be the mayor of Newark, with the Negro majority that exists in that city. Gary, Indiana, is another tinderbox city; but its black mayor, Richard Hatcher, has given Negroes a new faith in the effectiveness of the political process.

One of the most basic weapons in the fight for social justice will be the cumulative political power of the Negro. I can foresee the Negro vote becoming consistently the decisive vote in national elections. It is already decisive in states that have large numbers of electoral votes. Even today, the Negroes in New York City strongly influence how New York State will go in national elections, and the Negroes of Chicago have a similar leverage in Illinois. Negroes are even the decisive balance of power in the elections in Georgia, South Carolina and Virginia. So the party and the candidate that get the support of the Negro voter in national elections have a very definite edge, and we intend to use this fact to win advances in the struggle for human rights. I have every confidence that the black vote will ultimately help unseat the diehard opponents of equal rights in Congress—who are, incidentally, reactionary on all issues. But the Negro community cannot win this victory alone; indeed, it would be an empty victory even if the Negroes *could* win it alone. Intelligent men of good will everywhere must see this as their task and contribute to its support.

The election of Negro mayors, such as Hatcher, in some of the nation's larger cities has also had a tremendous psychological impact upon the Negro. It has shown him that he has the potential to participate in the determination of his own destiny—and that of society. We will see more Negro mayors in major cities in the next ten years, but this is not the ultimate answer. Mayors are relatively impotent figures in the scheme of national politics. Even a white mayor such as John Lindsay of New York simply does not have the money and resources to deal with the problems of his city. The necessary money to deal with urban problems must come from the Federal Government, and this money is ultimately controlled by the Congress of the United States. The success of these enlightened mayors is entirely dependent upon the financial support made available by Washington.

The past record of the Federal Government, however, has not been encouraging. No President has really done very much for the American Negro, though the past two Presidents have received much undeserved credit for helping us. This credit has accrued to Lyndon Johnson and John Kennedy only because it was during their Administrations that Negroes began doing more for themselves. Kennedy didn't voluntarily submit a civil rights bill, nor did Lyndon Johnson. In fact, both told us at one time that such legislation was impossible. President Johnson did respond realistically to the signs of the times and used his skills as a legislator to get bills through Congress that other men might not have gotten through. I must point out, in all honesty, however, that President Johnson has not been nearly so diligent in *implementing* the bills he has helped shepherd through Congress.

Of the ten titles of the 1964 Civil Rights Act, probably only the one concerning public accommodations—the most bitterly contested section—has been meaningfully enforced and implemented. Most of the other sections have been deliberately ignored. The same is true of the 1965 Voting Rights Act, which provides for Federal referees to monitor the registration of voters in counties where Negroes have systematically been denied the right to vote. Yet of the some 900 counties that are eligible for Federal referees, only 58 counties to date have had them. The 842 other counties remain essentially just as they were before the march on Selma. Look at the pattern of Federal referees in Mississippi, for example. They are dispersed in a manner that gives the appearance of change without any real prospect of actually shifting political power or giving Negroes a genuine opportunity to be represented in the government of their state. There is a similar pattern in Alabama, even though that state is currently at odds with the Democratic Administration in Washington because of George Wallace. Georgia, until just recently, had no Federal referees at all, not even in the hard-core black-belt counties. I think it is significant that there are no Federal referees at all in the home districts of the most powerful Southern Senators—particularly Senators Russell, Eastland and Talmadge. The power and moral corruption of these Senators remain unchallenged, despite the weapon for change the legislation promised to be. Reform was thwarted when the legislation was inadequately enforced.

But not all is bad in the South, by any means. Though the fruits of our struggle have sometimes been nothing more than bitter despair, I must admit there have been some hopeful signs, some meaningful successes. One of the most hopeful of these changes is the attitude of the Southern Negro himself. Benign acceptance of second-class citizenship has been displaced by vigorous demands for full citizenship rights and opportunities. In fact, most of our concrete accomplishments have been limited largely to the South. We have put an end to racial segregation in the South; we have brought about the beginnings of reform in the political system; and, as incongruous as it may seem, a Negro is probably safer in most Southern cities than he is in the cities of the North. We have confronted the racist policemen of the South and demanded reforms in the police departments. We have confronted the Southern racist power structure and we have elected Negro and liberal white candidates through much of the South in the past ten years. George Wallace is certainly an exception, and Lester Maddox is a sociological fossil. But despite these anachronisms, at the city and county level, there is a new respect for black votes and black citizenship that just did not exist ten years ago. Though school integration has moved at a depressingly slow rate in the South, it *has* moved. Of far more significance is the fact that we have learned that the integration of schools does not necessarily solve the inadequacy of schools. White schools are often just about as bad as black schools, and integrated schools sometimes tend to merge the problems of the two without solving either of them.

There *is* progress in the South, however—progress expressed by the presence of Negroes in the Georgia House of Representatives, in the election of a Negro to the Mississippi House of Representatives, in the election of a black sheriff in Tuskegee, Alabama, and, most especially, in the integration of police forces throughout the Southern states. There are now even Negro deputy sheriffs in such black-belt areas as Dallas County, Alabama. Just three years ago, a Negro could be beaten for going into the county courthouse in Dallas County; now Negroes share in running it. So there *are* some changes. But the changes are basically in the social and political areas; the problems we now face—providing jobs, better housing and better education for the poor throughout the country—will require money for their solution, a fact that makes those solutions all the more difficult.

The need for solutions, meanwhile, becomes more urgent every day, because these problems are far more serious now than they were just a few years ago. Before 1964, things were getting better economically for the Negro; but after that year, things began to take a turn for the worse. In particular, automation began to cut into our jobs very badly, and this snuffed out the few sparks of hope the black people had begun to nurture. As long as there was some measurable and steady economic progress, Negroes were willing and able to press harder and work harder and hope for something better. But when the door began to close on the few avenues of progress, then hopeless despair began to set in.

The fact that most white people do not comprehend this situation—which prevails in the North as well as in the South—is due largely to the press, which molds the opinions of the white community. Many whites hasten to congratulate themselves on what little progress we Negroes have made. I'm sure that most whites felt that with the passage of the 1964 Civil Rights Act, all race problems were automatically solved. Because most white people are so far removed from the life of the average Negro, there has been little to challenge this assumption. Yet Negroes continue to live with racism every day. It doesn't matter where we are individually in the scheme of things, how near we may be either to the top or to the bottom of society; the cold facts of racism slap each one of us in the face. A friend of mine is a lawyer, one of the most brilliant young men I know. Were he a white lawyer, I have no doubt that he would be in a $100,000 job with a major corporation or heading his own independent firm. As it is, he makes a mere $20,000 a year. This may seem like a lot of money and, to most of us, it is; but the point is that this young man's background and abilities would, if his skin color were different, entitle him to an income many times that amount.

I don't think there is a single major insurance company that hires Negro lawyers. Even within the agencies of the Federal Government, most Negro employees are in the lower echelons; only a handful of Negroes in Federal employment are in upper-income brackets. This is a situation that cuts across this country's economic spectrum. The Chicago Urban League recently conducted a research project in the Kenwood community on the South Side. They discovered that the average educational grade level of Negroes in that community was 10.6 years and the median income was about $4200 a year. In nearby Gage Park, the median educational grade level of the whites was 8.6 years, but the median income was $9600 per year. In fact, the average white high school dropout makes as much as, if not more than, the average Negro college graduate.

Solutions for these problems, urgent as they are, must be constructive and rational. Rioting and violence provide no solutions for economic problems. Much of the justification for rioting has come from the thesis—originally set forth by Franz Fanon—that violence has a certain cleansing effect. Perhaps, in a special psychological sense, he may have had a point. But we have seen a better and more constructive cleansing process in our nonviolent demonstrations. Another theory to justify violent revolution is that rioting enables Negroes to overcome their fear of the white man. But they are just as afraid of the power structure after a riot as before. I remember that was true when our staff went into Rochester, New York, after the riot of 1964. When we discussed the possibility of going down to talk with the police, the people who had been most aggressive in the violence were afraid to talk. They still had a sense of inferiority; and not until they were bolstered by the presence of our staff and given reassurance of their political power and the rightness of their cause and the justness of their grievances were they able and willing to sit down and talk to the police chief and the city manager about the conditions that had produced the riot.

As a matter of fact, I think the aura of paramilitarism among the black militant groups speaks much more of fear than it does of confidence. I know, in my own experience, that I was much more afraid in Montgomery when I had a gun in my house. When I decided that, as a teacher of the philosophy of nonviolence, I couldn't keep a gun, I came face to face with the question of death and I dealt with it. And from that point on, I no longer needed a gun nor have I been afraid. Ultimately, one's sense of manhood must come from within him.

The riots in Negro ghettos have been, in one sense, merely another expression of the growing climate of violence in America. When a culture begins to feel threatened by its own inadequacies, the majority of men tend to prop themselves up by artificial means, rather than dig down deep into their spiritual and cultural wellsprings. America seems to have reached this point. Americans as a whole feel threatened by communism on the one hand and, on the other, by the rising tide of aspirations among the undeveloped nations. I think most Americans know in their hearts that their country has been terribly wrong in its dealings with other peoples around the world. When Rome began to disintegrate from within, it turned to a strengthening of the military establishment, rather than to a correction of the corruption within the society. We are doing the same thing in this country and the result will probably be the same—unless, and here I admit to a bit of chauvinism, the black man in America can provide a new soul force for all Americans, a new expression of the American dream that need not be realized at the expense of other men around the world, but a dream of opportunity and life that can be shared with the rest of the world.

It seems glaringly obvious to me that the development of a humanitarian means of dealing with some of the social problems of the world—and the correlative revolution in American values that this will entail—is a much better way of protecting ourselves against the threat of violence than the military means we have chosen. On these grounds, I must indict the Johnson Administration. It has seemed amazingly devoid of statesmanship; and when creative statesmanship wanes, irrational militarism increases. In this sense, President Kennedy was far more of a statesman than President Johnson. He was a man who was big enough to admit when he was wrong—as he did after the Bay of Pigs incident. But Lyndon Johnson seems to be unable to make this kind of statesmanlike gesture in connection with Vietnam. And I think that this has led, as Senator Fulbright has said, to such a strengthening of the military-industrial complex of this country that the President now finds himself almost totally trapped by it. Even at this point, when he can readily summon popular support to end the bombing in Vietnam, he persists. Yet bombs in Vietnam also explode at home; they destroy the hopes and possibilities for a decent America.

In our efforts to dispel this atmosphere of violence in this country, we cannot afford to overlook the root cause of the riots. The President's Riot Commission concluded that most violence-prone Negroes are teenagers or young adults who, almost invariably, are underemployed ("underemployed" means working every day but earning an income below the poverty level) or who are employed in menial jobs. And according to a recent Department of Labor statistical report, 24.8 percent of Negro youth are currently unemployed, a statistic that does not include the drifters who avoid the census takers. Actually, it's my guess that the statistics are very, very conservative in this area. The Bureau of the Census has admitted a ten-percent error in this age group, and the unemployment statistics are based on those who are actually applying for jobs.

But it isn't just a lack of work; it's also a lack of *meaningful* work. In Cleveland, 58 percent of the young men between the ages of 16 and 25 were estimated to be either unemployed or underemployed. This appalling situation is probably 90 percent of the root cause of the Negro riots. A Negro who has finished high school often watches his white classmates go out into the job market and earn $100 a week, while he, because he is black, is expected to work for $40 a week. Hence, there is a tremendous hostility and resentment that only a difference in race keeps him out of an adequate job. This situation is social dynamite. When you add the lack of recreational facilities and adequate job counseling, and the continuation of an aggressively hostile police environment, you have a truly explosive situation. Any night on any street corner in any Negro ghetto of the country, a nervous policeman can start a riot simply by being impolite or by expressing racial prejudice. And white people are sadly unaware how routinely and frequently this occurs.

It hardly needs to be said that solutions to these critical problems are overwhelmingly urgent. The President's Riot Commission recommended that funds for summer programs aimed at young Negroes should be increased. New York is already spending more on its special summer programs than on its year-round poverty efforts, but these are only tentative and emergency steps toward a truly meaningful and permanent solution. And the negative thinking in this area voiced by many whites does not help the situation. Unfortunately, many white people think that we merely "reward" a rioter by taking positive action to better his situation. What these white people do not realize is that the Negroes who riot have given up on America. When nothing is done to alleviate their plight, this merely confirms the Negroes' conviction that America is a hopelessly decadent society. When something positive is done, however, when constructive action follows a riot, a rioter's despair is allayed and he is forced to re-evaluate America and to consider whether some good might eventually come from our society after all.

But, I repeat, the recent curative steps that have been taken are, at best, inadequate. The summer poverty programs, like most other Government projects, function well in some places and are totally ineffective in others. The difference, in large measure, is one of citizen participation; that is the key to success or failure. In cases such as the Farmers' Marketing Cooperative Association in the black belt of Alabama and the Child Development group in Mississippi, where the people were really involved in the planning and action of the program, it was one of the best experiences in self-help and grass-roots initiative. But in places like Chicago, where poverty programs are used strictly as a tool of the political machinery and for dispensing party patronage, the very concept of helping the poor is defiled and the poverty program becomes just another form of enslavement. I still wouldn't want to do away with it, though, even in Chicago. We must simply fight at both the local and the national levels to gain as much community control as possible over the poverty program.

But there is no single answer to the plight of the American Negro. Conditions and needs vary greatly in different sections of the country. I think that the place to start, however, is in the area of human relations, and especially in the area of community-police relations. This is a sensitive and touchy problem that has rarely been adequately emphasized. Virtually every riot has begun from some police action. If you try to tell the people in most Negro communities that the police are their friends, they just laugh at you. Obviously, something desperately needs to be done to correct this. I have been particularly impressed by the fact that even in the state of Mississippi, where the FBI did a significant training job with the Mississippi police, the police are much more courteous to Negroes than they are in Chicago or New York. Our police forces simply must develop an attitude of courtesy and respect for the ordinary citizen. If we can just stop policemen from using profanity in their encounters with black people, we will have accomplished a lot. In the larger sense, police must cease being occupation troops in the ghetto and start protecting its residents. Yet very few cities have really faced up to this problem and tried to do something about it. It is the most abrasive element in Negro-white relations, but it is the last to be scientifically and objectively appraised.

When you go beyond a relatively simple though serious problem such as police racism, however, you begin to get into all the complexities of the modern American economy. Urban transit systems in most American cities, for example, have become a genuine civil rights issue —and a valid one—because the layout of rapid-transit systems determines the accessibility of jobs to the black community. If transportation systems in American cities could be laid out so as to provide an opportunity for poor people to get meaningful employment, then they could begin to move into the mainstream of American life. A good example of this problem is my home city of Atlanta, where the rapid-transit system has been laid out for the convenience of the white upper-middle-class suburbanites who commute to their jobs downtown. The system has virtually no consideration for connecting the poor people with their jobs. There is only one possible explanation for this situation, and that is the racist blindness of city planners.

The same problems are to be found in the areas of rent supplement and low-income housing. The relevance of these issues to human relations and human rights cannot be overemphasized. The kind of house a man lives in, along with the quality of his employment, determines, to a large degree, the quality of his family life. I have known too many people in my own parish in Atlanta who, because they were living in overcrowded apartments, were constantly bickering with other members of their families—a situation that produced many kinds of severe dysfunctions in family relations. And yet I have seen these same families achieve harmony when they were able to afford a house allowing for a little personal privacy and freedom of movement.

All these human-relations problems are complex and related, and it's very difficult to assign priorities—especially as long as the Vietnam war continues. The Great Society has become a victim of the war. I think there was a sincere desire in this country four or five years ago to move toward a genuinely great society, and I have little doubt that there would have been a gradual increase in Federal expenditures in this direction, rather than the gradual decline that has occurred, if the war in Vietnam had been avoided.

One of the incongruities of this situation is the fact that such a large number of the soldiers in the Armed Forces in Vietnam—especially the front-line soldiers who are actually doing the fighting—are Negroes. Negroes have always held the hope that if they really demonstrate that they are great soldiers and if they really fight for America and help save American democracy, then when they come back home, America will treat them better. This has not been the case. Negro soldiers returning from World War One were met with race riots, job discrimination and continuation of the bigotry that they had experienced before. After World War Two, the GI Bill did offer some hope for a better life to those who had the educational background to take advantage of it, and there was proportionately less turmoil. But for the Negro GI, military service still represents a means of escape from the oppressive ghettos of the rural South and the urban North. He often sees the Army as an avenue for educational opportunities and job training. He sees in the military uniform a symbol of dignity that has long been denied him by society. The tragedy in this is that military service is probably the only possible escape for most young Negro men. Many of them go into the Army, risking death, in order that they might have a few of the human possibilities of life. They know that life in the city ghetto or life in the rural South almost certainly means jail or death or humiliation. And so, by comparison, military service is really the lesser risk.

One young man on our staff, Hosea Williams, returned from the foxholes of Germany a 60-percent-disabled veteran. After 13 months in a veterans' hospital, he went back to his home town of Attapulgus, Georgia. On his way home, he went into a bus station at Americus, Georgia, to get a drink of water while waiting for his next bus. And while he stood there on his crutches, drinking from the fountain, he was beaten savagely by white hoodlums. This pathetic incident is all too typical of the treatment received by Negroes in this country—not only physical brutality but brutal discrimination when a Negro tries to buy a house, and brutal violence against the Negro's soul when he finds himself denied a job that he knows he is qualified for.

There is also the violence of having to live in a community and pay higher consumer prices for goods or higher rent for equivalent housing than are charged in the white areas of the city. Do you know that a can of beans almost always costs a few cents more in grocery chain stores located in the Negro ghetto than in a store of that same chain located in the upper-middle-class suburbs, where the median income is five times as high? The Negro knows it, because he works in the white man's house as a cook or a gardener. And what do you think this knowledge does to his soul? How do you think it affects his view of the society he lives in? How can you expect anything but disillusionment and bitterness? The question that now faces us is whether we can turn the Negro's disillusionment and bitterness into hope and faith in the essential goodness of the American system. If we don't, our society will crumble.

It is a paradox that those Negroes who have given up on America are doing more to improve it than are its professional patriots. They are stirring the mass of smug, somnolent citizens, who are neither evil nor good, to an awareness of crisis. The confrontation involves not only their morality but their self-interest, and that combination promises to evoke positive action. This is not a nation of venal people. It is a land of individuals who, in the majority, have not cared, who have been heartless about their black neighbors because their ears are blocked and their eyes blinded by the tragic myth that Negroes endure abuse without pain or complaint. Even when protest flared and denied the myth, they were fed new doctrines of inhumanity that argued that Negroes were arrogant, lawless and ungrateful. Habitual white discrimination was transformed into white backlash. But for some, the lies had lost their grip and an internal disquiet grew. Poverty and discrimination were undeniably real; they scarred the nation; they dirtied our honor and diminished our pride. An insistent question defied evasion: Was security for some being purchased at the price of degradation for others? Everything in our traditions said this kind of injustice was the system of the past or of other nations. And yet there it was, abroad in our own land.

Thus was born—particularly in the young generation—a spirit

of dissent that ranged from superficial disavowal of the old values to total commitment to wholesale, drastic and immediate social reform. Yet all of it was dissent. Their voice is still a minority; but united with millions of black protesting voices, it has become a sound of distant thunder increasing in volume with the gathering of storm clouds. This dissent is America's hope. It shines in the long tradition of American ideals that began with courageous minutemen in New England, that continued in the Abolitionist movement, that re-emerged in the Populist revolt and, decades later, that burst forth to elect Franklin Roosevelt and John F. Kennedy. Today's dissenters tell the complacent majority that the time has come when further evasion of social responsibility in a turbulent world will court disaster and death. America has not yet changed because so many think it need not change, but this is the illusion of the damned. America must change because 23,000,000 black citizens will no longer live supinely in a wretched past. They have left the valley of despair; they have found strength in struggle; and whether they live or die, they shall never crawl nor retreat again. Joined by white allies, they will shake the prison walls until they fall. America must change.

A voice out of Bethlehem 2000 years ago said that all men are equal. It said right would triumph. Jesus of Nazareth wrote no books; he owned no property to endow him with influence. He had no friends in the courts of the powerful. But he changed the course of mankind with only the poor and the despised. Naïve and unsophisticated though we may be, the poor and despised of the 20th Century will revolutionize this era. In our "arrogance, lawlessness and ingratitude," we will fight for human justice, brotherhood, secure peace and abundance for all. When we have won these—in a spirit of unshakable nonviolence—then, in luminous splendor, the Christian era will truly begin.

QUESTIONS FOR DISCUSSION AND WRITING

1. What is "white paternalism"? How important a factor is it in racial relations?
2. What factors contribute to King's optimism?
3. Compare King's definition of "progress" with that of LeRoi Jones (p. 259).

4. Compare King's point of view with that of Carmichael (p. 329) on (a) the problems that beset black people in the United States and (b) the solutions to these problems. (For instance, what value do the two spokesmen give to integration?) In what ways do their opinions differ? Why?
5. "Ultimately, one's sense of manhood must come from within him." Compare and contrast King's point of view on this subject with DuBois' (p. 83), Jones' (p. 263), Elkins' (p. 229), and Grier and Cobbs' (p. 309).

RONALD STEEL IS THE AUTHOR OF TWO BOOKS ON AMERICAN FOREIGN POLICY, *Pax Americana* AND *The End of Alliance: America and the Future of Europe*. HE FORMERLY WORKED FOR THE STATE DEPARTMENT AND IS CURRENTLY A FREELANCE POLITICAL JOURNALIST.

RONALD STEEL

LETTER FROM OAKLAND: THE PANTHERS

I went to Oakland, dead end of the westward course of empire, and home of the Black Panthers, to take a look at a conference of the revolutionary Left. Oakland, where the American dream ends at the Pacific, and the nightmare begins, is a familiar kind of industrial city: high-rise office buildings and apartments downtown, plasticene shopping centers on the fringe, and slowly decaying wooden houses in between. West Oakland, facing the Bay and the gleaming hills of San Francisco beyond, is the ghetto where the Black Panthers were born. It is a California-style ghetto, with one-family houses and neglected yards, where poverty wears a more casual face and despair is masked by sunshine.

The Panthers in July summoned their friends—a mixed bag of

revolutionaries, radicals, pacifists, and liberals—to assemble in Oakland to form what they called a "united front against fascism." The phrase itself had a defensive ring, reminiscent of the ill-fated Popular Fronts of the 1930s, and it seemed to indicate that the Panthers were in trouble. White radicals, few of whom were consulted about the agenda, privately expressed doubts about the usefulness of such a conference, and many SDS chapters did not send representatives. As it turned out, they would not have had much of a role to play anyway, since the Panthers were very much running their own show and not accepting criticism from those who came to hear them.

Like so many other gatherings of the radical Left, the conference produced little unity but a great deal of dissatisfaction. Most of the sessions were disorganized and, with a few exceptions, the speeches were little more than an interminable series of spot announcements denouncing the evils of rampant fascism. No one seemed interested in discussing whether fascism had indeed arrived in America. This, like so much of the other rhetoric of the revolutionary Left, was simply taken for granted.

When the three-day conference finally rambled to an end, the dwindling band of white radicals drifted away in dismay, wondering what kind of bag the Panthers had got themselves into. The more militant radicals from Berkeley feared that the Panthers had turned reformist, while socialists and Trotskyites complained about their dictatorial methods. The "united front," whose creation was the ostensible purpose of the conference, had not been formed and most participants expressed doubts that it ever would be. The general consensus was that the Panthers didn't have a very clear idea of what they were up to. They wanted to enlist allies, and they hoped that some kind of united front would develop. But they had no real plan worked out, and certainly no intention of letting anyone else supply one.

Why did the Panthers call such a conference in the first place? At least in part because they have been under increasing harassment and intimidation by the police and the FBI. During the past few months more than forty leaders and 100 members have been arrested, and some of them are now facing life imprisonment or the death penalty. The party's founder and chief theorist, twenty-seven-year-old Huey P. Newton, is serving a fourteen-year sentence for allegedly shooting an Oakland policeman. Its most articulate spokesman, Eldridge Cleaver, has chosen to go into exile rather than return to prison on dubious charges of parole violation. Its treasurer, seventeen-year-old Bobby

Hutton, was killed by police during last year's Oakland shoot-out. And its acting chairman, Bobby Seale, is under federal indictment for conspiring to incite a riot at last year's Democratic convention, although he was not a member of any of the organizations sponsoring the protests, and spent less than a day in Chicago.

The Panthers see a concerted plot by the federal government, with the assistance of local police, to destroy them. Recently Spiro Agnew has described them as a "completely irresponsible, anarchistic group of criminals," and J. Edgar Hoover has called them, among black militants, the "greatest threat to the internal security of the country." This summer the Justice Department set up a special task force to investigate the party in the hope of nailing it on violation of some twenty federal laws, including those making it a crime to cross state lines to foment civil disorder, to interfere with persons participating in programs supported by the federal government, and to damage government buildings. Senator McClellan's Permanent Subcommittee on Investigations has been providing a forum for police officers and their informants to denounce the Panthers, as well as white radical groups. Recently they heard Larry Clayton Powell and his wife Jean tell how the Panthers forced them to rob for the party. The Panthers, however, claim that the Powells were kicked out of the party because they were criminals, and that they are telling the McClellan committee what it wants to hear in order to win clemency.

From the record it is clear that the campaign against the Panthers has been stepped up in recent months. In March Bobby Seale was linked to the Chicago conspiracy case and placed under federal indictment. On April 4 New York District Attorney Frank Hogan announced in banner headlines that his office had smashed a Panther plot to blow up several midtown department stores, a police station, and, inexplicably, the Bronx Botanical Gardens. A grand jury indicted twenty-one Panthers and bail for thirteen of them was set at $100,000 each. No bondsman will touch the case, and the party, of course, is unable to raise such an amount of money. Meanwhile the Panthers remain in jail, some under maximum security, not for having actually committed a crime, but for having *conspired* to do so, an extremely vague charge that rests on circumstantial evidence and the testimony of informers.

On May 22, in a case which police claim was linked to the New York twenty-one, eight New Haven Panthers were arrested and charged with kidnapping and murdering Alex Rackley, a New York

Panther. Police claim he was killed because he was an informer, the Panthers charge that the police murdered him themselves in order to justify nation-wide raids on chapter offices in a search for his alleged assassins. Whatever really happened to Rackley, federal agents did in fact carry out raids in Washington, D.C., Salt Lake City, Denver, and Chicago in conjunction with the case. Two Denver Panthers are being held on $200,000 bail—not for murder or even conspiracy but on the vague catchall charge of unlawful flight to avoid prosecution.[1]

In the Chicago raid, which took place on June 4, FBI agents blocked off the street at 5:30 in the morning and confiscated Panther literature, a list of donors, and copies of a petition signed by 15,000 people calling for the release of Illinois party chairman Fred Hampton, who is in prison on a two-to-five-year sentence for allegedly stealing $71 worth of ice cream bars distributed to ghetto children.

The day after the Chicago raid, police broke into the Panther office in Detroit, photographed documents, and arrested three Panthers, who were later released. On June 7, during racial disturbances, police entered the Panther office in Indianapolis and arrested thirty people. On June 10 a grand jury in Chicago indicted sixteen Panthers on charges of conspiracy, kidnapping, and threatening to murder two people who allegedly refused to return weapons entrusted to them by the Panthers. Bond was set at $100,000 each for six of the sixteen. One of the charges, aggravated kidnapping, carries a maximum death penalty. On June 15 San Diego policemen shot their way into Panther headquarters, where they claimed a sniper had taken refuge.

That same day in Sacramento the Panther office was torn apart by police during a shoot-out. On July 31, again in Chicago, police raided Panther headquarters during the pre-dawn hours, destroyed office equipment, medical supplies, and food for the children's breakfast program, and arrested three unarmed men for shooting at policemen from the office windows. The Panthers insist they were attacked by the police and tried to defend themselves.

Now that the federal government has joined the local police in operations against the Panthers—Attorney-General Mitchell is trying

[1] On August 19, shortly after this article was completed, Bobby Seale was arrested in Berkeley by FBI agents in connection with the Rackley case. So far, fourteen other Panthers have been arrested in various states on similar charges. The day before Seale's arrest David Hilliard, the Panther Chief of Staff, was ordered to face trial on charges of attempted murder arising from last year's Oakland shootout. With these arrests, the chief national Panther leaders are in exile, in jail, under or facing indictment, or dead.

to get the courts to admit wiretap evidence against the Panthers and other groups ostensibly threatening "national security"—the strengthening of their links with white radical groups is more important than before. This is partly a question of ideology, for the Panthers—popular impressions to the contrary—are not racist. Indeed, they are virtually the only black militant group that actually welcomes white allies. It is also a question of survival, for without support from the white community they fear they will be picked off and destroyed.

Vilified and distorted by the press, which has little understanding of their program, they are generally viewed as an anarchistic band of gun-toting, white-hating thugs. This allows the police and federal officials to abridge their constitutional rights in a way they would not dare to use against whites. Provocation, false arrests, trumped-up charges, illegal detention, barbaric treatment, excessive bail, and even legal murder—this is everyday treatment for the Panthers. They have been defined as threatening to white society, and therefore beyond the normal protection of the law.

Is it likely that members of a white political organization, even the Ku Klux Klan, would be rounded up in the middle of the night, thrown into jails dispersed around the city, kept under maximum security and even solitary confinement, detained in prison for months on exorbitant bail for a crime that was never committed, and charged with plotting irrational actions, without the liberal press voicing its indignation? Yet this is precisely what has happened to the New York twenty-one. If you let it happen to us, the Panthers are saying to white liberals, it will happen to anyone who dissents. After the lessons of Chicago and Berkeley, white radicals, at least, are beginning to believe the Panther contention that we're all niggers now.

The Panthers are convinced that those in power are out to get them as much for their socialist ideology and their efforts to organize the black community into an effective political force as for their defensive actions against the police. Heavily into the economics and sociology of Marxism, the Panthers see racism in this country as an integral part of the capitalist system. "Capitalism deprives us all of self-determination," Huey Newton has said. "Only in the context of socialism can men practice the self-determination necessary to provide for their freedom."

The Panthers are absolutely serious when they talk of the need for "socialism"; and this is what distinguishes them from the other black militant and black power groups. They see themselves as "revolutionary nationalists," as opposed to "cultural nationalists," who seek black pride in separatist movements, religious cults, and emulation of ancient African culture. "The revolutionary nationalist," according to Huey Newton, "sees that there is no hope for cultural or individual expression, or even hope that his people can exist as a unique entity in a complex whole as long as the bureaucratic capitalist is in control." On the other hand, "cultural nationalism," explained David Hilliard, "is basically related to the physiological need for a return back to Africa in the culture, and we don't see that that is really relevant to any revolution, because culture never frees anyone. As Fanon says, the only culture is that of the revolution."

The reference to Fanon is instructive, for the Panthers, as can readily be seen from the writings of Huey Newton and Eldridge Cleaver, have been deeply influenced by the black psychiatrist from Martinique who died in the service of the Algerian revolution. *The Wretched of the Earth* is a kind of revolutionary Bible for them, and one with far more emotional impact than the Little Red Books which are so often quoted. Both Newton and Cleaver, freely acknowledging their debt to Fanon, have described black people as forming an oppressed colony within the white mother country, the United States. The colony is kept in line by an occupying army—white policemen who live outside the ghetto—and is exploited by businessmen and politicians.

The exploiters can be black as well as white, for the enemy, they insist, is not so much racism as capitalism, which creates and nourishes it. As would be expected of socialist revolutionaries, the Panthers are opposed to black capitalism, which Huey Newton has described as a "giant stride *away* from liberation . . ." since ". . . the rules of black capitalism, and the limits of black capitalism are set by the white power structure." Explaining his opposition, Newton has written:

> There can be no real black capitalism because no blacks control the means of production. All blacks can do is have illusions. They can dream of the day when they might share ownership of the means of production. But there is no free enterprise in America. We have monopoly capitalism which is a closed society of white industrialists and their protectors, white politicians in Washington.

According to the Panthers, black power has been absorbed into the establishment, shorn of its horns, and transformed into innocent black capitalism, which even Richard Nixon can praise because it poses no threat to the white power structure.

As an alternative they offer "revolution," to liberate oppressed minorities in the United States and break the stranglehold of capitalism on the economically underdeveloped countries of the Third World. Until there is some form of socialist "revolution" in America, they believe, small countries will remain prey to neo-colonialism and imperialism. The revolutionary in America, therefore, carries the world upon his shoulders. The black man in America will not be free until the white man is free, and until the white man is free, until America is transformed by a socialist revolution, the underdeveloped countries of the world will remain in economic chains.

Such a comprehensive theory clearly has its inadequacies. Although blacks can be described as forming an internal colony within the United States, they do not supply raw materials, labor, or markets to capitalism in the same way as the colonies did. There is, moreover, no evidence at present that the US is entering a revolutionary crisis that will involve the mass of workers. Nor can the Panthers have much success in breaking away into a separate state. What happens, as has been asked, when there's a border dispute? (It is not fair, however, to charge the Panthers with advocating political separatism. They claim neither to favor it nor to discourage it; they simply demand that a UN-supervised plebiscite be held on the issue in the black colony. In any case, this is not an immediate problem, and certainly not a major objective for them.)

The Panthers' Marxist-Leninist language, combined with their Fanonist theories of psychological alienation and Third World solidarity, makes them particularly appealing to middle-class white militants, who share their ideology but lack their discipline. White radicals also lack the black man's non-reducible commitment to black liberation: the fact that he is black. A white radical can cop out any time he wants by cutting his hair and behaving like a square. A black man cannot escape. In fighting against the system he becomes, by his very act of resistance, a hero to white radicals. As Huey Newton has explained:[2]

> Black people in America, in the black colony, are oppressed because we're black and we're exploited. The whites are rebels, many of them from the middle class, and as far as any overt oppression

[2] The quotations from Huey Newton are from an interview in *The Movement*, August 1968, republished as a pamphlet, and available from SDS.

> this is not the case. So therefore I call their rejection of the system somewhat of an abstract thing. They're looking for new heroes. . . . In pressing for new heroes the young white revolution found the heroes in the black colony at home and in the colonies throughout the world. . . .

While Newton favors alliances with white radicals, he points out that "there can be no black-white unity until there first is black unity." Only blacks can decide the proper strategy for the black community.

White radicals, divided on tactics and ideology, and split into a plethora of competing, often hostile, groups, have only recently begun to deal with some of the problems of "black liberation." There has always been sympathy for the black struggle, and even participation when it was permitted during the civil rights movement. But things have changed greatly since Stokely Carmichael kicked the whites out of SNCC and the Panthers moved into the streets with guns. Unable to lead the black movement, white radicals are no longer even sure how they can aid it. Uncertain of their tactics, and confused about their goals, they revert to ready-made formulas, like "revolution," to deal with a multitude of complexities that are too difficult to analyze right now. Some assert that groups like the Panthers are the "vanguard" of the revolution—as though this justified white radicals' inability to work out a coherent theory or strategy.

The Vietnam war no longer serves as the great rallying point for the Left that it used to. Radicals have a good deal to protest about, but they seem to focus their energies on largely symbolic issues, such as the People's Park, or on the predictable seizure of university administration buildings. The radical Left is hung up on revolution, but doesn't seem to have the vaguest idea of how it should be organized, or how the country would be run if such an event ever took place.

For the time being the Left is divided, confused, and hopelessly weak and inept, and there is no more telling sign of the insecurity of those who hold power in America than that they are seriously worried about its activities. The McClellan committee solemnly listens to the "threats to national security" posed by campus agitators, while Congress debates[3] unconstitutional limitations on dissent and hysteri-

[3] The level of congressional discussion is exemplified by the following dialogue, from *The Congressional Record,* between Senators Long (D. La.) and Byrd (D. Va.):

cal punishments against demonstrators. Not only do conventional politicians fear the Panthers, who at least carry guns and who can be described as a para-military organization, but even the scholastic debaters of the Students for a Democratic Society. In spite of all the spies and *agents provocateurs* it planted at the SDS convention in Chicago this past June, the politicians and the police apparently failed to learn that the Left is too schismatic and ego-centered to threaten anybody.

Everyone now knows that SDS split in two this year, with the national leadership, through its RYM (Revolutionary Youth Movement) faction, expelling the rival Progressive Labor group for being, of all things, "counter-revolutionary." Among its sins the Maoist-oriented PL, through its Worker-Student Alliance (WSA), opposed the People's Park fight in Berkeley as a liberal-reformist move, branded many student demonstrations as "adventurous, diversionary, and alienating to the working people," accused Ho Chi Minh of selling out to the Washington-Moscow axis, criticized Fidel Castro, and condemned the Panthers for "bourgeois nationalism" in fighting the struggle on racial rather than exclusively class lines.

When the Panthers at the convention accused PL of deviating "from Marxist-Leninist ideology on the national question" and called its members "traitors," the SDS national leadership had the issue it needed to read PL out of the organization (although this violated SDS's own constitution) and establish itself as the defender of the black liberation movement.

While PL's position is indeed bizarre on many issues, it is a

---

Long: Has the Senator ever heard of the Students for a Democratic Society?

Byrd: Yes, I have heard of that group.

Long: Does he agree with me that they are about the scum of the earth?

Byrd: I do not know whether I would use the same phraseology the Senator uses.

Long: They're about the most contemptible people I know of. They're the most overprivileged group in this country. Is the Senator familiar with the fact that the parents of these people have put up the money to pay all their expenses and buy soap for them? But they refuse to take baths. That they have put up the money to buy them razor blades? But they refuse to shave. That they put up the money to buy food for those children? And they spend it on marijuana. They are the most sorry, contemptible, overprivileged people in the world and I say those people are a good element for the Communists to move in on.

determined, well-disciplined, ideologically trained organization. In the past it has supported the Panthers, but a break was inevitable, since PL argues that even the revolutionary nationalism of the Panthers is "counter-revolutionary." People are oppressed, PL argues, as workers, not as blacks, browns, or women. Naturally this has won PL the enmity not only of the Panthers but of militant women opposed to "male chauvinism," as well as Puerto Rican groups like the Young Lords, and Mexican-American (Chicano) militants.

The RYM group tried to summarize its position in a lengthy not always coherent document it called Weatherman ("you don't need a weatherman to know which way the wind blows"). Among other things, it took the curious position that "the blacks could do it [the revolution] alone if necessary because of their centralness to the system," and signed off with friendly greetings to such enlightened outposts of proletarian freedom as Albania and North Korea.

In Oakland a few hundred SDS people joined others from some forty organizations to form a gathering of about 3,000 people: Trotskyites and women striking for peace, communist party veterans and anarchists, factory workers and ministers. And, of course, a contingent of Panthers who, in spite of the inter-racial theme of the meeting, sat in a roped-off section at the back of the Oakland auditorium.

The conference not only got off to a late start, owing to the Panthers' frisking everyone who entered the auditorium, but a bad one, with an interminable address by Communist Party stalwart, Herbert Aptheker, who cut into the time allotted to the women's panel (thereby producing cries of "male chauvinism"—a serious issue for the Panthers and certain radical groups), and, even worse, a charge that the Panthers had sold out to the bourgeois, reformist Communist Party. The Trotskyites and PL people were particularly upset by this, but the complaint is unjustified. The CP is useful to the Panthers because it furnishes bail money and teams of hard-working organizers who go out and get names on petitions. While the CP is happy to ride the Panthers' tail, it by no means calls the shots.

The Panthers ran the conference without help from the CP or anyone else. There were no workshops and no discussion from the floor, until the final night when a few questions were permitted. "When you begin to develop a united front you do not start off with a bunch of jive ideological bullshit," Bobby Seale declared to cries of "Right on" from the Panther cheering section and much waving of Little Red Books. But as the Trotskyite ISC observed in one of the leaflets it surreptitiously distributed at the conference, ". . . A left which lacks respect for its own ideas and programs and cannot stand internal debate cannot possibly hope to win the support of the masses." The Panthers, however, weren't interested in internal debate or jive ideological bullshit (although they produced a good deal of their own in the course of three days), but support for their own programs—or, as they would say, "solidarity."

The major program they are now emphasizing is community control of police, with cities divided into districts, each with its own police force controlled by an elected neighborhood council, and with policemen living in the district they control. "If a policeman's brutalizing somebody in the community and has to come back home and sleep that night," Bobby Seale explained, "we can deal with him in our community." Participants at the conference were urged to get out and work on such petitions for decentralization—whites in white communities, browns in Latin communities, and blacks in the ghettos. For blacks and other minority groups such decentralization makes sense. It would not bring about the millennium, but it could sharply reduce the slaying and beating of ghetto people by trigger-happy, frightened, or racist white cops.

The white revolutionaries, however, were put off by such reformist proposals—particularly the Berkeley contingent, which seemed hung up on violence, with some members talking about guerrilla warfare in the streets. Even the pro-Panther SDS leadership felt that decentralization, however good it might be for the ghettos, was a bad policy for white neighborhoods, where it might lead to the creation of vigilante teams under the guise of police forces. The SDS interim committee voted against endorsement of the petition campaign unless it were limited to black and brown communities.

This didn't go down well with the Panthers. On his return from Algiers, where he attended the Pan-African Arts Festival, chief of staff David Hilliard told newsmen that "The Black Panther Party will not be dictated to by people who are obviously bourgeois procrastinators, seeking made-to-order revolution which is abstract, metaphysical and doesn't exist in the black or white community." He derided the SDS argument that community control would make police forces in white areas worse than they already are, and defined the issue as one of revolutionary solidarity. "We're not going to let SDS worm their way out of their revolutionary duties," he warned. "If they are revolutionary, then this is what we, as the vanguard of the revolution in

Babylon, dictate—that they circulate that petition, not in our communities, but in their own."

Never very comfortable with SDS, the Panthers feel much more at home with the "brothers off the block," the street people, the lumpen proletariat, to use another phrase they are fond of, than with the guilt-ridden children of the white bourgeoisie. With a few exceptions, such as Huey Newton and Bobby Seale, they have had little formal education beyond high school, and some of the most intelligent do not even have that. "We got our education on the street, in the service, or in jail," the Panthers' soft-spoken minister of education, Ray "Masai" Hewitt, told me. The Panther leaders are self-made intellectuals or, in political scientist Martin Kilson's term, "para-intellectuals."[4]

"We relate to the Young Patriots" (a white, recently radicalized Chicago group that is organizing nationally), David Hilliard stated, "because they're operating on the same class level as the Black Panther Party." They also share a similar rhetoric. Speaking at the conference on the eve of the moon landing, a leader of the Young Patriots named Preacherman, in black beret and shades, gave a moving speech which was, in effect, a tribute to the Panthers' ability to reach traditionally apolitical, racist white groups:

> Our struggle is beyond comprehension to me sometimes, and I felt that poor whites was (and maybe we felt wrongly, but we felt it) was forgotten, and that certain places we walked there were certain organizations that nobody saw us until we met the Illinois chapter of the Black Panther Party and they met us. And we said, "Let's put that theory into practice about riddin' ourselves of that

[4] Describing such leaders as Malcolm X and Eldridge Cleaver, Kilson has written:

> Unlike the established elements in the Negro intelligentsia, the para-intellectuals share a cultural experience similar to that of the black lower classes. They share too the lower classes' brutalizing experience with the coercive arm of white-controlled cities, especially the police power. These common experiences enabled the paraintellectuals to be spokesmen for the Negro masses as they emerged into a militant politicalization through riots. The paraintellectuals came onto the scene as legitimate and *natural* leaders. Moreover, they advance the politicalization of the black urban masses, after a fashion, by formulating descriptions of black-white relations, past and present, and policies for altering these relations that the Negro lower class finds meaningful. Few of the established elements among the black intelligentsia have, until very recently, had such success. (Martin Kilson, "The New Black Intellectuals," *Dissent*, July–August 1969, p. 307.)

> racism." You see, otherwise, otherwise to us, freeing political prisoners would be hypocrisy. That's what it'd be. We want to stand by our brothers, dig? . . .

The Young Patriots started out as a street gang and gradually developed a political consciousness that led them in the direction of the Panthers. A similar attempt at radicalizing organized labor is being made with the creation of the League of Revolutionary Black Workers, a federation of several Detroit-based workers' groups such as the Dodge Revolutionary Union Movement (DRUM) and its equivalents at Ford (FRUM), Chrysler (CRUM), and elsewhere. The all-black League was started, according to John Watson, one of its founders, "because the working class is already divided between the races, and because it is necessary for black workers to be able to act independently of white workers."

White workers have been encouraged to form radical organizations of their own to work out a common strategy with black union revolutionaries, but progress has been slow. Speaking of such a group at the Detroit *News*, Watson observed, ". . . although a number of the white guys who were down there had risen above the levels of racism and understood the exploitative nature of the company and of the system, they had very little experience in organizing to fight oppression and exploitation." As with the Panthers, these black workers consider themselves to be in the "vanguard of the revolutionary movement," and see most whites still on the fringes of the real struggle.

These "revolutionary" union groups were started to protect black workers who felt they were being treated unfairly and even victimized by racist white union leaders. Also, they believed, together with like-minded white workers, that union chiefs were in collusion with the bosses to speed up work schedules and ignore grievances over intolerable working conditions. The radical union groups are, first of all, self-protective associations for people unprotected or abused by the regular, bureaucratized unions. Secondly, they hope to stimulate a political awareness that will lead to a revolutionary situation in America.

For the time being, however, it is clear that the ghettos are potentially the most explosive places in the country. This is where the Panthers are organized (although they are trying to establish closer contacts with the revolutionary union movements, as well as with student groups) and where they draw their main support. Much of their appeal for ghetto youths (shared by many whites) is their image of a powerful black man with a rifle. In his recent book of essays[5] Eldridge Cleaver describes his own first encounter with the Panthers at a meeting in the Fillmore district ghetto of San Francisco: "I spun round in my seat and saw the most beautiful sight I had ever seen: four black men wearing black berets, powder blue shirts, black leather jackets, black trousers, shiny black shoes—and each with a gun!"

Since then Cleaver has learned that there is more to being a Panther than carrying a gun. But the image of power and violence is still the basic one created by the Panthers. When ghetto youths learn that party membership is not like joining a street gang but more like taking religious vows, many of them become disillusioned and turn away from the Panthers. They are put off by the strict discipline,[6] the political indoctrination, the discouragement of racism, and such community service projects as the Panther program to provide free breakfast to ghetto children. The Panthers have had to purge people who turned out to be basically criminals or racists unable to relate to the party's political and intellectual program.

Unlike many of the ghetto youth, who want action, retribution, and loot, young black idealists are drawn to the Panthers' philosophy of social justice and equality through power. Where there have been spontaneous black riots, such as those following the assassination of Martin Luther King, the Panthers have tried to cool it, to discourage violence that could lead only to further repression without any political gains. Unfortunately the political leadership in most cities is too dense to realize that the Panthers are actually a force for stability in the ghettos. An intelligent white ruling class would encourage the Panthers rather than try to destroy them; that it has failed to understand this does indeed argue for its own inherent instability.

[5] *Eldridge Cleaver*, Random House, 211 pp.

[6] There are twenty-six rules of discipline that all members must follow, of which the first is "no party member can have narcotics or weed in his possession while doing party work." In addition, there are eight "points of attention":

1. Speak politely.
2. Pay fairly for what you buy.
3. Return everything you borrow.
4. Pay for anything you damage.
5. Do not hit or swear at people.
6. Do not damage property or crops of the poor, oppressed masses.
7. Do not take liberties with women.
8. If we ever have to take captives, do not ill-treat them.

Lately the Panthers have been emphasizing programs directly related to the needs of the ghetto community, such as free breakfasts and health clinics. This summer they have also been setting up black "liberation schools," where children between two and sixteen are taught some things about American history, economics, and politics that they never learn in the public schools. Clearly much of this is indoctrination, although the Panthers claim that they are correcting the distorted image that black children receive of themselves and their society.

White middle-class revolutionaries tend to patronize such activities as reformist. But the breakfasts, the schools, and the clinics have won the Panthers support within the ghetto that they never could have gained by guns alone or by Marxist-Leninist analyses of the internal contradictions of capitalism. In Oakland, where the party has existed for nearly three years, it is an important element of the black community, respected even though it is not often fully understood. Just as the police have been forced to respect the power of the Panthers, so the white power elite has had to deal with an organized, politically conscious force within the black community. Throughout much of the Bay Area, where the Panthers are particularly well organized, they are an articulate, alert defender of black people's interests. The Panthers are there when the community needs them, and they are there when no one else seems to be listening.

An example that comes to mind, simply because it occurred while I was in San Francisco, concerned a sixteen-year-old boy who was shot in the back by a member of San Francisco's Tactical Squad while he was fleeing the scene of an alleged auto theft. The shooting occurred near his home and was heard by his mother, a practical nurse, who was thrown to the ground by the police when she ran to his side screaming. "Don't shoot my boy again." The wounded boy was thrown into a police truck and nearly an hour elapsed before he actually reached the hospital. It is the sort of thing that happens every day in Hunter's Point and a hundred other black ghettos around America. The only difference is that, miraculously, the bullet was deflected by a rib bone and the boy was not killed, and that the Panthers brought it to the attention of the public by calling a press conference which Bobby Seale, David Hilliard, and Masai, the party's three top leaders, attended.

At the conference were a few representatives of the local press (the television stations were invited but refrained from sending anyone), myself, a few Panthers, their lawyer, Charles Garry, the boy,

Jimmie Conner, and his parents. The boy, soft-spoken and composed, spoke of the incident as though it were a normal part of life and when asked why he ran away, replied, with the tedium of one explaining the obvious, "Why did I run? Because I'm scared of police." With him sat his parents, an attractive, quiet woman in her mid-thirties and a handsome, somewhat stocky, graying man who works in aircraft maintenance. Both very light-skinned, eminently respectable, and both bitter and confused about what had happened to them.

Had they been white, their son would have been reprimanded, or at most taken to court. But they are black and their son was almost killed, as other boys have been killed in Hunter's Point and elsewhere for even lesser crimes—if indeed Jimmie Conner was guilty of a crime. When asked about the incident, Mrs. Conner replied, "Just another Negro gone, that's the way we believe that they think about the kids up here. Too many of our kids are dying for nothing. They see police three blocks away and they start running because they're scared. I'm gonna fight them. If I have to go to jail OK. If I have to work for the rest of my life, I will. If they shoot me that's fine. I'm gonna fight, this has got to stop." The story so far has included the radicalization of Mrs. Ozella Conner, housewife, mother, nurse, and now friend of the Black Panthers.

How did the Panthers get involved in this incident, although none of the Conners is a member of the party? Because a doctor at the hospital where Jimmie was taken was so shocked at his treatment by the police that he called Charles Garry, who in turn called Bobby Seale. What followed was a press conference, followed by a lawsuit under the 1964 Civil Rights Act, followed by press coverage—which of course could never have occurred had the Panthers not been called in.

The cynical would say that the Panthers have something to gain from this publicity, which indeed they have. But that is to miss the point, which is that by such actions they are establishing themselves, in the eyes of the black community, as the defenders of the black man too humble to interest anyone else. They can sink their roots in the black community and win its allegiance partly because no one else is fulfilling that role. This is one of the things that the Panthers mean by "educating" the people, informing them of their rights and making them activist defenders rather than passive victims. This education is carried on through meetings, discussions, leaflets, and the party newspaper. While their tactics have shifted several times since the formation of the party in October 1966, their objectives remain the ones set out in their ten-point program of black liberation.[7]

Looking at this program and talking to the Panthers, as well as reading their newspaper, *The Black Panther* (which everyone interested enough to read this essay ought to do in order to gain, if nothing else, an idea of the atrocities that are going on under the name of law and order), make one realize that the "revolution" they talk about is not necessarily the cataclysmic upheaval that sends the white middle class into spasms. Rather, it is the achievement of constitutional guarantees and economic justice for black people. These gun-carrying, Mao-quoting revolutionaries want what most middle-class Americans take for granted. As Huey Newton has said, if reformist politicians like the Kennedys and Lindsay could solve the problems of housing, employment, and justice for blacks and other Americans at the bottom of the social heap, there would be no need for a revolution. And, it goes without saying, little support for such groups as the Black Panther Party.

The Panthers have a voice in the black community (although not necessarily so large as many whites imagine) because they offer hope for change to ghetto people whom the civil rights movement and the poverty program bureaucrats have been unable to touch. They walk proudly through the streets of Oakland in their black

[7] 1. We want freedom. We want power to determine the destiny of our Black Community.

2. We want full employment for our people.

3. We want an end to the robbery by the CAPITALIST of our Black Community. [N.B. Recently changed to "capitalist" from "white man."]

4. We want decent housing, fit for shelter of human beings.

5. We want education for our people that exposes the true nature of this decadent American society. We want education that teaches us our true history and our role in the present day society.

6. We want all black men to be exempt from military service.

7. We want an immediate end to POLICE BRUTALITY and MURDER of black people.

8. We want freedom for all black men held in federal, state, county and city prisons and jails.

9. We want all black people when brought to trial to be tried in court by a jury of their peer group or people from their black communities, as defined by the Constitution of the United States.

10. We want land, bread, housing, education, clothing, justice and peace. And as our major political objective, a United Nations-supervised plebiscite to be held throughout the black colony in which only black colonial subjects will be allowed to participate, for the purpose of determining the will of black people as to their national destiny. [Followed by an explanatory paragraph taken from the US Constitution: "When in the course of human events . . . ."]

leather jackets, and they hold mass rallies for the liberation of Huey Newton in the shadow of the Alameda County Court House where he was sentenced. They speak to the black man's image of himself. They tell him that he is no longer powerless against the forces that oppress him, and that his struggle for freedom is part of a world-wide liberation movement. In this sense they fulfill a real psychological need.

While they have not yet shed white blood, except in self-defense, does this mean that they never will, that their talk of guerrilla warfare is simply rhetoric? It would be rash to say so, for the Panthers have declared that they are ready to kill anyone who stands in the way of "black liberation." And they are convinced that racism in this society is so pervasive and deeply rooted that there can be no freedom for black people until it is extirpated by some form of revolution. Even Gene Marine, who, in his highly informative book, *The Black Panthers*,[8] freely admits his admiration for the Panthers, confesses, "I am frightened by them." Like some of the white revolutionaries who emulate them, the Panthers seem to have over-learned *The Battle of Algiers*, and have tried to apply its lesson to a society where the situation is totally different. The United States today is not Algeria of 1954, nor Cuba of 1958, nor even France of 1968. It is a deeply troubled, but nonetheless largely stable society which is capable of putting down an insurrection ruthlessly and quickly.

Don't the Panthers realize this? They seem to, at the present moment anyway. This is why they are serving free breakfasts to ghetto children; attempting to form alliances with white radicals, liberals, workers, and pacifists; and urging people to sign petitions for the decentralization of the police. They may be going through a temporary stage, but the direction in which they are heading is clearly marked reformism. Right now they seem interested in maximum publicity, which is why they hold meetings and press conferences, and complain about the way the mass media ignores or distorts their actions. Some of their sympathizers fear that the Panthers are pushing themselves too much in the public eye, and that this only aids the enemies who are trying to destroy them. But since the police and politicians are out to get the Panthers in any case, perhaps such an effort to convince the public that they are not really monsters is their only chance for survival.

It is curious, to say the least, that the federal government has

[8] Signet, 1969, 224 pp. (paper).

decided to come down hard on the Panthers at the very time that they are emphasizing ballots and petitions, community self-help, and political alliances, rather than shoot-outs. The severe harassment and repression they are now suffering may, if anything, improve the Panthers' appeal among the black bourgeoisie and white liberals. It would be one of the ironies of our irrational political life if John Mitchell and J. Edgar Hoover, together with the so-called "liberal" mayors of cities like San Francisco and Chicago, succeeded in giving the Panthers a new vitality just at the time when the party seemed in difficulty.

Mention of the word "revolution" is enough to send most politicians and police officers into a rage. Like radicals in general, the Panthers naturally talk a good deal about revolution, and use such other catch-words as fascism, imperialism, and the dictatorship of the proletariat. They connect racism with the evils of capitalism, and quote freely from the sacred texts of Marx, Lenin, and Mao. Walk into any Panther office and you are likely to find not only Little Red Books lying about, but the officer of the day with his nose buried in the works of Mao, or one of Lenin's many pamphlets. Slogans, often vague and even meaningless in the context of which they are used, become part of the revolutionary vocabulary. This is true not only of the Panthers, who use such slogans to reach an audience with little formal education, but of young radicals generally. The deliberate inflation and distortion of language is a disease of the Left.

The Panthers, however, realize that racism is deeply embedded in the cultural history of Europe and America and is not, as certain Marxists still argue, simply a by-product of class society. As Huey Newton has said, "Until you get rid of racism . . . no matter what kind of economic system you have, black people will still be oppressed." What revolution seems to mean for the Panthers is the transformation of the ghetto and the "liberation" of black people, and of all oppressed people, from lives of poverty, degradation, and despair. The steps by which this will take place are not specified precisely, but they need not be violent ones unless every other road to radical change is closed. Having defined the problem, the Panthers now ask white America what kind of solution it proposes. So far as the Panthers are concerned, the answer has been harassment, repression, and even murder.

The Panthers are not racist; but they refuse to take any instructions from their white sympathizers. Indeed, this may be what makes it possible for them to be anti-racist. Commenting on the anti-white sentiment in SNCC before it became an all-black organization, Huey Newton recently said, "We have never been controlled by whites, and therefore we don't fear the white mother-country radicals." Their willingness to work with allied white radicals is not shared by most black militant groups. When Stokely Carmichael recently left the Panthers, his stormy letter of departure[9] centered on just this issue.

As the Carmichael-Cleaver exchange indicated, the black militants are just as fragmented into feuding factions as are the whites. Their rivalry, however, is a good deal more violent, and the struggle between the Panthers and the "cultural nationalist" US group of Ron Karenga led to the murder of two Panthers in Los Angeles last year. The Panthers are serious about wanting to carry on programs of education, and in spite of the terrible repression they are now facing have an enduring faith in the democratic system of petitions and ballots—far more than do the young white radicals. But like most revolutionaries, they are highly authoritarian and want loyal and unquestioning followers (as Stokely Carmichael rightly pointed out in his letter) rather than critical colleagues.

Unlike the white revolutionaries, however, the Panthers do have some fairly clear ideas of what they want—even though they are uncertain about the best way to get it. Whatever their shortcomings,

[9] In spite of his official title of Prime Minister, Stokely Carmichael was not much more than a figurehead in the party. From his self-chosen exile in Guinea, he sent an open letter to the party, distributed by his wife at Kennedy airport to the press, in which he declared:

> The alliances being formed by the party are alliances which I cannot politically agree with, because the history of Africans living in the US has shown that any premature alliance with white radicals has led to complete subversion of blacks by the whites through their direct or indirect control of the black organization.

He also criticized the "present tactics and methods which the party is using to coerce and force everyone to submit to its authority," and declared that unless the Panthers change their political direction they "will at best become a reformist party and at worst a tool of racist imperialists used against the black masses."

To this denunciation Eldridge Cleaver, Minister of Information in enforced exile, replied in the pages of *Ramparts*:

> That you know nothing about the revolutionary process is clear, that you know less about the United States and its people is clearer, and that you know even less about humanity than you do about the rest is clearest of all. . . . You should know that suffering is color blind and that the victims of imperialism, racism, colonialism, and neo-colonialism come in all colors and that they need unity based on revolutionary principles rather than skin color.

they did not seem to me self-indulgent, romantic, or part-time players at revolution. They are in this struggle for keeps. Anyone who is a Panther today, or who contemplates joining the party, knows that there is a good chance that he will be jailed or die a violent death. Panthers have already been murdered by the police, many have been beaten and wounded, and others are almost certain to be killed in the months and years ahead. It takes courage to join the party, to submit to its discipline, and to face the likely prospect of imprisonment or death. But for some there is no other way. As Eldridge Cleaver has written, "A slave who dies of natural causes will not balance two dead flies on the scale of eternity."

The Panthers have come a long way since Huey Newton and Bobby Seale first formed the party three years ago in Oakland. It has spread across the nation and has eclipsed such groups as SNCC and CORE to become the most powerful black militant organization in America. This rapid expansion has created problems—not only increasing police harassment and repression as the Panthers become more influential within the black community, but also the difficulty of maintaining the high standard of membership that its leaders would like. Not all Panthers have the organizing ability of Bobby Seale or the analytical minds of David Hilliard, Eldridge Cleaver, and Huey Newton. Which is to say that the Panthers are not super-human, as some white radicals would like to believe, any more than they are devils.

Beneath an inflammatory vocabulary of ghetto hyperbole and a good deal of facile Marxist sloganizing, the Panthers seemed to me serious, hard-working, disciplined, and essentially humanistic in their work within the black community and in their vision of a more just society. For the Panthers, weapons are an instrument of self-protection, and ultimately the means to achieve the revolution that, in the absence of a peaceful alternative, will make liberation possible. For some of the white militants I spoke to around Berkeley, however, it seemed that revolution is the means, and denouncing or shooting up the "fascists" (who seem to include just about everyone who disagrees on tactics or strategy, and many readers of this magazine) is conceived as the end. Since Chicago, and particularly since the brutal suppression by the police during the battle of People's Park, some West Coast militants seem to have become traumatized by violence, convinced there is no other way to carry on radical politics.

But Che's prescription is no more relevant in the tree-lined streets of Berkeley or Cambridge than it was in the mountains of

Bolivia. The Panthers are prepared for guerrilla warfare, as a last-ditch stand, because they think they may have no other alternative. There are white revolutionaries, on the West Coast and elsewhere, who, in the impatience of their rage and their inability seriously to change a society whose policies they find oppressive, accept this prescription uncritically, and, in view of the forces marshalled against them on the Right, with a half-conscious quest for martyrdom. As its frustration increases, the New Left becomes more shrill in its rhetoric and dogmatic in its politics. Instead of focusing on the most blatant inequalities and injustices of American life, it is assaulting the periphery. Instead of trying to educate the people to inequities of the social-economic system and the cost of maintaining an empire, it has successfully alienated the working class—without whose support no radical change, let alone "revolution," is possible.

In its resistance to the draft, the war, and racism, the radical Left has aroused parts of the nation. More people now realize there is something seriously wrong with American society but are not certain how to deal with it. Many are frightened and attribute all unrest to a conspiracy of "troublemakers." Others know that change must come, but would like it to be as unobtrusive as possible. It remains to be seen how many can be reached, whether it be on the plane of morality or self-interest, and convinced that change need not be personally threatening to them. To do this radicals must have plausible ideas on how a transformed society would produce a better existence for the mass of people. It does little good for the radical Left to dismiss everyone who disagrees as "fascist," for these are a majority, and if they are treated as fascists long enough, they may begin behaving in such a way as to make the current repression seem like libertarianism in comparison.

America is not now a "fascist" country, nor is it likely soon to become one, although this is not impossible. Probably it will continue to be an advanced capitalist society in which cruel inequalities and repression, unlivable cities, and inhuman conditions of work continue to exist along with considerable liberty to take political action, while our rulers control an empire of poor nations abroad. It is the duty of the Left to find ways to change this system: to educate people rather than simply abuse them; to understand what is happening in the factories and farms and lower-middle-class neighborhoods and be in touch with the people in them; to use the universities as places where the complex problems of replacing repressive capitalism and imperialism with a better system can be studied seriously; to stop playing Minutemen and begin acting like radicals. If there is ever going to be a revolution in this country, it will have to happen first in people's heads. What takes place in the streets of a society like this one has another name. It is called repression.

QUESTIONS FOR DISCUSSION AND WRITING

1. Why does the white community fear the Black Panthers?
2. In what ways do the goals of "cultural nationalists" differ from the goals of the Black Panthers? What are the assumptions of the two groups?
3. According to Black Panther spokesmen, how does capitalism support a racist society? Do you agree? Why?
4. What interest does the "New Left" have in the Black Panthers? In what ways do "New Left" organizations differ from the Panthers?
5. Compare the goals of the Black Panthers with the "civil rights" goals advocated by King (p. 341) and with the goals of "black power" advanced by Carmichael (p. 338).

ROBERT S. BROWNE IS ASSISTANT PROFESSOR OF ECONOMICS AT FAIRLEIGH DICKINSON UNIVERSITY. THE FOLLOWING ESSAY OFFERS A DRAMATIC SOLUTION FOR THE BLACK MAN IN AMERICA.

ROBERT S. BROWNE

THE CASE FOR BLACK SEPARATISM

If the mass media are to be believed, the most sensational information leaked to the general public from the closed sessions of the Conference on Black Power, recently held in Newark, New Jersey, concerned the adoption of a resolution which favored the partitioning of the U.S. into two separate nations. Understandably, any effort to split the U.S., or any other major power, is certainly prime news—witness the storm which President de Gaulle aroused by his support for French separatism in Canada. Consequently, the attention which the press has focused on this resolution is not unexpected. Unfortunately, however, there has been some confusion as to exactly what the resolution says, and considerably more misunderstanding of the traumatic agony which lies behind it. As the individual who had the responsibility for reading this resolution to the Conference for adoption, I should like to clarify some of this confusion for black and white

THE CASE FOR BLACK SEPARATISM From *Ramparts* Magazine (December 1967). Reprinted by permission of the author.

readers alike. (I wish to make it clear at the outset that I do not speak in any official capacity for the Conference.)

With respect to the content of the resolution, it reads as follows (as amended from the floor):

Whereas the black people in America have been systematically oppressed by their white fellow countrymen

Whereas there is little prospect that this oppression can be terminated, peacefully or otherwise, within the foreseeable future

Whereas the black people do not wish to be absorbed into the larger white community

Whereas the black people in America find that their interests are in contradiction with those of white America

Whereas the black people in America are psychologically handicapped by virtue of their having no national homeland

Whereas the physical, moral, ethical, and aesthetic standards of white American society are not those of black society and indeed do violence to the self-image of the black man

Whereas black people were among the earliest immigrants to America, having been ruthlessly separated from their fatherland, and have made a major contribution to America's development, most of this contribution having been uncompensated, and

Recognizing that efforts are already well advanced for the convening of a Constitutional Convention for the purpose of revising the Constitution of the U.S. for the first time since America's inception, then

Be it resolved that the Black Power Conference initiate a national dialogue on the desirability of partitioning the U.S. into two separate and independent nations, one to be a homeland for white and the other to be a homeland for black Americans.

Clearly, this is not a radical resolution. Like the Declaration of Independence, it enumerates some of the felt grievances of the people. But it is more moderate in tone than Jefferson's Declaration and its action clause stops considerably short of that of the 1776 document. Significantly, it asks not for separation but merely for dialogue. In this sense, it is possibly the mildest resolution which the Conference adopted.

Nevertheless, as the press reported, this resolution received perhaps the most thunderous ovation of the entire Conference. Obviously, this enthusiasm was not due to the resolution's moderation but to the fact that reference to an all-black state touched deep sensitivity in the emotions of the audience. All of those who applauded and approved the resolution can by no stretch of the imagination be considered active partisans of the idea of a separate state. But just as surely, as black people have become progressively more disillusioned at the prospect of ever finding a dignified niche for themselves in American society, so have they become more eager to explore any avenue which may offer greater promise. What the support for the resolution unmistakably revealed was the depth of the despair about white America which is now prevalent in the black community; and therein lies its significance.

Taken at face value, the resolution is far from an expression of racism or hate. Rather, it is a straightforward effort to explore an obvious means of minimizing racial friction by suggesting some fair basis for the physical separation of the contending parties. Partitioning of the U.S. into separate black and white nations will conceivably appeal to both the Southern white racist and the Northern black nationalist, and it can with equal inaccuracy be characterized as painfully conservative or wildly radical. The intent of the resolution, however, is to free the partition concept from the deadly embrace of extremists and to afford it consideration by moderates of both races. The social climate in America is being transformed at a dizzying pace, and those who summarily dismiss the partition concept as being too radical to merit serious consideration risk committing the classic error of ignoring the pleas of the moderate center and thereby sentencing the country to the terror of the irresponsibles on the two extremes.

A certain amount of hostility toward any modification of the American political structure is only natural. Indeed, the nation's bloodiest war was fought under the banner of "preserving the Union," so that on sentimental grounds alone the resistance to partitioning can be expected to be massive. But primitive emotion is scarcely a sound guide for policy. Besides, sensitive persons must with increasing frequency ask themselves if there really remains much of a Union to preserve.

One of the few lessons which history teaches us is that nothing created by man is immutable, least of all his political architecture. Only those who are completely lacking in historical perspective are likely to believe that the U.S. has settled its political form and its geographical boundaries for all time. The political realist is not only aware that man-made institutions are never eternal; he realizes that it is not even desirable that they should be. Rather, they must be amenable to constant reshaping to meet changing conditions. The hope which underlies the partition resolution is that the anticipated initial hostile reaction to the proposal can be gradually stripped away and replaced by non-hysterical discussion and analysis as to whether or not partitioning of the national territory offers a promising solution to our racial quandary.

As this dialogue progresses, serious exploration and research will be required probing the legal, political, economic and sociological implications of partitioning and of population relocation. Assumptions will have to be made regarding just what portions of the present territorial U.S. will be included in each of the two new nations and how assets will be apportioned. The mechanisms for negotiating such a partitioning will have to be examined intensively, as well as the basis for recognition of official negotiators for the black community. The answers to such questions obviously cannot be found in one month or in one year. Ultimately, the proposal may well prove unworkable because some of these questions may prove unanswerable. But the mere fact that the modalities of implementation are difficult to formulate is certainly no reason to prejudge the merits of the proposal and to dismiss it from consideration as a viable alternative if it seems to speak to the needs of a large segment of the population.

There is ample historic precedent for national partitioning, the most appropriate contemporary model probably being the division of the former British India into today's India and Pakistan. This schism, which was made along religious rather than racial lines, was accompanied by personal hardships of such magnitude that one hesitates to refer to it as a model. A substantial portion of these human tragedies, however, appear to have stemmed from the precipitous manner in which the entire matter of partitioning was agreed to and effectuated. Only during a brief period was partition given really serious consideration and then, suddenly, because of political pressures, it was abruptly approved and implementation begun—an implementation which involved the relocation of tens of millions of people. An atmosphere of extreme bitterness and hostility prevailed throughout the area and in such circumstances atrocities were easily predictable. The grossly inadequate administrative preparations for so gigantic an undertaking also contributed to the widespread hardships which occurred. By encouraging a national dialogue, the Black Power resolution hopes to diffuse the intense emotionalism which the proposal is certain to arouse, and to stimulate serious planning as to how such a project could best be carried out, thus avoiding many of the pitfalls which befell India and Pakistan.

It should not be overlooked that such racially white and culturally Western countries as Canada, Belgium and Spain all harbor strong separatist movements. The separatists in these countries are not considered a lunatic fringe but constitute a significant political force. In these countries the dialogue proceeds at a leisurely pace and continuous efforts are made to accommodate the nation to the demands of the ethnic or linguistic minority. It is also noteworthy that in the examples of classical decolonization, violence has tended to occur principally when dialogue and national planning were absent (e.g., Ireland, Indonesia, Algeria) and to have been largely avoided where honest dialogue was permitted (Ghana, Zambia, French Africa).

I frankly do not know how many blacks would favor a separatist solution of the type proposed. Many of us suffer from a serious inferiority complex about our race and may doubt our ability to operate a successful nation, despite the inspiring example of several of the African countries which came into independence with handicaps of illiteracy and lack of capital far more serious than those we would face. My experience suggests that the number of blacks who would support the idea of partitioning is nevertheless sufficient to warrant serious national consideration of its feasibility. I have listened to the voices of my people and I know that they are desperate. Talk of violence and of revolution hangs heavy in the atmosphere of both black and white America. Not surprisingly, black leadership is in the vanguard of those who recognize and articulate the need for drastic changes in American society. However, the black community's role in effecting these changes remains unresolved. Partition has the significant advantage of offering a path which, with proper goodwill, can be trod nonviolently. It has the disadvantage of speaking primarily to the basic problem facing black America and not to the problems of the total society. Clearly, *some* new path will have to be taken to relieve the desperation of black Americans. Partition is being offered as one way out. Does white America have an equally reasonable counter-proposal?

The sources of this desperation of the Negro should have been fairly well known by now. In case they were not, the resolution's drafters took the Jeffersonian view that "a decent respect of the opinions of mankind requires that they should declare the causes which impel them to the separation." Yet, in their formalized brevity, the "whereas" clauses of the resolution hardly convey the full panoply of frustrations which have driven some blacks to an endorsement of separatism.

Unquestionably, the gloomy statistics on black unemployment, income, housing and disease create the general framework for this despair—statistics which the Negro must read against the background of a decade of both unprecedented national civil rights activity and unprecedented national prosperity. The black community clearly sees itself getting a progressively smaller share of the pie as the pie itself grows ever larger. Coupled with these economic statistics are the sociological ones: schools are more segregated than ever before; cities are more ghettoized in 1967 than in 1937.

For the upper middle class Negro, as for most whites, these figures on the deterioration of the Negro's position since World War II are sometimes difficult to grasp, for on the surface much progress is in evidence. Well scrubbed, nattily dressed Negroes are to be seen working in myriad sorts of establishments from which they were formerly barred; they are increasingly seen at private social functions of upper class whites; they are even to be glimpsed occasionally in advertisements for well known products, and in non-stereotype roles in TV and film entertainment. A Negro sits on the Supreme Court, another sits on the Federal Reserve Board, and one has been elected to the Senate from a primarily white constituency.

Indeed, it is these very strides which have been, at least in part, responsible for the current crisis in Negro leadership. The traditional leaders point with pride to their accomplishments and conclude that they are pushing matters at as fast a pace as the white society will permit. Meanwhile, the great bulk of the black community sinks ever lower, increasingly resentful of its worsening position vis-à-vis the black elite as well as vis-à-vis the whites. As a result, the black masses are becoming politicized, are developing a class consciousness, and are rejecting the existing Negro leadership. An unexpected, although possibly temporary, interruption in this process of polarization of the black community occurred last winter as fallout from the Adam Powell incident. The manner in which virtually all segments of the white community openly supported the attack on Congressman Powell, the supreme symbol of black achievement of power in America, served as an eye-opener to all blacks, whatever their level of sophistication and economic achievement. If Powell, the epitome of power, was not safe, then clearly no black man was safe and it was obviously naive to think otherwise. The Powell incident, by the very grossness of its racism, built a precarious bridge between the increasingly bitter, increasingly segregated black masses, and the increasingly affluent, increasingly integrated black middle class. Their interests were once again shown to be identical, even if involuntarily so.

Clearly, it is as a measure of self-defense that the black community has begun to draw together and even to discuss separatism. Let every liberal white American ponder this.

The bridge between the two segments of the black community is by no means a stable one, largely because of the schizophrenia of the black middle class. Whereas the black masses, both those in the rural South and those who have flooded into Northern cities in the past quarter century, aspire primarily for a higher standard of living and for freedom from the indignities and oppressions which their blackness has attracted to them, the middle-class Negroes have developed more subtle tastes. To varying degrees, these Negroes have become "assimilated" into white society and lead lives which are spiritually dependent upon the white community in a way that the mass of Negroes could never comprehend. For them, an integrated America is fast becoming a reality and the thrust of their effort is to extend the integration concept to every corner of the country. Their schizophrenia arises from the inescapable reminders of their vulnerability. Even with a Ph.D., a Nobel prize, a Congressional Medal of Honor or a vast fortune, a Negro is still a "nigger" to many (most?) white Americans and the society does not let him forget it for very long. Nor does the sensitive Negro really want to forget it; he wants to change it.

But perhaps the most unsettling of all the factors affecting the mental health of the black man in this white society is the matter of identification. It can be exemplified by the poignant, untold agony of raising black, kinky-haired children in a society where the standard of beauty is a milk-white skin and long, straight hair. To convince a black child that she is beautiful when every channel of value formation in the society is telling her the opposite is a heart-rending and well-nigh impossible task. It is a challenge which confronts all Negroes, irrespective of their social and economic class, but the difficulty of dealing with it is likely to vary directly with the degree to which the Negro family leads an integrated existence. A black child in a predominantly black school may realize that she doesn't look like the pictures in the books, magazines and TV advertisements, but at least she looks like her schoolmates and neighbors. The black child in a predominantly white school and neighborhood lacks even this basis for identification.

This identity problem is, of course, not peculiar to the Negro. Minorities of all sorts encounter it in one form or another—the immigrant who speaks with an accent; the Jewish child who doesn't celebrate Christmas; the Oriental whose eyes are slanted. But for the Negro the problem has a special dimension, for in the American ethos a black man is not only "different," he is classed as ugly and inferior. This is not an easy situation to deal with, and the manner in which a Negro chooses to handle it will both be determined by and a determinant of his larger political outlook. He can deal with it as an integrationist, accepting his child as being ugly by prevailing standards and urging him to excel in other ways to prove his worth; or he can deal with it as a black nationalist, telling the child that he is not a freak but rather part of a larger international community of black-skinned, kinky-haired people who have a beauty of their own, a glorious history and a great future. In short, he can replace shame with pride, inferiority with dignity, by imbuing the child with what is coming to be known as black nationalism. The growing popularity of this viewpoint is evidenced by the appearance of "natural" hair styles among Negro youth and the surge of interest in African and Negro culture and history.

Black Power may not be the ideal slogan to describe this new self-image which the black American is developing, for to guilt-ridden whites the slogan conjures up violence, anarchy and revenge. To frustrated blacks, however, it symbolizes unity and a newly found pride in the blackness with which the Creator endowed us and which we realize must always be our mark of identification. Heretofore this blackness has been a stigma, a curse with which we were born. Black Power means that this curse will henceforth be a badge of pride rather than of scorn. It marks the end of an era in which black men devoted themselves to pathetic attempts to be white men and inaugurated an era in which black people will set their own standards of beauty, conduct and accomplishment.

Is this new black consciousness in irreconcilable conflict with the larger American society? In a sense, the heart of the American cultural problem has always been the need to harmonize the inherent contradiction between racial (or national) identity with integration into the melting pot which was America. In the century since the Civil War, the society has made little effort to find a means to afford the black minority a sense of racial pride and independence while at the same time accepting it as a full participant in the larger society. Now that the implications of this failure are becoming apparent, the black community seems to be saying, "Forget it! We'll solve our own problems." Integration, which never had a high priority among the black masses, is now being written off by them as being not only unattainable but actually harmful—driving a wedge between the black masses and the so-called Negro elite. To these developments has been added the momentous realization by many "integrated" Negroes that, in the U.S., full integration can only mean full assimilation—a loss of racial identity. This sobering prospect has caused many a black integrationist to pause and reflect, even as have his similarly challenged Jewish counterparts. Thus, within the black community there are two separate challenges to the traditional integration policy which has long constituted the major objective of established Negro leadership. There is the general skepticism that the Negro, even after having transformed himself into a white blackman, will enjoy full acceptance into American society; and there is the longer-range doubt that even should complete integration somehow be achieved, it would prove to be really desirable, for its price may be the total absorption and disappearance of the race—a sort of painless genocide.

Understandably, it is the black masses who have most vociferously articulated these dangers of assimilation, for they have watched with alarm as the more fortunate among their ranks have gradually risen to the top only to be promptly "integrated" off into the white community—absorbed into another culture, often with undisguised contempt for all that had previously constituted their heritage. Also, it was the black masses who first perceived that integration actually increases the white community's control over the black one by destroying black institutions, and by absorbing black leadership and coinciding its interests with those of the white community. The international "brain drain" has its counterpart in the black community, which is constantly being denuded of its best trained people and many of its natural leaders. Black institutions of all sorts—colleges, newspapers, banks, even community organizations—are all experiencing the loss of their better people to the newly available openings in white establishments, thereby lowering the quality of the Negro organizations and in some cases causing their demise or increasing their dependence on whites for survival. Such injurious, if unintended, side effects of integration have been felt in almost every layer of the black community.

If the foregoing analysis of the integration vs. separatism conflict exhausted the case for partition then we might conclude that the problems have all been dealt with before, by other immigrant groups in America. (It would be an erroneous conclusion, for while other groups may have encountered similar problems, their solutions do not work for us, alas.) But there remains yet another factor which is cooling the Negro's enthusiasm for the integrationist path: he is becoming distrustful of his fellow Americans.

The American culture is one of the youngest in the world. Furthermore, as has been pointed out repeatedly in recent years, it is essentially a culture which approves of violence, indeed enjoys it. Military expenditures absorb roughly half of the national budget. Violence predominates on the TV screen and the toys of violence are best selling items during the annual rites for the much praised but little imitated Prince of Peace. In Vietnam, the zeal with which America has pursued its effort to destroy a poor and illiterate peasantry has astonished civilized people around the globe. In such an atmosphere the Negro is understandably restive about the fate his white compatriots might have in store for him. The veiled threat by President Johnson at the time of the 1966 riots—suggesting that riots might beget pogroms and pointing out that Negroes are only ten per cent of the population—was not lost on most blacks. It enraged them, but it was a sobering thought. The manner in which Germany herded the Jews into concentration camps and ultimately into ovens was a solemn warning to minority peoples everywhere. The casualness with which America exterminated the Indians and later interned the Japanese suggests that there is no cause for the Negro to feel complacent about his security in the U.S. He finds little consolation in the assurance that if it does become necessary to place him in concentration camps it will only be as a means of protecting him from uncontrollable whites: "Protective incarceration," to use governmental jargonese.

The very fact that such alternatives are becoming serious topics of discussion has exposed the Negro's already raw and sensitive psyche to yet another heretofore unfelt vulnerability—the insecurity which he suffers as a result of having no homeland which he can honestly feel his own. Among the major ethno-cultural groups in the world he is unique in this respect. As the Jewish drama during and following World War II painfully demonstrated, a national homeland is a primordial and urgent need for a people, even though its benefits do not always lend themselves to ready measurement. For some, the homeland constitutes a vital place of refuge from the strains of a life led too long within a foreign environment. For others, the need to reside in the homeland is considerably less intense than the need for merely knowing that such a homeland exists. The benefit to the expatriate is psychological, a sense of security in knowing that he belongs to a culturally and politically identifiable community. No doubt this phenomenon largely accounts for the fact that both the West Indian Negro and the Puerto Rican exhibit considerably more self-assurance than does the American Negro, for both of the former groups have ties to an identifiable homeland which honors and preserves their cultural heritage.

It has been marveled that we American Negroes, almost alone among the cultural groups of the world, exhibit no sense of nationhood. Perhaps it is true that we do lack this sense, but there seems to be little doubt that the absence of a homeland exacts a severe if unconscious price from our psyche. Theoretically, our homeland is the U.S.A. We pledge allegiance to the stars and stripes and sing the national anthem. But from the age when we first begin to sense that we are somehow "different," that we are victimized, these rituals begin to mean less to us than to our white compatriots. For many of us they become form without substance; for others they become a cruel and bitter mockery of our dignity and good sense; for relatively few of us do they retain a significance in any way comparable to their hold on our white brethren.

The recent coming into independence of many African states stimulated some interest among Negroes that independent Africa might become the homeland which they so desperately needed. A few made the journey and experienced a newly-found sense of community and racial dignity. For many who went, however, the gratifying racial fraternity which they experienced was insufficient to compensate for the cultural estrangement which accompanied it. They had been away from Africa for too long and the differences in language, food and custom barred them from experiencing the "at home" sensation which they were eagerly seeking. Symbolically, independent Africa could serve them as a homeland: practically, it could not. Their search continues—a search for a place where they can experience the security which comes from being a part of the majority culture, free at last from the inhibiting effects of cultural repression and induced cultural timidity and shame.

If we have been separated from Africa for so long that we are no longer quite at ease there, then we are left with only one place to make our home, and that is this land to which we were brought in chains. Justice would indicate such a solution in any case, for it is North America, not Africa, into which our toil and effort have been poured. This land is our rightful home and we are well within our rights in demanding an opportunity to enjoy it on the same terms as the other immigrants who have helped to develop it. Since few whites will deny the justice of this claim, it is paradoxical that we are offered the option of exercising this birthright only on the condition that we abandon our culture, deny our race and integrate ourselves into the white community. The "accepted" Negro, the "integrated" Negro, are mere euphemisms which hide a cruel and relentless cultural destruction which is sometimes agonizing to the middle class Negro but which is becoming intolerable to the black masses. A Negro who refuses to yield his identity and to ape the white model finds he can survive only by rejecting the entire white society, which must ultimately mean challenging the law and the law enforcement mechanisms. On the other hand, if he abandons his cultural heritage and succumbs to the lure of integration, he risks certain rejection and humiliation along the way, with absolutely no guarantee of ever achieving complete acceptance. That such unsatisfactory options are leading to almost continuous disruption of our society should hardly be cause for surprise.

Partition offers one way out of this tragic situation. Many will condemn it as a defeatist solution, but what they see as defeatism might better be described as a frank facing up to the realities of American society. A society is stable only to the extent that there exists a basic core of value judgments which is unthinkingly accepted by the great bulk of its members. Increasingly, Negroes are demonstrating that they have some reservations about the common core of values which underlie American society—whether because they had little to do with formulating these values or because they feel them to be weighted against their interests. For the Negro in the ghetto especially, the society's values are often as alien and as damaging to him as is its standard of beauty. They are both built on premises which are for him unattainable and often irrelevant.

The alleged disproportionately large number of Negro law violators, of unwed mothers, of non-working adults *may* be indicators that the supposed community of values is much weaker than had been supposed, although I am not unaware of additional racial socio-economic reasons for these statistics. But whatever the reasons for observed behavioral differences, there is clearly no reason *why* the Negro should not have his own ideas about what the societal organization should be. The Anglo-Saxon system of organizing human relationships has certainly not proved itself to be superior to all other systems, and the Negro is likely to be more acutely aware of this fact than most Americans.

Certainly partition would entail enormous initial hardships. But these hardships should be weighed against the prospects of prolonged and intensified racial strife stretching into the indefinite future. Indeed, the social fabric of America is far more likely to be able to withstand the strains of a partitioning of the country than those of an extended race war. Indeed, if it happened that the principle of partition were harmoniously accepted by most Americans as the preferable solution, it is possible that only voluntary transfers of population would be necessary. Conceivably, no one would be forced to move against his will. Those Negroes who wanted to migrate to the new nation ("New Africa"?) could do so, and their counterparts could move to the United States. The France-Algeria arrangements could be used as a model. (To put the question of mass transference of populations into its proper perspective, it is well to remember that the U.S. is currently witnessing one of history's great demographic movements, although most Americans are totally unaware of it. In the past 25 years, some four million Negroes, roughly 20 per cent of the total Negro population, have migrated from the rural South to the cities of the North and West. History records few such massive population transfers.)

There is an excellent chance that, following partition, neither nation would be overtly racist. The basis for the present racial animosity would be largely removed by the very act of separation. Reciprocal tourism might very well become a leading industry for both nations, for the relations between the races would finally be on a healthy, equalitarian basis. A confederation of the two states, perhaps joined by Canada, Mexico and other nations, could conceivably emerge at some future time.

Divorce is an inherent aspect of the American tradition. It terminates the misery of an enforced but unhappy union, relieves the tension and avoids the risk of more serious consequences. It is increasingly apparent to blacks and whites alike that their national marriage has been a disastrous failure. Consequently, in the search for ways to remedy this tragic situation, divorce should obviously not be ruled out as a possible solution. The Black Power Conference resolution asks America to do no more than to give it serious consideration.

Even in the black ghettos it may require considerable time before the idea of partitioning can be evaluated dispassionately, for the Negro has never rejected the indoctrination which he receives in "Americana"; rather, his problem is that he has accepted it too readily, only to discover that it was not meant to apply to him.

But the mood of the ghetto is in a state of unprecedented change and in this new climate a sense of nationhood is groping for expression. It may hold within it the key to mental health for black America, and its ultimate outcome cannot now be foreseen. It may lead to two separate nations or it may lead us toward some as yet untried type of human community vastly superior to the present system of competing nationalisms. The new world community which mankind so desperately needs may rise phoenix-like from the collapsing, unworkable old order. Intelligent, imaginative men must not shrink from exploring fearlessly any avenue which might lead mankind to this new world community. Men may sometimes hate other men. Fortunately, they do not hate mankind. This is the solid foundation upon which we must try to build.

QUESTIONS FOR DISCUSSION AND WRITING

1. According to Browne, what social groups will have their goals recognized by black separatism?
2. What conditions have brought about acceptance of the proposal for black separatism as a "moderate" one? In what context is the proposal "moderate"?
3. "Even with a Ph.D., a Nobel prize, a Congressional Medal of Honor or a vast fortune, a Negro is still a 'nigger' to many (most?) white Americans and the society does not let him forget it for very long." Evaluate this statement.
4. Compare and contrast Browne's point of view on "integration" with that of Carmichael (p. 333). In what ways do the viewpoints of both writers differ from that of King (p. 347)?
5. Compare and contrast Browne's point of view on separatism with Garvey's (p. 103) and Malcolm X's (p. 317).

"CLOROX" IS THE PEN NAME OF FRANK CLEVELAND, A NEW YORK HIGH SCHOOL STUDENT. HIS POEM AND OTHERS WRITTEN BY "GHETTO" CHILDREN WERE RECENTLY COLLECTED BY STEPHEN JOSEPH IN *The Me Nobody Knows.*

CLOROX

WHAT AM I?

I HAVE NO MANHOOD—WHAT AM I?
YOU MADE MY WOMAN HEAD OF THE HOUSE—WHAT AM I?
YOU HAVE ORIENTED ME SO THAT I HATE AND DISTRUST MY BROTHERS
AND SISTERS—WHAT AM I?
    YOU MISPROUNCE MY NAME AND SAY I HAVE NO SELF-RESPECT—
    WHAT AM I?
    YOU GIVE ME A DILAPIDATED EDUCATION SYSTEM AND EXPECT
    ME TO COMPETE WITH YOU—WHAT AM I?
    YOU SAY I HAVE NO DIGNITY AND THEN DEPRIVE ME OF MY CUL-
    TURE—WHAT AM I?
    YOU CALL ME A BOY, DIRTY LOWDOWN SLUT—WHAT AM I?
    NOW I'M A VICTIM OF THE WELFARE SYSTEM—WHAT AM I?
    YOU TELL ME TO WAIT FOR CHANGE TO COME, BUT 400 YEARS
    HAVE PASSED AND CHANGE AINT'T COME—WHAT AM I?
I AM ALL OF YOUR SINS
I AM THE SKELETON IN YOUR CLOSETS
I AM THE UNWANTED SONS AND DAUGHTERS-IN-LAW, AND REJECTED
BABIES
I MAY BE YOUR DESTRUCTION, BUT ABOVE ALL I AM, AS YOU SO
CRUDELY PUT IT, YOUR NIGGER.

QUESTIONS FOR DISCUSSION AND WRITING

1. To whom is the poem addressed? Why?
2. What aspect of the new black consciousness does the poem suggest?
3. The author makes several references to the black stereotype—for example, "I am the skeleton in your closets." In what sense is the stereotype one of "skeletons in the closet"?
4. What does the author mean by "nigger"?
5. How might Washington (p. 65) have responded to the question posed by this poem? How would Carmichael (p. 329) respond? In what ways would their answers differ from Clorox's?

B 0
C 1
D 2
E 3
F 4
G 5
H 6
I 7
J 8